Public Theology for the 21st Century

Public Theology for the 21st Century

Essays in honour of Duncan B. Forrester

Edited by

WILLIAM F. STORRAR and ANDREW R. MORTON

Foreword by

PROFESSOR RAYMOND PLANT

T & T CLARK
A Continuum imprint
LONDON • NEW YORK

T&T CLARK LTD
A Continuum imprint

The Tower Building   15 East 26th Street
11 York Road   New York 10010
London SE1 7NX   USA
UK

www.tandtclark.com

First published 2004

British Library Cataloguing-in-Publication Data
A catalogue record for this book is available from the British Library.

Library of Congress Cataloging-in-Publication Data
Public theology for the 21st century : essays in honour of Duncan B. Forrester /
    William F. Storrar, Andrew R. Morton, editors.
        p. cm.
    Includes bibliographical references and index.
    ISBN 0–567–08895–2 – ISBN 0–567–08892–8 (pbk.)
    1. Theology, Doctrinal – Popular works.   I. Title: Public theology for the
twenty-first century.   II. Forrester, Duncan B., 1933–   III. Storrar, William.
IV. Morton, Andrew, 1928–

    BT77.P78 2003
    261–dc22   2003060042

ISBN 0 567 08895 2 (hardback)
ISBN 0 567 08892 8 (paperback)

Typeset by Waverley Typesetters, Galashiels
Printed and bound in Great Britain by MPG Books Ltd, Bodmin, Cornwall

Contents

Foreword

I am delighted to have been invited to contribute a Foreword to this volume of essays, which is a real tribute to the wide-ranging and influential work of Duncan Forrester. His scholarship and engagement in theology have been inspirational and, as I can testify, his personal kindness is legendary. I can think of few academics who can emulate this mixture of high-level scholarship combined with personal warmth and generosity of time and engagement in the work of others.

I am not a theologian but a rather odd combination of political and legal philosopher and practical politician and thus the judgement of others represented in this volume will be better guides to Duncan's contribution to theology. What I can say, however, is that Duncan's writings on public theology are full of interest both to academic theologians and to those involved in the formulation and implementation of public policy. This has come about both through his writing and also through the remarkably sustained effect of the Centre for Theology and Public Issues in the School of Divinity at the University of Edinburgh. The work of the Centre and Duncan's own creative theological writings seem to me to have been of vital importance because public policy is always in danger of being taken over by those with instrumental expertise. There is a deep reason for this. Public policy depends very much on questions of value: do we want more or less freedom? more or less equality? Is the purpose of punishment retribution, deterrence, rehabilitation, restitution? Does social or distributive justice make sense as a political principle and, if it does, how should it guide policy? What rights should we have and how extensive should they be? What is the relationship between social solidarity and welfare provision? What moral significance, if any, do national boundaries have in terms of international aid? And so on. These sorts of questions are central to public policy but the moral resources that we bring to seeking to debate these issues are nowadays very attenuated. Because we seem to lack a common moral vocabulary in terms of which we can address these issues, it seems easier to allow the debates about policy to be taken over by experts. But we have to be clear that there are no experts in respect of the nature and ranking of the values, which lie at the heart of public policy, and hence our predilection to leave these matters to experts is ultimately illusory. We cannot avoid something that is at the heart of our humanity, namely how we should live and how we should live in collective as well as individual personal terms. To engage in debate about the morality of what is done in our name is immensely difficult but it is a human responsibility that we cannot avoid. Duncan's work and that of the Centre has been devoted to keeping these moral issues at the centre of our minds and by so doing reminding us of our responsibilities. His work shows that it is possible to address these moral problems in creative and resonant ways and the Centre has provided a public forum in which such debates can take place between policy-makers, practitioners, theologians and philosophers. This is likely to be the only sort of way in which we shall ever be able to arrive at moral and civic insight into these issues. These insights have to be arrived at through deliberation if they are to be achieved at all and Duncan's theology and the work of the Centre have been very important in the development of such a capacity.

Of course, in a modern or postmodern society we cannot expect the laying down of a set of compelling values by some kind of central moral authority, whether sacred or secular. This does not however mean that we should abandon the search for some kind of moral agreement to frame and ground the public practices of our society. This naturally brings us onto questions about the kind of voice that both the churches and theology should have in the deliberation about and articulation of these issues. So a public theology has the doubly difficult task of not only attempting to formulate a theologically coherent account of the moral issues facing public policy in a complex society but also facing up to what might be seen as sort of *meta-task* to do with arguing for a role for theology amongst the voices in society brought to bear upon these questions. Duncan, and indeed the Centre for Theology and Public Issues, have made very significant contributions to both of these aspects of a modern public theology and both of these are represented in this volume of essays.

I therefore see the publication of this volume as a very significant moment in the history of public theology over the past fifty years or so, taking stock of and renewing a sense of social vision in theology which we saw in earlier times exemplified in Gore and Temple and more recently in the work of Ronald Preston. Duncan's work stands in the same tradition of seeking to articulate a Christian social vision, which can be brought to bear upon the problems of civil and political life and arguing a very strong case for the seriousness of that voice to be heard and respected within the conversation of modern society.

PROFESSOR RAYMOND PLANT
King's College, London

Acknowledgements

The editors wish to express their gratitude and acknowledge their indebtedness to those who in various capacities have contributed to the preparation and production of this book.

So we thank:

the British Academy for a generous grant towards the costs of an academic colloquium that brought together the authors;

those who hosted the colloquium, the then Dean of the Faculty of Divinity of the University of Edinburgh, Professor J. Stewart Brown, and the staff of the Carberry Conference Centre, Edinburgh;

the contributors to both the colloquium and the book itself, especially those who travelled from afar, from Argentina, India, the Netherlands, South Africa and the United States of America, as well as from around the United Kingdom;

Professor Duncan Forrester for responding to the contributions both at the colloquium and in an Afterword to the book;

Lord Plant of Highfield, who as a friend and colleague of Professor Forrester has contributed the Foreword to the book as well as a chapter of it;

Dr Geoffrey Green, Dr Fiona Murphy and their colleagues in T&T Clark/Continuum, the publishers;

our colleagues in the Centre for Theology and Public Issues, its Associate Director, Dr Alison Elliot OBE, who helped to organize the colloquium, and its Organizing Secretary, Alastair Hulbert, who has given substantial assistance to us in the editing process. Further information on the work of the Centre for Theology and Public Issues, including its publications, is available from:

Centre for Theology and Public Issues
School of Divinity
The University of Edinburgh
New College
Mound Place
Edinburgh EH1 2LX

email: *ctpi@ed.ac.uk*
website: *www.div.ed.ac.uk/research*

WILLIAM F. STORRAR and ANDREW R. MORTON
Editors

Contributors

Dr Marcella Althaus-Reid is an Argentinian theologian and senior lecturer in Christian Ethics and Systematic Theology at the University of Edinburgh. She has written extensively on issues related to theology, sexuality and economy, including *Indecent Theology: Theological Perversions on Sex, Gender and Politics* (Routledge, 2000). She is a member of the advisory board of *Concilium*.

Richard J. Bauckham is Professor of New Testament Studies and Bishop Wardlaw Professor in the University of St Andrews. He has published widely in theology and biblical studies. Recent books include: *God and the Crisis of Freedom: Biblical and Contemporary Perspectives* (Westminster/John Knox Press, 2002); and *Gospel Women: Studies of the Named Women in the Gospels* (Eerdmans, 2002).

Alastair Campbell is the inaugural Professor of Ethics in Medicine in the School of Medicine, University of Bristol, and Director of the Centre for Ethics in Medicine. He is a member of the Medical Ethics Committee of the British Medical Association and a former President of the International Association of Bioethics. Recent publications include *Health as Liberation* (Pilgrim Press, 1995) and *Medical Ethics*, co-authored with Max Charlesworth, Grant Gillett and Gareth Jones (Oxford University Press, 1997).

David Fergusson is Professor of Divinity at the University of Edinburgh. From 2000 to 2002 he served as President of the Society for the Study of Theology. He is the author of *Community, Liberalism and Christian Ethics* (Cambridge University Press, 1998) and co-editor of *John Macmurray: Critical Perspectives* (Peter Lang, 2002).

Robin Gill is the Michael Ramsey Professor of Modern Theology in the University of Kent at Canterbury. Previously he held the William Leech Research Chair of Applied Theology at the University of Newcastle. Among his books are *Moral Leadership in a Postmodern Age* (T&T Clark, 1997), *Churchgoing and Christian Ethics* (Cambridge University Press, 1999) and *Changing Worlds* (T&T Clark, 2002).

Timothy Gorringe has taught in India, Oxford and St Andrews, and is now Professor of Theological Studies at the University of Exeter. His most recent publications are *The Education of Desire* (SCM Press, 2000) and *A Theology of the Built Environment* (Cambridge University Press, 2001).

Elaine Graham is Samuel Ferguson Professor of Social and Pastoral Theology at the University of Manchester. She is the author of *Making the Difference: Gender, Personhood and Theology* (Mowbray, 1995) and *Transforming Practice* (Mowbray, 1996), as well as numerous articles. Her latest book, *Representations of the Post/Human* (Manchester University Press, 2002), considers the relationship between science, religion and popular culture in a digital and biotechnological age.

Mary C. Grey is D. J. James Professor of Pastoral Theology at the University of Wales, Lampeter, and Sarum College, Salisbury. Her interest in the field of Ecofeminist Liberation Theology and Globalization involves questions of a spiritual response. Her theological work is underpinned by regular visits to desert areas of Rajasthan, India, through the work of the NGO 'Wells for India'. Her most recent book is *The Outrageous Pursuit of Hope: Prophetic Dreams for the Twenty-first Century* (Crossroad, 2001).

John W. de Gruchy is the Robert Selby Taylor Professor of Christian Studies and Director of the Graduate School in Humanities at the University of Cape Town, South Africa. He has published widely on the Church in South Africa, on the theology of Dietrich Bonhoeffer and on issues in public theology. His most recent books are *Christianity, Art and Transformation* (Cambridge University Press, 2001) and *Reconciliation* (Fortress Press, 2002).

Stanley Hauerwas is the Gilbert T. Rowe Professor of Theological Ethics at the Divinity School of Duke University. His most recent publication is *With the Grain of the Universe: The Church's Witness and Natural Theology* (Brazos Press, 2001) which were his Gifford lectures given at the University of St Andrews.

Alistair Kee is a graduate of the University of Glasgow and Union Theological Seminary, New York. He taught in Rhodesia (Zimbabwe), Hull and Glasgow before being appointed as Professor of Religious Studies at the University of Edinburgh. His main research field is ideology and religion. Publications include *Marx and the Failure of Liberation Theology* (SCM Press, 1990) and *Nietzsche against the Crucified* (SCM Press, 1999).

Kees J. Klop is Professor of Political Ethics in the Faculty of Philosophy and Centre of Ethics at the Catholic University, Nijmegen. From 1978 to 2001 he was Deputy Managing Director of the Abraham Kuyper Foundation, the Institute for Policy Research for Dutch Christian Democracy. He now serves as Chairman of the Dutch Protestant Broadcasting Company, NCRV. He has written several publications on morality in the public sphere.

C. T. Kurien is Emeritus Professor and currently Chairman of the Madras Institute of Development Studies. Formerly he taught economics in the Madras Christian College. Recognized as one of India's leading economists, he was President of the Indian Economic Association in 2002. His books include *Growth and Justice: Aspects of India's Development Experience* (Oxford University Press, 1993) and *Rethinking Economics: Reflections Based on a Study of Indian Economy* (Sage, 1996).

Ann Loades is Professor of Divinity in the University of Durham where she was the first woman to be given a 'personal' chair in the history of that university. She was awarded a CBE in 2001 'for services to Theology'. Her publications include *Evelyn Underhill* (Font, 1999) and *Feminist Theology: Voices from the Past* (Blackwell, 2001).

José Míguez-Bonino is Emeritus Professor of Systematic Theology and Ethics at the Instituto Universitario ISEDET in Buenos Aires. A former Deputy in the National Constitutional Assembly of Argentina and, since 1975, President of the Permanent Assembly for Human Rights, he is the author of several books, including *Toward a Christian Political Ethics* (Fortress Press, 1982) and *Faces of Latin American Protestantism* (Eerdmans, 1995).

Jürgen Moltmann is Emeritus Professor of Systematic Theology at the University of Tübingen. He was editor of the journal *Evangelische Theologie*, and from 1979 to 1994 one of the directors of the Catholic journal *Concilium*. Of the many books he has written, the most recent are *Experiences in Theology* (Fortress Press, 1999) and *Science and Wisdom* (Fortress Press, 2002).

Dr Andrew R. Morton is an Honorary Fellow in Divinity in the University of Edinburgh and until recently the Associate Director of its Centre for Theology and Public Issues. He edited and contributed to many CTPI publications. Following parish ministry and university chaplaincy, he worked for the British Council of Churches as its secretary for public affairs, then served the Church of Scotland as its ecumenical and European officer and later as its Church and Nation secretary. He goes in for cross-frontier living.

George Newlands has been Professor of Divinity in the University of Glasgow since 1986, and is Principal of Trinity College. A former Dean of Trinity Hall, Cambridge, his research publications are in the field of systematic theology, and include *Generosity and the Christian Future of God* (SPCK, 1997) and *John and Donald Baillie: Transatlantic Theology* (Peter Lang, 2002).

Dr Michael Northcott is Reader in Christian Ethics in New College in the University of Edinburgh and a priest in the Scottish Episcopal Church of St James', Leith. He is also Academic Chair of the Centre for Human Ecology. His publications include *The Environment and Christian Ethics* (Cambridge University Press, 1996), *Urban Theology: A Reader* (Cassell, 1998) and *Life After Debt: Christianity and Global Justice* (SPCK, 1999). He has held permanent or visiting positions in the University of Sunderland, the Seminari Theologi Malaysia, Dartmouth College, New Hampshire and the Claremont School of Theology, California.

Lord Raymond Plant of Highfield is Professor of Legal Philosophy in the School of Law at King's College, London. He was formerly Master of St Catherine's College, Oxford. From 1991 to 1993 he was Chair of the Labour Party Commission on Electoral Systems and from 1988 to 1992, a *Times* columnist. His major works include *Modern Political Thought* (Blackwell, 1991) and *Politics, Theology and History* (Cambridge University Press, 2000).

Christopher Rowland is Dean Ireland's Professor of Exegesis of Holy Scripture at the University of Oxford. In addition to interests in the apocalyptic tradition, he has written on radical movements in Christianity, most recently with Andrew Bradstock in *Radical Christian Writings: A Reader* (Blackwell, 2002) and is at present completing two books on the reception history of the Apocalypse and on the contribution of early Jewish mysticism to New Testament theology.

Max L. Stackhouse is Stephen Colwell Professor of Christian Ethics at Princeton Theological Seminary. He was previously H. Gezork Professor of Christian Social Ethics at Andover Newton Theological School. He is author or editor of twelve books, including *Public Theology and Political Economy* (Eerdmans, 1987) and *God and Globalization* (3 Vols; Trinity Press International, 2000–2).

William F. Storrar is Professor of Christian Ethics and Practical Theology and Director of the Centre for Theology and Public Issues at the University of Edinburgh. He previously held lecturing appointments at the Universities of Aberdeen and Glasgow, after serving as a parish minister. From 1992 to 2000 he was Convener of Common Cause, a Scottish civic forum on democracy. His publications include *Scottish Identity: A Christian Vision* (Handsel Press, 1990), and the co-edited work, *God in Society: Doing Social Theology in Scotland Today* (CTPI, 2003).

Alan J. Torrance is Professor of Systematic Theology in the University of St Andrews. He has taught in universities in Germany, Australasia and the UK. Formerly Director of the Research Institute in Systematic Theology at King's College, London, he has given the Hensley Henson lectures in the University of Oxford and presently participates in three USA-based research groups. Recent books include *Persons in Communion: An Essay on Trinitarian Description and Human Participation* (T&T Clark, 1996) and, with Michael Jinkins, *Invitation to Theology* (Inter-Varsity Press, 2001).

Introduction

WILLIAM F. STORRAR and ANDREW R. MORTON

A Public Theology

What is a *public* theology? One of the most influential theologians of the twentieth century, Jürgen Moltmann, a contributor to this volume, has expressed it well. Public theology has to do with the public relevance of a theology which has at the core of its Christian identity a concern for the coming of God's Kingdom in the public world of human history:

> Its subject alone makes Christian theology a *theologia publica*, a public theology. It gets involved in the public affairs of society. It thinks about what is of general concern in the light of hope in Christ for the kingdom of God. It becomes political in the name of the poor and the marginalized in a given society. Remembrance of the crucified Christ makes it critical towards political religions and idolatries. It thinks critically about the religious and moral values of the societies in which it exists, and presents its reflections as a reasoned position.[1]

Moltmann is not alone in this understanding. Here is how another distinguished theologian has described public theology:

> It is not domesticated and tamed within a particular class or community. No – public theology is rather a theology, talk about God, which claims to point to publicly accessible truth, to contribute to public discussion by witnessing to a truth that is relevant to what is going on in the world and to the pressing issues which are facing people and societies today … It offers convictions, challenges and insights derived from the tradition of which it is a steward, rather than seeking to articulate a consensus or reiterate what everyone is saying anyway. Public theology is thus confessional and evangelical. It has a gospel to share, good news to proclaim. Public theology attends to the Bible and the tradition of faith at the same time as it attempts to discern the signs of the times and understand what is going on in the light of the gospel.[2]

The author of that last statement is Duncan Forrester, whose contribution to such a public theology is celebrated in this book, published in his honour. It is the editors' hope that the essays in it will offer the reader a deeper, richer understanding of public theology for the twenty-first century.

A Public Theologian

Duncan Baillie Forrester is the Professor Emeritus of Christian Ethics and Practical Theology in the University of Edinburgh, Scotland. He held the Chair of Christian Ethics and Practical Theology there for the twenty-two years from 1978 to 2000 and the Personal Chair of Theology and Public Issues for the year from 2000 to 2001. He was also the founding Director of the University's Centre for Theology and Public Issues from 1984 to 2000.

Born in Edinburgh on 10 November 1933, he was educated at St Andrews University from 1951 to 1955, at Chicago University from 1955 to 1956 and, after a year in industry, at Edinburgh University from 1957 to 1960. His St Andrews degree was in Arts, with specialization in Politics, and his Edinburgh degree in Divinity. In 1960 he became a minister of the Church of Scotland and served for a year as assistant in St James' Mission and Hillside Church in Edinburgh. At the end of 1961 he was sent by the Church of Scotland to serve the Church of South India and was ordained as a presbyter of that Church by the Diocese of Madras. He was Professor of Politics in Madras Christian College for the following eight years, returning in 1970 to be Chaplain and Lecturer in Politics and Religious Studies in Sussex University. Eight years later, in 1978, he was appointed to the Edinburgh Chair. From 1986 to 1996 he was also Principal of New College and from 1996 to 1999 Dean of the Faculty of Divinity.

His degrees are: MA, St Andrews, 1955; BD, Edinburgh, 1960; DPhil, Sussex, 1976; ThD, Iceland, 1997; DD, Glasgow, 1999; DD, St Andrews 2000. In 1999 he was also recipient of the Templeton Prize (UK), in particular recognition of his work in the Centre for Theology and Public Issues.

Under his leadership, the discipline of Practical Theology in the University of Edinburgh has flourished, with new developments both in its scope and in its methodology, and with a new clarity in its definition. Through his enterprise, many new programmes have been established, not least in the theology and ethics of communication and media and of development and liberation. It may be no surprise that, as a professor in an institution which is at one and the same time a church college (New College) and a university school of divinity (formerly the Faculty of Divinity), he has been much concerned with the method of Christian moral theology in a secular context. He has described his own great concern as dual – with worship, including preaching, and with political ethics, these two being regarded not as separate but as in constant interplay. One of his special interests has been the contextual study of particular moral theologians, such as Karl Barth, Reinhold Niebuhr and Jacques Ellul. But some of his deepest convictions have been manifested most in the work of the Centre for Theology and Public Issues, which he has described as a forum of people in public life and in the churches which 'on the one hand endeavours not to speak about people behind their backs but to attend to the voice of the weak and the marginalised, and on the other hand attempts to exert some positive influence in public affairs.'

A Centre for Theology and Public Issues

In its nineteen years, this Centre has involved a wide range of people from different academic disciplines, different spheres of public and professional service, different churches and faith-communities – and different forms of suffering. They have gathered in open conferences, invited consultations, specialized seminars, commissioned working groups and specially funded research projects. They have shared their diversity of experience, knowledge, skills and convictions in an atmosphere of mutual respect and trust and in an effort to uncover their underlying values and visions. If the range of participants has been wide, so too has the range of public issues, as is shown by this list of some of the topics which it has addressed:

Welfare state or welfare society
The end of professionalism?
The ethics and economics of the distribution of income and wealth
Education and community
Finance and ethics
Northern Ireland – a challenge to theology
The renewal of social vision
Justice, guilt and forgiveness in the penal system
The market and health care
Aids, sex and the Scottish Churches
Third World debt – First World responsibility

Security, solidarity and peacemaking
Scottish devolution and national identity
Work, worth and community: responding to the crisis of work
Christianity and violence against women in Scotland
The sorrows of young men: exploring their increasing risk of suicide

In what is essentially a collaborative exercise, it is impossible and perhaps invidious to distinguish Duncan Forrester's particular contribution. However, if one of the threads through many of the themes is justice, it would be reasonable to detect his influence; for he has struggled both with philosophical issues of justice and with political measures to develop it, whether distributive or restorative, whether in fiscal and welfare policy or in penal policy; for two groups of people about whom he will not 'speak behind their backs' are the impoverished victims of economic injustice and the imprisoned perpetrators of criminal injustice. But perhaps his special roles in the work of the Centre have been threefold – to discern and formulate the crucial issues deserving treatment; to design and refine the method of their treatment; to distil from this essentially interdisciplinary enterprise the uniquely theological insights.

In his very active and productive life of teaching, administration, preaching and pastoring, not to mention not-for-profit entrepreneurship from which many have profited, he has also published the products of much of his scholarship and reflection; a selection of those publications is listed in an appendix. They show the diversity of his interests.

A Colloquium on Public Theology for the Twenty-first Century

It seemed good to the editors of this volume, themselves much involved in the work of the Centre for Theology and Public Issues, to honour this significant contributor to public theology in the twentieth century by organizing an academic colloquium of his peers to consider 'public theology for the twenty-first century' and to publish its thinking.

The colloquium duly took place from 31 August to 3 September 2001 in Carberry Tower Residential Conference Centre, Musselburgh, Edinburgh, after an opening session in New College, the home of the University of Edinburgh's then Faculty and now School of Divinity. Twenty-four scholars participated; four others submitted papers; in addition, around 80 people attended the opening session, which was public, and around twelve other local academics attended one or other of two sessions to which there were specific invitations. The organizers gratefully acknowledge a grant from the British Academy in support of this remarkable international scholarly gathering in the field of public theology.

The colloquium addressed the central question 'What legacy from public theology in the twentieth century should be carried over into the new millennium?', together with the question 'What issues and approaches will be important in the twenty-first century?' As will be evident from what follows, the colloquium took account of major contemporary developments such as pluralism, globalization, postmodernity and the vast expansion of technological capability, and it addressed a number of the cultural, social, economic and political implications of these historic changes.

The participation of distinguished academic scholars from the Americas, from Africa and from Asia, as well as from Britain and other European countries, helped to prevent the work from becoming Eurocentric, and the cross-continental element in the dialogue was a major enhancement of it.

The design of the colloquium, with its combination of plenary sessions and parallel ones, made it possible to handle a large number of topics with a reasonably high degree of scrutiny and interaction and allowed the participants to contribute both from their specialisms and from their more general understanding of theology and of public life. In the light of those proceedings they have revised their contributions. These now form this collection, which is offered as a resource for academics and students, for churches and other faith-communities, and for all who in any way seek to contribute to the making of public policy.

A Volume on Public Theology

Overview

The book is in four parts, as follows:

Part I: Critical Contributions – the Twentieth-century Legacy

Part II: Contested Ideas – Modernity's Legacy

Part III: Changing Contexts – Globalization's Impact

Part IV: Emerging Concerns – Twenty-first-century Issues and Approaches

Parts I and II, consisting between them of ten chapters, look mainly at what has been inherited from the past. Part III, consisting of four chapters, forms a kind of hinge between the past and future, by examining the current great change that is denoted by the term 'globalization'. Part IV, consisting of ten chapters, looks mainly at what is to be anticipated in the future. It has to be said immediately that this distinction between retrospect in Parts I and II and prospect in Part IV is far from absolute, in that the experiences and ideas of Part I contain seeds of the future and the issues and approaches of Part IV emerge from the past. The continuity is striking.

The first chapter of Part I focuses attention on one person, the one in whose honour this volume is published, Duncan Forrester. It is an interpretation of his contribution by one of the editors, Andrew Morton, who examines a number of senses in which Forrester's theology is 'public'. It shows why this particular theologian provides a good way in to the topic of public theology for the twenty-first century. It deals not so much with the content of his work as with its presuppositions and style of approach, an approach which is highlighted at various points in the volume, appreciatively or occasionally critically. (The other editor, William Storrar, returns to Forrester's work in the closing chapter and considers its content in more detail, in the light of the contributions to this volume, and the overall theme of public theology for a global era.)

After this initial attention in the first chapter to the legacy of one theologian whose work has spanned the second half of the twentieth century, the remaining three chapters in Part I and the six chapters in Part II look more broadly at the recent legacy as sources of theological wisdom. The three in Part I reflect twentieth-century experience from three continental perspectives, European, African and South American. This is a mapping of the topic of public theology in terms of social context. The six chapters in Part II look back not just at the twentieth century but at modernity as a whole, and they map the topic in terms not of social geography but of the history of ideas, in particular some of the controlling and contested notions of modernity such as freedom, moral neutrality, tolerance, rights, pluralism and progress. It could be said that the traumatic experiences of the twentieth century reflected in Part I show the darker side of modernity, whereas the history of ideas reflected in Part II presents a more attractive face. But all these chapters indicate the ambiguities and tensions represented by both the experiences and the ideas.

The shorter Part III, consisting of Chapters 11–14, focuses on a major change which appears to be taking on prime significance at this juncture of history, namely globalization.

In Part IV, which consists of Chapters 15–24, five topics are treated, each in a complementary pair of chapters. The fact that in each of these five cases two contributors independently chose the same topic is some indication of the importance of the five, as well as helpful in providing different perspectives and in fostering dialogue. While we are not claiming to be exhaustive or suggesting that these are the only emerging issues, we hazard the view that they are a bit more than merely illustrative of those that are emerging in this century from origins in the previous one. The five can be summarized as: medical ethics, justice, equality, exclusion and politics. It so happens that most of these topics have also featured prominently in the work of Duncan Forrester. He has served on an eminent body concerned with bioethics. He has devoted himself to justice in the context of both criminal behaviour and communal conflict. His position is strongly egalitarian. Indeed one could say that his emphasis on restorative justice has been applied to both 'a world of evils' and 'a world of goods'. Much of his work has taken as its starting point the experience of those 'outside the gate', the excluded. The final topic, politics, is of particular importance not only to Forrester but also to his successor both as Professor of Christian Ethics and Practical Theology and as Director for the Centre for Theology and Public Issues, William Storrar. It is appropriate that he as the other of the two editors should provide the concluding chapter, which also has an element of reprise.

Though this fourth part of the volume, with its main title of 'Emerging Concerns', is arranged in terms of *issues for* public theology, it is every bit as much about *approaches to* public theology. We do not have two sections, one entitled 'Issues' and the other 'Approaches', because these two, though conceptually distinct, are operationally inseparable. It is in the handling of specific issues that one's general approach or methodology is manifested. There is only very occasional explicit reference to the distinctive approach of an author, whether contributing or cited; for example one contributor contrasts the methodological presuppositions of John Yoder and Duncan Forrester. However, the approaches, though implicit, are not hard to discern. The decisions facing public theology in the twenty-first century will be as much about approaches as about issues. At stake are its contents *and* its methods, what it considers important *and* why, what it does *and* what it is.

WILLIAM F. STORRAR and ANDREW R. MORTON

Part I: Critical Contributions – the Twentieth-century Legacy

Chapter 1

Andrew Morton's interpretation of Duncan Forrester's approach to public theology takes the term 'public' through a series of explorations as to its possible meaning, directed by the map offered by Forrester's life and work as a public theologian. With Duncan Forrester as guide, Morton sees theology as a public activity, conducted in the midst of public life and committed to the pursuit of public truth. Theology must therefore be done in public, and face to face with members of the public. But this raises the question for Morton of which public? He picks up on David Tracy's idea of theology's different publics, in Church, academy and the public domain of society, and reflects on the different public theological styles that each may elicit. Then Morton describes the ways in which Forrester does his own public theology, inhabiting and crossing among these different publics with ease, but not without a passion for practical engagement with public issues, an attention to the particular and a profound empathy with the pain of the many poor people who are all too often on the margins of such publics. In closing, Morton opens up the possibility that Forrester's preference for offering theological fragments to the discussion and resolution of particular public issues in a pluralist public world, rather than universal theological systems, may yet disclose the divine wholeness.

Chapter 2

The eminent German theologian, *Jürgen Moltmann*, gives an historical account of public theology in the latter part of the twentieth century. He traces the links between the political theology of the 1960s and a range of later theologies – black, *minjung*, liberationist, socialist, feminist and ecological. Central to the account is recognition of the tragic failure of Christianity represented by the Holocaust, together with the inescapably political nature of Christianity and the idolatry that is political religion. Through all run the concept of the Kingdom of God, the three principles of contextual theology – context, *kairos* and community, the centrality of the cross and with it 'the authority of the suffering'. Moltmann then points forward to the new need to take account of globalization and economization.

Chapter 3, 4

This mainly European perspective is then complemented through testimony by *John de Gruchy* from South Africa, a society which learned from European theology but also had to discover its own distinctive lessons, and similar testimony from Argentina by *José Míguez-Bonino*. Both these contributions highlight the contextuality of public theology and therefore the limits to the transference of theological insights from one context to another, whether across space or across time. In one context the Christian Church may find its Gospel confronting an obviously false gospel, such as German Nazism or South African apartheid, whereas in the context of a liberal democracy such either-or starkness may be absent or at least less obvious. South Africa illustrates the change over time from a society in which the Christian Church was the most influential religious community to one in which it is but one member of a multi-faith group of religious communities. Argentina illustrates the change over time from a more to a less dictatorial regime and the effect of this change on the Church's opportunities and responsibilities. De Gruchy's contribution from South Africa brings home the way in which, in situations of conflict and oppression, traditional theological vocabulary and live political vocabulary tend to coincide, with the language of guilt, forgiveness, justice, reconciliation and reparation becoming apposite. Míguez-Bonino's experience in Argentina leads him to reflect on a similar appositeness between the concerns with justice and law of the newly agrarian and monarchic society of the ninth to seventh centuries BCE in Palestine, as reflected in much of the Old Testament, and the Latin American concerns of the late twentieth century. With this biblical background he describes the dialectical relation between justice and law, in which the claims of justice lead to law, and law in turn enriches the concept of justice.

Part II: Contested Ideas – Modernity's Legacy

After these examinations of the immediate past, namely the latter half of the century just gone, the focus is widened to the whole modern era, of which the twentieth century was perhaps the climax, and to the new 'postmodernity'. The large questions that are faced include: whether modernity, including the Enlightenment tradition, is a child of Christianity, and if so, what happened to it when it 'left home' and took on secular form; how far postmodernity is an extension of modernity and how far a departure from it; and what Christian theology makes of the present cultural situation, variously characterized as liberal or secular or pluralist as well as postmodern, in which there is scepticism about objective truth and in which everything is regarded as contingent, diverse and indeterminate.

Chapter 5

Within this context *Richard Bauckham* focuses on the modern liberal concept of the freedom of the autonomous self and what he sees as its dependence on, and departure from, Christian antecedents. His treatment is particularly directed to the work of Jürgen Moltmann and his critical acceptance of modernity. While accepting modernity's concept of freedom, Moltmann rejects its accompanying individualism, with its atomization, domination and competitiveness, favouring instead a more communicative and mutual form of freedom. Bauckham argues that, though the Enlightenment emphasis on subjectivity and choice may have been derived from the Reformation doctrine of justification by faith, once it left behind the original Christian context, the selfhood grounded in God became a selfhood grounded in self.

Questions that arose in the colloquium in this context included: whether religion is the inner architecture of culture; whether ritual is the lifeblood of institutions; whether, more specifically, Christianity is the soul of modernity, without which it becomes vacuous; and whether therefore the currently dominant individualist secularism might be about to collapse and share the fate of the collectivist secularism which has already collapsed.

Chapter 6

Kees Klop from the Netherlands examines another implicit concept of liberal modernity, that of moral neutrality in the political sphere; he judges it hard to sustain. He engages with the crucial postmodern debate in which the case for moral neutrality and equality of respect is set against the case for a comprehensive narrative which is socially shared. In particular he defends the comprehensive narrative of the Spirit in creation, and applies it to the environmental debate with its seven competing models: ruthless pioneer, enlightened ruler, secular steward, participant in nature, religious steward, partner of nature or mystical union with nature.

Chapter 7

The important and related Enlightenment concept of tolerance is then examined by *David Fergusson*. He shows how the Reformed Church's aim of wholesale social transformation, to form a godly commonwealth, sat uneasily with tolerance and indeed could justify compulsion. Consequently, tolerance had to wait for later, more secular notions of human autonomy, state neutrality and social diversity. Now, however, when this concept of tolerance is being criticized as encouraging indifference, subjectivism and relativism, it

10

may need to be complemented by earlier, more religious notions of it, which were not wholly absent at the time of the Reformation. These included the non-coercive, persuasive approach of Jesus, the freedom and voluntariness of faith and a doctrine of Word and Spirit that calls for truth-seeking conversation. This earlier tradition contrasts with the later secularist one in its greater emphasis on group identity and on social, as distinct from individual, goods. In one way it goes beyond tolerance of others to the more active notion of empathetic understanding of them and to the articulation of common standards. In another way it may restrict tolerance through censorship in the interests of the common good.

All this highlights the hard task, in a world both one and plural, of both honouring diversity and serving the common good. This difficult search for moral coherence in a plural world and for a safe passage between the Scylla of moral authoritarianism and the Charybdis of moral chaos points increasingly towards the vocabulary of human rights.

Chapter 8

Relating this Enlightenment concept of human rights to theological understanding of transcendence is the topic of the contribution by *George Newlands*. Like Fergusson, he recognizes that Christianity's relation to human rights has been ambiguous, with the Church often supporting autocratic rule; but he finds intimations of human rights thinking throughout Christian history as expressed, for example, by Lactantius, Augustine, Aquinas, Luther and Calvin, and he sees a flowering of this in the Christology of the twentieth century, with the concept of the Christomorphic image of God providing a strong transcendental basis. Human rights language, though promising, is not problem-free, and Newlands points out some of the philosophical, political and legal, as well as theological, difficulties. He draws on the thinking of the philosopher, Martha Nussbaum, and notes the contributions of two fellow contributors to the volume, Jürgen Moltmann and Max Stackhouse. He illustrates his argument from four issues, homosexuality, the place of women, India and race. For him the central theological clue is in the 'Christological matrix' of generous, vulnerable, self-giving, self-affirming love.

The colloquium saw the issue of human rights as deserving of sustained examination, which might include such issues as: the relation of individual rights to the common good; the rights of organizations as distinct from individuals; the similarity or dissimilarity between politico-civil rights and socio-economic rights; and the dilemma of 'tolerating the intolerant', i.e. the possible limits to the freedom to express opinions conducive to behaviour which militates against the common good.

Any theological writing which attempts, as this volume does, to look back at a century and forward to another one, which, in other words, surveys a large tract of history, can hardly avoid the issues raised by those who make big assertions about history; for there are those who still dare to pronounce on 'where we are at' in the human story, though others now deny that there is any story. At a time when it is more common to eschew 'grand narratives' and big pictures, at least one writer has been bold enough to make such a metaphorical movie and declare that the human wagon train has completed its journey and reached *the end of history*, namely Francis Fukuyama.

Chapter 9

Ann Loades's contribution is to address this issue, challenging Fukuyama's thesis with the help of the somewhat neglected theology of Immanuel Kant. This is at the same time an exercise in theodicy, exploring how God acts in history with all its horrors. The trivializing operetta-like character of Fukuyama's and others' grand narratives, their suppression of human particulars and evasion of the terrors of history and, above all, their closed eschatology is contrasted with a more theological eschatology, including Kant's, which is open and which gives more room for responsible human action precisely because of transcendent divine grace. In the course of this contribution Loades reviews sympathetically a wide range of contemporary commentators on 'where we are at', but her main focus is on the distinctive role of public theology in transforming human action, especially through the restoration to public life of the language and the practice of grace.

Chapter 10

Raymond Plant addresses a dilemma facing liberal societies. If the justification for their political framework (which is liberal in the sense that it accommodates an internal plurality of moralities and 'comprehensive doctrines') is 'thin', as in John Rawls' very thin 'modus vivendi' or his not quite so thin 'overlapping consensus', it may be too thin to be sustainable; but if it is thicker in the sense of morally or metaphysically richer, it becomes itself a comprehensive doctrine, which overrides, and may conflict with at least some of, those espoused by its inhabitants, including religious believers.

Plant agrees with Rawls that a modus vivendi based on merely prudential calculation and not on moral principle (a Hobbesian tolerance rather than a

Millian toleration) is too unstable. But he also finds Rawls's preferred option of an 'overlapping consensus' ultimately unsatisfactory, since it veers either towards the thinness of a modus vivendi or to the thickness of a morality or metaphysic, involving as it does, according to Rawls, the belief that persons are free and equal. There seems to be an unresolvable conflict between liberal society's morality of *the right* and at least some moralities of *the good*. Certainly the primacy which it gives to Kantian individual autonomy and Millian equality of rights is not universally accepted.

Plant then examines an attempt by Thomas Nagel to resolve the dilemma by distinguishing between public and private assessment of beliefs; however, with Brian Barry, he rejects this as involving an unsatisfactory dichotomy between public and private and between two standards of evidence.

Finally, he offers his own justification for a liberal polity. He acknowledges his debt to Alan Gewirth's notion of goods which are *preconditions* of action, whatever goods may be the *object* of action. He regards this as a form of natural law theory, since the goods belong to human nature as such. He also sees an analogy between these goods as preconditions of all agency and truth-telling as a precondition of all language. On the basis of Gewirth's two conditions of action, namely voluntariness and purposiveness, he develops his own concepts of freedom and well-being. By spelling out at least some of 'the basic generic goods of agency', he hopes to start a far-reaching dialogue which will get beyond the current 'loose talk about moral diversity and incommensurability within a late modern society'.

Part III: Changing Contexts – Globalization's Impact

A feature of 'late modern society' (with possible intimations of it in earlier modernity) is 'globalization' – a frequently used but ambiguous term. The controversies around it, both as to its meaning and on whether from a theological perspective it is benign, malign or neutral, are the subject of the next four contributions.

Chapter 11

Max Stackhouse from the United States views globalization as a multifaceted phenomenon, social–cultural–political–economic–technological, and one to be welcomed and handled creatively. He explores four areas: a shift from the theological concept of 'orders of creation' to one of 'dynamic spheres of relative sovereignty'; global powers understood as principalities, authorities, thrones and dominions; how religions shape civilizations; and covenantal thought as a mode of public theology for global society. For him, the public in 'public theology' is no longer national but global and no longer just the state but the whole of civil society.

Chapter 12, 13, 14

The other three contributors on globalization, the Indian economist *Christopher Kurien* and the two British theologians, *Michael Northcott* and *Mary Grey*, see less welcome features in so-called globalization, which they regard as a particular kind of narrowly economic development, allied to political, military and ideological domination – a new colonialism.

Kurien points to the ambiguity of globalization as both unifying and dividing, both empowering and coercing. While he recognizes its technological and cultural dimensions, he focuses on its economic content, tracing its centuries-long history and its particular development in the last few decades. He considers the main economic development to be the growth of money-mediated transactions, which in most recent years have led to huge global inequalities of opportunity, income and power. He explores the relation between economic and political agents, between market and state, and pleads for political and social forms of globalization to balance the economic ones.

Michael Northcott and Mary Grey explore the conflicting world-views that underlie what they see as a fundamental conflict between contemporary economic globalization and Christianity. In Northcott's understanding there is an integral relation between liturgy, theology and ethics, with the latter two grounded in the first; and so, how food is handled in the global economy and how it is handled in the sacramental feast that is the Eucharist should be at one; but, given the present global economy, they are not. He illustrates this from the very particular case of salmon farming in Scotland, incidentally arguing that the distinctiveness of recent constitutional reform in Scotland, and of theological thinking that has influenced it, has not saved Scotland from subordination to the corporatist global culture. His contribution also includes an exposition of the public theology of the influential Mennonite, John Yoder, whose approach differs from Forrester's but who comes to not dissimilar conclusions.

For Grey, spirit is central to theology as 'the depth dimension of God'. She sees the present global culture, dominated by an American and Western European economic system, as spiritually pathological, with life commodified, diversity lost, material gratification deified and, above all, imagination and aspiration atrophied. She argues the need for a new common language and spirituality of dreaming and finds anticipations of it in Gandhi's search for embodied truth, which she expounds and links with a Christian understanding of spirit.

The discussion of globalization in the colloquium, not surprisingly, included discussion of 'the market', which was seen as an ancient institution that was either morally neutral or enhancing of humanity, or, by contrast, dangerous if it is idolatrously elevated or if associated, as it is at present, with highly concentrated and unequally distributed power.

There was also discussion of the scope and limits of theologians' influence on major institutions. Those theologians who are close to the leaders of institutions such as the World Bank or World Trade Organization are aware of those individuals' desire for theological guidance. Others, however, point to the extent to which even the most influential members of large institutions are constrained by institutional forces, for example by the way in which industrial and commercial enterprises influence states, which in their turn influence intergovernmental organizations. There was also a warning of the danger of the ideological abuse of theology.

Part IV: Emerging Concerns – Twenty-first-century Issues and Approaches

Medical Ethics

A striking feature of the twentieth century was the rapid and accelerating increase of scientific knowledge and technological capacity. Scientific discovery and technical innovation have been particularly dramatic in the biological realm and have given human beings awesome influence over life itself. The twenty-first century is likely to see yet more of this development. *Robin Gill* and *Alastair Campbell* focus attention on theological implications of this.

Chapter 15

Gill's treatment of 'genetic engineering' concentrates on the ethical decisions and dilemmas produced by these new human powers, and discusses the role of religion in handling them. He expounds the contrasting approaches of Michael Banner and Audrey Chapman, the former making sharply particularist Christian claims and the latter being more consensual, and both involved as theologians on public bodies concerned with genetics and medical ethics. Chapman is equally critical of theologians who in this context abandon theistic language and those whose theological claims are simplistic or show a pre-evolutionary understanding of creation. Banner's position is that Christian medical ethics is based on the quite distinctive knowledge of humankind given by the Word of God. He is highly critical of the consequentialist ethics of secular moral philosophers and resistant to notions of human co-creation; his own arguments are a blend of deontological and consequentialist ones. Gill himself stresses the importance for theologians of listening to scientists and moral philosophers; given this, he believes that theology brings to the ethics of health care and genetics critical motivation, commitment and depth.

Chapter 16

Campbell reflects a recent shift in ethical thinking, in which attention is directed not only to right acting but also to virtuous being. This leads to a fresh approach to medical ethics, which does not confine itself to the right action and proper practice of the providers of health services but attends also to the ethical stance of the patient, seeking to identify a virtuous response to the common human experience of being ill. He regrets the hubris of medicine that has substituted the technological fix for the Hippocratic modesty of curing sometimes, alleviating often, comforting always, and so he addresses those parts of medical care in which cure is not an option. In particular, with the help of his research assistant, Teresa Swift, he gives a full account of their recent empirical study of the relevance of virtue ethics to patients with chronic illnesses. This study showed that such illness threatens not only physical capacity and social life but also self-respect, and that living well with illness involves above all the maintenance of self-respect and the associated virtues of courage, realism, acceptance and communality. Campbell then relates these findings to the thinking of two writers, Karen Lebacqz and Stanley Hauerwas, especially the latter's concept of Christian patience. After expanding Martha Nussbaum's notion of 'thin' and 'thick' accounts of virtue, he develops his own 'rich' concept of self-respect and finally claims that there is no real expertise in ethics, the patient being the best teacher.

Justice

If biomedical intervention has been one of Duncan Forrester's preoccupations, another and even more sustained preoccupation, as already noted, has been justice, both retributive and distributive. Indeed he himself stimulated the colloquium to forward-looking thought on justice, pointing out that the boundary is being eroded between civil and criminal justice, which have been judiciable, and social and economic justice, which have not. He also made a plea for a justice which is more proactive, not just reactive, and therefore closer to the biblical than to the classical concept.

Chapter 17

Stanley Hauerwas's contribution on punishment reflects his characteristic challenge to what he sees as the capitulation of Christian theology to a secular liberal consensus. Not that he accuses Duncan Forrester of this. He respects Forrester's work on criminal justice and the way in which it has contributed to valuable reform of the practice of punishment in the civil order. However, Hauerwas's contribution is to emphasize the distinctiveness of Christian punishment, which is to be expressed primarily in the Christian community and only thereby influencing the civil order, the boundary between Church and world being both real and permeable. The conviction that God's justice is the cross and that Christ is the end of expiation leads to a distinctive understanding of the relation between retribution, penitence, forgiveness and reconciliation.

Chapter 18

If Hauerwas rejects the apparently commonsensical contrast between retribution and forgiveness, Alan Torrance rejects that kind of contrast between justice and forgiveness. His focus is on forgiveness for major atrocities, such as those by Nazis on Jews or in the conflicts in the Balkans, Rwanda and Northern Ireland. So it is not surprising that he pays particular attention to the Croat theologian, Miroslav Volf. Torrance contends that unconditional and unbounded forgiveness applies as much to political as to personal relations and that it belongs not only to the ethic but also to the ontology of both the Testaments. He takes seriously the argument that only immediate victims are in a position to forgive perpetrators, but he eventually rejects it on the basis of the divine–human and human–human solidarity implicit in the atonement. He shows how the possibilities of justice are limited by 'partiality' and 'irreversibility'; justice is to be achieved not through a vain and damaging attempt to restore a supposed balance of nature, but through forgiveness.

Equality

Duncan Forrester's even more sustained concern for distributive justice is the stimulus of the next two contributions. *Tim Gorringe* and *Chris Rowland* both focus on equality, which has featured in Forrester's work from his first book, *Caste and Christianity*, to his most recent, *On Human Worth*.

Chapter 19

Gorringe examines the question whether inequality is inescapable or avoidable, and whether or not it is a manifestation of sin. He looks at various theories of its origins in the course of human development, such as the development of agriculture and urbanization. His special interest is in the respective weights of material and ideological factors in historical trends both towards inequality and towards equality; while he takes seriously the Marxist concept of base and superstructure, he finds it wanting. A key concept for him is Barth's *Mitmenschheit* or cohumanity.

Chapter 20

Rowland, as a biblical scholar, is particularly concerned with the place of equality in the biblical and Christian tradition. He sees it as having a central place and directs his contribution to an exposition of what he regards as the most extensive and systematic of theologies of equality, namely that of the seventeenth-century founder of the 'Digger' colony, Gerrard Winstanley. In addition, he provides the volume with its one exposition of exegetical method, showing how biblical exegesis relates to public theology.

In these contributions, the theology of equality is traced throughout the tradition, from the Bible through the early Fathers to the conciliar movement and then through more recent Christian movements typified by such thinkers as Winstanley, Blake and Tawney. However, it is also recognized here, as in the contributions on toleration and human rights, that Christian history has been ambiguous, being sometimes liberative and sometimes restrictive.

Exclusion – Chapters 21, 22

The next two contributions, those by *Alistair Kee* and *Marcella Althaus-Reid*, take up respectively two of Duncan Forrester's special emphases, namely on excluded people and on a theology of fragments. The two have much in common. It is not just that they share a worldscope, Kee drawing particularly on black experience in North America and in South Africa and Althaus-Reid on Latin American and Indian sources; it is that both are saying that the future, the hope is with the people who don't belong, don't fit, don't get included or integrated *and* with their ideas that don't belong, don't fit, are hard to include or integrate. Their moral is not to try to include or integrate them. So the recent fragmentary and unfitting theologies, which characterize the end of the twentieth and beginning of the twenty-first century, not least the feminist and post-colonial ones, present a sharp challenge. Is the relation of the centuries-long, well-established traditional theology to the novel and radical theologies of the twentieth and twenty-first centuries that of sun to planets, core to fragments, theme to variations, *cantus firmus* to counterpoint, the given to the constructed, or are such contrasts fundamentally flawed? Whatever the answer, public theology on the cusp of the second and third millennia is an exciting and exacting enterprise.

Politics – Chapters 23, 24

Elaine Graham analyses the crisis of citizenship in contemporary Britain. She explores possible reasons for the low level of political participation, reflected in low levels of voting, and calls for a broader understanding of 'public' to include civil society and to hold together political, cultural and spiritual power. She sees the present disenchantment with political institutions as indicative of major changes in the configuration of social life, to which the response should not be complaints of 'apathy' but attempts to discover the nature and implications of these changes. While she recognizes the importance of what is happening to values, she lays as much stress on what is happening to procedures and processes and on the need for new forms of social infrastructure. She calls for a public theology that holds together 'universal' and 'preferential' dimensions.

The discussion of this in the colloquium raised such issues as the commodification and individualization of leisure, the affluence that enables some people to opt out of social participation and, by contrast, the pressures of work and limited income that leave others no time for the voluntary activity involved in responsible citizenship.

Finally *William Storrar* relates the volume's overall theme – the twentieth-century legacy and twenty-first-century agenda for public theology – to the meeting of two extremes, the global and the local. Can globalization be combined with localization? And can theology itself avoid being either so global and universal as to be imperialist or so local and particular as to be incommensurable? He expounds the notion of 'glocalization', developed by the sociologist Roland Robertson and the Catholic theologian Robert Schreiter; this is the claim that in what is called globalization there is actually an interactive *global–local* dynamic, combining homogenization with heterogenization. Storrar then argues that Duncan Forrester's public theology is through and through 'glocal', illustrating this from four salient features of his work: his rooting in the Scottish Reformed tradition including its 'Radical Orthodoxy'; his immersion in Indian life including the impact of degrading inequality; his constant ecumenical engagement in both transconfessional and transcontinental senses; and his no less continuous collaboration with a wide range of disciplines, academic, professional and 'experiential'. Storrar then surveys the full range of contributions to this volume in the light of those four Forrester perspectives. Finally, he describes in some detail the role of theology in the Scottish constitutional politics of the late twentieth century; he does so on his own authority as a participant but also through the eyes of Gregory Baum, the Canadian Catholic theologian of German and Jewish origins, who has studied the theological contribution to progressive nationalism in Scotland, as well as in Quebec and East Germany. The optimistic Scottish Christian interpretation of nationalism is presented as a 'potentially emancipatory site of glocalization'. It is also taken to illustrate the positive value of the 'middle axiom' approach made famous in the 1930s by a Scottish pioneer of the World Council of Churches, J. H. Oldham. Storrar, in his treatment of middle axioms as interactive rather than deductive, takes issue with Forrester's criticism of them. So, while the last word of the co-editor of this volume is a tribute to the theologian in whose honour it is published, the penultimate word is disagreement with him! Let public theology in the twenty-first century continue such constructive controversy.

In an *Afterword*, which the editors have entitled *Working in the Quarry*, *Duncan Forrester* responds to the papers presented at the colloquium in his honour, from which this volume has emerged. Reflecting on his own understanding of public theology, and the contributions and discussion at the colloquium, he offers two arresting metaphors for public theology's calling in the twenty-first century. First, he sees it as a barque that must always steer between the Scylla of an orthodoxy detached from the insights of contemporary thought or the language of contemporary people, and the Charybdis of an extreme liberal accommodation to secular thought, speaking the language of godless morality without any distinctive content. Forrester wishes public theology to steer a course that relies on the tradition as compass to travel into unknown waters. That compass for public theology has as its true north the Church, as an inclusive community of faith, and Scripture, read through the eyes of the excluded. The task of those who would serve public theology today is to keep alive the dream of ending global human misery and to speak in public debate in ways that are prophetic, passionate and yet accessible. Having avoided the rocks of Scylla and Charybdis, Forrester returns to his favoured metaphor and method for doing public theology: the quarrying of theological fragments. The calling of the public theologian is to work humbly and hard in the quarry of the rich resources of the Bible, the Christian tradition, and other world faiths and ideologies in their interaction with that Christian tradition, to produce the fragments of insight, challenge and truth that may help to pave the way in the coming of God's Reign.

We end, then, where we began. Public theology is concerned with the public affairs of society in the light of hope in Christ for the Kingdom of God. But now we see more clearly something of what this involves, in the extraordinary range and reach of the chapters in this volume. From the twentieth century, public theology inherits its contextual and emancipatory engagement with society pioneered mainly by non-Western Christians, while still wrestling with modernity's contested ideas of universal human flourishing. The emerging concerns of the twenty-first century, whether on the new frontiers of human genetics or in the old heartland of human suffering, challenge public theology to find fresh and relevant approaches to address such complex public issues. And, as if that were not enough of a challenge, the compressions of time and space under the impact of globalization make public theology an increasingly interdependent and collaborative activity. In as much as this book has brought together scholars from around the world, already linked by friendship and respect for Duncan Baillie Forrester, a public theologian whose life and work embody the fruitful interchange of the local and the global, it offers theological fragments from a global quarry for many publics and changing times.

Notes

1 Jürgen Moltmann, *God for a Secular Society* (London: SCM Press, 1999), p. 1.
2 Duncan B. Forrester, *Truthful Action* (Edinburgh: T&T Clark, 2000), pp. 127–8.

Part I

Critical Contributions – the Twentieth-century Legacy

Chapter 1

Duncan Forrester: A Public Theologian

ANDREW R. MORTON

A Personal Perspective

Discovering what a friend has learned from you can be a surprise, as it may bear little resemblance to your own self-understanding. If Duncan Forrester does not recognize himself in this personal interpretation of his contribution to the theory and practice of public theology, I can only apologize. I am confident, however, in asserting that his work – happily, to be continued – is powerful testimony to the public nature of theology. It is public theology in many senses, of which I can mention only a few.

Public Activity

The most obvious sense in which he has engaged in public theology is that his theological activity has not been confined within the walls of either the Church or the academy, but has also been out in the public domain, in the political arena. This may be no surprise in one whose scholarship is in both theology and politics; but even if he were not a political scientist and theorist, it would be an implicate of his theology, which is public in two deeper senses. He rejects two prevalent notions: one is that religion, and hence also theology, affects only private life; the other is that it is solely a function of individual subjectivity.

Public Life

The distinction between private life and public life is useful, provided that these are understood as parts of a continuum. Person-to-person relations, person-to-group ones and group-to-group ones, though distinguishable, are inseparable. The intimate and the institutional are in constant interaction. What we do and are as families and friends and what we do and are as fellow-workers and citizens affect each other. Sadly there has been a tendency, at least in the twentieth century in the English-speaking world, to oversharpen the private/public distinction, to obscure or downplay the influence of the public on the private, and to confine religion to the latter. To all this, Forrester's work says a loud 'no'. It is not just that his sober observation – and he is a stickler for empirical evidence – has shown him that the private and the public form a seamless robe. It is above all that his theology is all-encompassing, being based on the biblical conviction that 'the earth belongs to the Lord and *all* that it contains'; therefore he is resistant to any reduction of the Gospel to the purely private; his is a full-spectrum evangel.

Public Truth

The other prevalent notion which he rejects is that religion or theology is a form of subjective act or condition that does not refer to anything in the 'real world'. On this view, it is something which an individual person thinks or feels or prefers or chooses, which is not subject to any objective, in the sense of public, test. It tells us nothing about the way things are; it tells us only about the way the person in question is, and there is no reference beyond her. In that sense it is purely private, not public. In rejecting such privatizing or subjectivizing of religion, Forrester is not alone among theologians. For theologians like him, theology is about the reality which all share, the world which all inhabit, and in that sense the public reality, the public world. Of course the subject matter of theology is God; but if God means anything like Anselm's 'that than which nothing greater can be conceived', then theology's subject matter is the whole of reality. It is cognitive, it makes truth claims, claims to know about the way things are, about what is the case. Such making of truth claims is an inherently public activity. Forrester would agree with Eberhard Jüngel's comment that 'the political relevance of the Christian faith consists first and last in its capacity for truth and its obligation to truth.'

To summarize – inasmuch as theology's subject matter is public as well as private life, public theology is *part* of theology; but inasmuch as theology makes claims about the way things are and therefore lays itself open to public test, *all* of it is public theology.

26

In Public

Forrester's theology, however, is public in further senses, which distinguish him from many other theologians. For him, theologizing is an activity in which one engages in face of a public. To put it more figuratively, it is always done in the open, in some forum or agora. One could say that he does not make a distinction between a theological product which is for self-use and one which is for export; all is for export, as well as self-use. I am not implying that he does not distinguish between market places, between publics; he does and, indeed, as we will see later, the multiplicity of market places, of publics is extremely important for him; but all theologizing is in *some* market place.

Being in the open, in face of a public, profoundly affects the nature of theology. First of all, it is not soliloquy; it is dialogue or, in plainer English, conversation. It always involves interlocutors, whether singly or in groups, whether the forum has one occupant or a crowd. One might say that it is about the ear as much as the mouth and about the connection between them. To be more precise, it is about the connection between my mouth and the *other*'s ear and between my mouth and *my* ear. In other words, it is always both persuasive speaking, focusing on the other's ear, and attentive listening, focusing on one's own ear.

Regarding the first, the persuasive speaking, Forrester is clear that all theology is advocacy; he says quite simply that it is evangelism. He resists the notion that public theology is a kind of secondary, away-from-home activity of the theologian, in which she makes small, theologically related contributions to public debate, but is not doing her primary job. To say, as he does, that public theology is evangelism is to say that it *is* the primary theological activity and that this is nothing other than to convey evangel or good news, which is a form of attempt to convince hearers of what is the case.

On the second, the attentive listening, he is equally clear that all theology involves receptiveness to the other, whoever that other may be. In all the many conversations that have been the stuff of the interdisciplinary activities which he has facilitated and in which he himself has engaged, under the auspices of his Centre for Theology and Public Issues, a notable feature has been mutual listening, in which givers have also been receivers, teachers also learners.

Of course he has also sat at his solitary desk, writing lectures and a goodly number of books. How then can one say that for him all theology is public

27

in the sense that it is in face of a public and is inherently a dialogue or conversation? The answer is that the solitary writer is not really alone, that his thought is internalized conversation, shot through with the persuasiveness of an advocate and the attentiveness of a listener. Internalized conversation is a necessary complement to the external conversation, each being creative, provided that it is in interaction with the other. But what Forrester would reject, if I understand him, is any notion that the conversation, the engagement with a public, is only the communication of a theology that is produced internally or in some other way; for him the conversation produces the theology and does not just communicate it. And such conversation involves throughout both the persuasive eloquence of advocacy and the attentive silence of receptivity – and in passing let it be said that when these two inseparables are sundered and ascribed respectively to 'evangelicals' and 'liberals', counsel is darkened.

Publics

I said that for Forrester, theology is public in the sense that it is 'in face of *a* public'; I did not say '*the* public'. For he makes quite clear that there are several publics; we are dealing with a plural not a singular. He acknowledges his indebtedness to David Tracy, in *The Analogical Imagination*, for the terminology of 'publics of theology'; but this plurality is a reality with which his whole career has made him familiar. Theology is practised in face of a plurality of particular publics. Whatever he may think about the reality or accessibility of a single universal human public – and this is not altogether clear – he is clear that theology is done in the context of particular publics.

In this he is at one with the recent widespread movement of thought (is it 'postmodern', 'late modern', 'second modern' or what?), according to which all thought is within the context of a particular 'community' of shared life. He shares that movement's suspicion and scepticism about great systems of thought which claim universal coverage and propound timeless, placeless principles. So theology, being in face of a particular public, must surely be limited by the limitations of that particularity, in at least two ways, in the scope of the truth claims it makes and in its comprehensibility or accessibility to those beyond the particular public. I believe that Forrester accepts this; in various ways he acknowledges the modesty of the theological enterprise; its claims to truth and its comprehensibility are indeed restricted. He would go on to say, however, that those claims, though restricted, are nonetheless real.

Public or Community

Since the particularity of a particular and not universal public is similar to the particularity of a particular and not universal community, one could say that Forrester is in the same camp as 'communitarians', both the sceptical ones who stress the limits of truth claims and the devout ones who stress the need to share the communal life if one is to grasp its truth. However, there are important differences. In at least two ways 'public theology', in Forrester's understanding of it, sets him apart from 'communitarian' theology. First, the concept of 'public' is significantly different from that of 'community'. Secondly, Forrester operates simultaneously in several publics.

The difference between public and community might be caught by a phrase of Khalil Gibran, popular in recent time in certain do-it-yourself marriage services; the phrase is, 'let there be spaces in your togetherness'. In a public, as distinct from a community, there is space or distance in the sense of difference and either disagreement or absence of agreement. It is indeed a forum or agora, a space which allows and indeed encourages encounter with that which is different; hence the role, already described, of advocacy and attentiveness. The whole thing is pervaded by questioning, doubting and challenging, as well as asserting, confirming and agreeing. This is of the nature of dialogue or converse. It presupposes difference and disagreement or absence of agreement, and with these it brings vulnerability and insecurity.

Of course words do not have fixed meanings and those who, for whatever reason, like the word 'community' may ascribe to it all that has just been ascribed to the word 'public'. We are not dealing with two separate entities, but two points on a spectrum. Nonetheless it is a difference, for which the two terms are convenient counters. Whereas 'community' places strong emphasis on what is common to its members, shared by them, 'public' puts more emphasis on what is not common, not shared.

Of course a public would not be a public unless its members had *something* in common. At the very least a public has a common language and form of discourse, without which there could be no exchange in the forum, no dialogue, no conversation. Its existence also presupposes *some* measure of common experience and common practice and possibly also of common belief and common purpose. But alongside this is a great area in which there is nothing in common. What is shared in a public is space more than substance; there is some togetherness but with large spaces in it; its weave is open.

29

ANDREW R. MORTON

Two Publics?

But what are the publics in which public theology is practised? Professional theologians are most aware of two of them, the Church and the academy; for it is to these two that most of them belong, these two which in some sense they serve, these two which have given them their qualification or appointment. Some are solely church-appointees – in church seminaries; some are solely university-appointees – in university faculties or departments; some, like Forrester, are appointed by institutions that contrive to be both university faculties and church colleges. Very many, however, in all three of these settings, belong in some way to both and regard their theology as exercised in both.

Now that we have specified two of the publics in question – and brought this term down from the clouds of abstraction – it may be objected that at least one of them is not a public but a community or even that both are communities not publics. Why does Forrester (and Tracy) call them 'publics' not 'communities'? It could be that 'public' just means audience or readership, those to whom theologians address their lectures or books. My argument is that, in Forrester's case (whatever Tracy's may be), it is more than that. It is that academia *and* Church, though in different ways, are dialogic forums, settings of advocacy and attentiveness, spaces within which there is distance, difference and possibility of disagreement. Of course Forrester is far from denying differences between these two publics, the ecclesial and the academic; he would certainly consider the Church to be farther than the academy towards the community end of the public/community spectrum. Indeed he is second to none in his emphasis on shared life as characterizing the Church (about which he is every bit as eloquent as any Alasdair MacIntyre or Stanley Hauerwas). For him it is above all in worship and especially the sacrament of the Lord's Supper that there is this shared life. It is shared experience more than shared belief, practice or purpose. His particular joy in the sacrament, about which he waxes most eloquent, is precisely that people, between whom there are vast spaces of difference in what they are and think and say and do, experience the grace of oneness. This is not tight community in the sense of either internal conformity or external exclusivity; it is not a 'ghetto' in either of these senses. It is indeed a dialogic forum, within which there is distance, difference and possibility of disagreement. Surely this is *ecclesia* in the original sense of an open assembly, which was the classical and classic type of a public. That the modern university is a public more than a community need hardly be argued.

30

If Forrester's position is to be distinguished from the typical communitarian one with the help of this distinction between a community and a public, it is also to be distinguished from it by his understanding and practice of simultaneous membership of several publics. It is this simultaneity – being in several places at once – which gives his theologizing particular power. The tension and even pain involved in such split living is highly creative.

Three Publics?

What then are these publics? So far we have mentioned two, the Church and the academy. But there is at least a third, and it is odd that we should only now be mentioning it, as it is the public that is usually regarded as the one and only real public, namely the population of a society as a whole, the public with a capital P, *the* public. My very first reference to Forrester's public theology was to his activity outside the Church and the academy in the 'public' domain. I also referred to it as 'the political arena'; but to be more precise, the domain or arena of *the* public is not only political, but also social and cultural and economic. A glance at the list of work of the Centre for Theology and Public Issues would immediately show that the Forrester canvas of public theology covers all these subdivisions, these further publics within the public in the big sense. There is an important further distinction, to which I will return, between two elements in the society-wide public, which makes it almost into two publics; but for the moment it makes sense to treat it as one and thus to speak of the big three – Church, academy and public with a capital P. The Centre for Theology and Public Issues has often referred to this trio of its interlocutors – Church, academy and public – and described itself as a meeting place of the three. The point about the Forrester theology is that it is fashioned within that conjunction and simultaneity, when the three publics are faced in the same place at the same time. I repeat that I am not talking only of the communication of that theology but of its creation. The conjunction is the crucible. As with any crucible, it is not comfortable to inhabit; it is a grinding experience; the tension is painful, a kind of passion.

Public Styles

Tracy speaks of three modes of theology as appropriate respectively to these three publics – systematic theology for the Church, fundamental theology for the academy, practical theology for society. He allows for a little overlap, but on the whole the allocation is clear-cut. I think of two other trios of styles of theology, somewhat though not exactly allocated to different publics. There is Schleiermacher's trio – poetic, rhetorical and didactic – and there is Rowan Williams's – celebratory, communicative and critical. It would be all too easy to treat such trios as three gears appropriate to three environments and involving a smooth gear change from one to other. But this presupposes that one inhabits only one environment at any one time. The point about the Forrester approach is that one is in several publics at the same time. This means that one has to be simultaneously in the three, or however many, modes. I would go further and suggest that Forrester would regard all three modes as necessary *within* any one of the three publics. Seeing him in action suggests that he would be hard put not to be celebratory *and* communicative *and* critical in any context. Admittedly there needs to be some modulation of style. While one may always be facing the three publics, there is usually one in the foreground and two in the background. If such a distinction, between foreground and background, can be applied to the environments or publics, it can also be applied to the modes. So, for example, the celebratory mode tends to be foregrounded in the Church and the critical mode in the academy. Forrester's own reference to 'reverence' in the former and 'rigour' in the latter is in line with this, though I have reservations about this particular antithesis; his own leadership of worship, for example, is as impressive for the rigour of its wording as for the reverence of its spirit; perhaps his homiletic love of alliteration has led him slightly astray here.

Transpublic

I believe that Forrester's theology has been particularly creative because of this tension of living simultaneously with several publics and of working simultaneously in several modes. He has described himself as a 'stickit minister'. This Scottish phrase usually refers to someone trained to be a minister who for some reason gets 'stuck', i.e., does not become a minister. I do not know quite why he applies this to himself; I guess that he is saying that he is *really* a minister, and I suspect that he may also be saying that he is surprised to be an academic. What he should be saying by this phrase is that he has not ceased to be a minister all the time he has also been an academic. I do not just mean that in New College he has been an outstanding pastor of people and president of worship as well as a teacher and a scholar. I mean that his theology has been Church-focused as well as academy-focused, and never other than evangelic. But perhaps the deepest insight hidden within his 'stickit minister' comment is the element of surprise and even discomfort. It is a sense of not being quite in the right place, not quite at home. This is precisely the creative tension that living simultaneously in different environments produces and that issues in genuine theology. To face several publics is not to be at home in any of them, but to be always away from the place where one really belongs. This experience of displacement is theology-generating discomfort, part of the grinding in this crucible of the simultaneity of publics.

Two Publics in One

I have already hinted that to speak of the society-wide public in the singular needs to be qualified. That the public with a capital P is made up of many publics is almost a platitude. There are societies within societies, Scottish, British, European and so on, and, as already noted, there are economic, cultural and other sub-publics. The public with a capital P is indeed publics. However, the subdivision which has been particularly significant in much of the practice of Forrester and his Centre is that between the most and the least powerful in society. Stress has already been laid on the high degree of difference which there can be in a public in contrast to the greater degree of commonality in a community. So it is no surprise that there can be a wide range of difference in power within the civic public of, say, Scotland. What has particularly influenced Forrester's practice has been the realization that this difference can be so great that it constitutes not only a difference in people's experience but also a difference in their very language and form of discourse, such a great difference that it spells not one public but two. Much of the Centre's work has derived from the recognition that the most and the least powerful people in Scotland constitute in effect two publics. There is something specially poignant about two publics in one society, which is absent from two publics in the sense of two neighbouring societies. It is the paradoxical pain of being two despite being also one. It is the dynamic of distribution of power within the one society that produces the two publics.

Forrester's work throughout his career has attempted to take seriously the realities of power and to correct a tendency in church circles to be blind to those realities both in the public with a capital P and in the public that is the Church. It is not that he is numbered among those who demonize power; he sees its central importance and he would, I guess, agree with Paul Tillich, for whom love, power and justice formed a kind of trinity. But he is very conscious of the inequality of power, and while he would not reject the current language of 'social exclusion', he would stress the way in which inequality of power within a society excludes the most powerful as well as the least powerful, shutting both off from one another and forming two publics with little common language or means of discourse. So creating simultaneity and shared space for these two publics has been a major part of his work through the Centre. When handling matters of public policy, he has brought together people from the two sharp ends of policy-making, i.e., those with most effect on public policy, legislators and administrators, and those who, because of their severe lack of power over their own lives to say nothing of others', tend to be most affected by public policy, in its actions and omissions. This has been a specially creative part of the crucible of theology constituted by the tension between publics.

In this connection Forrester contrasts two approaches to public theology, the 'magisterial' and the 'liberationist', the first being more 'top-down' and the second more 'bottom-up'. The first tends to reflect the perspective of theologians who are used to talking to the powers that be, whereas the second tends to reflect that of theologians close to the least powerful. While he rejects the authoritative style of the first (and his use of the term 'magisterial' for it is significant) and while his style is closer to that of the second, he cannot really be put in either camp. Because he seeks to relate simultaneously to the most and the least powerful, facing these two publics simultaneously and helping them to face each other, he holds the tension between them.

Public Issues – Practical, Particular and Painful

This brings me to a specially important feature of the Forrester approach to public theology, namely the focus on public *issues*. It is no accident that the name of the Centre does not have a term like 'public *life*' or 'public *responsibility*' or any other term that is singular and comprehensive. The term 'issues' is plural and what might be called 'bitty'. It does not suggest wholeness or completeness. This is indeed a *fragmentary* approach – and with that I come to a word about which Forrester has much to say. He stresses the importance of fragments. It might be thought that in this he is simply reflecting the spirit of the age, the postmodern emphasis on the fragmentary nature of knowledge and the impossibility, or alternatively the danger, of systems of thought. Is he simply reflecting the contemporary scepticism about any attempt to 'see things steadily and see them whole'? I think not. His emphasis on fragments is traceable much further back, certainly to Søren Kierkegaard and I think also to Karl Barth. In the great Kierkegaard/Hegel divide, he would have been on the side of the author of *Philosophical Fragments*. For Forrester, the place where theology is created is not up high where you see everything from end to end but down low where you seek to do and scarcely see enough to be able to do. It is the place of faithfulness, that is of attempting to do the will and on that basis know the doctrine. It is a place of practicality, where any seeing is bound up with doing or at least attempting to do. There *is* seeing; it is not blind doing. For one thing, there is a seeing of what is, as one pays attention to all available data. There is also a seeing of what is possible and of what is to be done. But this latter is no straightforward seeing. It is not prediction, but 'vision'. It is not prescription, but 'discernment'. This is fragmentary seeing; it comes in flashes, in glimpses. For this place of practicality is also necessarily a place of particularity; and its practicality and particularity mean that it is down low, far from Olympus, and in the middle or thick of things, far from Alpha and from Omega. So it is redolent of Kierkegaard's understanding of Christian living of truth, and with him it looks askance at systems, which are castles one builds but does not inhabit. I believe that it is also redolent of Barth's understanding of God's sovereign freedom, and with him it looks askance at principles which become idols that infringe that transcendent freedom.

A glance at the list of public issues that Forrester and his Centre have faced will show that they have been very practical and very particular. What may not be so immediately evident is the method of approach to them, the way in, the point of entry. It has been 'where the shoe pinches'. So one needs to add a third 'p' to practicality and particularity, namely pain. It is not any pain; it is that which is associated with practice, with action. It is the pain of the struggle to act, which is the struggle to overcome the limitations and frustrations of practice, the limited power both to know what to do and to do it. To add yet another 'p' – it is about powerlessness, in two forms of it. It is the powerlessness of the *obviously* powerless, for example, the prisoners, the homeless, the impoverished. But it is also the powerlessness of those who on the face of it have power, the professionals charged with serving the prisoners, the homeless, the impoverished. For in the Forrester approach a typical place of theological creativity is where two such categories of people are brought together, those suffering the obvious limitations of power – no freedom, no shelter, no money – and those charged with helping them, who are themselves painfully aware of the limits of *their* power. This is a typical way in which the Forrester approach, as I have already suggested, transcends the opposition between the top-down and bottom-up approaches.

ANDREW R. MORTON

A Revelation?

What comes out of such an approach that starts where the shoe pinches and creates a conjunction of the pains of powerlessness? In what way is it creative? The answer is twofold. It is firstly that out of the shared perplexity and powerlessness come some vision of change and some power for change. But it is secondly – and this is the special interest here – that it generates theology. By that is not meant that one more chapter is added to an expanding volume of particular *applications* of an already understood universal gospel; this is no more the application of a pre-existing theology than the communication of it. What is meant is that there is discovery or revelation of God. It is in that sense that theology is created out of the places of practicality, particularity and the pain of the limits of power known only to those who push against them. It is, quite simply, though it is far from simple, that God is encountered.

That being so, one is not left with mere particularity and nothing universal, mere fragments and no wholeness; for within the particularity is universality, within the fragments is wholeness, but it is the universality and wholeness not of a system or of a set of principles but of God. It is half a century since some theologians talked of the 'scandal of particularity' of the Christ event, that place of the pain of the limits of power from which came power and disclosure. Is it legitimate to extend this notion to those other places of discovery or revelation of God and to say that William Blake's 'minute particulars' and T. S. Eliot's 'sordid particulars' are capable, for all their fragmentariness, of disclosing the divine whole? Be that as it may, the Forrester handling of public issues, especially at those places where the shoe pinches most, has been valuable not only because of its influence on public policy but also because of its creation of public theology.

Some of this public theology is publishable and has been published. Some of it is not publishable, being hidden in the lives of those who have participated in the Forrester-inspired enterprise. In the interaction of people of many publics, including those on the margins and those in the middle, God has been made known to not a few, including ones who thought they knew but didn't and ones who thought they didn't but did.

Chapter 2

Political Theology in Germany after Auschwitz[1]

JÜRGEN MOLTMANN

About thirty years ago, Johann Baptist Metz introduced the term 'political theology' into the theological and public discussion in Germany. With this term he wanted to break out of the narrows of middle-class 'theology as a private affair', and to escape from the confines of the transcendental, existential and personalistic theologies of the time.[2] But his other purpose was to formulate prophetically Christianity's eschatological message in the conditions of modern society: 'Every eschatological theology has to become a political theology, a theology critical of society.'

Metz had been influenced by the 'new anthropological direction' of Karl Rahner's theology, and by stressing the eschatological horizon of theology and its political context he found a new contemporaneity with the conflicting social forces of those years. The point was not to politicize the churches. The purpose was to find a 'theology with its face turned towards the world', and a way of 'talking about God in our own time'.

I first met Metz in 1965 in Tübingen on the occasion of Ernst Bloch's eightieth birthday. It was Bloch, the 'atheist for God's sake', to whom we owe our ecumenical friendship. Together we joined in the last Christian–Marxist dialogue in Marienbad in 1967, which was called to life by the Paulus Society and the Prague Academy of Sciences – a great encounter because it was so moving.[3] An eschatologically orientated talk about God – 'the God of hope', 'the God ahead of us' – bound Metz and myself together in critical responsibility for society.

On the Protestant side, a number of different paths pointed in the same direction: Leonhard Ragaz's Kingdom of God theology, with its social criticism; Karl Barth's concept of 'political preaching' and his resolute intervention in political events; Ernst Wolf's teaching about 'political virtues' in the light of Romans 13; Ernst Käsemann's concept of 'worship in the everyday of this world'; Helmut Gollwitzer's practical application of 'Christian political obedience'. I myself contributed ideas about a political hermeneutics of the Gospel (1968). In the Political Night Prayers in Cologne, Dorothee Sölle put the ideas of political theology into practice in her own way.[4]

For all this, the time was ripe. In Latin America, 'the emerging continent', liberation theology was born, and exerted its influence on the episcopal conference in Medellin in 1968. In Europe, the East–West conflict intensified into the Cold War. Divided Germany became the arena for the greatest concentration of military power in the world. Anti-Communism on the one side and anti-capitalism on the other dominated the friend–enemy thinking of the political ideologies. The anti-Vietnam War movement mobilized students all over the world. New radically democratic and socialist ideas kindled criticism of the condition of the universities, the state of society and the political restorations of the post-war years.

At that time, with political theology we certainly took up Bloch's messianic ideas and Adorno's apocalyptic concepts, and tried to come to terms with them theologically. But the deepest motivation for the rise of political theology was horror over the failure of the churches and the theologians in the face of the German crime against humanity symbolized by the name Auschwitz.[5]

Why the appalling silence on the part of Christians? Had the middle-class privatization of religion secularized politics to the depths of this abyss? Was it anti-Semitism, unconscious and conscious, that kept Christians silent? Was it the misappropriated doctrine of the two kingdoms – Christ for the soul, Hitler for the people? Was it Lutheran submissiveness to the powers that be ('all authority is God-given')? Was it the Roman Catholic option for the anti-Communist dictatorships in Italy, Spain, Portugal, Croatia, Poland and, in 1933, in Germany too?

Our publications show that 'talk about God in our own time' increasingly became talk about God in the face of Auschwitz, and after Auschwitz. For Metz, what emerged was the anamnetic culture of 'dangerous remembrance' and the open theodicy process of modern political history. For me, it was the theology of the cross, a theology of the suffering God, the passion of the passionate God and Christian criticism of all political and civil religions.[6] For us, Auschwitz means the hermeneutical conditions in which we think about Christian talk about God in post-war Germany.

The term 'political theology' was not new. It unfortunately laboured under an unpleasant previous history. In 1922 and 1934 the later National

Socialist and highly anti-Semitic Carl Schmitt made it the slogan for his anti-revolutionary, anti-liberal and anti-democratic predilection for political dictatorships. 'That person is sovereign who can declare the state of emergency', he declared, meaning by that in 1922 the dictatorship of the German president according to Article 48 of the Weimar Constitution, and then in 1933 Hitler's Enabling Law.[7] Theologically he justified political dictatorship by way of a secularized doctrine of original sin: 'Against absolute evil . . . there is only dictatorship' – as if dictatorship were not itself absolutely evil! Because human beings are evil and chaotic by nature, they need a strong hand to control them. For Carl Schmitt, as Nicolas Sombart points out in his acute analysis, this meant the trinity of 'monotheism, monarchy and monogamy'.[8] The anarchist Michael Bakunin had cried, 'Neither God nor state!'; Schmitt wanted to be his opposite number and to come forward on behalf of 'God and state'. The subject of his political theology is state power, not the Church and not Christianity in the world. But it is these which are the subjects determining political theology in our sense. This fundamental distinction has continually to be made, so it is good that – following our practice from 1970 onwards – Metz should have called his 1997 collection of essays 'On the Concept of *the New* Political Theology'.[9] But clear though the distinction is, it has unfortunately failed to prevent confusion in recent years between these different senses of political theology, and the assimilation of the two.

From the very beginning, this new political theology in Germany enjoyed a stimulating give and take with the other contextual theologies which were springing up everywhere. In 1969, through Fred Herzog, I came into contact with Jim Cone's Black Theology, which grew out of the Black Power movement, and took its way between Martin Luther King's integration ideal and Malcolm X's will for separation. In Korea, Suh Nam Dong and Ahn Byun Mu developed *minjung* theology, the theology of the people, seeing the resistance of the humiliated Korean people to military dictatorship, and their protest on behalf of freedom and human rights, in the light of the role of the *ochlos* in the Gospel of Mark. From both black theology and *minjung* theology we could learn that if 'talk about God in our own time' is to get anywhere it must keep its sights set on its context, its *kairos* and its own social community.[10]

For Metz, the tie with Catholic liberation theology in Latin America was in the foreground. That already resulted from work on the editorial board of the periodical *Concilium*. There theology in the East–West conflict met theology in the human conflict between North and South. What we all shared, as the writings of Gustavo Gutiérrez show, is theology's eschatological horizon and its critical responsibility towards society. What differed was the context.[11] The 'location' of liberation theology – its *locus theologicus* – was the misery of the poor. Consequently its criticism was targeted at the rich countries which exploit Latin America. In the years that followed, this led to a breach with us too, and with what the liberation theologians called our 'progressive theology' of the rich First World. It was difficult to make clear to them our situation in divided Germany, faced as we were with the immediate nuclear threat. In order for them to find their own theology, they had to cut themselves free from European theology. Separation is always the first step dependants take in their search for freedom.

What deeply moved all of us was what Metz described as the Latin American 'landscape of cries'. This was 'the authority of the suffering, in which the authority of the judging God manifests itself in the world for all human beings' (Metz). But it was not easy to follow up the theology of the liberation of the oppressed, which is self-evident, by a corresponding theology of the liberation of the oppressors; for they are generally blind to what they are doing. Yet liberation from historical suffering has to go hand in hand with liberation from historical guilt. Unless it does, there can be no reconciliation and new community. Sympathy with the sufferers is not as yet a liberation from the burden of guilt.

In Europe, the approaches to a new political theology soon became diversified. Helmut Gollwitzer saw in the conversion from destructive greed to a love for life the dawn of the Kingdom of God in this capitalist world, which is so out of joint. In the group he gathered round him in Berlin a socialist theology developed in which capitalism was seen as a contradiction to God's kingdom – a contradiction hostile to life – and new democratically socialist forms of community were sought which would be in accord with that kingdom.[12]

In the long run, however, political theology in Europe and liberation theology in America were overtaken by two new theological movements: feminist theology and ecological theology, sex-role politics and earth politics, the liberation of women from age-old patriarchy and the liberation of the earth from the destruction of nature brought about by human beings. In both feminist theology and ecological theology the problems are not momentary. They are long term, and are bound up with the fate of humanity itself.[13]

Feminist theology was not an offshoot of political theology, but the new feminist theology sees itself as a political theology too, although after initial attempts with the term, the description 'feminist liberation theology' has taken over and is now generally accepted. There is considerable sensitivity towards the political side of the feminist movement, however, and in their resistance to identification with the white American middle class Afro-American women prefer to speak of 'womanist theology' and Latin American women of '*mujerista-teología*'.[14]

This fresh departure for women is political in a wider sense too, for it takes in theological reflections and visions of a cultural revolution which will radically change the position of women, and with that the position of men as well.

Ecological theology, like feminist theology, was not an offshoot of political theology, although every ecological theology is political. This is evident from the protests against nuclear power and in favour of renewable energies. In 1972 the Club of Rome showed 'the limits of growth'. The Chernobyl catastrophe of 1986 has led to the death (up to now) of 150,000 people, and made large areas of the country uninhabitable. 'Natural' catastrophes, which are in fact man-made, are on the increase.

The ecological theology which is developing, like the other contextual theologies, will move Christians to participate in the necessary changes to our civilization, and in these changes to implement their own visions. Liberation theology in its narrower sense has now become embedded in a wider 'theology of life', and political theology has in recent years expanded into a Kingdom of God theology, so that new convergences between these movements have become evident.[15]

What has remained? What has gone? What has remained is largely speaking the recognition of the political dimension for the Christian faith of the cross of Christ and the Kingdom of God. What has remained is necessary criticism of the idols of political and civil religion. What has become generally accepted is God's preferential option for the poor. What has developed are the principles of every contextual theology: context, *kairos*, community.

What is now a thing of the past is the undue weight given to political exist-ence, which in 1934 Carl Schmitt maintained was 'the whole'. The end of the East–West conflict has been followed by the globalization of the economy and the total marketing of everything, including the private sphere. Politics has deregulated and privatized the economy, and is now itself controlled and regulated by the economy. This means that political life is now the subsystem of a greater economic system. Politics are still important, but they are no longer 'the world', the only world to which theology must turn its face.

The road leads from political theology to economic theology, and from economic theology to ecological theology. In a theology of life which comprehends God and the earth, the different contextual theologies, with their diverse contributions, can find themselves once more.

Notes

1 Text translated from the German by Margaret Kohl.
2 J. B. Metz, *Theology of the World*, trans. W. Glen-Doepel (London and New York: Burns & Oates, 1969).
3 E. Kellner (ed.), *Schöpfertum und Freiheit in einer humanen Gesellschaft: Marienbader Protokolle* (Vienna: Europa, 1969).
4 D. Sölle, *Political Theology* (English trans.; Philadelphia, PA: Fortress Press, 1974).
5 E. Kogon and J. B. Metz (eds), *Gott nach Auschwitz: Dimensionen des Massenmords am jüdischen Volk* (Freiburg: Herder, 1979).
6 J. B. Metz, *Faith in History and Society*, trans. D. Smith (London: Burns & Oates, 1980); J. Moltmann, *The Crucified God: The Cross of Christ as the Foundation and Criticism of Christian Theology*, trans. R. A. Wilson and J. Bowden (London: SCM Press, 1974).
7 C. Schmitt, *Politische Theologie: Vier Kapitel von der Souveränität* (Munich and Leipzig: 1922, 1934; English trans., Cambridge, MA: MIT Press, 1985).
8 N. Sombart, *Die deutschen Männer und ihre Feinde: Carl Schmitt – ein deutsches Schicksal zwischen Männerbund und Matriarchatsmythos* (Munich: Hanser, 1991).
9 J. Moltmann, *Politische Theologie: Politische Ethik* (Munich: Kaiser, 1984); J. B. Metz, *Zum Begriff der neuen Politischen Theologie 1967–1997* (Mainz: Matthias-Grünewald, 1997).
10 J. Moltmann, *Experiences in Theology: Ways and Forms of Christian Theology*, trans. Margaret Kohl (London and Minneapolis, MN: SCM Press, 2000), Part III: *Mirror Images of Liberating Theology*.
11 G. Gutiérrez, *A Theology of Liberation* (1973), trans. C. Inda and J. Eagleson, revised edn. (Maryknoll, NY: Orbis and London: SCM Press, 1988).
12 H. Gollwitzer, *Krummes Holz – aufrechter Gang: Zur Frage nach dem Sinn des Lebens* (Munich: Kaiser, 1970).
13 J. Moltmann (ed.), *Friedenstheologie – Befreiungstheologie* (Munich: Kaiser, 1988).
14 E. Moltmann-Wendel, *Menschenrechte für die Frau* (Munich: Kaiser, 1974); D. Williams, *Sisters in the Wilderness: The Challenge of Womanist God-Talk* (New York: Orbis, 1994); A. M. Isasi-Diaz, *Mujerista Theology* (New York: Orbis, 1996).
15 In an addition to the revised edition of his *Theology*, published in Germany in 1992, Gutiérrez writes: 'Every healthy, fruitful liberation theology is embedded in the theology of the kingdom of God . . . *already* thrusting into history, it still does

not yet find its full development in history. That is the reason why the kingdom of God must not be confused with a particular historical achievement, however important and valuable that may seem. The kingdom of God certainly has its realizations in the Here and Now, but these realizations are neither "the coming of the kingdom" nor "the whole of salvation". They are anticipatory fragments – with all their ambiguities – of a fullness which will only come about beyond history. It is precisely their provisional character which theological criticism must bring out' (*Theologie der Befreiung*, 10th German edn. (Mainz, 1992), p. 242). In saying this Gutiérrez gives his subsequent assent to our early criticism during the beginnings of Latin American liberation theology.

Chapter 3

From Political to Public Theologies: The Role of Theology in Public Life in South Africa

JOHN W. DE GRUCHY

There are two diametrically opposing temptations facing theologians who engage the public sphere. The first is the temptation to convince ourselves that theology makes more of a contribution and difference than it does; the second is to underestimate the significance of its role. Both temptations arise out of a misunderstanding of the task of theology in public life. If the first smacks of an immodest triumphalism, the second indicates a crisis of confidence and false modesty. Many theologians in South Africa, as in other post-Christian contexts, wonder whether theology, which has certainly lost the public status that it once had, has any public significance at all. Who listens and who cares? But we should not confuse the one-time public status of theology with the real contribution it can make when rightly pursued within public life.

At the outset, we need to recognize that there is no universal 'public theology', but only theologies that seek to engage the political realm within particular localities. There are, however, shared commonalities, both confessional and ecumenical, in approach and substance between theologies that seek to do this. This makes it possible to engage and fruitfully learn from each other at this colloquium. In doing so, both here and in many other places around the world, the contours and content of a broader ecumenical public theology begin to emerge. But these, in turn, have to be tried and tested in specific localities, critically informing each other and being recast in ways appropriate to specific contexts.

South Africa provides an interesting case study of the way in which theology has developed and functioned within the public sphere during the past fifty years. Located as it was within the Church struggle against apartheid, public theology was deeply rooted in the life and witness of the

45

churches. Those engaged in doing public theology in the academy were invariably embedded in the life of the churches. But academic reflection and teaching were not pursued in isolation from the praxis of witness. It was, rather, a theology of witness in which theology and ethics, and especially ecclesiology and social ethics, were integrated. Furthermore, doing theology against apartheid in South Africa was ecumenical despite confessional differences. The dividing lines were drawn not between the historic confessions but around the issue of what it means to confess Christ concretely here and now. So the historic cleavage within ecumenical circles between faith and order, on the one hand, and life and work, on the other, was unthinkable.[1]

In what follows I shall briefly explore some of the ways in which public theology in South Africa has emerged and taken shape during the past half century. Obviously I will do so from my own perspective, so in a sense what follows is autobiographical and idiosyncratic, though by no means entirely so. Much that could be discussed must necessarily be left out or mentioned only tangentially. For example, the public theology that derives from the rich Anglo-Catholic heritage of Christian socialism and which found expression in South Africa through the influence of Trevor Huddleston, Desmond Tutu and many others. Or the public theology that derived from British Nonconformity, and found expression in South African equivalents of the 'Nonconformist conscience' and the social gospel. Or the public theology, of quite a different kind and character, that has emerged within some of the African Initiated Churches, an incipient theology that is expressed solely in praxis rather than in critical reflection and construction. All of these, and more, would be essential to any comprehensive account of public theology in South Africa. Moreover, I will leave you to discern what may be of wider relevance within your own context.

My chapter has two main sections. In the first part I will show how theological developments in Europe, North America and Latin America were appropriated in South Africa in the struggle against apartheid, from the late 1960s to the watershed years of the early 1990s. This appropriation inevitably led to both subtle and significant changes to that which was received, and resulted in what became a distinct set of South African theologies.[2] These in turn attracted the attention of theologians and churches in other parts of the world and, in some instances, even helped to shape public theology in those contexts. Evidence of this can be found in many sources, not least in Duncan Forrester's own writings.[3] This leads me to acknowledge with much appreciation Professor Forrester's interest in and encouragement of what we have attempted to do in South Africa over the past years.

46

In the second part of my chapter the focus will shift to the current post-apartheid period. Insofar as the legacy of apartheid remains, much of what was learnt in doing theology in the struggle years remains pertinent. So it would be incorrect to assume that the task of doing theology has fundamentally altered to suit a changing context. But the transition from apartheid to a non-racial democracy has obviously reshaped public life, and this inevitably requires a different theological response than that which was appropriate within a totalitarian apartheid context. At the same time, the particular challenges now facing South Africa, the region and the world as a whole are setting new priorities. How public theology in South Africa will cope with these challenges and contribute to the common good is the challenge facing churches and theologians. As previously, South African theologies continue to be influenced by theological and intellectual trends elsewhere, but how our native theologies will also contribute to the global Church and theology remains to be seen. As yet, public theology in the new South Africa does not have the clarity it once had, and it is doubtful whether it will ever again have such clarity.

Political Theologies in the Struggle Against Apartheid

Looking back to the 1960s, I suppose the term 'political theology' would have been the equivalent term to what we now refer to as 'public theology', though somewhat different in character, reflecting changes in our historical contexts. Both terms are, of course, European constructions and not widely used in South Africa. But I purposely choose them in order to connect what we are engaged in with the wider global theological enterprise.

Political theology originally referred to those theologies in Europe that gave legitimacy to the state and its claims within the context of Christendom. This understanding prevailed well into the second half of the twentieth century when political theology was radically reconstructed by Johannes Baptist Metz and Jürgen Moltmann to mean precisely the opposite.[4] Writing in the context of the Cold War and amidst the debate about secularization in the 1960s, Metz recognized the ambiguity in the extent to which the phrase was 'burdened with specific political connotations'.[5] But he nevertheless opted for its use because it best described the critical role of theology in both correcting the privatization of bourgeois religion,[6] and in challenging the political status quo. In fact, for Metz, under certain historical conditions, political theology might well support revolutionary protest.[7]

Political theology of this kind had a secondary task. Whereas previously it reinforced the connection between Church and state, between throne and altar, as retrieved by Metz its task now became that of determining 'anew the relation between religion and society, between Church and societal "publicness," between eschatological faith and societal life'.[8] The critical distinction was avoiding the mixing of faith and politics in a reactionary way and, coupled with that, providing a critique of the Church that enabled it to become an institution of social transformation. It was not a matter of politicizing the Church, but of developing what Moltmann refers to as the 'public testimony of faith and political discipleship of Christ'.[9]

Metz insisted, however, that while his use of political theology was novel, it was not a new discipline, but rather 'a basic element in the whole structure of critical theological thinking'. In particular, this meant a new understanding of the relation between theory and praxis.[10] Political theology was another way of describing practical fundamental theology. Hence the recognition that the substance of political theology was nothing other than the main themes and concerns of theology as such. The novel element was that the central themes of the New Testament message of the reign of God, of salvation, forgiveness and reconciliation, of freedom, justice and peace, were no longer understood in a privatized way, but rather in terms of the transformation of public life and society. The key theological category that held this together was hope, the hope that, in Moltmann's words, 'sets about criticising and transforming the present because it is open towards the universal future of the kingdom'.[11] It is difficult to overemphasize the extent to which this influenced the development of theologies against apartheid, and the extent to which it remains influential at this time of democratic transformation.

As intimated, the term 'political theology' has not been widely used in South Africa, but both types of 'political theology' have been significantly present. Afrikaner neo-Calvinism, which gave its blessing to apartheid ideology and promoted the notion of a white Christian nation, was in direct continuity with the political theologies of Christendom. As later defined by the *Kairos Document*, it was a 'state theology'.[12] But equally clearly, the anti-apartheid theologies that emerged in the course of the struggle and in critical opposition to neo-Calvinism were akin to the way in which Metz and Moltmann used the term 'political theology'. Indeed, they were profoundly influenced by that use.

But political theology, as redefined by Metz and Moltmann, was a distinctly European theology. Its historical background was the post-Enlightenment secularization of European society. For Metz, as for other political theologians in the 1960s, secularization was the starting point for critical theological reflection. But there were two more immediate contextual realities that informed political theology. The first was the Cold War. This made dialogue with Marxism imperative, and led to a critique of both Western imperialism and capitalism, and the failures of Communism. The second was the Holocaust or Shoah. This raised fundamental questions about Christian theology and the Church, and demanded a wholly new way of understanding the role of the Church in the modern world.

In South Africa, as in Latin America, the situation was rather different even though in both cases the Cold War played a role in shaping political attitudes and policies. Secularization was at most a secondary factor, given the prevailing religious character of society as a whole, and the Holocaust was overshadowed by more immediate circumstances of racist oppression and suffering. So while theologians engaging the public arena in South Africa and Latin America were influenced by this new political theology, we had to plough our own furrows. Even then, South African and Latin American theologies could not be the same for the realities facing us were not identical either. The rise of Latin American liberation theology was in response to the failure of development policies, whereas South African theologies were primarily engaged with the realities of colonialism, racism and apartheid, though these were inseparable also from economic issues. Moreover, the theological legacies of those churches in South Africa that opposed apartheid were more shaped by the liberal 'social gospel' or Anglo-Catholic socialism, than they were by theologies emanating from continental Europe.

But a new generation of South African theologians was in the making that was looking elsewhere for inspiration and guidance. Allow me to inject here some personal memories. During the late 1960s I was busy writing my doctoral dissertation on Barth and Bonhoeffer's ecclesiology, and was engaged with the writings of Metz and Moltmann in doing so. At the same time I was working for the South African Council of Churches, where my main brief was to follow up the publication of the *Message to the People of South Africa* that had been published jointly by the SACC and the Christian Institute in 1968. Those were heady days of confrontation between the political theologies of the right and of the left, and I well recall the extent to which the 'theology of hope' spoke so clearly to us as we sought to engage the apartheid state and its ecclesiastical supporters.

Elsewhere I have referred to the theology of the *Message to the People of South Africa* as a 'confessing theology'.[13] 'Confessing' indicates a theology that arises out of a commitment to confess Jesus Christ within the public sphere. This implies both the prophetic critique of idolatry and the liberatory thrust of struggle against oppression, but it anchors them in what is an unambiguous Christian confession: 'Jesus Christ is Lord'. Confessing theology, as distinct from 'confessional theology', was the first theology that really engaged apartheid on a basis other than a more liberal social gospel platform. And it did so because it confronted the 'state theology' of apartheid with an alternative 'political theology' rather than with an appeal to more individualist liberal norms. This was, I believe, a major advance, and one which opened up possibilities that were previously closed simply because liberal theology was really no match for the comprehensive neo-Calvinism that shaped the political thinking of the Dutch Reformed Church. Eventually, 'confessing theology' led to the recognition of apartheid as a *status confessionis*, to its denunciation as a heresy and to the *Belhar Confession*.[14]

Critics argued that such anti-apartheid theology was, in principle, no different from the political theology that gave support to apartheid. Some, from a more radical theological perspective, were unhappy about the emphasis on the 'Kingdom of God' and the Lordship of Christ, a critique to which we will later return. But others, from a more conservative perspective, were critical of what they regarded as the politicizing of faith and the life of the Church. What was needed, such critics declared, was a 'third-way theology' that was above such dirty business where inevitably the Church became a political instrument of some ideology. Such criticism was faulty for two reasons. In the first place it simplistically equated political theologies that legitimated an unjust status quo, and those which sought its overthrow. This is akin to the equation made between the use of violence by the state and security forces to implement apartheid and repress opposition, and the armed struggle against apartheid. The second fault was the more obvious one, namely the assumption that theology can be politically neutral. Those who claim to be so are often the most guilty of ideological captivity, not least because they often lack a built-in mechanism of self-critique.

Permit me to return to personal reminiscences. At the same time as I was working on my dissertation, immersed in the 'theology of hope', in an office just above mine theologians involved in the Black Theology Project were busy at work digesting James Cone's *A Black Theology of Liberation*. They recognized the importance of the *Message to the People of South Africa* but they were also critical of its failure to get to grips with the issues raised by black consciousness, especially the connections between ethnicity and poverty. This was related to the fact that the *Message* was written mainly by white theologians. If Barth, Bonhoeffer and Moltmann spoke to us, Cone and

Gustavo Gutiérrez spoke to our black colleagues. It was, of course, largely a matter of social location. For those of us who were influenced by Bonhoeffer with his insistence that we should see things 'from below, from the perspective of those who suffer', the time had come to rethink the way in which we did theology. Without equating apartheid and Auschwitz, they had similar implications for doing theology. But black theologians did not have to try and see things from below; they were below!

Thus, once the leadership in the Church struggle against apartheid was wrested from white liberal or confessing theologians and taken over by the black theologians in the early 1970s, political theology assumed the character of an African 'black theology'. As intimated, this shared similarities with Latin American liberation theology, but it was much closer to the black theology movement of North America. The development of 'black theology' did not mean the end of 'confessing theology', nor did it preclude the emergence of other forms of liberation theology, notably feminist, but it did make an indelible impression on such theologies. By way of example, feminist theology was soon divided along racial lines, as in the United States, with 'womanist' becoming the description of feminist theology 'from below'. The critical issue now was not simply solidarity with the poor and oppressed, not just 'seeing things from below', but the social location of those doing theology in the struggle against apartheid.

By the mid-1980s, however, a new approach to doing theology, which was non-racial in character, began to emerge. This reflected the emergence of the United Democratic Front, an internal front for the African National Congress, which arose in response to P. W. Botha's attempt at reform and the resulting 'state of emergency' which plunged South Africa into escalating civil conflict. This was the context in which the *Kairos Document* was produced. What was critical in this process was whether one identified with what, in hindsight, was the final push against apartheid repression. As is now well known, the *Kairos Document* not only attacked the heresy of 'state theology', but it also attacked the attempt by what it called 'church theology' to try and find a middle 'third way' way. Political theology had become 'prophetic theology', and the key issue was that of political strategy. What was required for Christians to bring about the demise of the apartheid regime? Hence the debate around the armed struggle and the use of violence to counter state violence.

The *Kairos Document* came in for heavy criticism from the state and from many of the churches. It was also criticized by others involved in the struggle, such as Desmond Tutu, and from some theologians who believed that it did not take seriously the concerns of 'black theology'. For Tutu the problem had to do with the phrase 'church theology' and the idea that all such theology propagated 'cheap reconciliation'. For the advocates of 'black theology', the problem was a failure to take seriously the connection between ethnicity and economics. *Kairos* or prophetic theology, nonetheless, became the dominant political theology of the final phase of the struggle, and it laid the foundations for the theology of transition that led to the debates about justice, reparation and reconciliation that have surrounded the work of the Truth and Reconciliation Commission.

Allow me, once again, a personal reminiscence. I recall attending the Annual General Meeting of the Institute for Contextual Theology, held at Marianhill Monastery, in 1991. The ICT, it should be noted, was largely responsible for the *Kairos Document*, and those attending its AGM were all strong advocates of its theology. However, history was moving on. Nelson Mandela was free and the transition process to democracy was under way even though there were immense obstacles that had to be dealt with. A large part of the agenda at that AGM was on the significance of the transition to democracy for theology or, to put it the other way round, what was the theological response which the transition demanded of us from the perspective of the *Kairos Document*. The metaphor that emerged was no longer that of the Exodus, a favourite of liberation theology, but that of the Wilderness experience, the experience of post-liberation struggling to reach the promised land. One temptation was to believe that liberation meant arrival and therefore we could now return to private piety and our ecclesial ghettos while the nation rushed to build temples in which to celebrate our freedom. Another was the opposite temptation, that is, to try and replicate the days of struggle back in Egypt when at least the issues were clear and the task obvious even if fraught with danger.

Looking back, the way in which the various theologies against apartheid emerged and developed differed in character, focus and strategy, deriving from various theological traditions, different social and ethnic locations and operating on the basis of a different hermeneutic. Yet they were all critical of the way in which the dominant white forms of Christianity and the Church in South Africa had, paradoxically, become privatized on the one hand, and supportive of an unjust political status quo, on the other. They were also theologies of transformation, seeking a new just and democratic social order. As such they were engaged in working out anew the relationship between 'eschatological faith' and politics, between society and salvation, forgiveness, justice and reconciliation. They were theologies in search of a new land.

South Africa did enter the Promised Land, though we soon recognized that the Promised Land is not flowing with unlimited quantities of milk or honey. Indeed, the very question of land, its distribution and use, has become central to both theology and politics. The transition to democracy has thus introduced the need for a new approach to doing theology in the public arena. On the one hand, the legacy of apartheid still has to be overcome; on the other, there is the task of building a just and democratic nation. The question, then, is what does it mean to do public theology in the new South Africa? This has brought us directly into the debate with public theology as it has emerged more globally, aware nevertheless that our own context must, yet again, determine the contours of such theology. But public theology, like political, liberation, black or feminist theologies, is not simply a generic term; it is historically located in the Western European theological world. How, then, is it being appropriated in post-apartheid South Africa?

Public Theologies and Christian Conviction in a Democratic Society

A significant theological event took place in Cape Town in February 1999. Called 'Multi-Event 99' to capture its multidisciplinary, multi-faith and multicultural character, its purpose was to examine the role of religion in public life with specific reference to South Africa during this period of democratic transition and transformation.[15] Amongst the participants were both local and international academics, politicians (including the then Vice-President Thabo Mbeki), community workers, church leaders and theologians. Reflecting back on that occasion, four observations can be made that indicate the changing political and religious framework within which we are now doing theology in the public sphere.

Firstly, the event was explicitly multi-faith rather than Christian, even though Christians were in the majority, and the event focused on religion rather than theology, even though there was an abundance of theologians present. Looking back on the anti-apartheid struggle, there can be no doubt that it involved people of different religious faiths and convictions alongside Communists and others with no religious commitment. But, in terms of religious communities' involvement in the struggle, it is also evident that churches and church leaders predominated as senior partners. There was a time when a public pronouncement from the South African Council of Churches or from one of the major churches was something of a public event. This is no longer the case.

53

There are several reasons why the churches had such a high profile. One was that the struggle was understood at its core as an ideological struggle between the Christian Gospel and the false gospel of apartheid. As a result we engaged in debates that had a classical theological resonance: Church and state, heresy and *status confessionis*, liberation and reconciliation. But the four key themes that were identified and debated at 'Multi-Event 99' had a very different feel about them: the role and status of religion in public life; religious communities and government; moral leadership and cultural values; and religion and political economy. This did not exclude reference to church and theology, or mosque and shariah, synagogue and Torah, except in a way that would preference one tradition over another. The Scriptures and traditions of the various faith-communities still play a decisive role within them, and sometimes result in public contestation over matters of social morality, but the Bible is no longer the definitive text. The text that now seeks to bind South Africans together is the new Constitution.

Secondly, whereas previously the liberation struggle was the core around which everything else was debated, now the focal point is democratic transformation, and within that the enormous challenge of inequality and poverty. The following list of seminar topics at 'Multi-Event 99' gives some idea of the range of issues that were discussed and remain central to our concerns:

> Nation state and xenophobia
> Poverty and Jubilee 2000
> Religion and labour
> Corporate values and practice
> Land and faith-communities
> Eco-justice
> Beyond the TRC
> Crime and corruption
> Abuse of women and children
> HIV/Aids

Few of these issues are really new, but previously most were either placed on the backburner or dealt with within the context of the struggle for liberation. The latter took priority. Previous neglect of such issues, coupled with the legacy of colonialism and apartheid, partly explain why some of the problems facing us now are so difficult to resolve. In particular, I refer to massive inequality, poverty and landlessness, and the racism that remains embedded in society, the core issues for any public theology in South Africa in touch with reality.

The issues are many and big. HIV/Aids, to name but one, is an issue of horrifying proportions, and it demands the attention and co-operation of all citizens, the vast majority of whom belong to a multiplicity of diverse religions and a startling array of Christianities. This is of fundamental importance, linking our second observation with our first. Even while Christians still outnumber members of other faith-communities in many of our countries, there is no way that Christians can tackle the problems alone, or simply on the basis of a Christian approach. Just as the new Constitution has become the nation's text, so all the tasks facing us require the participation of all citizens.

Thirdly, the 'Multi-Event 99' was a multidisciplinary event. During the Church struggle there was, of course, some engagement between theologians and social scientists. But because we were focusing so sharply on the ideological issues in the Church struggle, this critical interaction was not particularly well developed other than in providing resources for that struggle. That usually meant picking and choosing from the social sciences in order to reinforce our theological attack. But we are now much more aware that theology cannot really engage in public life if it is ill-informed about the substantive issues, unwilling to learn from those whose task it is to investigate them and incapable of entering into a meaningful discussion with them. Doing theology in public must still be done from the perspective of those who are at the receiving end of injustice. But it has to be well-informed, multidisciplinary and able to engage the issues in a way that relates to those who now exercise power and influence. This brings us to the fourth observation.

Fourthly, participants at 'Multi-Event 99' included members of government and others who had been in the Church struggle but were now in important positions of political responsibility. This signals the fact that the new government has democratic legitimacy, and that those in authority acknowledge the important role of religion and religious communities in building a non-racial democracy. Previously the government claimed to be Christian, claimed to be a defender of Christian civilization, claimed the support of its state theologians, and yet maligned, attacked and sought to destroy those churches and other religious communities opposed to it. Now the government is not formally Christian, but it is encouraging all the churches and other religious communities to participate in the task of nation-building, and chiding them for not doing so with the same intensity that some opposed apartheid.

What I have briefly described in these four observations is what one anticipated would follow from the transition from a totalitarian racial oligarchy to
an open multiracial democratic society. But there is one further element that
must be included in our account of the changing historical context, namely,
globalization. Suddenly South Africa has been swept into the mainstream
of globalization with all its pitfalls and promises, become a major player in
African and regional politics and a significant one in international affairs.

The implications all this has for doing theology in the public arena
are obviously far-reaching, holding out great promise but also raising new
problems and serious dangers. None of this is unique to South Africa. It is
the new global context within which we have to work out the particularities
of doing theology in local situations. Last year I was engaged in theological
conversations in Germany and Denmark that centred on similar issues to
those facing us in South Africa. In short, we all, irrespective of where we are
located have, in Duncan Forrester's words 'to re-examine the basis, content,
and manner of theology's contribution in the light of rapidly changing
circumstances'.[16]

But the challenge, as Forrester also recognizes, is how do we locate the
Church and our own theological discourse within this multi-faith, multidisciplinary, democratic and global framework? What does all this imply for an
explicitly Christian confessing and prophetic theology, and for the life and
witness of the Church, in public life? Does the fact that we in South Africa
now live in a pluralistic democracy fundamentally change what we say and
do? Do we have to ditch the theological heritage that nurtured us for the sake
of passing relevance, or turn our backs on our experience, some of it learned
at considerable cost? The answer must surely be a dialectical 'yes' and 'no'.

Given the fact that there are many different currents, different contexts,
different influences, different forms of discourse and different points of
reference, it seems self-evident that there will be and must be different
approaches to public theology. This was certainly the case previously in the
struggle against apartheid when political theology was reworked in various
ways in terms of South African realities. So it is necessary to talk now about
public theologies, rather than a public theology, both within the global post-
colonial context and within our new multicultural democracy in South
Africa. The public sphere is, after all, not one reality but rather a complex set
of interacting groups and institutions, political parties, religious communities, NGOs, trade unions, cultural organizations. In all of these, Christians of
various confessions and people of other faiths or no religious commitment are
involved together in terms of their own perspectives, agendas and, hopefully,

their commitment to the common good. This is the framework within which public theologies emerge, whatever names we will eventually give them. We recall David Tracy's comment at the beginning of *The Analogical Imagination*: 'Behind the pluralism of theological conclusions lies a pluralism of public roles and publics as reference groups for theological discourse.'[17]

Tracy's well-known delineation of the three 'publics' (the academy, the Church and society) of theology has influenced attempts to construct theologies of public life in South Africa. But his approach has not been uncontested. I recall a graduate seminar in the late 1980s at which I introduced Tracy's proposal. My students at that time were deeply engaged in what was, in hindsight, the final days of the struggle against apartheid. For them, Tracy's approach not only lacked the passionate, incisive clarity of confessing, liberation and prophetic theologies. It was too nuanced, too carefully qualified, too inclusive of approaches to be helpful in confronting evil in the public square. Given our situation, the students were right, but I do not think they would take precisely the same position today. Even so, as I pointed out at the time, although Tracy recognized the need for a plurality of theologies, he also stressed the connections between them around the question of authenticity and truth. 'Every theologian', he wrote, 'must face squarely the claims to meaning and truth of all three publics' precisely for the fact that theologians have a responsibility for 'authentically public discourse'.[18] Whatever shape public theologies take, whatever name given to them in our new historical context, there has to be synergy and coherence around the key issues facing us today, both globally and locally.

But what constitutes an authentic public theological discourse in a democratic society such as South Africa is striving to become? In response to that question, let me again pay tribute to Duncan Forrester's contribution to the subject. The more I read the growing number of books that have come from his pen in recent years, the more I realize the extent to which his approach resonates with much of what we are seeking to do in South Africa. Maybe that is because he has participated at various times in some of our projects! But there is undoubtedly more to it than that. As I wrote in a blurb for his book, *On Human Worth*: 'Forrester writes out of a lifetime of wrestling with such questions, and also with passion, clarity, and conviction.'[19] These, I suggest, are hallmarks of authentic public theological discourse.

Much was said at the colloquium about these and related issues. However, I wish to focus rather on the third of the hallmarks, namely Christian conviction. Forrester is a model public theologian in the sense that he is fully cognisant of the multi-faith, multidisciplinary dimensions to doing theology. He is equally passionate about the issues and about the need to engage the structures of power from that perspective both critically and constructively. But throughout he remains committed to his convictions as a Christian theologian. For theology can only make its unique and decisive contribution to public life if it is faithful to the Gospel of God's reign in Jesus Christ in the service of both Church and society. The problem is how this is to be done given the new historical context in which we live. How do we contribute to public life from an authentic Christian theological perspective?

In a very helpful essay, written for 'Multi-Event 99', in which she examined the contribution of black and feminist theologies to public discourse Rebecca Chopp considered how these theologies function, how they shape discourse and how they imagine the public arena.[20] Different as they are, as Chopp indicates there are 'some common theoretical resources in ideology critique, hermeneutics, and the retrieval of the prophetic or mystical/prophetic strands in Christianity'.[21] By this Chopp means seeking 'to tell the truth or the real represented in and through narrative identity'. It is, as Forrester reminds us, 'telling the story with all its inner vitality and depth of meaning which is the truest Christian contribution to the public realm'. [22] The point of such testimony is to provide a critique of dehumanizing ideologies, to evoke social imagination in a way that engenders compassion for the 'other' and hope for society, and thereby reshapes public discourse. Put differently, such testimony allows the transcendent to break into the present without which politics is distorted.[23]

In this regard we might refer to those moments during the work of the Truth and Reconciliation Commission in South Africa which, through the testimony of victims, broke the chains of the past, evoked empathy and solidarity and opened up fresh possibilities of healing, both individual and corporate. In many ways, whatever its faults and failures, and there is ongoing debate about this, the TRC provides one of the most significant challenges for doing public theology in South Africa today. In particular, it has been a catalyst for rethinking the meaning of justice and reconciliation in the process of nation-building.

One of my present theological tasks is to reconsider the Christian doctrine of reconciliation in the light of the work of the Truth and Reconciliation Commission in South Africa. This is not the place to elaborate on this project, except as a way of illustrating the point I am making. Theological concepts such as guilt, forgiveness, reparation, restorative justice and reconciliation have all become parts of our current political vocabulary.

Each of them has a particular Christian history and meaning which is in many respects distinct from the way in which it is understood in other traditions or by secular political players. As a result, each has become a highly contested concept. Indeed, the fact that these key Christian theological concepts, which encapsulate the Gospel, became central to the work of the TRC reflects the preponderance of Christianity in South Africa and the role which church leaders played in the transition from apartheid to democracy. But the fact that these terms are now so hotly contested indicates that their meaning and significance is in the public domain with all this implies for critical theological reflection, discourse and ecclesial praxis. If truth-telling, confessing guilt, offering forgiveness, making reparation, restoring justice and witnessing to reconciliation are to mean anything, they cannot be confined to an ecclesial ghetto.

An authentic public theology has to be self-critical and sensitive to other perspectives and approaches, as well as to the historical context, in order to function in the market place and public square. Yet, self-critical does not mean apologetic in a way that denies its specific Christian content, or undermines prophetic clarity and responsibility. There is a fine line between a theology that is arrogant and triumphalist in its witness, and a theology which seeks to bring insight into the debate and, when necessary, to speak the truth clearly and unequivocally in the most concrete way possible. There is always, as Bonhoeffer insisted, the need to speak the Word of God here and now in the most concrete way possible out of knowledge of the situation.[24] It is precisely the distinctive element which theology brings to public discourse that makes it relevant. In Forrester's words: 'Something has surely gone seriously amiss if the role of theology in the public realm is no longer seen as in any sense confession of a faith which is at odds with the world, or confrontation with the powers.'[25]

The task of the Church in society is, after all, not to confirm the status quo, however good it may be, but to seek its ongoing transformation, however difficult. The Church must surely prefer a democratic society to one that is totalitarian, but its task is not primarily to legitimate democracy. Rather, it is to inject into the democratic system a vision that pushes democracy beyond its present achievements towards a greater expression of what we believe is God's will for the world.[26] Indeed, prophetic witness always remains a necessity in public life, and there are subtle, and not so subtle, dangers embedded in democracy that demand a watchful eye on the part of the churches. The Church can be as captive to the powers under democracy as under other forms of government and, sometimes, even more so.

59

As part of the preparation for 'Multi-Event 99', the organizers arranged for small groups of rural community Christians, many of them belonging to the African Initiated Churches, to reflect on the issues facing South Africa today from their particular perspective. When the Event itself was held, a representative number from these groups participated, along with a rather high-powered number of theologians and academics from South Africa and overseas. But it was during one of the public sessions addressed by the then Vice-President Thabo Mbeki that the group came into its own. Just before Mbeki's speech they took the platform and presented a statement on their concerns about current social and political issues. I wish to quote at length from their presentation before making a concluding comment. The reason is that what they said should not only be heard within the corridors of power, but also by the Church and its theologians as we seek to do theology in public but as members of the community of Christian faith:

> We do not claim to speak for many religious community groups who work on the fringes of society but, like so many in South Africa, we are religious *and* community-based *and* from the fringes *and* we have something we believe is worth saying.
>
> It is we – the ordinary people – who are not only the backbone of our religious institutions but also the foundation on which our democratic state is built. When we constantly demand and work for justice, the foundation is broad and strong. When we are apathetic and do nothing the foundation is like sand on which no stable structure, be it religious or political, can be built.
>
> Our religious character – for us our Christianity – makes us a significant entity. One may say religion is obviously one social institution alongside others such as economics and politics and is found in church buildings, synagogues, mosques, temples and shrines. This is true in one sense but it is definitely not true of the religion of the Community Groups we represent. Our religion does not end in church buildings. It propels us into public space to function as agents of trans-formation, but people merely see us as 'agents of transformation'. They miss one thing and that is our religious or Christian calling and conviction. It is our faith conviction, that we have a responsibility towards out fellow human beings, that brings us where we are. This conviction urges us not only to be concerned with what happens at the bottom of the hierarchy of our society but to act. Our faith and values drive us to be involved in social transformation and in the improvement of the lives of ordinary members of our communities by mobilizing our resources and energies into establishing various community-based projects relevant to the needs of our communities.[27]

Speaking as the poor rather than on behalf of the poor, their voice carried far more power than the rest of us were able to muster, and it spoke directly to government. Moreover, their voice articulated issues that concern those who experience inequality and poverty directly, those who know that the legacy of apartheid continues and that globalization is as much a threat as it is a promise. Listening to that voice surely goes to the heart of the matter of what it means to exercise political responsibility and do theology today for the sake of a genuinely transformed public life. Whoever else theologians concerned about public life should be listening to, it is to those who suffer most, and to those whose Christian faith and conviction gives them a way of coping with adversity, evaluating policies which affect them and transforming their circumstances.

Notes

1 John W. de Gruchy, 'Church unity and democratic transformation: perspectives on ecclesiology and ethics in South Africa', *The Ecumenical Review*, 49(3) (July 1997).

2 See John W. de Gruchy, 'African theology: South Africa', in David F. Ford (ed.), *The Modern Theologians: An Introduction to Christian Theology in the Twentieth Century* (Oxford: Basil Blackwell, 1997).

3 See, for example, Duncan B. Forrester, *Beliefs, Values and Policies: Conviction Politics in a Secular Age* (Oxford: Clarendon Press, 1989), pp. 53, 61.

4 See Jürgen Moltmann, 'Political reconciliation', in Leroy S. Rouner (ed.), *Religion, Politics, and Peace* (Notre Dame, IN: University of Notre Dame Press, 1999), pp. 24ff, 46ff; Jürgen Moltmann, *Experiences in Theology: Ways and Forms of Christian Theology* (London: SCM Press, 2000), pp. 116f.

5 Johann Baptist Metz, *Theology of the World* (London: Herder & Herder, 1968), p. 107.

6 Johann Baptist Metz, *Faith in History and Society: Toward a Practical Fundamental Theology* (New York: Seabury, 1980), pp. 34f.

7 Johann Baptist Metz, 'Political theology', in K. Rahner (ed.), *Encyclopedia of Theology: A Concise Sacramentum Mundi* (London: Burns & Oates, 1975), p. 1242.

8 Metz, *Theology of the World*, p. 111.

9 Moltmann, 'Political reconciliation', p. 49.

10 Metz, 'Political theology', pp. 1239; Metz, *Faith in History and Society*, pp. 50f.

11 See Jürgen Moltmann, *Theology of Hope* (London: SCM Press, 1967).

12 *The Kairos Document* (Johannesburg: Institute for Contextual Theology, 1986).

13 John W. de Gruchy, 'From Cottesloe to the "Road to Damascus": confessing landmarks in the struggle against apartheid', in G. Loots (ed.), *Listening to South African Voices* (Port Elizabeth: Theological Society of Southern Africa, 1990), pp. 1–18; de Gruchy, 'African theology: South Africa'.

14 John W. de Gruchy and Charles Villa-Vicencio (eds), *Aparthed is a Heresy* (Cape Town: David Philip, 1983).
15 James R. Cochrane, *Circles of Dignity: Community Wisdom and Theological Reflection* (Minneapolis, MN: Fortress Press, 1999).
16 Forrester, *Beliefs, Values and Policies*, p. 1.
17 David Tracy, *The Analogical Imagination: Christian Theology and the Culture of Pluralism* (London: SCM Press, 1981), p. 5.
18 Tracy, *Analogical Imagination*, p. 29.
19 Duncan Forrester, *On Human Worth* (London: SCM Press, 2001).
20 Rebecca Chopp, 'Reimagining public discourse', *Journal of Theology for Southern Africa*, 103 (March 1999). Chopp's essay was prepared for a workshop held in Cape Town in September/October 1998 on 'constructing a language of religion in public life'.
21 *Ibid.*, p. 34.
22 *Ibid.*, p. 28.
23 *Ibid.*, p. 81.
24 Dietrich Bonhoeffer, *No Rusty Swords: Letters, Lectures and Notes 1928–1936, Collected Works of Dietrich Bonhoeffer*, Vol. 1 (London: Collins, 1965), p. 158.
25 Forrester, *Beliefs, Values and Policies*, p. 42.
26 John W. de Gruchy, *Christianity and Democracy: A Theology for a Just World Order* (Cambridge: Cambridge University Press, 1995).
27 Welikazi Sokutu, 'A voice from the periphery: a community group's perspective of the role of religion in public life', in Cochrane, *Circles of Dignity: Community Wisdom and Theological Reflection*, pp. 58f.

Chapter 4

From Justice to Law and Back:
An Argentinian Perspective

JOSÉ MÍGUEZ-BONINO

A discussion about justice involves different disciplines, going all the way from religion and philosophy to juridical issues and penal and administrative decisions. Each of these dimensions has its own characteristics and demands which we have to recognize and respect. As we move in this area, however, we can easily forget that, at the start and at the end of all this process, there are human beings, specific situations, fortunate and unfortunate consequences of the decisions at which we have arrived from the 'mix' of the ingredients of all these disciplines which we have consulted. Precisely when we want to recognize and honour a person like Duncan Forrester we could not for a moment forget this fact. If there is a person who has moved wisely and consistently from the academic discussion to the condition of the victim and what the victim experiences, this is our teacher, colleague and friend, Duncan. What I will be trying to do in this brief chapter is to underline this aspect of the question of justice by looking briefly at some moments in the past and more concretely to a specific situation in my country. But let me first offer three different quotations on the question of justice.

Old and New Voices

Three brief quotations can introduce us to the subject. The first comes from a Brazilian writer:

> As a fickle and voluble dancer, justice changes partners as the game of historical contradictions moves on. Today we see her dancing with the powerful and tomorrow with the poor, now with the lords and then with the small and humble. In this dynamic game, everybody wants to be her partner and, when

she moves into another's hands, those who are slighted will call her a prostitute. Justice survives all rhythms and all partners because she flies above all of them … as if she floated in an atmosphere where collisions and conflicts do not exist. But in this great dance everybody is engaged … and justice, thinking of herself as eternal and well-balanced, does not realize that she is getting old, empty, an object of derision, and those who for a long time have been ignored and never had this woman in their arms, begin to think that what they want is not a distant and well-balanced woman but a committed and passionate one, who would dance the new rhythms of hope and commitment … the rhythms and the music of life, joy, bread and dignity.[1]

The second is a story remembered by the Portuguese Nobel Prizewinner José Saramago at the closing of the 'II Foro Mundial Social' (São Paulo, Brazil, 2002):

I will begin telling very briefly a striking event in the life of a rural village in the vicinity of Florence four hundred years ago.

The people of the village were in their homes or working on their farms . . . when, suddenly, they heard the sound of the Church bell. In those times (we are speaking of something that happened in the sixteenth century) bells rang several times throughout the day, so there would have been no reason for being disturbed at its sound, but that bell was now tolling for a funeral. It was strange because they did not know that anybody had died in the village. So the women came out into the street, the children gathered together, the men left their work and in a moment they were all gathered in the courtyard of the Church, waiting to be told whose death they should mourn. The bell kept sounding for some more minutes and it finally stopped, the door of the bell tower opened and a peasant came out. But it was not the bell-ringer and the neighbours asked him where the bell-ringer was and who had died. 'The bell-ringer is not here, it was me who sounded the bell,' was the answer. 'Then, nobody died?' answered the neighbours, and the peasant responded, 'Nobody with a human name or figure. I have sounded the funeral bell for Justice, because Justice is dead.'

What had happened? What happened was that the rich lord of the place – some unscrupulous count or marquis – had for a long time been moving the markers of his land into the small parcel of the peasant, which kept becoming smaller and smaller. The victim began by protesting and demanding, then he claimed mercy, and finally he decided to take the matter to the authorities and ask the protection of justice. Nothing happened, the plundering continued. Then, in despair, he decided to announce *urbi et orbie* . . . the death of Justice . . . I don't know what happened afterwards, I do not know whether the whole town came out to return the markers to their proper place or, once the death of justice had been declared, they returned with resignation, head down and soul resigned to the sad life of everyday. The truth is that History never tells us everything.

64

The third quotation comes from the social philosopher John Rawls:[2]

> Justice is the primary virtue of social institutions just as truth is in respect of thought systems. A theory, no matter how attractive and illuminating it may be, has to be rejected or revised if it is not true; in the same way, it does not matter that law and institutions may be well ordered and prove efficient; if they are unjust they must be reformed or abolished. Every person owns an inviolability grounded in justice which not even the welfare of the whole society can overrun.

It is not my intention to enter the philosophical and juridical debate on the meaning of justice. Two things seem to me to emerge from these very different quotations. The first is that concrete issues, as they become problems of justice, bring together basically three elements: namely, a fundamental understanding of the notion of justice – the justice about which Rawls speaks or for which the peasant claims; a need for a law – the markers in the land, law and institutions; and the question of power – with whom is justice dancing, who controls the duke or the count. The second is a consequence: whatever may be the clarity about each of these 'ingredients', unless they are combined in such a way that they become one single product, justice as a human condition has no meaning.

In what follows I will simply try, very briefly, to illustrate the question involved in the relation of justice to law and power: (1) with a reference to a specific moment in the history of Israel – let us say, 'a religious–theological approach'; (2) to suggest the new conditions in which our modern world has had to face the question of justice – an historical location; and (3) to look through a concrete case – my own country – how our recent Latin American societies are confronted with the question of justice.

The Claim of Justice and the Quest for Law: A Biblical Story

In the course of the ninth and eighth centuries BC, the Israelite nation moved from being a predominantly pastoral people, small farmers, to an agrarian society, from a tribal political organization resting on a charismatic leadership to a monarchy. The social consequences were the appearance of a nobility, the accumulation of land, the transformation of the small independent farmer into a salaried worker, etc. It is in the crisis of this transition that the 'prophetic protest' of Amos, Isaiah and Micah took place. The prophets did not have 'a revolutionary plan'. In fact, they appealed to tradition: the pastoral tribal society of small landowners who cultivated their piece of land and cared for their sheep and made of that society a 'Utopia' which demanded equality, egalitarian treatment for all, shalom, mercy and freedom. For them, faithfulness to the covenant hung on justice for the poor, the destitute, the foreigner. They denounced the corruption of the royal court, the enrichment of the new property owners at the cost of the misery of the poor and the connivance of the religious authorities – priests and false prophets – with this system of exploitation and servitude.

Could this protest for the sake of *mishpat* and *tsedaqah* (justice and righteousness) be transformed into 'law', 'commandment', 'ordinance', even casuistry? This is what 'Josiah's reform' attempted to do by enacting the Deuteronomic law – scholars will debate whether an older form was rewritten or a new one emerged. Josiah's reform had several goals. One was political and international: to recover the unity of the nation and to take advantage of the weakening of the Assyrian Empire to retrieve autonomy. It was also a religious recovering of the classical importance of worship – which in turn, had a political dimension – the centralization in a national sanctuary. But, in relation to our present subject, it means to reconstruct society through the enactment of laws of protection of the poor, the weak – orphans, widows and foreigners – redressing injustices or imbalances and protecting the use of the land through the seventh-year 'rest', by laws like the condoning of debts and (as in the Levitical law) even the fiftieth-year Jubilee.

As we know, the effort had only a temporary and partial success. International conditions – Babylon was emerging as the controlling power – made Josiah's political project impossible; internal conditions deteriorated and successive heirs of the throne did not follow Josiah's programme. Jeremiah would later transform Josiah's reform in a paradigm for his vehement accusation of the successors of Josiah (Jer 22:15ff) and his court and the reason for the exile to which it led. But even as a plan, it illustrates at least two things: one is the power of the claim of justice to awaken the need for reform; the other is that the reformed law helps to redefine and sharpen the understanding of justice. On that basis, the authors of the Books of Kings and Chronicles were able to pronounce judgement on the behaviour of the people in government – specifically the kings.

There is no doubt that the prophetic protest and the Deuteronomic law lie at the base of the Lukan report of Jesus' Galilean programme as described in the Nazareth (Luke 4:16ff) announcement and in the Lukan interpretation of Jesus' understanding of the 'Kingdom of God'.

66

A New Organization of Justice, Power and Law

The long and complex process of conflict and encounter of the biblical interpretation of justice and law, now in the new universal Christological dimension, and the Greco-Roman philosophical and political culture of the Empire, resulted in the new organization of the social, economic and political variables which we define as 'the medieval synthesis' which dominated – not without conflicts – until the fourteenth and fifteenth centuries. Then, new conditions began to challenge the existing order. The logic of the nations that sought to emancipate themselves from the Empire, of the cities which began to control trade and commerce, of the emerging bourgeoisies which gained space, of the 'financial' role of the Fugger and other groups, of the peasants' revolts, forced a new organization of justice, power and law. Christianity could not escape the demands of the new situation. The 'two kingdoms' theology of Luther, the Calvinist interpretation of the 'threefold use of the law', the Anabaptist communal organizations represent new attempts to find criteria for the organization of a 'just' society, the definition of new political, social, economic laws and the creation of political mechanisms to ensure an order without which a society cannot exist.[3]

Although we cannot enter now into a detailed discussion of these interpretations, they are a necessary background – which we need to take for granted – for the issues we are facing today. These new nations which emerged from the Western Empire, the building of colonial empires, the transition to a different economy, the emerging of a bourgeoisie and working classes pose the need to create new laws and regulations and thus in some way to redefine justice. There are new partners demanding their turn to enter the dance with justice. There are 'peasants' whose space is invaded.

One way to face the new conditions appears in the new laws that began to be defined in the early stages of 'globalization' in the sixteenth and seventeenth centuries. People like Grotius, Vitoria and others, working on the basis of theological premises, Roman law and the new conditions, began to offer new formulations of the *jus gentium*, the laws of transit on the seas (even the strange rule for *praedo*, the right to piracy and booty), the *de iure belli ac pacis* and later of the (bourgeois) 'rights of man and citizen', which are only a few results of the efforts and struggles of the new partners to find access to the dance. I will not try to describe this process, but it is important to take account of it because it is the background of a second wave of 'globalization' which has reached new dimensions and expressions in the last decades. The UN *Universal Declaration of Human Rights* and the successive covenants, charts and organisms respond to the struggles in which women, children, original peoples, older people, handicapped, affirm their right to enter the dance with justice.

But a parallel process has been developing alongside these efforts to find laws that establish the 'landmarks' for the necessary space for all to live, to grow, to be fully human. Globalization has also been a creation of power structures that control the different areas of human life: finances, production, use of the earth's resources, control of the media of communication, are 'privatized' in a number of world organizations which in theory do not deny the universal rights to which we made reference in the previous paragraph but actually determine the conditions to which these rights are subject. The Bretton Woods agreements of 1945 which resulted in the creation of the International Bank for Reconstruction and Development (World Bank), the International Monetary Fund (IMF), the former General Agreement on Tariffs and Trade (GATT) and the political decisions that ensure that a few nations which are permanent members of the Security Council of the 'United' Nations establish the place for the 'landmarks' and the 'pace' of the dance.

To ignore the tension between these two responses to the process of globalization is to blind ourselves to the fundamental issues of justice. To put it in Rawls's terms: 'it does not matter that law and institutions may be ordered and prove efficient; if they are unjust they must be reformed or abolished.' How is our world faring in relation to this demand at the beginning of the new millennium?

The Argentinian Case

How could we bring together, in relation to a particular case, the 'game' between the three forces we have been mentioning: justice, law and power? A game in which, as Rawls puts it, 'everybody has a right' to justice, whatever may be the cost for a society. My choice of Argentina – my own country – is somewhat arbitrary. Perhaps it is because I am part of the game, or because I know more about it. *Mutatis mutandis* – in terms of history, culture, including religion, social and economic conditions, international relations – we could have chosen almost any country of what is usually called the 'Third World' (and some people now define as the 'Two-Thirds World'). In fact, however, some of the issues and conditions which we will have to consider are intrinsically 'global' and operate, although with diverse conditions and intensities, in all areas of our world.

In the first place, we have to identify the scenery and the actors. In the context of the Cold War, the United States perfected the 'doctrine of national security' – which had originated in northern Europe early in the twentieth century – and exported it to Latin America under the 'Condor Plan' drawn up for the control of Latin America (particularly Central and South America) through US ideologically educated and trained Latin American military forces. In the decade of the 1970s, the military dictatorships which had begun in Brazil in 1964 took power in Bolivia, Chile, Uruguay and Argentina. One well-known aspect of the picture has to do with summary executions, the disappearance of people, new and perfected forms of torture, the appropriation and selling of children born in captivity. A second, less visible area of control – which has become more and more central – has to do with the control of the economy – privatization of state services, control of banking, brands and patents, control of trade through transnational corporations. Finally: who are the 'partners' who lead the dance? The military, the financial establishment, the social (including political) national elites who have been incorporated in the 'process' and the international organizations: the World Bank, the IMF, WTO.

In the second place, we have to look at the stages in the process. In the case of Argentina, we identify three periods. The first goes from 1976 to 1982 and corresponds to the military regime. The second is from 1983 to 1989 with the first democratically elected government, and the third begins in 1989 and culminates in the present critical situation which has attracted so much attention in the world press.

Finally, we need to try to understand the relations of justice, law and power at different stages of this history.

In the *first period* (1976–82), we face an illegitimate military government (following the military coup of 1976) – which, however, de facto exercises the power and functions of the state. As is well known, and has been later established in regular trials, illegal detention, the forced disappearance of people, torture and murder were systematically used. The power of the military state was absolute and uncontrollable (at least, from the inside of the country). The 'human rights' issue was the only way in which society could try – with the necessary risks – to pose the issue of 'justice' and 'law'. It was done through internal and international denunciation on violations of human rights as defined in the National Constitution and the Universal Declaration of Human Rights. The only accessible power was the appeal to Committees on Human Rights of international organizations, including the UN, the Organization of American States and human rights NGOs.

The purpose was twofold: to establish the case for future trials of those responsible for human rights violations and to bring to bear public internal and international pressure on the military regime. One could say that, as in Jeremiah, the law was used as a prophetic instrument of denunciation of an unjust use of power.

The *second period* (1983–9) changed the interplay of power and law. Several factors – the incapacity of the military regime to provide the minimum economic satisfaction, the internal conflicts within the military, the senseless engagement in a war for the possession of the Falkland Islands, the lack of international support and a growing rejection by the people – forced the military to call for an election. Now, the question of justice would be raised as a request for the rule of law exercised by a legal authority. The problem of power was posed in a different way: as both a demand and a support in relation to a government whose actual power was still fragile. So, the relation between justice, law and power became critical. If we take literally Rawls's dictum of a justice which even the welfare of the whole society cannot run over, we should demand trials and punishment of all those who had been involved in the violation of human rights, even if that demand would mean the risk of a new military coup or a civil war. The government decided to follow an intermediate road – to try and punish the main actors of the violations but to put a time limit and certain conditions of responsibility to the trials.[4] Was this a wise decision? Whether we think that it was the only possible action at the time or not, it is clear that the basic question of justice was not adequately solved and would come back again and again in different forms.

This dissatisfaction has given rise to the quest for a new international legislation which could offer a response to violations of human rights in our globalized world. The project of an International Court for the judgement of 'crimes against humanity', the right of any country to try crimes committed against a citizen of that country even if it took place in another country, the right of any country to try crimes against humanity committed in another country, are some of the issues which demand careful attention. But, again, the relation to power is present in all these cases. For instance, who will control a UN-organized International Court? Will that court be responsible to the UN General Assembly or will it be left in the hands of the Security Council where a few 'powerful countries' are the permanent majority and can use at their discretion a power which could easily become an instrument for their own interests?

The *third period* (1989 to the present) continues to pose some of the problems of the second period and underlines issues that were already present in the previous periods. The question of 'impunity' for many identified participants in criminal action during the military dictatorship continues. A 'pardon' to the members of the military junta by President Carlos Menen created a strong reaction from the population. We cannot speak of 'impunity' in this case – it is a constitutional privilege that the president can use, which does not absolve from guilt but suspends the effects of punishment – but there is no doubt that releasing from prison those people who had designed and led the brutal repression was felt by the population to be a blow to their sense of justice.

Be that as it may, the main problems in this period arise at a different level: one is the real or feigned powerlessness of the state to investigate, indict and punish the authors of a number of threats, acts of intimidation, aggression and even the murder of journalists, political analysts and members of the judicial power – judges and public prosecutors – and the two terrorist attacks against the Jewish community (the bombing of the embassy of Israel and, two years later, of the building of the Jewish Association – AMIA – resulting in almost a hundred dead). Moreover, it is increasingly felt that there is a systematic blocking of both police and judicial action and that this is the result of mafias with strong influence in government.[5] The result is a feeling of 'judicial insecurity', a growing sense that the government has resigned or is unable to fulfil its proper functions.

An even more critical problem of justice is occupying the centre of the stage. A number of international declarations, charts and agreements have to do with 'social and economic rights'. Some of these are now included in Argentina as part of the National Constitution. But who is responsible for ensuring the enforcement of these rights? Who defines the crimes? And who administers justice and provides for the fulfilment of the sentence? An early attempt in the 1970s to create some such international instrument in the framework of the United Nations was sabotaged by the powerful states (including the Soviet Union) and finally died out. The 'partners' of the Bretton Woods agreements continue to determine the rhythm of the dance, and the International Monetary Fund, the World Bank, GATT and their different instruments are the only recognized partners in this fantastic festival mysteriously called 'The Market'. In Latin American countries, growing millions of people looking from behind the fence – children dying of hunger, old people begging for a crumb, 15 to 40 or 50 per cent of unemployed, tens of millions of abandoned women, whole countries whose total income goes into 'the payment of the interests of *the debt*'– ask themselves when is it their turn to dance with justice? For how long will they wait? Will they simply be dying again and again in their misery, looking at the holy land from afar? Will they try to jump or tear down the fence and enter the feast by force? Will they die in that attempt? Or is there a possibility that the beautiful lady might herself call a new rhythm, jump the fence and make every one her partner? If she does, our world might be finding a new meaning of justice – closer to Amos, Isaiah . . . or Jesus![6]

What About Us?

Are there any specific responsibilities for a Christian community as the depositary of a long and rich tradition but also of a complex, sometimes ambiguous but in any case unavoidable participation in relation to power, justice and law? There is a need for a permanent constructive and critical debate to evaluate, correct and empower this responsibility. Let me end this 'dialogue' with some possible issues for debate.

There could be *a function of inspiration*: a permanent programme, within and outside the Christian community, of education in the values that back and support the will to have and obey a law that expresses 'justice'. Religious communities are spaces of socialization in the values and guidelines for life. When the 'children of Israel' were invited to remember their own epic of liberation, they were told: 'teach them to your children and to their children after them' (Deut 4:9). This (covenant) would incorporate into their lives these 'basic' ethical values – justice, righteousness, mercy, peace – which could support the 'minimum' behaviour habits without which no society can function.

Then, there is *a critical function*, in the prophetic tradition, which challenges the existing 'ways of doing things' from the point of view of 'justice'. In other words: God's justice is a permanent challenge to existing human laws, which does not deny the need of 'laws' but pushes them forward for a permanent 'quest for justice'. One could see the question of human rights – and the process, let us say, from the French Revolution to the contemporary diversity of particular – children, women, handicapped, ethnic, etc. – rights as an example of the need for this 'prophetic' function of the Christian community.

The biblical 'deuteronomic and prophetic tradition' calls the Christian community to *a permanent function of 'advocacy'* – to be the defence lawyers of all the unprotected social groups or individuals. The 'option for the poor' has been the 'symbolic' formulation which expresses a fundamental axiom of the biblical tradition. In the words of Karl Barth: 'God is always, passionately and unconditionally on one side and one alone: against the powerful and arrogant and with the poor and humiliated.'[7]

Perhaps the most radical demand to the Christian community in this area is the *disobedience to the law*. Without any doubt, when a Christian or a Christian community is convinced that a law is contrary to justice, it has a moral obligation to denounce it, to use all the available instruments of information, appeal, democratic procedures, to abrogate or modify such law. There may be, however, extreme cases in which protest has to become 'disobedience'. In our recent history, issues like apartheid in South Africa or the rights of the black population in the USA have led Christians and churches to go back to Peter's and John's response to the Sanhedrin: 'Judge for yourselves whether it is right . . . to obey you rather than God' (Acts 4:19). Naturally, such a decision should not be banalized or claimed capriciously and it would have to be taken only when all other options have been tried, when the community has analysed and discussed the issue and when concrete measures to change the situation have been advanced. But, in principle, this remains a possible and even a necessary and unavoidable option for the Christian community.

Although this may look like a 'pious digression' from our main concern, our own experience in relation to the role of the Christian community in these different forms of response to the struggle for justice teaches us that they reach their deepest meaning and greatest strength both inside and outside the Church when they are born of *a committed, militant and profound faith, accompanied by intercessory prayer*. Just as a Christian has no right to pray for the poor and do nothing to change their condition, a Christian equally has no right to protest, oppose or fight against people, government or enemies for whom he/she has not prayed.

Notes

1 Roberto A. R. de Aguiar, *O que é a justiça* (São Paulo, Brazil: Alfa y Omega, 1982), p. 15.

2 John Rawls, *A Theory of Justice* (Cambridge, MA.: Harvard University Press, 1971), pp. 19ff.

3 I have to excuse myself from entering into discussion of this complex chapter of history which remains an object of debate. It would be a necessary background for a serious discussion of a Christian conception of justice and law, but I have had to take it for granted for evident reasons of space.

4 The same issue has arisen for other South American countries (Brazil, Chile, Uruguay) and the different roads chosen are strictly related to the balance of power and the internal situation of the populations. Other approaches to the question in South Africa, Central America and Central Europe deserve to be carefully assessed in this respect.

5 In a similar situation, the judicial power in Italy launched a programme to indict, try and punish these mafias and, although it paid a high price in the threats and deaths of judges and judicial officers, by and large succeeded in controlling the situation and counteracting the power of the mafias.

6 At the very moment when I wrote these lines (in the Spring of 2002) a committee from the IMF was negotiating in Buenos Aires the possibility of a loan of 9000 million US$. The conditions are: (1) the loan would go to pay the interests of earlier loans from the IMF and the World Bank – so, the 9000 million would simply move in the books of the IMF and begin to generate a new debt; (2) the budget for 2002–2004 would cut funds from public health and education. Meanwhile, salaries were frozen, unemployment had reached 30 per cent and the cost of living had increased by 5 per cent – mostly in the areas of food, oil (and thus transportation) and services (which have all been privatized).

7 Karl Barth, *Church Dogmatics* (Edinburgh: T&T Clark, 1957), Eng. trans., Vol. II/1, p. 386.

Part II

Contested Ideas – Modernity's Legacy

Chapter 5

Freedom in the Crisis of Modernity

RICHARD J. BAUCKHAM

Centrally at issue in the widely perceived crisis of modernity that character-izes the beginning of the twenty-first century are the meaning and value of human freedom. So essential has freedom been to the metanarrative modernity told about itself that it has become impossible to think about freedom without engaging with that metanarrative of progressive emanci-pation. Whether modernity has in fact delivered the emancipation it saw as its goal, whether it has proved a movement of liberation or a project of domination, whether the freedom it has delivered is a boon or a burden, whether the kind of freedom it envisaged was the authentic goal of human fulfilment or a deformation of human freedom – that such questions are now inescapable constitutes the crisis of modernity. That they must be questions for public theology in the twenty-first century hardly needs arguing. For modernity itself the question of human freedom was a theological ques-tion, even when its answer entailed atheism. In the crisis of modernity the question of the death of God still lurks behind every discussion of human liberation in which it is not explicit. In public *theology* above all one must expect it to be explicitly addressed.

Duncan Forrester has recently reminded us that R. H. Tawney claimed: 'In order to believe in human equality it is necessary to believe in God.'[1] In view of the close connection he correctly saw between equality and freedom, he might well have said the same of freedom. In a straightforward sense it would obviously not be true: not all atheists are determinists, though many are. The question as it will arise in this chapter is rather whether freedom is sustainable, whether it does not become a kind of slavery, demeaning human life and destroying human community, without a context of other values and practices of life in which human life is related to God. We shall call in evidence two secular thinkers, a novelist and a political theorist, and two Christian theologians.

Freedom at the End of History: Michel Houellebecq and Francis Fukuyama

According to Michel Houellebecq's extraordinary novel, *Les Particules élémentaires*[2] (in English translation, *Atomised*), the idea of personal freedom was, by the end of the twentieth century, 'a concept which had already been much devalued … and which everyone agreed, at least tacitly, could not form the basis for any kind of human progress' (p. 383).[3] Individual autonomy is the central feature of late twentieth-century Western society as Houellebecq portrays it in this savage satire. The modern age, as he sees it, has reached its nadir in the egotistical and especially sexual hedonism by which most individuals are now driven, dominated as they are by the ideals of personal freedom projected by the entertainment industry and commerce generally (p. 63). The breakdown of community through the excesses of modern individualism entered its final phase with the sexual revolution, which, by destroying the traditional couple and the family, removed the last social factor protecting the individual from the market (pp. 28, 135–6). Most people loathe the 'atomised society' (p. 185) that is the result, but are condemned to the lonely lives it creates.

Against a background of violence and beggars on the urban streets, the banality of commercially regulated culture and the mindless triviality of New Age alternatives, Houellebecq's characters live loveless and meaningless lives. Three of the four main characters kill themselves, the other passes the latter part of his life in a psychiatric clinic, drugged beyond the possibility of unhappiness. Most people in this culture, the novel claims, are terrified, not of death itself, but of ageing, the loss of sexual attractiveness and capacities, and the indignity of dependence on others:

> Each individual has a simple view of the future: a time will come when the sum of the pleasures that life has to offer is outweighed by the sum of pain (one can actually hear the meter ticking, and it ticks inevitably towards the end). This weighing up of pleasure and pain which, sooner or later, everyone is forced to make, leads logically, at a certain age, to suicide. (p. 297)

This is the logic of a society in which most people have no other aim than the pursuit of physical pleasure. One reviewer complains of the 'long and arid tracts of anti-erotic pornography':[4] the wearisome detail conveys the joyless obsession with sex for mere sexual pleasure's sake in a society whose 'remaining myth was that sex was something to do' (p. 155).

The story aspires to the status of metanarrative. It centres on the lives of two half-brothers: Bruno, who typifies his generation, and Michel, who becomes one of the architects of the future. Emotionally crippled by parental neglect (especially by their mother, a precursor of the me-generation), neither is capable of love. Bruno's life is completely driven by the pursuit of sexual pleasure, while Michel, a brilliant molecular biologist, leads an almost purely intellectual life, devoid of emotion, but sadly aware of his own incapacity to love and of the near impossibility of love in the world he observes. Discussing the work of Aldous and Julian Huxley with his brother, Michel enunciates the novel's theory of the modern age: 'Metaphysical mutation, having given rise to materialism and modern science, in turn spawned two great trends: rationalism and individualism' (p. 191). A 'metaphysical mutation' is a global transformation in the values by which most people live (p. 4). The rise of Christianity was one such mutation; modern science was responsible for the next; and Michel and Bruno live in the generation when the implications of this modern mutation are pressing relentlessly to their logical and destructive conclusion, stoppable only by another metaphysical mutation.

Michel reads Huxley's *Brave New World* not as a satire, but as a Utopia. It is 'our idea of heaven: genetic manipulation, sexual liberation, the war against age, the leisure society. This is precisely the world that we have tried – and failed – to create' (p. 187). Why then has the metaphysical mutation of scientific modernity not led to such a Utopia? Michel continues:

> [Aldous] Huxley's mistake was in not being able to predict the power struggle between rationalism and individualism – he crucially under-estimated the power of the individual faced with his own death. Individualism gives rise to the idea of freedom, the sense of self, the need to feel that one is superior to others. A rational society like the one he describes in *Brave New World* defuses the struggle. Economic rivalry – a metaphor for animals competing for territory – should not exist in a society of plenty, where the economy is strictly regulated. Sexual rivalry – genes competing over time – is meaningless in a society where the link between sex and procreation has been broken. But Huxley forgets about individualism. He doesn't seem to understand that, stripped of their link with reproduction, lust and greed still exist – not as pleasure principles, but as forms of egotism … [T]he metaphysical mutation brought about by modern science depends on individuation, narcissism, malice and desire. Any … philosopher worthy of the name knows that, in itself, desire – unlike pleasure – is a source of suffering, pain and hatred. The Utopian solution – from Plato to Huxley by way of Fourier – is

79

> to do away with desire and the suffering it causes by satisfying it immediately. The opposite is true of the sex-and-shopping society we live in, where desire is marshalled and organised and blown up out of all proportion. For society to function, for competition to continue, people have to want more and more until it fills their lives and finally devours them. (pp. 191–2)

Thus, in Michel's view, the rationalism of the modern age seeks a society of Utopian happiness but is prevented from achieving it by the competitive individualism also characteristic of the modern age. Consumerism is both the product of this individualism and ensures that its desires can never be satisfied.

Why has the modern metaphysical mutation produced this egotistical individualism? Michel's answer seems to be simply that it has replaced religion and its other-worldly hope with materialism and the inevitable finality of death. Scientific awareness of mortality makes it impossible to return to the religious world-view which curbed egotism and fostered community. So Michel's problem becomes: 'How could society function without religion?' (p. 193). His life-work is to solve this problem and thereby enable the next metaphysical mutation, which takes place after his death during the twenty-first century. The solution is purely biological: the production, through genetic engineering of a new, post-human species. The new species is asexual, in that it does not reproduce sexually, though it has the means of experiencing much greater sexual pleasure than humans have. A perfected process of cloning makes possible exact reproduction, such that all members of the species, including all future members of the species, are related as identical human twins are, individuated by experience but 'maintaining a mysterious fraternity' by virtue of their genetic identity (p. 375). Love now comes naturally, rooted in the post-human DNA. Humanity has overcome the biological competitiveness of Darwinian evolution by creating a new species with a radically new biological constitution. As the post-humans, revealed at the end to be the putative writers of the narrative, observe how relatively peacefully the extinction of the old species has occurred, they comment: 'It has been surprising to note the meekness, the resignation, perhaps even the relief of humans at their own passing away' (p. 378).

As science fiction goes, this is a modest speculation. But Houellebecq surely means it seriously at least in this sense: he does not think the problem of the contradiction between individual freedom and community is soluble while humans remain humans. This is a profoundly misanthropic form of the long tradition of thought about post-history (*posthistoire*), stemming in France especially from Auguste Comte and more recently expressed in Hegelian form by Alexandre Kojève, the main inspiration of Francis Fukuyama's now famous American version.[5] Throughout this tradition runs the vision of transcending the historical condition of humanity that is characterized by dissatisfaction, aspiration, suffering and conflict: history itself will lead to a post-historical condition which has a finality about it at least in its transcendence of the conflictual character of history. If the human is defined as the historical, then humans in attaining their post-historical goal will cease to be human. Thus Kojève, whose work has almost certainly had some influence on Houellebecq, understands the end of history as humanity's rational self-destruction.[6] Houellebecq also sees it in this way, but introduces genetic engineering to solve the problem his radically pessimistic view of modernity produces for the notion of human history's self-transcendence into post-history. Humans, in his novel, finally realize the impossibility of attaining the human dream of happiness beyond conflict and suffering through the pursuit of freedom, just at the moment when the achievements of scientific rationality make the creation of a post-human species, liberated from human individualism, possible. The struggle between rationalism and individualism in the modern era, a notion not unknown in the tradition of thinking about post-history, Houellebecq perceives as an irreconcilable one, but he can retain the dream of a post-historical solution of it, because he also envisages a scientific means of ensuring a complete triumph of rationalism over individualistic freedom.

Freedom is almost inescapably a central theme in theories of post-history, just as it is in virtually all forms of the modern metanarrative of progress. This makes it illuminating for our theme to compare and to contrast Houellebecq and Fukuyama. There are significant similarities that reflect their common ideological background in the tradition of post-historical thought. They are both Hegelian in their conviction that ultimately consciousness and ideas, rather than material factors, determine history, and that in the long run ideological principles will work themselves out to their logical conclusion in the course of historical events. They also both see the goal of history as the achievement of the rational, but differ crucially in their understanding of the relationship of individual freedom to the rational ordering of life in the interests of happiness. For Houellebecq these are fundamentally antithetical, whereas for Fukuyama, the liberal optimist, they are not only compatible but indispensable to each other. These judgements are integral to their evaluation of the modern age as one of progress (Fukuyama) or decline (Houellebecq). But we should also note that their concerns about freedom focus on different forms of freedom. Houellebecq seems unconcerned with the constitutional freedoms of liberal democracies, whereas for Fukuyama it is in the irreversible recognition of the ideal of liberal democracy as the final political ideology that the end of history is achieved.

However, some elements in Fukuyama suggest that the two perspectives are not as clearly incompatible as at first appears. Fukuyama has his own criticism of excessive individualism. He dissociates himself somewhat from the Anglo-Saxon liberal tradition stemming from Hobbes and Locke, in which liberal democracy is founded on the selfish interests of the individual, and embraces a more Hegelian emphasis on the social being of humanity, such that democratic societies must be held together by shared democratic values (pp. 145, 160–1).[7] Moreover, he allows that liberal democracy only provides a framework for the good life, rather than defining or ensuring it.[8] But he comes much closer to Houellebecq when he himself speaks of 'the tendency of democratic societies toward social atomization' (p. 324) and the tendency of 'liberal economic principles … to atomize and separate people' (p. 325).

The Anglo-Saxon version of liberal theory, on which the United States was founded, bases society solely on the enlightened self-interest of individuals. As this liberal theory has permeated all aspects of American society, it has inevitably, according to Fukuyama, weakened or destroyed community at every level, including now the family. He also observes that 'the pressures of the capitalist marketplace' destroy community because they require of individuals constant shifts both in locality and in the nature of their work (p. 325). What really support and strengthen community, he continues, are shared religious values, which the authors of the American Revolution did to some extent presuppose: they 'did not hesitate to assert that liberty required belief in God' (p. 326). This religious support for liberty has necessarily, with the onset of greater pluralism in American society, led to 'a purer form of liberalism', in which the basic liberal theory of the right of individuals to pursue enlightened self-interest has had to survive in, as it were, naked form. In this naked form it was bound to destroy community.

Thus Fukuyama, who considers secularization essential to liberal democracy (pp. 216–17), is obliged to argue that liberalism itself creates a gaping whole at the heart of liberal societies:

> Liberal democracies … are not self-sufficient: the community life on which they depend must ultimately come from a source different from liberalism itself. The men and women who made up American society at the time of the founding of the United States were not isolated, rational individuals calculating their self-

interest. Rather, they were for the most part members of religious communities held together by a common moral code and belief in God. The rational liberalism that they eventually came to embrace was not a projection of that pre-existing culture. It existed in some tension with it. 'Self-interest rightly understood' came to be a broadly understandable principle that laid a low but solid ground for public virtue in the United States, in many cases a firmer ground than was possible through appeal to religious or pre-modern values alone. But in the long run those liberal principles had a corrosive effect on the values predating liberalism necessary to sustain strong communities, and therefore on a liberal society's ability to be self-sustaining. (pp. 326–7)

This is a remarkable qualification of Fukuyama's overall thesis that 'liberal democracy in reality constitutes the best possible solution to the human problem' (p. 338), and therefore represents the end of history. If liberal democracy both depends on and itself tends to corrode 'pre-liberal traditions' (p. 335), if it cannot survive without values which it cannot itself produce and even tends to debilitate, it would appear to be much more radically unstable than Fukuyama allows, and quite incapable by itself of constituting 'the best possible solution to the human problem'. The search for such a solution and with it the continuing history of humanity would seem rather to shift to a concern for what might promote human solidarity and community in the face of the atomizing power of triumphant liberalism.[9]

At this point it seems that Fukuyama's argument, despite his resolute optimism, could easily come to meet Houellebecq's: he too perceives a very serious contradiction between freedom and community at the heart of the liberal society that he, unlike Houellebecq, lauds. But there is also a key point at which Houellebecq connects liberalism and egotistical individualism, but which Fukuyama, for understandable ideological reasons, does not perceive or ignores. This is the economic power and culture of consumerism. For Fukuyama, free market capitalism is part and parcel of the ideal of liberal democracy. The spread of Western consumerist culture throughout the world is an index and agent of the spread of liberal values. As we have seen, he does admit that capitalism tends to social atomization through mobility. But he does not see that consumerism is destructive of social values. Houellebecq, on the other hand, clearly sees consumerism as part and parcel of the egotistical individualism that is reducing life in Western society to banal hedonism and threatening its survival. Moreover, in the passage quoted above from Michel in the novel, he puts his finger on a significant flaw in Fukuyama's position. The consumerist 'sex-and-shopping society' depends on keeping human desire endlessly unsatisfied, in constant and competitive pursuit of more and new, whereas a post-historical society, a rational Utopia such as Michel helps to achieve, depends for its stability on the immediate satisfaction of desire. Fukuyama's end of history is inherently unstable and insecure because it requires the endless prolongation of exponential economic growth.

It is not my intention to endorse either Fukuyama's or Houellebecq's diagnosis of the contemporary world as such. Partly because the post-history thesis requires of both a particularly strong form of the typically modern desire for a metanarrative of modernity and its future, their accounts are undoubtedly selective and exaggerated. Both are illuminating in different ways. But the point of most interest for our present purpose is the surprising one that, despite their apparently opposite evaluations of freedom in contemporary Western society, both perceive a serious contradiction between the kind of freedom nurtured by the liberal values of that society and the requirements of human community. Both think that the decline of religion in Western society has left a void that liberal individualism cannot fill. Neither considers a lasting resurgence of religion in Western society either possible or desirable. Michel's problem, 'How could society function without religion?', is taken with extreme seriousness by Houellebecq and answered only with an extreme solution: the biological creation of a new species. Fukuyama, despite his enthusiasm for technology, indulges in no such futurology and does not have the luxury of the genre of the novel to provide an ironic distance from such extreme solutions. Moreover, to recognize the full seriousness of the dilemma would endanger his whole argument.

An uncharacteristically theological passage, from a response Fukuyama wrote to a volume of essays on his thesis about the end of history, is revealing in its incoherence. In a perceptive essay in the volume,[10] Peter Lawler compared Fukuyama unfavourably with the work of Kojève on which he is heavily dependent. According to Lawler, Kojève is a consistent atheist, Fukuyama not. Kojève recognized that belief in God sustains human freedom because it cannot allow that there can be a historical resolution of the irrationality of human history. Within a historical framework human aspirations can never be finally satisfied. Kojève, on the other hand, is the consistent atheist who sees the implications of Enlightenment rationalism to their logical conclusion. There can be an end of history in a finally rational satisfaction of human desires and this will be the end of human freedom. God, history and humanity, entailing human dignity and freedom, stand or fall together. Fukuyama, on the other hand, envisages an end of history in which human beings remain human beings, with the conditions for their dignity and freedom established, paradoxically, by this end of history. Lawler writes:

The most misleading incoherence of Fukuyama's book is his combination of a seemingly moderate defense of human dignity and liberal democracy with comprehensive atheism. He seems to hold that human liberty can be perpetuated in the absence of the distinction between man and God. With this suggestion, he departs from the rigor of the comprehensive atheism of his mentor, Kojève … Kojève and Nietzsche agree that the death of God, or, as Fukuyama puts it, the banishing of religion from the West by liberalism, signals the end of human liberty or distinctiveness.[11]

Fukuyama's response to Lawler's essay, which he understands to be posing the question whether it is possible to have a sense of human dignity without God, is this:

My answer to Lawler's question is: if the question of man's dependence on God is meant in a practical sense, that is, if he is asking whether a liberal society is sustainable without religion and other pre-modern sources of constraint and community, the answer is probably *no*. If his question is meant in a theoretical sense (i.e., are there other sources of cognition [of human dignity] besides God?), the answer is, *I don't know*. It may be that God is the only possible source for such knowledge; if so, and if God has indeed died, then we are in a lot of trouble and need desperately to find another source on which to base our belief that human beings have dignity. Enlightenment rationalism is not the solution but part of the problem.[12]

The incoherence of the penultimate sentence here is breathtaking. If God is 'the only possible source' for knowledge of human dignity, then we cannot find 'another source'. The trouble must be terminal. Fukuyama here escapes only by blatant self-contradiction from agreeing with Kojève and Lawler (as well as with Houellebecq) that the death of God entails an end of history that is also the end of humanity's distinctively human being: human dignity and freedom. Moreover, the desperate search Fukuyama invokes, beyond Enlightenment rationalism, for 'another source on which to base our belief that human beings have dignity' must mean the continuance of history.

Fukuyama's thesis about the end of history cannot but raise the question of God, and the ludicrous inadequacy of his response to it reveals that the question of God is the most serious flaw in his whole argument. Is the freedom Fukuyama values and for the sake of which he values liberal democratic and liberal economic principles a consequence of the death of God or undermined by it? Fukuyama appears to say both. We must at least conclude that the question of human freedom in the crisis of modernity is inescapably also the question of God.

The Crisis of Modernity in Theological Perspective:
Jürgen Moltmann and Ellen Charry

In recent years Moltmann has devoted a number of lectures and essays to reflecting on the crisis of modernity.[13] His reflections on this theme are of particular interest in that he is not willing, with some theologians, to accept a complete, postmodern repudiation of the values of modernity, but, on the other hand, he is far from sharing Fukuyama's optimism about the spread of Western liberal values in the contemporary world. He recognizes the individualism and atomization of Western society, and goes further than Houellebecq in implicating economic liberalism in the destruction of community. Communities are threatened from one side by increasing individualism and from the other by 'the global marketing of everything', which, he points out:

> is much more than pure economics. It has become the all-embracing law of life. We have become customers and consumers, whatever else we may be. The market has become the philosophy of life, the world religion, for some people even 'the end of history'. The marketing of everything destroys community at all levels, because people are weighed up only according to their market value. They are judged by what they can perform or by what they can afford. (p. 153)

What could perhaps be clearer in Moltmann's treatment is the intimate connection between the global free market and individualism. Not only does the market destroy community by reducing people to their economic value and subjecting their lives to its imperious needs, which are not those of community. It also, insofar as it treats people as subjects, treats them as acquisitive individuals who must be seduced into wanting more and more. Though these connections cannot be reduced to simple one-way causative relationships, consumerism constitutes a deeply interconnected relationship between increasing individualism and the global free market and, highly significantly for our subject, enables the oppression of the latter to be perceived as liberating. The most important aspect of this is that it is liberating for the affluent who enjoy consumer choice, while oppressing others whose conditions of life and work make that possible, but it is also the case that even for those who enjoy consumer choice – the vast majority of people in Western societies – the perception of this as liberating masks the way in which the market oppresses them also by its destruction of community.

It is characteristic of Moltmann's analysis of modernity and its crisis that he not only speaks, like Houellebecq and Fukuyama, of freedom and individualism, but also of domination. The modern period has produced not only modernity and its 'progress' but also sub-modernity, the condition of the victims at whose expense modern 'progress' has occurred. For the modern project has been a project of exploitative domination – both the domination of the Third World by the West, and the domination of nature by humanity. When he asks, 'What interests and concerns, and what values, rule our scientific and technological civilization?', the simple answer is: 'the boundless will towards domination' (p. 97). Both forms of domination create a world situation that cannot be stable: the growing impoverishment of the Third World cannot but react in some way against the prosperity of the rich countries, while the finite resources of nature cannot be exploited to meet the ever accelerating standard of living of the affluent without catastrophe. This conviction of unstable contradictions within the global economic system grounds Moltmann's dissent from Fukuyama's thesis about the end of history. Even if it is true, as Fukuyama holds, that there are no longer any alternatives to liberal democracy and the global free market, this does not indicate the end of history, so long as there are 'challenging contradictions' that 'thrust forward to a new solution'. If new solutions are not found, the consequence will be not only the end of history, but the end of humanity (pp. 154–5).

Domination is a means of securing the freedom of some at the expense of the freedom of others. As Moltmann has it, domination is one definition of freedom. It connects freedom with the struggle for power and therefore sees it as competitive. Freedom is that of the master who makes others his slaves. But in this way Moltmann not only represents the dark side of modernity, its domination of others, as the correlative of its freedom. He also sees the individualism of European and American democratic societies as stemming from this idea of competitive freedom. In the democratic revolutions the freedom of the feudal lord was democratized. Each one's freedom is his (and later her) independence of others; each is related to others only insofar as they are limits on his freedom and he may not encroach on theirs. The result is 'individuals in an atomized world' (pp. 155–6). Moltmann's next move is not unusual in late twentieth-century theology: in contrast to this notion of freedom as domination or individualism, he commends another definition of freedom: 'communicative freedom' or 'freedom as free community', according to which mutual respect and friendliness create free relationships between community members. In a shared life, the freedom of each is not bounded by the freedom of others, but is extended in the mutual sharing of love or solidarity (p. 158). Moltmann's distinction here between two types of freedom – individualistic and communicative – is valuable, and a major advantage over the much less discriminating talk of freedom and individualism in both Houellebecq and Fukuyama.

At first sight it may seem that Moltmann is contrasting the typically modern concept of freedom as individual autonomy with an alternative that is less typically modern. But there is an important element in his argument that shows that the notion of communicative freedom as he understands it remains typically modern in a basic respect. Moltmann asks how people can resist increasing individualism and live in a more communitarian way. He immediately states that 'we cannot revert to the predetermined affiliations of traditional societies.' Rather, the way forward is through committing ourselves and keeping promises, such as to engender trust between people (p. 157). It seems that *freedom of choice* remains basic. Unlike pre-modern communities, modern or postmodern communities will be formed as people choose relationships and freely commit themselves to them: 'The paradigm of a free society is not predetermined membership. The paradigm is the covenant. A free society rests on social consensus' (p. 88). Elsewhere Moltmann has spoken of friendship as the paradigm of free relationships, in that it is a chosen rather than given relationship. His model does correspond with major social trends in urban life, where the given ties of family and neighbourhood have been increasingly eroded, while instead people form networks of friends (cf. pp. 85–6).

Whether such a model of free relationships is adequate, however, can be questioned by the observation that it is very easy for people to be left out of such freely chosen associations. Cases where people have been found dead in their homes long after they died illustrate what can happen when no one relates to neighbours but only to friends. Moltmann seems to accept as axiomatic the modern sense that what is given, predetermined by history or circumstances, is necessarily a constraint on freedom, even when the given is not oppressive in any sense other than that one has not selected it from a choice of options. But this excessive revolt against the given may well, in fact, be a factor in the crisis of modernity, closely allied to egotistical individualism. Recovery of community may require a rediscovery of the ability to find freedom within given relationships and circumstances – to choose, for example, to befriend a person people find hard to like but for whom one accepts a responsibility simply because circumstances put one in the position to do so. While the freedom and commitments of friendship are one important model of relationships, perhaps the parent–child relationship (including the responsibility of adult children for their parents) should remain another, in which givenness rather than chosenness is constitutive of the relationship without detriment to freedom properly understood. Is it really slavery to recognize obligations to people to whom we have not freely made even implicit promises of commitment? To insist that a person is only truly free when every aspect of life becomes a matter of choice between available alternatives is really to understand freedom as a rejection of finiteness. Arguably this is indeed a strong tendency in the modern ideal of individual freedom. It is revealing to observe Moltmann's thought tending in the same direction.

There is a profound ambiguity in Moltmann's evaluation of modernity. As well as his claim, already quoted, that the ruling principle of the modern age is 'the boundless will towards domination' (p. 97), there is also the claim: 'The first principles and supreme values of the modern world are to be found in *the self-determination of the determining human subject* ... [H]uman dignity lies in individual self-determination' (p. 212). These two claims are not simply contradictory, for according to the definition of freedom as domination, 'the boundless will towards domination' is the corollary of individual self-determination. They can be seen as two sides of the one coin. From the Enlightenment principle of individual self-determination derive both 'the humanitarian ideas of human dignity and the universality of human rights', to which Moltmann passionately asserts there is no alternative except barbarism (p. 17), and the rampant individualism that is destroying community (pp. 212–13). It is the apparent tension between individual self-determination and community that, as we have just noticed, Moltmann attempts to overcome by a notion of community formed by individual self-determination in promise and dependability. He evidently treats individual self-determination as an absolute not to be compromised by any concession to a notion of community that might qualify it. In this sense Moltmann remains profoundly modern in his thinking about the self and community.

The ambiguity of the modern principle of individual self-determination appears even more emphatically in an essay entitled: 'Protestantism: "The Religion of Freedom"' (pp. 191–208). Here Moltmann attributes the origins of modern concepts of freedom to the Protestant tradition: initially the Reformation, then the German and American Enlightenments. Notable in this account is Moltmann's apparent contentment with describing the whole development of modernity's understanding of freedom as an authentically Christian one. He seems quite at home in the nineteenth-century German Liberal Protestant view of nineteenth-century German culture as the logical and authentic development of the Reformation. His abstention from critical theological assessment of the theology of the German Enlightenment is apparent in the following:

> Protestant subjectivism has led religiously and culturally to all possible kinds of individualism, pluralism and egoism. But it has also brought into modern culture the dignity of every human person, and individual human rights, so that these can never be forgotten (pp. 202–3).

But why has it had such mixed consequences? Was there some flaw at the heart of modernity in its origins? Were there more ideological factors at work than 'Protestant subjectivism'? By what theological or other principles can we justify applauding and retaining part of this modern heritage while resisting other aspects?

Most remarkably, in attributing to the Christian tradition both the credit and the blame for the modern notion of individual freedom, with its positive and negative consequences, Moltmann never asks whether an idea such as the dignity and freedom of the individual, originating within a framework of Christian belief, can be expected to remain the same notion when removed from that context and divorced even from belief in God. What, we might ask, becomes of the freedoms of the Enlightenment, with their focus on individual choice, when they no longer supplement, but replace the essentially God-related freedom proclaimed by the Reformers? Moltmann does recognize the loss of God as an aspect of the crisis of modernity (pp. 16–17), but never explores the relationship of this to other aspects of that crisis. Arguably he shares a kind of theological prejudice common both to theologians and to opponents of the Christian tradition, i.e., a propensity to seek the origins of key features of modernity deep in the Christian tradition rather than in modernity's increasingly self-conscious detachment of itself from that tradition. Another very striking example in this same collection of Moltmann's essays is an argument that traces modern individualism all the way back to Augustine (pp. 82–4). So why was community so strong and why is individualism in the modern sense so difficult to discern in precisely the many centuries in which Augustine's influence over Western Christendom was at its height? Such an argument seems entirely to ignore the obvious fact that the individualism of contemporary atomized society emerges just in the period when Christianity's influence in Western society has spectacularly waned. Houellebecq draws the obvious conclusion: atomization is the consequence of the demise of religion. It is extraordinary that Moltmann never seems to notice this possible explanation. This may be due to his strong consciousness of the fact that often in the modern period an authoritarian Church opposed movements of freedom and lent its ideological support to authoritarian political regimes.[14] A Christian critique of the modern understanding of freedom may seem altogether too much like a reversion to this ecclesiastical suppression of freedom.

At this point we may usefully refer to the critique of Moltmann offered by American theologian Ellen Charry.[15] She interprets Moltmann as accepting the modern understanding of the self, which she sees as decisively different from the Christian self. In its fundamental notion of individual autonomy the modern understanding of the self does not derive from Christian tradition but is a departure from Christian tradition:

> The modern values of individuality, autonomy and freedom that define the modern self may have some distant links to Christian themes, but they now have a life of their own. The secular self is grounded in itself, while the Christian self is grounded in God. (p. 95)

The roots of the crisis of modernity lie in this decisive difference: 'a certain secular understanding of the self that disagrees with the Christian tradition on just one small point: that we (really) need God' (pp. 95–6). Instead of stressing the Christian tradition's responsibility for the crisis of modernity, as Moltmann does, Christians need to gain a critical distance from modernity by recovering a key insight of their own tradition, precisely the key insight that modernity lost: 'we need God' (p. 93).

At stake is a decisively different notion of freedom. The modern understanding of the self assumed that the individual self inherently has all it needs for its own happiness and requires only to be set free from external constraints. It is this supposed self-sufficiency of the modern self that sets it in opposition both to socialization in human community and to dependence on God. These are seen as restrictions from which the self must be free in order to flourish. Charry sums up her narrative of the way this has led to the problems of hyper-individualism in contemporary American society in this way:

> [By] turning from confidence in God to confidence in itself alone, the secular self proves to be quite alone. It is thrown on the world to seek its fortune, without history, without guidance, with scant moral boundaries, and without a framework of meaning within which to interpret failure and suffering. The modern self is discouraged from supporting social and political life, for these necessarily place limits on the self and demand compromise, self-restraint, and even self-sacrifice that are no longer supported by the culture. Freedom, self-sufficiency and an expectation of happiness render it anomic, amoral, asocial, and alone. Having no access to God, sin, and grace, it has only itself to confide in or worry about. Families and bonds of community cannot be sustained on this highly individualistic and

> morally vacuous basis. This asociality and amorality are, I suggest, the source of the crisis of modern values. (p. 104)

In place of this modern idea of the liberation of the self as mere release from all constraint, Charry proposes 'a Christian theological understanding of emancipation that is keyed to transformation', a critical retrieval of the tradition's insights that emancipation is needed 'from the unlovely side of the self' and 'that the way to emancipation is through self-mastery achieved by attending to God' (p. 93). While the secular self is on its own, the Christian self is formed by intimacy with God within the Christian community with its helps to finding identity in God. Charry is well aware that much of the traditional language of Christian formation – self-denial, humility, self-control, submission to God – is easily associated with the repressive authoritarianism against which Western society is still in reaction and of which the Church certainly has been guilty all too often. But her argument that the hyper-individualism of the contemporary West is now in serious overreaction against such authoritarianism coheres with observation from many quarters. The intrinsic tendency to amorality and asociality in contemporary individualism surely does suggest that Moltmann's attempt to accommodate the modern self within a form of community that does not require any qualification of its absolute autonomy is quite insufficient to meet the need. The elements of oppression and repression in the Christian tradition need not prevent a retrieval of the tradition's realistic recognition of the neediness and dependence of the self, its need of ordered and intentional growth and formation, supremely its need of God.

Conclusion

What is quite clear is that the history of freedom in the modern period is double-edged. On the one hand, there is the affirmation of individual human dignity, the foundations of democracy in the equal right to freedom of all individuals and the fundamental freedoms of individuals over against the powers of state and Church. Moltmann is correct that the struggles for such freedoms are far from complete and that in fact the growing economic domination of the Third World by the First requires a new chapter in the history of the liberation of all from oppressive rule and oppressive circumstance.

On the other hand, the Enlightenment belief in the wholly self-sufficient and self-determining self has led to the asocial, amoral and isolated individual of contemporary atomized society in the West, portrayed so contemptuously by Houellebecq and characterized more analytically by Charry. It is striking that all four of the authors we have discussed converge on the contradiction between this hyper-individualism and community, while all except Moltmann also connect it with the demise of religion or the rejection of God. It is also noteworthy that this individualism itself threatens the positive values of modern freedom. Consumerism is one, if not *the*, vehicle of egotistical individualism, as well as being integral to the global economic system of domination.

We can usefully relate Charry's argument to Moltmann's by seeing it as bringing to light a further implication of the false understanding of freedom as domination. In Moltmann's argument this is exemplified in the two major contemporary forms: the West's economic domination of the Third World, and humanity's technological domination of nature. Charry adds that the modern understanding of the self as wholly self-determining has led to the postmodern reduction of the self to the will to power. Freedom as self-liberation from every last vestige of constraint and as the freedom to construct one's life and one's self wholly according to choice is another form of freedom as domination.

How is it that the modern age has bequeathed both the idea of the inherent dignity of the human individual, entailing the right to freedom *from* domination, and also its contradiction: freedom *as* domination? It must be that respect for the dignity and freedom of the individual requires a context of other convictions and beliefs without which the right to self-determination degenerates into the banal pursuit of pleasure or the cynical pursuit of power. It may be as simple as Charry puts it: human beings need God. If it is adequately to address the problematic of freedom in the twenty-first century, public theology should not be hesitant also to address the question of God. That means, of course, not only whether there is God but what sort of God there is.

Notes

1 D. B. Forrester, *On Human Worth* (London: SCM Press, 2001), p. 137, quoting J. M. Winter and D. M. Joslin, *R. H. Tawney's Commonplace Book* (Cambridge: Cambridge University Press, 1972), p. 53.

2 Paris: Flammarion, 1999.

3 Page references to the novel are to the English translation, *Atomised*, trans. by F. Wynne (London: Heinemann, 2000).

4 Andrew Marr in *The Observer*.

5 F. Fukuyama, *The End of History and the Last Man* (London: Penguin, 1992).

6 P. A. Lawler, 'Fukuyama versus the End of History', in T. Burns (ed.), *After History? Francis Fukuyama and his Critics* (Lanham, MD: Rowman & Littlefield, 1994), p. 70.

7 Page numbers refer to Fukuyama, *The End of History*.

8 Cf. H. Williams, D. Sullivan and G. Matthews, *Francis Fukuyama and the End of History* (Cardiff: University of Wales Press, 1997), p. 81, citing F. Fukuyama, 'A reply to my critics', *The National Interest*, 18 (Winter 1989–90) pp. 26–8.

9 Fukuyama's subsequent book, *Trust: The Social Virtues and the Creation of Prosperity* (London: Hamish Hamilton, 1995), attempts to pursue this issue, but does little more than observe at length what he already stated concisely in *The End of History*: that modern liberal democracy and capitalism depend on the survival of pre-modern 'cultural habits'.

10 P. A. Lawler, 'Fukuyama versus the End of History', in Burns (ed.), *After History?*, pp. 63–79.

11 *Ibid.*, p. 64.

12 F. Fukuyama, 'Reflections on *The End of History*, five years later', in Burns (ed.), *After History?*, p. 254.

13 I refer especially to the essays collected in English in *God for a Secular Society: The Public Relevance of Theology*, trans. M. Kohl (London: SCM Press, 1999). Page numbers in the text in what follows refer to this book. Three of the same essays also appear in J. Moltmann, N. Wolterstorff and E. T. Charry, *A Passion for God's Reign: Theology, Christian Learning, and the Christian Self*, ed. M. Volf (Grand Rapids, MI: Eerdmans, 1998), pp. 1–64.

14 J. Moltmann, *The Spirit of Life*, trans. M. Kohl (London: SCM Press, 1992), pp. 107–8.

15 E. T. Charry, 'The crisis of modernity and the Christian self', in Moltmann, Wolterstorff and Charry, *A Passion*, pp. 88–112. Page numbers in the text refer to this essay.

Chapter 6

Equal Respect and the Holy Spirit: The Liberal Demand for Moral Neutrality in the Political Sphere and Christian Respect for the Creation

KEES J. KLOP

The Spirit[1]

> *In the beginning God created heaven and earth. The earth was waste and desolate and darkness was in the abyss; and the Spirit of God moved upon the face of the waters.*

These are the pregnant sentences with which the Bible starts telling the story of God and humankind. If religious fundamentalists struggle against secular evolutionists, this is their foundation. Whatever the position may be that someone takes in the debate about evolutionism, every party recognizes the basic character of these sentences. There seems to be no position of indifference. You agree with them or you struggle with them. It is an impressive declaration with which the Bible commences, a declaration that reaches into the foundations of human existence.

These two opening sentences of the Bible are full of meanings that invite us to interpret them. In doing that we should be aware that these sentences themselves are interpretations too. Jewish priests wrote them during the exile in Babylon. So their view of the creation was not their first interpretation of their experience with God. They knew him already as a caring God who calls his people to take the road with him to the Promised Land. Originating from that experience they formulated a view of the beginning of the earth as an emanation of life and light, an emanation by a God who is not part of nature: 'the Spirit moved upon the face of the waters', they wrote. God is not the sun, the moon or the stars – as the surrounding peoples thought – but

God is a power that spread his caring wings above nature. Human beings are not overwhelmed by powers in nature whose purposes cannot be understood and who should be kept satisfied by sacrificing to them.

On the contrary, they wrote that the one who calls himself 'I am here for you', created cosmos against chaos. These priests were not answering questions that Darwin was to put thousands of years later, nor were they interested in the question of later philosophers whether God created the earth *ex nihilo* or not. They were convinced that their God created the earth *contra nihil*. The creation brought order to a chaotic mass of being. Levinas called this 'being-without-identity': an absolute, impersonal, neutral anonymous, which overwhelms and absorbs everything in such a way that it loses its separateness and identity. Chaos is the impermeable darkness in which all distinctions and shapes disappear. God's act is to overcome the disorder of this wriggling mass of being by creating order, by developing a dynamic direction in which different beings are distinguished.

They also wrote that God's eternal Spirit was already in the temporal world when this world was still chaos. Neither Pentecost nor Jesus' baptism in the River Jordan were the first appearances of the Holy Spirit. She was already there. I say 'she' because the word for spirit that the Hebrew bible uses, *ruach*, is female. I was surprised when I discovered that God is present in the temporal world as a power that already in the biblical stories was experienced as a storm that is grammatically female. I wonder why feminist theology, that so often and understandably wrestles with the male fatherhood of God, so rarely stresses that God is present in the female Spirit as a power of inspiration and perseverance.

This is quite another experience from the image of God as the Lord Almighty who has already decided everything in advance and directs every human act or manages nature in detail. It is an image that is not very convincing anymore. Recently I happened to read an interview with the Secretary-General of the Dutch Reformed Church. The interviewer asked him what he would do first when he, after his death, should arrive in Heaven. 'I would look for John Calvin', he answered, 'and ask him if he really had meant what the Calvinist tradition has made of his ideas about predestination.'

God is present in the temporal world as a power that is there for his creatures: a strength amidst other powers, powers that want to reduce the creation once again to the wriggling mass of being-without-identity. In the case of human beings we may understand this as depersonalization, as stripping a person of individuality and identity. This raises a feeling of horror. It is an experience to make you shudder, in which people have a presentiment of the reduction into chaos. This chaos is not an accidental relict of oriental mythology in a biblical story about creation, but a persisting and time-and-again re-emerging terror of the powers of darkness. The Holy Spirit always was and still is the strength that breaks through that terror at surprising moments and that gives creatures the energy to act in the world according to the distinctions that the Creator has made and to struggle with the powers that are reduced to chaos.

The order and the distinctions that God creates may be interpreted as a well-known order that should be restored if it is damaged. But I think that we should not think in terms of a 'Paradise lost' that needs to be regained. Christians should remain critical of deification of any historical situation. There is no place for naturalism. The Spirit is a renewing power that not for the first time inspires us to restore a lost order, but that creates order time and again. God is present in our temporal world as a renewing power.

The problem I will study in this chapter is the role of this story of God and humankind in Western political praxis, developed into respect for the creation as a driving force for sustainable development. Maybe Duncan Forrester himself formulated my problem in the best way it can be stated. That is when he states that, compared to Fukuyama, 'others see the present situation of the West as a far more problematic intellectual vacuum: not so much a victory of liberalism and decency, as a house swept and garnished, ready for seven worse devils to enter in it.'[2] This sentence reflects Matthew 12:43–5 and Luke 11:24–6 where Jesus says that he who does not open his heart to God's Spirit will see the devil that was expelled from it return with seven mates. Now my problem is: is there a place in Western political praxis, which has liberated itself from theology, for the Spirit that inspires respect for the creation?

Moral Positions Towards Sustainability

In environmental ethics different moral positions towards sustainability may be discerned. A common list of positions that starts from anthropocentrism and finishes with ecocentrism sums up the roles of the ruthless pioneer, the enlightened ruler, the secular steward, the participant in nature, the religious steward, the partner of nature and the mystic union with nature.

The *ruthless pioneer* does not see any limits to his or her exploitation of the natural world. He or she believes that science and technology will always produce new possibilities to create prosperity. This attitude may have been a position of moral integrity in the beginning of the Enlightenment in the Western world. With our knowledge it no longer is, although many people – among whom is the President of the United States – still stand in this position.

The *enlightened ruler* – like the pioneer – does not recognize any intrinsic value of nature apart from the value nature has for humankind. Only human beings have intrinsic value, according to this position. But the enlightened ruler does see limits to the exploitation of nature. In the first place she sees limits because of her own needs in the future. She foresees that her way of living is not sustainable for herself.

If the enlightened ruler accepts liberal justice as a moral principle for her actions, she also recognizes that she should not damage other human beings, whether contemporary or future generations. We could call her the *secular steward*. The secular steward feels responsible for others. Not responsible to God, but to humankind. The secular steward says 'By drawing on the earth's resources, we are living off our children's inheritance; we should also enable them to meet *their* needs.'

The *participant* recognizes that she is dependent upon nature and that nature is dependent on humankind. Humankind is part of nature. She belongs to it, although she is the only being that is able to be aware of her position. For her, technology is not a power of human beings opposed to nature, but a power within nature. For the participant, as for the secular steward, however, nature still does not have intrinsic value.

This is different for the *religious steward*. For her, nature has intrinsic value because it is God's creation that is not her own property, nor the property of humankind. For her, God is the stakeholder to whom she is responsible. Instead of anthropocentric or ecocentric this moral position is therefore also called theocentric. I call this theocentric stewardship religious and not Christian, because it is not found in the Christian tradition alone, but also in Islam (as in the caliphate) and in the Jewish tradition.

The *partner* of nature is acquainted with the participant, but she respects the intrinsic value of nature. There is no mutuality between human beings and nature, as is the case for the participant, but both have intrinsic value. Nature should be respected, independently from the needs of human beings. The partner has ecological sensibility.

In the *mystic union* between humankind and nature, nature is seen as divine. Preservation of nature has a higher priority than human needs. This is the radical ecologist point of view.

So the different moral positions towards nature have a dividing line between the participant and religious stewardship. The positions of the pioneer, the enlightened ruler, the secular steward and the participant do not recognize any intrinsic value in nature. The religious steward, the partner and the mystic union do. Among environmental moral philosophers there is agreement on the conclusion that sustainability asks for more than the position of the enlightened ruler. Recognizing limits to the exploitation of the natural world on the basis of safeguarding one's own future needs is not enough. The needs of others should also be brought into the decision-making process. At the very least the position of the secular steward is necessary. The last is the position of the United Nations, as seen in the *Brundtland Report* of 1985 and in the *Declaration of Rio de Janeiro* in 1992. In the Rio Summit an effort to agree on a preamble about respect for nature as God's creation did not get a majority. Since then the policies of the global community and of the member-states have been inspired by anthropocentric moral arguments in which future generations fulfil the role of a secularized god, to whom humankind declares itself responsible.

Although the concept raises many questions, in theory this anthropocentric moral position in favour of future generations could bring humankind some way on the road to sustainability. The questions circle around the fact that – because these generations are defined as the yet unborn – we do not know who they are and what they want. An intriguing problem with future generations is also that sustainability makes it necessary to prevent a huge number of them being born. But if we define the needs of future generations as in any way to be clean soil, water, air and energy, if we understand furthermore that we should preserve a high level of biodiversity, which also means less of the greenhouse effect, and if we understand that our history is their history, so we should also preserve important cultural artefacts for them; there are therefore already a lot of things to do. Doing them would at least put the world on to the road to sustainability.

Liberalism and the Problem of History

But the Western world is not doing that now. Nor is the possibility of fulfilling basic needs respected either for the future, or for contemporary generations outside the Western world. Why not? Maybe the motivational force of this moral position is the weak point of the secular steward. We cannot be sure about that. There are also observers who state that the road to sustainability will take at least as long as the road to universal human rights took. In that

99

case it would merely be a question of time. But there are also observers who point to the paradigm-shift that is needed for the moral motivation of the secular steward. They observe that Western states have become used to looking to themselves as having the organized conditions for a peaceful society of free and equal individuals, who live contemporaneously. Ideas like Rousseau's social contract, Durkheim's division of labour or Habermas' *Herrschaftsfreier Diskurs* reflect this basic contemporary view. There is no reason to see it differently. Such political philosophies are ahistorical in the sense that states are supposed to be founded at any moment in history.

Our situation at the beginning of the twenty-first century, however, compels us to think along other lines. Symmetry or mutuality in repeated original positions cannot any longer be the way of thinking. Instead, the relationship between people in time, between generations that pass on the planet to other generations, becomes the dominant perspective. Is it possible for modern human beings to look at themselves as generations that are involved in a common process of transmission through time? Does the welfare state, with its accent on prosperity in the here and now, contain the possibility of keeping the doors of history open? Why should it pass the earth on undamaged, if it does not see it as a gift? Does this not ask for a comprehensive view of history, also on the political level?

Creation and Stewardship

Christianity offers such a view. It is the story of the Creator who gave human beings creation to work in but at the same time told them to preserve it. So to be active in nature this way is not just to handle a mass of natural resources, but also to engage in a kind of sanctifying activity. Creation and salvation are not nice ornaments around a physical and technical matter; they are the foundational qualities of intercourse with the ecological system. The mission to sanctify is total, it is binding and motivating for all intercourse with nature.

The steward is the person who takes care of the property of someone else in the way that the owner meant it should be done. That does not make the steward a functionary without a will or a responsibility of her own. On the contrary, she has to make decisions and she can make mistakes. The Bible gives parables about such responsible people and their mistakes and successes. Examples are the story about the steward who dissipated the property of the master (Luke 16:1–8a), the story about the successful farmer (Luke 12:13–21), the story about the criminal servants of the owner of the vineyard

100

(Mark 12:1–11) and the story of the vinegrower, who pays the same just wage to every worker, those who came first and those who came last (Matt 20:1–16).

These parables do not give a blueprint for action, they raise questions. They shock us out of our customary practices by showing the possibility of another way of doing the same things. Parables do not do that by bringing meaning from outside into daily life, but they reveal it within our practices. This meaning is already there in the order of the creation. The parable about the last that will be first even describes the way things are going to be in the Kingdom of Heaven. A good parable is a successful connection of daily life with transcendence. The parable opens people's minds for the Spirit so that they can see the same things differently.

God placed humankind in a world of time, as a people on the road, the road to the end of time, where the workers that came last earn as much as the workers that came first. All generations are connected in this comprehensive view of history. They have good reasons for a stewardship that places the fruits of the earth at the disposal of any contemporary living human being and preserves the planet for future generations.

At the same time, we must recognize that sociological investigations do show a negative, or neutral, relationship between Christian belief and positive environmental behaviour. Christianity does not attract public attention by its environmentalism. Nor does Islam or Jewish culture. The declaration is sought in the close relationship between Christianity and the welfare state that was justly seen as the prosperous and socially secure product of hard-working people. We should not speak with disdain about this product. It put an end to a lot of poverty and illness and it raised a lot of possibilities for a really good life that must not immediately be condemned as consumerism. Looking to sociological research into environmental attitudes and behaviour, we see that the overall environmentally friendly consumer and entrepreneur do not exist. Environmental values, like stewardship, are not rejected; they are part of value hierarchies related to practices in which other values have priority. The practices of housekeeping, of transport and traffic, of entrepreneurship serve values like health, communication and craft that are esteemed of high value, also within the Christian moral tradition. The awareness of the environmental shadow side of this welfare state is only slowly growing in circles of church members, although the church leaders have been speaking about the integrity of creation for two decades. Maybe we must conclude that the Spirit is doing its work more in the hearts of the activists of the environmental movements that nowadays gain broad popular support, than in the hearts of church members? Established Christianity still has a long way to go towards sustainability, just as it was not the first to criticize the ruthless capitalism of the nineteenth century.

That does not, however, diminish the relevance of the comprehensive Christian story for the political and business realms of society. This story is worth telling, not only in the private sphere where liberalism places it, but also in the public house that was swept of theology and garnished.

The Liberal Demand for Moral Neutrality in the Political Sphere

The question is whether the political realm is open to such comprehensive stories about history. Open for the Christian story, but the question is the same for other stories that bring comprehensive views about history to the public forefront, that are relevant for a politics of sustainable development. This brings me to the liberal demand for moral neutrality in the political sphere as a problem for politics in relation to sustainability.

The core of the liberal argument that comprehensive stories should not be accepted on the political agenda is that laws that diminish individual freedom may be justified only with arguments that everyone can accept as valid and reasonable. Because people are divided about such comprehensive stories, arguments from these stories are not acceptable to everyone as valid and reasonable arguments to diminish their freedom. The liberal idea is that free citizens owe each other equal respect. Therefore in the political sphere they should use only arguments that are acceptable to everyone. This is the equal respect argument for the moral neutrality of the state. Government may not have its own idea of the good life, nor may government promote one of the different ideas of the good life that lives among its citizens.

Now if Western political praxis becomes dominated by this idea of equal respect and the moral neutrality of the state and if, at the same time, I am right in stating that sustainable development makes it necessary that governments have a comprehensive idea about the relationship between different generations in history, then there is a serious problem. How can this problem be solved?

The first step to a solution is to look to the liberal argument of equal respect. That argument has attractive force for a lot of people. Who would not like to be treated as free and equal? There are still many people, such as homosexuals, women and blacks, who are not treated as free and equal. And who would not approve the idea that their freedom may only be restricted on the basis of arguments that they accept as valid and reasonable? Calvinists who struggled for freedom of conscience will be especially open to this idea.

Yet this idea of moral neutrality for the sake of individual freedom is criticized. One argument is that it expels religious arguments from the political agenda not only in favour of freedom of conscience, but in favour of the basic assumption of men and women as free, autonomous and rational calculating individuals with restricted altruism. This basic assumption functions in itself as some sort of religion. If a religion is a story about the meaning of life in which people trust, a story that cannot be proved by scientific arguments, then the liberal idea of humankind is at least a quasi-religion. This quasi-religion presents itself as a jealous god that does not accept any other god in its sphere. In my opinion, it is important to unmask this liberal idea of equal respect as a comprehensive story about people.

That is very possible. The idea may be criticized not only from outside, from the point of view of another comprehensive doctrine, but also from inside. Is it really equal respect, it may be asked, if liberals invite other citizens to enter the political debate by leaving their most fundamental convictions about the good life at home in their private lives? Does that not strip them of their identity? Is it not true that liberals ask other citizens to go through some sort of detection gate that forces them to leave not only physical weapons behind, but also serious arguments that may be relevant for the common cause? Does political liberalism not mould citizens first into rational machines before they may participate in the political debate? May this really be called equal respect or is it in fact a very one-sided sort of respect? A respect that other citizens should have for liberals? In my opinion it is. The liberal argument of equal respect may be criticized because it is not mutual. It is a comprehensive doctrine among other comprehensive doctrines that have ideas about the public sphere.

If this is the conclusion regarding the first step necessary to solve the problem that sustainable development raises, then the public forum could become really a house swept and garnished that is open for all citizens. Two new questions arise: who should enter the house and does such a house really exist?

An Empty Public Sphere?

Let me start with the last question. The French political philosopher Claude Lefort argues that since the period of the divine right of kings ended with the French Revolution the place of political power is empty. Kings by divine right had two bodies: they were the ruling force but at the same time they embodied in themselves the place of political power. In our times nobody embodies political power. Because in a democracy it is open to everybody, no one can claim that she will be the ruler for ever, and because she needs to be re-elected by other people, the place of political power should be principally empty.

I wonder whether this is true. In my opinion the place of political power is shaped at the moment someone develops that power. This was the situation in the time of the divine right of kings and it is the situation in our times. There is no house that is swept and garnished. Kings with their divine right built such a house when they took power by military strength and rationalized it with a doctrine that was written for them by the clergy who served in their royal courts. In Western Europe this was done in opposition to the secular power of the Church. In Eastern Europe the Church itself did it. And in our times the house is built by politicians who get power by winning votes for ideas about the common good, ideas that come out of comprehensive views of the good life.

By doing that they give shape to a possibility that was already there, a possibility to institutionalize the political sphere of society by discerning between justice and the powers of darkness. In Western states Christianity and humanism shaped this political house. They built the house on the dignity of the human person, of which the new Charter of Fundamental Rights for the European Union in its opening sentences says that any government should recognize, respect and safeguard it. Calvinism stressed the religious calling of the individual to live according to the will of God. Immanuel Kant's idea of individual autonomy meant that people are able to put themselves under the moral law of the categorical imperative. I think John Rawls is right in stating that the house was built on an overlapping consensus between such comprehensive views. It is fundamentally a house that was built on moral ideas about man and society and it is not morally neutral. But I do not agree with him that the comprehensive views should be asked to leave the building in favour of free and equal individuals who leave their comprehensive views at home. In fact this opened the door for the calculating and competing autonomous individual of whom modern liberal utilitarianism can only say that it seeks pleasure and avoids pain. It is this, in our times dominant, idea that rationalizes the withdrawal of the state in favour of the global market that absorbs everything in such a way that it loses its separateness and identity. The public square is never naked. There is no house that is swept and garnished. The house is always built and ruled at the same time by the people who enter the public sphere.

104

Moral Compromise

If the political house is shaped by the ideas of the politicians who get the majority of votes, then it is necessary to bring ideas about the good political life into that political sphere. If Christians think that their comprehensive ideas are good ideas to build on, keep in repair and rule the house, then they should not be restricted from doing so by a liberal idea of the moral neutrality of the state, that in fact is also a comprehensive view. The public sphere is a place with practices that differ from the vineyard in the parables to the extent that politicians do not harvest grapes. But it does not differ in that in political practices, as in the practices of the vineyard, meaning can be revealed – meaning that is already there in the order of the creation; meaning that has to do with the role that politics may fulfil in order to let biblical justice flourish in society. I would call that meaning public justice. Revealing that meaning is the successful connection of daily political life with transcendence. Why should the Spirit be able to open the minds of vinegrowers so that they see the same things differently, but keep the minds of politicians closed?

If Christians strive for such public justice and abide with the Spirit in the political life, they are not nostalgic restorers of a former public monopoly of Christian theology that is no longer there. In the first place, they are not because moral experience is an experience in the praxis of political life. I do not think theologians should take over the moral responsibility of practical politicians and tell politicians what to do. That is an old model that should not be restored at all. Theology does not have the monopoly of the Spirit. Theology studies the way the Spirit inspires people. Theology may articulate and interpret the stories of people that do have moral experience in the political praxis. In that way it helps the praxis.

If Christians strive for public justice in the political sphere they are not alone in that arena. Other powers also have their adherents there, even the powers of darkness that may be recognized in any political idea that reduces creation to a wriggling mass of being-without-identity and strips human beings as well as nature of their dignity. Nowadays Christians who strive for an idea of public justice are becoming a minority in politics. It is not necessary for them to stand aside and pretend that they are keeping their hands clean by not sharing political power with others. I do not think this is really a clean position. What they can strive for is moral compromise. Moral compromise means that it is possible to found laws on different moral arguments – arguments that are not shared by everyone as valid and reasonable, but which are convincing for the citizens who adhere to the arguments. For instance, if Christians strive for laws that implement sustainable development, they may make moral compromises on the basis of their Christian stewardship of creation with other politicians that agree to have this compromise on the basis of enlightened rulership or secular stewardship. If such compromises last long enough and become stable through time, with John Rawls we could even speak of a new overlapping consensus between different comprehensive views which in their basic ideas are incommensurable. Such moral compromises or overlapping consensus should be the expression of mutual respect.

Conclusion

If the Spirit was already there when there were as yet no distinctions in the wriggling mass of being-without-identity, why should she not be able to inspire politics in our times to save creation? I think that openness to the Spirit's creative break through the pragmatic routine of quasi-technical politics should be the rule for Christians in the political sphere of life. The Spirit is surprising. The biblical story of creation is a way of imagining the future of our history that is not yet there and that we may even not be able to grasp with scientific research. That places the questions about sustainability in a perspective in which a plea for moral or religious neutrality should be treated with critical suspicion. The story of the Spirit that renews everybody and everything may inspire Christians to take their political responsibility with perseverance, trust and expectation, even in times of secularization.

Notes

1 In this text I want to think about the relationship between the Gospel and the political sphere of society. Since I am a moral philosopher and not a theologian, for that part of my text that has to do with theology I rely on two Dutch theologians: Professor Dr G. D. J. Dingemans, *De stem van de Roepende* (Kampen: Kok, 2001) and the constructive comments I received on my first draft from Professor Dr A. J. M. van den Hoogen, Professor of Fundamental Theology at the Faculty of Divinity of the Catholic University of Nijmegen.
2 Duncan Forrester, *Christian Justice and Public Policy* (Cambridge: Cambridge University Press, 1997), p. 26.

Chapter 7

The Reformed Tradition and the Virtue of Tolerance

DAVID FERGUSSON

For the Reformed tradition, public theology is firmly rooted within the confessional and other programmatic documents of the sixteenth century. The stress upon church order, discipline and the creation of a godly society, a distinguishing feature of Reformed church life, is apparent in the work of Bucer, Calvin, Knox and others. In Scotland, *The First Book of Discipline* (1560)[1] is often hailed for its commitment to the ideals of comprehensive education and poor relief. The struggle to reform and reorganize embraced not so much the gathered congregation of the faithful as the whole of civil society.[2] In part, this may explain why the practice of baptizing every newborn infant continued into the magisterial Reformation. Yet a less attractive feature of the effort to create a godly society was the difficulty in accommodating legitimate diversity. The attempt to create not merely a church but a civil polity according to the Word of God inevitably threatened the social position of anyone confessing a different faith. Thus in Scotland, ideals of religious tolerance commanded acceptance rather later than in England and in other parts of Europe. In the middle of the seventeenth century, leading Scottish theologians wrote treatises against ideals of religious toleration.[3] Believing toleration to be corrosive of the moral and spiritual identity of a covenanting society, they continued to cite Old Testament precedents for compulsion and discipline in matters of religion. In doing so, they maintained the Augustinian tradition of 'compelling them to come in'. Although compulsory measures tended to be regarded as remedial rather than retributive, the most notorious act of civil enforcement of religious orthodoxy was the execution for heresy in 1697 of Thomas Aikenhead, an Edinburgh divinity student. Similar problems attended Catholic social thought with its related tradition of the common good. If the *bonum commune* was to be secured by general adherence to the Catholic faith, then it could be argued that political rulers had a duty to promote such adherence if necessary by force. Gregory XVI, for example, resisted liberty of opinion and the separation of Church from state. The Catholic faith is true and ought to believed. Only in this way is the common good promoted.[4]

A survey of the modern history of arguments for tolerance reveals that these first emerged in the sixteenth and seventeenth centuries and were often defended on theological grounds.[5] By contrast, more modern convictions regarding tolerance have been promulgated on the basis of secular assumptions about human autonomy, rights and state neutrality. In what follows, I argue that a theology of toleration is better served by attention to arguments from the early modern period rather than acquiescence in later and more secular claims which sit uneasily with theological convictions. What emerges is an account of tolerance which in some respects demands more but in other respects may be less tolerant than secular ideals.[6]

At first glance, tolerance is an odd virtue in that it suggests the acceptance of beliefs and activities of which we disapprove. We only tolerate what we dislike or deplore. Thus I may be said to tolerate smoking in restaurants, the ringing of mobile phones in lectures and the commitment to creation science displayed by some of my students. The reasons for practising tolerance may include a pragmatic recognition that 'you cannot win them all', together with the realization that friendship, universities and society at large can only flourish where there is some tolerance of other people's differing habits and beliefs. We might add to these the dual hope that we can learn from those who are different and that they in turn will tolerate our own idiosyncrasies, defects and opinions. In these respects, the attitude of tolerance often functions negatively and can even border on the condescending, the patronizing and the indifferent.

The standard liberal arguments for tolerance are found in J. S. Mill's essay *On Liberty*. Here Mill appeals to the autonomous self which can flourish only where it is left free to make its own choices, form its beliefs, and adopt whatever lifestyle it judges most authentic. In pursuing this conviction, Mill was not advocating a moral relativism – some choices are better than others – but his argument was nonetheless predicated on the assumption that the individual must attain his or her fulfilment through the spontaneous exercise of freedom and responsibility. To secure these conditions under which persons can thus flourish it is necessary that the state not infringe individual liberties. Insofar as possible, it must maintain a position of neutrality with respect to the beliefs, actions and lifestyle options of its citizens. This account of tolerance is one which many today almost intuitively hold, though perhaps without Mill's conviction that some goods are intrinsically more desirable than others. Freedom to make our own lifestyle choices is a right, and we should therefore tolerate the decisions that others make. We live and let live. So attempts to criticize the particular choices of others will often meet the charge that these are judgemental and intolerant. On this account, moreover, a diverse society is not merely to be tolerated but is positively to be encouraged. Where there is a wider range of cultural alternatives, the scope for the exercise of autonomy is correspondingly extended. Thus a patchwork society in which there is a plurality of lifestyle choices is to be preferred for the reason that it enhances our freedom.

Despite its attractions, this justification of toleration has been subjected to some formidable criticism. Its account of the unencumbered self, detached from commitments and traditions, is illusory. The choices we make are inevitably shaped by our upbringing, education and social context. There is no possibility of judging competing alternatives from an Archimedean point of unattached simplicity. It is customary to complain in this context that where such attitudes are adopted with respect to religion the result is not impartiality so much as sheer indifference.[7] Religion is reduced to one consumer product amongst others. It is available in different forms for selection and use, but there is no overriding imperative from the perspective of the neutral observer to make any particular choice. Thus David Tracy remarks that religion 'is a private consumer product that some people seem to need. Its former social role was poisonous. Its present privatization is harmless enough to wish it well from a civilized distance.'[8]

Other cultural commentators complain that the exaltation of liberal ideals of tolerance breeds subjectivism and relativism. This is the theme of Allan Bloom's *The Closing of the American Mind*, in which he deplores the attitude of today's educated youth, an attitude he detects in his students. Everyone has his or her own values. These are to be tolerated and there can be no argument about which are right and which are wrong. This high level of tolerance, Bloom argues, leads to a narrowing of moral and intellectual possibilities. There are no standards which define the self and which provide opportunities for notions such as vocation, honour and heroism. The result is a mindset which fosters a bland indifference and scepticism in ethical debate.[9]

This difficulty is compounded by the impracticality of the unencumbered state. No polity can remain neutral in respect of the goods it values and promotes through the passing of laws. This is true on a range of measures

109

including broadcasting, sex education, pornography, Sunday trading, advertising standards, asylum-seekers and abortion. Decisions are made not on the thin basis of securing freedom and maintaining state impartiality. These may have their place, but thicker notions of the good are necessary to the formation of substantive policies in each of these fields. On a more pessimistic reading, Alasdair MacIntyre argues that decisions in the modern liberal state reflect not so much a consensus as the interests of those with the power to adjudicate. This itself is a function of the wider distribution of political, social and economic power.[10] In the light of these problems, it will be claimed that a theology of toleration may fare better by taking its bearings from early modern arguments emerging from the religious disputes of the Reformation, than from more recent liberal ideology.

The standard Whiggish interpretation of the history of religious toleration is that it was first articulated by Renaissance humanists, lost sight of by the first generation of magisterial reformers, but steadily recovered by later writers throughout the early modern period. As an account of religious practice, this has been challenged in recent historiography.[11] Tolerance was patchy in the sixteenth and seventeenth centuries. There are some surprising examples of toleration to be registered from times when latitude might be least expected. Yet one has also to note widespread persecution of marginal groups and individuals well into the seventeenth century. Heiko Obermann has remarked that it is at the margins of society that tolerance is best measured.[12] While a desire for peaceful co-existence emerges within Christianity – particularly after the Thirty Years' War ending in the Peace of Westphalia in 1648 – there remains, for example, evidence of intensified persecution of those accused of witchcraft. Yet whatever the difficulties with a steady evolutionary reading of the rise of religious toleration, we find some clear landmarks in the history of ideas. In the writings of Erasmus and other Renaissance humanists, arguments are encountered which, although muted in the magisterial reformers, became crucial in the growing demand for toleration in later centuries. These might be enumerated as follows:

1. Reference to the example of Christ and the Apostolic Church reveals that there was no attempt to coerce men and women to join the early Christian community or to embrace its doctrines. The way of persuasion was pursued by Jesus. At the heart of the Christian religion is the search for peace and concord, though not at any price. Locke would later speak of the holiness of conversation found in Christ and his disciples.[13]

2. A distinction between the moral essence of the Christian faith and some of its inessential dogmatic claims must be maintained. The upshot of this is that where ethical unanimity can be established it is unnecessary and futile to divide over more obscure issues on which certainty cannot be attained. 'You will not be damned if you do not know whether the Spirit proceeding from the Father and the Son has one or two beginnings, but you will not escape damnation, if you do not cultivate the fruits of the Spirit.'[14]

3. The coercion of belief is futile and even counter-productive of genuine piety. So Erasmus criticized the intervention of political rulers to resolve dogmatic disputes and to impose orthodoxy. 'That which is forced cannot be sincere, and that which is not voluntary cannot please Christ.'[15]

We might note that stress is not yet on the positive value of religious diversity. We are far from the modern pluralist ideal of the rainbow society comprising different cultures, religions and lifestyle options. Indeed there are illiberal strains in Erasmian thinking. If we cannot achieve certainty on dogmatic matters, he argues, then we must have recourse to the traditions of the Church. If moral rather than dogmatic conformity is what matters, then the civil ruler may have a duty to suppress anarchy and disorder. This appears to have constituted his response to Anabaptist rejection of the authority of the civil magistrate. Bainton concludes that on the issue of toleration Erasmus was a bell calling others to church while himself remaining in the steeple.[16]

In Calvin's Geneva, as in other societies, all citizens were subject both to civil and ecclesiastical law. The Consistory comprised ministers and elders, the latter group including prominent members of Genevan society nominated by the magistracy. It was intended to meet weekly with the purpose of enforcing ecclesiastical discipline in the entire community. Its remit was extensive and it developed a reputation for being unnecessarily inquisitorial and prying.[17] The partnership between the civil and religious represented the Reformed commitment to social transformation.[18] This ideal is one which characterized Reformed churches at other times and places, but from the early modern period onwards there arose a perceived need for a greater distancing of the state from the Church, and for a stronger account of religious liberty.[19] The earlier organic unity of Church and civil society thus declined as a greater measure of religious and cultural diversity had to be accommodated.

Calvin's Geneva is frequently criticized for producing a cramped social order with an imposed uniformity, an invasion of privacy and an overbearing moral censoriousness. His treatment of Servetus is symptomatic of the impossibility of religious dissent or nonconformity in this world. Yet the Reformed ideal of social transformation, with its stress on comprehensive education and the relief of poverty, is animated by the same theological impulse. While this desire for a godly commonwealth has occasioned much praise, this has not always been accompanied by the recognition that the deficits of the Reformed *polis* arise from a common source. If we desire transformation yet with a greater measure of toleration, some theological adjustments will be necessary to accommodate both aspirations within the Reformed tradition. This is a problem not adequately addressed in much of the literature. In extolling the social and political commitment of their tradition, Reformed writers have arguably paid too little attention to its potential for illiberal consequences.

By examining Calvin's writings and ministry, we can gain some further understanding at to why tolerance and religious diversity were not live options in his socio-political context. Later notions of state neutrality and religious pluralism are neither possible nor desirable. Intolerance was justified on a variety of grounds. These were apparent in Reformed Scotland in the seventeenth century and can be listed as follows:

1. The maintenance of the religious purity of the community is paramount. For the sake of this great good, those who deviate from the path of true religion must be suppressed or rooted out. This is a responsibility of civil rulers according to the magisterial reformers and many of the classical confessions of the Reformation churches. The spiritual health of a community requires the disciplining and even forceful exclusion of heretics.

2. It is for the good of heretics themselves that they be suppressed. If they are risking the fate of eternal damnation, it is better than they be subjected to some temporal discipline in order to avert a much greater eschatological evil. (How this squares with the doctrine of election is not clear.) Here there are several theological assumptions surrounding divine retribution, the significance of right belief and the nature of hell as eternal torment. Nonetheless, with some or all of these arguments in place a plausible argument can be rehearsed. It has been expressed in the following way.

> Since the most important thing in the world for any man is that he save his soul, it cannot matter how it is saved. Men may change their beliefs voluntarily, but they can also be compelled to do so. St Augustine himself compelled them to come in. If a man remains outside the faith, then he is

condemned to burn forever; thus it must be better to force a man, if that is required, where such force will provide him with eternal life. If a man dies in the process, this is nothing to what he will experience in Hell. If he is converted, however painful the conversion, the pain must be set against the hope of eternal life which is achieved thereby. The means, even torture, certainly cannot be worse than the end, which is salvation.[20]

3. The argument which really held sway with Calvin concerned the maintenance of divine honour. The First Commandment must be upheld. Blasphemy cannot be tolerated for it is an offence against God of the most serious and vile nature. Thus Servetus is not merely offering one theological opinion amongst others. He has denied the being of God and has therefore placed himself in a position in which he must be punished for the sake of restitution. And if we require restitution for crimes committed against human persons, how much more must we demand restitution of those who deny the divine persons.[21]

4. Although not often recognized, there may also be a further consideration in Calvin. It can be detected at the close of the *Institutes*.[22] Since religion is an universal human phenomenon, every society must have a theological identity. Therefore, in organizing the life of a people, the civil ruler has no alternative but to enforce a decision about which religion is to be promoted amongst his or her people for the glory of God and human well-being. The idea of state neutrality is still a long way off. It is not possible to conceive of a society which does not favour one form of religion over against another. Thus, at the Peace of Augsburg in 1555, we encounter the principle *cuius regio, eius religio*, which was reasserted at Westphalia almost a century later. The religion of the territory is determined by the religion of its ruler. Here we are reminded that religion is as much about group identity as individual preference.

The case for greater toleration emerges historically not so much from a welcome embrace of diversity as through the refutation of arguments for intolerance. Here the work of Sebastian Castellio deserves attention.[23] Though colleagues for a time in Geneva, Castellio found himself at odds with Calvin over the interpretation of the Song of Songs, the treatment of Servetus and the doctrine of election. He penned his pseudonymous defence for religious tolerance in reaction to the burning of Servetus and in concern at the civil wars raging in France. This work is an ingenious selection from the writings of humanists and reformers in support of tolerance.

Conversion is a voluntary matter, Castellio argues. Christ does not force people to follow him. It is pointless to attempt to coerce belief and a violation of another person's soul. Here emerges something like the positive value of liberty of conscience. Castellio suggests that the murder of a heretic is a greater evil than heresy itself. The freedom of the individual is a good, particularly where religious faith is concerned, and to violate that freedom by the taking of life is a greater evil than the failure to exercise freedom in correct judgement. As we shall see, this humanitarian argument, if valid, may require some revision of the earlier theological assumptions noted above.

Castellio also argues that, in practice, many of the differences between Huguenots and Catholics are neither very striking nor matters on which Scripture pronounces. Moreover, these are matters on which we cannot be certain. This recalls Erasmus' earlier stress on the insignificance of dogmatic disputes in distinction from the importance of good practice. The blend of arguments in his preface written for the Duke of Württemburg is worth noting. It anticipates strategies which were to be pursued by thinkers in the following centuries, particularly in Locke's 'Letter concerning toleration' (1689) which has become a *locus classicus* in the field. The teaching of Christ bids us to be merciful and forgiving. We are to consider the beam that is in our own eye before attending to the mote in our neighbour's. Heresy is not to be condoned, but we must beware of convicting others who will in the long run turn out to be vindicated, as Christ and his disciples were. If discipline is appropriate, it should not be excessive.

The essence of the Christian religion, Castellio proposes, is belief in God, Father, Son and Spirit, and approval of the commandments of true religion as set out in Scripture.[24] A distinction is made between the uncertainties of doctrinal points of difference and the widely acknowledged principles of true conduct. 'In the matter of conduct, if you ask a Jew, Turk, Christian, or anyone else, what he thinks of a brigand or a traitor, all will reply with one accord that brigands and traitors are evil and should be put to death.'[25] Yet, on matters of right belief there is widespread difference between Jew, Turk and Christian, even though all agree that there is one God. Amongst Christians there are many disagreements on points of doctrine. No one position is self-evidently true. 'Great controversies and debates occur as to baptism, the Lord's Supper, the invocation of the saints, justification, free will, and other obscure questions, so that Catholics, Lutherans, Zwinglians, Anabaptists, monks, and others condemn and persecute one another more cruelly than the Turks do the Christians.'[26]

114

There then follows a plea for peaceful toleration of one's theological opponents. Together, through forbearance and kindness, we may hope to arrive at the truth. Divided, we deny the name of Christ before the world. 'Who would wish to be a Christian, when he saw that those who confessed the name of Christ were destroyed by Christians themselves with fire, water, and the sword without mercy and more cruelly treated than brigands and murderers?'[27]

The case for peaceful co-existence in pursuit of the truth can be sustained by a theology of the Word and Spirit. Although the truth is discerned through the patient hearing of God's Word and the guidance of the Spirit, there is also a need to listen to the testimony of other Christians in the community of faith even when (or perhaps above all when) their opinions are diametrically opposed to one's own. This requires tolerance, humility and the proper conditions for respectful conversation. John Milton's argument for religious freedom in the *Areopagitica* is based on the assumption that a forum for free speech, dialogue and conversation is necessary if the truth is finally to emerge. The practice of conversation rather than mutual anathematizing is advocated for the sake of the truth and the well-being of all parties.

The case against intolerance proceeds on the basis that it is irrational to attempt to alter by force a person's most fundamental convictions. Outward behaviour and insincere speech can be coerced but our deepest allegiances cannot be eradicated in this way. Indeed, they may only be reinforced. This argument in turn leads to the valuing of liberty of conscience. We have a personal responsibility for our faith. This cannot be transferred to the state or even the Church. So in the slipstream of arguments against intolerance there is found an enhanced claim for the sanctity of individual conscience. Thus we find Roger Williams in Rhode Island in the 1630s promoting a religiously diverse society on the conviction that the only authentic faith is voluntary and grounded in the conscience of the individual. From his exile in the Low Countries in 1685, John Locke argues for an England that is more tolerant. 'It appears not that God has ever given any such authority to one man over another as to compel anyone to his religion ... Whatever profession we make, to whatever outward worship we conform, if we are not fully satisfied in our own mind that the one is true, and the other well pleasing unto God, such profession and such practice, far from being any furtherance, are indeed great obstacles to our salvation.'[28]

Arguments for the irrationality of intolerance and the sanctity of the individual conscience were not presented in isolation from wider cultural factors which shaped a greater latitude of opinion.[29] Expansion of world trade had brought closer contacts with other civilizations and religion. These had achieved cultural excellence independently of Christianity. International trade made tolerance an economic necessity, while some European cities reaped the economic benefits of providing a home for dissenters.[30] The broadening of intellectual horizons facilitated greater scholarly interest in other religions. The confirmation of the Copernican hypothesis cast doubt on the uniqueness of the earth as this had been described by the Church in its theological teaching. The single-state Church in England came finally to co-exist with traditions of dissent which it could not overcome. At the same time, the dissenters could not control the state without perpetual strife and damage to the commercial interests of the small shopkeeping classes to which many of them belonged. Moreover, society may have been further pacified by the gradual diminishing in intensity of apocalyptic hopes and the fear of hell. When John Mason attracted large crowds at Water Stratford in 1694 he was not prosecuted for proclaiming the imminent end of the world – he was advised to take his medicine. [31]

The theological case for tolerance in the early modern period is based on a cluster of related arguments – the example of Christ and the early Church, the limits of state power, the irrationality of coercion, the sanctity of each person's faith commitment, the need for peace and social cohesion and the promotion of conversation and debate amongst those who differ for the sake of a greater approximation to God's truth. These arguments retain their validity even if more modern claims for autonomy are found increasingly suspect. At a time when liberalism is under attack, we may need to be reminded of the preceding theological case for toleration for reasons along the following lines.

A fuller account of the implications of tolerance will require one to recognize not merely individual preferences, but the significance of group identity and solidarity. In this respect, early modern arguments for tolerance may be more relevant to securing contemporary multicultural freedom for groups, as opposed to later claims for individual autonomy. Society is not an aggregate of private consumers who make their own choices. It comprises a variety of groups, communities and traditions with their different and sometimes competing loyalties. It is these which shape our identity and influence the choices we make. If the goal of tolerance is not simply the protection and extending of individual choices, but rather the promotion of shared, social goods, then this may result in policies which are in different ways more or less tolerant. Christian theology, with its traditions of the godly society, the common good, the reign of God and the nation under the kingly rule of Yahweh, should be able to articulate these aspirations. At one level, it attests the importance of securing freedom of worship and association for the household of God, while at another level it can stress the bonds uniting all creatures and the contribution of the Church to the welfare of society and the world. This is illustrated by those early Christians who, in arguing for religious freedom, could frequently appeal to the wider social contribution of the Church.

For individuals and groups to participate in the common good of a society, what is required is not merely the absence of persecution but something more akin to recognition, acknowledgement or respect. Here there is a more positive investment in the meaning of the term 'tolerance' beyond its negative sense of the 'putting-up with of that which is disapproved'. This was noted by Hegel when he argued that, for persons to achieve self-consciousness it is necessary that their identity be affirmed by other self-conscious subjects. Moreover, what is true for persons is also true for communities and nations. What is sought is not only peaceful co-existence, but something stronger and more positive. In the context of a modern society which comprises differing solidarities and identities, this may require more tolerance for the different practices, customs and beliefs of subgroups. The insistence that all fit a paradigm of autonomous choice fails to comprehend the manner in which it is group identity which shapes individual desires and preferences. What tolerance requires is not simply an available menu of choices but recognition of the outlook, sensitivities and practices of different communities. In this respect, more than tolerance is demanded. Of course, the comprehension of differing convictions in a single society must create points of tension and conflict. Here we should return to the early modern desire for public space within which groups are accorded respect and provided an occasion for civil conversation. Thick communities of discourse must find ways of articulating for their members moral standards which can be assented to by all (or most) members of the wider civil society. These will typically require a capacity for self-criticism, and a willingness to hear and to empathize with traditions other than one's own.

Moreover, a stronger sense of the common good may also result elsewhere in a restriction of choice, an awareness that there are places where tolerance is overstretched. Where communities find their self-esteem eroded in the public domain by attitudes and practices of free individuals, there arises a prima facie case for intolerance. It is at this sensitive juncture that issues relating to censorship in the media and the advertising industry arise. An outlook which has some sense of the need to maintain the common good by supporting differing solidarities may find itself on occasion less tolerant when standards of public decency and self-respect are violated. It is not coincidental that amongst the most troubled critics of the portrayal of sex and violence in entertainment and commerce are parents struggling to socialize their children into a different form of life.

One further point demands attention. Theological arguments for freedom of conscience in religion require to be buttressed by the recognition that God is active in different faiths and philosophies, and that therefore the choices of others are to be affirmed on account of the goods that these realize for individuals, communities and the world. Without this assumption, a theology of tolerance will be inadequate. It is no coincidence that Vatican II is able to attach a high value to freedom of conscience in religion while also affirming the values realized in other faiths. Similarly, Reformed theologies today have generally abandoned the seventeenth-century assumption that those practising other religions cannot belong to the company of God's elect.[32]

In examining a range of arguments for the virtue of toleration, Michael Walzer has suggested that these can be located on a spectrum of views which run through five possible positions.[33] The first reflects the origins of religious toleration in the sixteenth and seventeenth centuries and is simply a resigned acceptance of peace for the sake of peace. A second possible attitude is passive, relaxed, benign indifference to difference. 'It takes all kinds to make a world.' A third approach is the principled recognition of the rights of others to express themselves in particular ways, even when we disapprove of what they do. Fourth, we can adopt an attitude of curiosity or respect; a willingness to listen and learn. Finally, there is the possibility of an enthusiastic endorsement of difference; this represents the wonderful diversity of human culture and extends human choice in a way that promotes greater self-expression.

If the foregoing argument is valid, a theology of tolerance can affirm at least four of these. Religious diversity can be tolerated for the sake of peace. It can be welcomed for the positive contribution it makes both to the self-understanding and witness of the Christian community, and also to the peace and prosperity of civil society. It does not require a bland reduction of all theological claims or the promotion of high levels of religious indifference. But it does necessitate a commitment to the salvation of the world and the action of God in Christ *extra muros ecclesiae*. At the same time, the theological underpinning of this proposal entails that some forms of diversity remain problematic. The First Commandment, the lordship of Christ, and the eschatological expectation of the Kingdom all suggest the unity of the human race under God. A philosophy of toleration which is indifferent to division, separation and conflicts over human goods cannot be supported. But one which recognizes the partial unities that can be achieved through the suppression of intolerance, and the promotion of mutual respect and a commitment to civil conversation, can anticipate something of that promised reign of God.

Notes

1 *The First Book of Discipline*, ed. J. K. Cameron (Edinburgh: Saint Andrew Press, 1972).

2 The extent to which Knox and his associates wished to impose Levitical standards of punishment upon the civil community (e.g., with adultery a capital offence) is explored by James Cameron in 'Scottish Calvinism and the principle of intolerance', in B. A. Gerrish (ed.), *Reformation Perennis: Essays on Calvin and the Reformation in Honour of Ford Lewis Battles* (Pittsburgh, PA: Pickwick Press, 1981), pp. 113–28. Cameron concludes that Scottish church life became more intolerant in the later seventeenth century than it was at the time of the Reformation.

3 E.g., Samuel Rutherford, *A Free Disputation Against Pretended Liberty of Conscience* (1649); George Gillespie, *Wholesome Severity Reconciled with Christian Liberty* (1645). Cf. W. Campbell, 'The Scottish Westminster Commissioners and toleration', *Records of the Scottish Church History Society*, 9 (1947): 1–18.

4 These problems are analysed from the perspective of Vatican II by David Hollenbach, *Justice, Peace, and Human Rights: American Catholic Social Ethics in a Pluralistic World* (New York: Crossroad, 1988), pp. 101–7.

5 Early modern arguments for tolerance were anticipated in some measure by Jewish and Christian writers of antiquity. Against coercive measures, Josephus, Tertullian and Lactantius could all appeal to the voluntary nature of religion. Cf. Peter Garnsey, 'Religious toleration in Classical Antiquity', in W. J. Shiels (ed.), *Persecution and Toleration* (Oxford: Basil Blackwell, 1984), pp. 1–27.

6 I am indebted here and elsewhere to the argument of Susan Mendus, *Toleration and the Limits of Liberalism* (London: Macmillan, 1988).

7 Cf. Kieran Flannigan, in Ian Hamnett (ed.), *Religious Pluralism and Unbelief: Studies Critical and Comparative* (London: Routledge, 1990), pp. 81–113.

8 D. Tracy, *The Analogical Imagination* (London: SCM Press, 1981), p. 13.

9 Allan Bloom, *The Closing of the American Mind* (New York: Simon & Schuster, 1987). Charles Taylor, however, argues that Bloom ignores a genuine ideal of sincerity in criticizing its debased forms in modern culture. In part, I share this argument by attempting to return to early modern ideals of tolerance to produce a viable alternative to more modern notions of autonomy. Cf. Charles Taylor, *The*

Ethics of Authenticity (Cambridge, MA: Harvard University Press, 1991).

10 E.g., Alasdair MacIntyre, 'Toleration and the goods of conflict', in Susan Mendus (ed.), *The Politics of Toleration: Tolerance and Intolerance in Modern Life* (Edinburgh: Edinburgh University Press, 1999), p. 141.

11 E.g., Ole Peter Grell and Bob Scribner (eds.), *Tolerance and Intolerance in the European Reformation* (Cambridge: Cambridge University Press, 1996). For a recent 'post-revisionist' account of the growth of religious toleration in England, see John Coffey, *Persecution and Toleration in Protestant England 1558–1689* (Harlow: Longman, 2000).

12 'The travail of tolerance: containing chaos in early modern Europe', in Grell and Scribner (eds.), *Tolerance and Intolerance in the European Reformation*, p. 29.

13 Locke, 'A letter concering toleration' (1689), in *Political Writings* (London: Penguin, 1993), p. 393.

14 From the preface to Hilary as cited by Roland Bainton in his edition of Sebastian Castellio, *Concerning Heretics* (New York: Columbia University Press, 1935), p. 33.

15 Castellio, *Concerning Heretics*, p. 34.

16 *Ibid.*, p. 42. The limits of toleration in Erasmus' thinking can be located at that point where religious, social and political concerns converge. Where a theological error manifests itself in sedition then civil suppression is justifiable. Cf. A. G. Dickens and Whitney R. D. Jones, *Erasmus the Reformer* (London: Methuen, 1994), p. 271.

17 Cf. the discussion in F. Wendel, *Calvin* (London: Collins, 1963), pp. 69ff.

18 This is less evident in Lutheranism which was dominated by the doctrine of the two kingdoms. The two-kingdoms doctrine, however, was interpreted in different ways, not all of which were radically different from Reformed views. Cf. Jürgen Moltmann, 'Luther's doctrine of the two kingdoms and its use today', in *On Human Dignity* (London: SCM Press, 1984), pp. 61–78.

19 Cf. David Little, 'Reformed faith and religious liberty', in Donald McKim (ed.), *Major Themes in the Reformed Tradition* (Grand Rapids, MI: Eerdmans, 1992), pp. 196–213.

20 Preston King, *Toleration* (London: Allen & Unwin, 1976), pp. 76–7.

21 Calvin's defence of his role in the Servetus affair is found in 'Defensio orthodoxae fidei de sacra trinitate contra prodigiosos errores Michaelis Serveti Hispani', *Calvini Opera*, Vol. VIII, pp. 452–643.

22 *Institutes*, 4.20.

23 I am indebted here to an unpublished paper by Michael Langford.

24 Castellio, *Concerning Heretics*, p. 130.

25 *Ibid.*, p. 131.

26 *Ibid.*, p. 132.

27 *Ibid.*, p. 133.

28 Locke, 'Letter concerning toleration' in *Political Writings*, p. 394.

29 Here I am following the summary of Christopher Hill, 'Tolerance in seventeenth-century England: theory and practice', in Susan Mendus (ed.), *The Politics of Toleration*, pp. 38ff.

30 Cf. Ole Peter Grell, 'Introduction', in Grell and Scribner (eds), *Tolerance and Intolerance in the European Reformation*, pp. 7ff.

31 Christopher Hill, 'Tolerance in seventeenth-century England: theory and practice', p. 41.

32 In twentieth-century Reformed thought Barth's Christocentric theory of universal election together with his account of 'secular parables of the Word of God' offers one influential revision of earlier exclusivism. For a discussion of this, see George Hunsinger, *How to Read Karl Barth* (Oxford: Oxford University Press, 1991), pp. 234–80. For an application to interfaith dialogue, see David Lochhead, *The Dialogical Imperative* (London: SCM Press, 1988).

33 Michael Walzer, *On Toleration* (New Haven, CT: Yale University Press, 1997), pp. 10ff.

Chapter 8

Human Rights, Divine Transcendence

GEORGE NEWLANDS

Try to think ahead for a moment to fifty years from now. By then the churches will have consolidated around their core membership and clarified their theology. The Anglican Communion will have its headquarters in Singapore, in Iain Duncan Smith House. The PCUSA will have relocated to Waco, Texas. And the Church of Scotland will be living contentedly in retirement together in a rather smart bungalow on the Isle of Skye. Where there was discord, there will be peace. Outside the sacred groves, the market will prowl abroad like a raging lion. Inverness, under its megadome, will look like the Aladdin Hotel in Las Vegas. But the market will still provide discounted opportunities for ecumenical travel and Festschrift colloquia. There is a God after all.

The churches will not need society and society will not need the churches. What I am suggesting in my chapter is that, whether or not there is a perceived need, whether we approve or disapprove, Christian faith believes that a God is indeed there, and that we shall have to find new ways of relating to God, to ourselves and to society to meet changed circumstances. Christendom is dying. Triumphalism is on notice. It is, however, the experience of human community that there is transcendence, and of Christian community that there is a Christ-shaped transcendence and that this transcendence has infinite value for human flourishing, corporate and individual. But how are we to articulate the impact of this transcendence in a strange land?

Here is where I think the concept of human rights can be of continuing value. Of course, like all basic concepts it has been thoroughly discredited. All the big words are discredited regularly – love, liberty, faith. Which of us would admit to being an agapeomonist, a libertarian or a fideist? But I still think the human rights cluster may be one of the best means available to articulate a Christian contribution to human welfare. Hence this chapter.

What legacy from public theology in the twentieth century should be carried over into the new millennium; and what issues and theological approaches will be important in the twenty-first century?

There is no automatic benefit in carrying over theology. Christianity has often been used in support of radically selfish policies. But this need not be the case. Christian faith which most Christians would recognize as authentic is other-related, promoting the selfless rather than the selfish. God is characterized as self-giving, self-affirming love, instantiated in the incarnation in Jesus Christ, in solidarity with the oppressed to the point of death. Faith is always eschatologically open, open to correction. We do not yet have the final understanding of God and the world, and must be open to learning from other human beings in mutuality and reciprocity. *Faith does not affirm complete relativism.* It affirms the values of the Kingdom of God, as indicated for example in the Sermon on the Mount. These values are non-negotiable. At the same time, it distinguishes between faith and knowledge. There remains an important dimension of epistemological humility, which should lead to a humility of praxis.

Of course this openness has been capable of endless distortion. Indeed, the hypostatization of cultural accidents into eternal verities remains a dangerous temptation. But to capitulate to failure would be a tribute to oppression and injustice. The struggle for the fruits of faith in love, peace and justice remains an ongoing and vital task.

Theology must always engage with culture and with society in their overlappings and their diversities, their continuities and disjunctions. It must engage with intellectual constructs like civil society. But it must not forget *the nuts and bolts of actual human interchange,* biological, economic and environmental realities. Because grace is its *raison d'être,* it will be free to engage in constructive tension and dialogue with different and contrasting conceptual frameworks. But because its central categories are themselves given with particular cultural constructions, it will not be able to presume a hegemony over other contributions to the human dialogue. It will be a partner with a vital and distinctive contribution, but still a contribution which works within mutuality and reciprocity.

There are considerable similarities between theological exploration of the distinctiveness and uniqueness of the Christian message and discussion in political theory about the limits of liberalism – how far there are core values and to what extent can relativism be taken to embrace respect for uncongenial positions. There may be attitudes which can be tolerated but which cannot be respected. There are actions which so curtail the freedom of others – violence and oppression – that the freedom to perform them has to be denied. To use Isaiah Berlin's language, we must have the negative freedom to be free from oppression. We may wish to advocate positive freedoms which we see as social goods – full employment, comprehensive health care. But we have to take care that these do not in turn become coercive.

Human Rights and Christian Tradition

Human rights has been one of the most powerful concepts in socio-political thinking in the last fifty years. Yet like other powerful concepts – freedom, God, justice – it has been and remains *much contested*. Lack of an agreed definition, or even agreement on the existence of human rights, has been a cause of much frustration among writers on the subject. Different writers have emphasized civil and political, economic and social, individual and collective rights. Some have started from philosophical ideas of individual freedom, others from legal debates about state sovereignty. Alan Gewirth has sought to ground human rights in the necessary conditions of human action. John Rawls imagines a system of basic liberties which are necessary in a just society, and these include individual rights. There are problems about cultures which claim exemption from critical scrutiny from outside. Peter Jones asks pertinently why some systems of value should be open to critical examination yet others not. The intensity of debate is itself a token of the importance of the issues involved. And, as Jones has written, 'Outside the cocooned world of the academy, people are still victims of torture, still subjected to genocide, still deprived of basic freedoms and still dying through starvation. We should remember these people before we decide to forget about rights.'[1]

What does *the Christian tradition* in the past and in the present have to contribute to human rights? Judging by a plethora of recent interest, the churches might claim that the Christian tradition has always been an advocate of human rights. There has always been recognition of the creation of man as a creature in the image of God, with his own dignity before God. There have been pleas for religious tolerance in the early Church (Lactantius) and the role of freedom of conscience (Augustine). Aquinas, following Aristotle, was much concerned for justice as central to the common good. Luther stressed justification by faith alone, and the freedom of the Christian man. Calvin followed Luther in supporting the individual judgement against the authority of church tradition.

But we have to wait for the legacy of the *Enlightenment*, in the French Revolution and the American Declaration of Independence, before we find a serious reckoning with human rights in society. Why should this be? It must be remembered that society up to 1750 was largely an autocratic and feudal society, in which claims to individual rights were commonly suppressed. After the Constantinian settlement the churches turned from pleas for tolerance to zeal for prosecuting those in error. *Error has no rights.* Only God has rights, and all men are subject to God, sinners in acute danger of eternal damnation. They are called to a life of repentance and obedience.

The churches were prepared to recognize rulers and states as the God-given arbiters of affairs. Rulers and states are autonomous, and individuals have no rights over against them. The development of states in modern Europe gave new impetus to the rights of states. Individual freedoms were the internal affair of sovereign states. The law and the Church offered mutual support to state power. It would therefore be stretching credulity to see the Christian Church as a player in the vanguard of human rights issues. The Church dealt too with its internal conflicts in a firmly authoritarian manner.

The situation is not of course entirely clear-cut. We noted that there were people of Christian convictions involved in some of the American declarations of the eighteenth century, and there were Christians prominent in the anti-slavery campaigns, and in the early work of the Red Cross. But these were largely individual actions, based on Christian convictions but carried out outside the institutional churches. As often, the values of the Kingdom were brought to the attention of the Church through agencies of the secular world.

Reflection on the Christomorphic shape of salvation suggests a further connection between the theological tradition and human rights. It is true that we have to wait for the Enlightenment for a considered focus on rights, and it is the case that human rights is a hugely powerful instrument for encouraging compassion in the politics of the contemporary world. *Human rights as a subject comes late to the theological agenda* – under Human Rights, the *Oxford Companion to Christian Thought*, published in 2000, refers the reader to articles on anti-Semitism, apartheid, democracy, justice and liberation theology. Yet there has always been, amid the failures of the churches, a witness to compassion and unconditional love as a thin line throughout the history of religion. For Christianity this is often focused on the notion of discipleship. This notion has its ambiguities and tendencies to triumphalism. Yet it has also inspired selfless service to our fellow human beings in unconditional acceptance and devotion. A classic but always relevant case is *discipleship* in the life and thought of Dietrich Bonhoeffer. In his later life and work he reflected often on the shape of 'the form of Christ in the world'. And Christians have seen Bonhoeffer himself as a classic modern instance of that form. Bonhoeffer has been venerated. But it is not always noted that Bonhoeffer and his circle almost all met with violent death at the hands of Fascism. Those who held back from this level of commitment largely survived into a new era in which they continued to flourish in Church and society. The Christomorphic shape is not something to be entertained lightly. There is a usually very high probability that it will lead to disaster within the prevailing culture, not least the ecclesiastical culture.

Much rights reflection has in fact been carried on in reflection upon justice, and upon social justice in a theological context, especially in recent decades. This is a most important stream of tradition. But conscious focus on human rights concepts may provide alternative approaches to asking fundamental questions about the nature of humanity and the reconstruction of civil society, especially in the light of the all too frequent experience of seeing justice denied within a state justice system. Beyond the letter of the law and the culture of a given juristocracy there may be further issues of the nature of the shape of community to be examined.

Human rights remain central to discussion of citizenship in the contemporary world. From a Christian perspective, they are grounded in a theological understanding of humanity as made in *the image of God*, calling for respect for others as unique individual selves. As such, human beings deserve to be treated with dignity. This implies equality and specific basic rights. Christian faith understands humanity to be moving towards a fulfilment which is characterized through the love of God as shown in the events concerning Jesus Christ. Christian faith offers this understanding as a contribution to the ongoing exploration of the nature of humanity and the development of society. This is, precisely, an ongoing exploration. Theology includes a basic eschatological dimension. It regards its basic themes as both reliable and provisional, reliable in their central structures, provisional in their modes of expression and articulation.

Rights and Ambiguity

Emphasis on human rights has brought and will continue to bring great benefits to society. This is all the more remarkable when we consider how real the problems are in defining and advocating rights. It is vital to be aware of these critical issues – and perhaps equally vital to be clear that

127

the abuse does not take away the proper use. Let us look at some of *the problem issues.*

From a *philosophical* perspective, there is nothing 'given' about human rights. Indeed, each decade highlights new dilemmas in the philosophical literature on the subject. The best overview is still perhaps provided by Alan Gewirth.[2] He examined the nature of rights as claim rights, for example, the question of whether rights are important even when they do not actually exist and the possibility and implications of absolute rights.

From a *political* viewpoint, rights can be seen as a two-edged weapon which is used and abused in international politics. David Forsythe[3] has explored these issues in a series of books. Human rights was used in the Cold War as an instrument of policy by Presidents Carter and Bush, with rather different agendas. As Isaiah Berlin long ago demonstrated in his *Two Concepts of Liberty,*[4] individual rights may conflict with social and economic rights. It is all too easy to major on the rhetoric of individual freedom and deny great sections of a population basic respect and the conditions for economic well-being.

From a *legal* perspective, there are again positive and negative aspects. Human rights legislation has brought and continues to bring benefits to individuals and groups marginalized by unfair laws. At the same time, it exposes conflicts of law, in which the interests of some groups inevitably conflict with those of others. Conor Gearty and Adam Tomkins' *Understanding Human Rights*[5] gives an excellent survey of these issues. But legislation is intimately connected with politics, and this may have controversial consequences. Legislation based on classical liberal views of individual freedom may conflict with ideals of social democracy which stress communitarian values.

From a *theological* perspective, there are at least as many different options and ambiguities. Churches on the one hand campaign, often very effectively, for the implementation of human rights in far-off countries. At the same time, they may campaign, sometimes with more and sometimes with less justification, for *exemption* from human rights regulation in their own practices on religious grounds. Members of national churches invoke ancient legislation which concedes their autonomy under God. How far does this extend to the practices of every group, and how do we know what God intends for these churches in any case? (Presbyterians sometimes say with conviction, 'We are not a democracy.' But is this something actually to be proud of? Do we really want a juristocracy?)

From a *cultural* perspective there has to be the recognition of pluralism at many levels of social grouping. It will not do to pit Eastern values against

Western, capitalist against socialist, white against black or whatever. Martha Nussbaum wisely suggests that we must seek not the parochial or the locally dominant but the *best* solutions in the world to problems of citizenship, and that these can arise from many different ethnic traditions. A cosmopolitan perspective is much superior to relativism.

Rights and God

One of the earliest theological discussions of human rights is to be found in Alan Falconer's collection *Understanding Human Rights*.[6] In an essay here on 'Christian Faith and Human Rights', Jürgen Moltmann sees the Reformed emphasis as being on human dignity through man's creation in the image of God, the Lutheran emphasis on a correspondence between Christian life in the sphere of faith and human rights in the sphere of the world, and the Roman Catholic emphasis on the analogy between nature and grace, in which grace illuminates the dignity of man in nature. Moltmann identifies another starting point in the experience of inhumanity, in a liberation theology context. The discussion has been taken forward by Max Stackhouse and others.

In the present, the language of human rights is frequently used in the churches, usually *on both sides of debates*, for example, on pro Choice and pro Life. As in secular politics, conservative groups have become at least as adept as liberal groups in seizing ownership of the language of human rights on behalf of their positions. Debates about love are polarized by such modifications as loving the sinner but not the sin. Debates about natural law and the common good may reach radically different conclusions from similar premises, as for instance in the debates about sexuality between Finnis and Nussbaum, both drawing on Aristotelian premises. The specific implications of human rights can be contested in numerous directions.

Arguments for the centrality of human rights would appear to be both complex and necessary, complex because of the range of different evaluations of rights, necessary because of the continued global violation of rights, especially of the most vulnerable. David Forsythe neatly sums up the history of the debate thus:

> We do not lack for differing theories about human rights. For Edmund Burke, the concept of human rights was a monstrous fiction. For Jeremy Bentham, it was absurd to base human rights on natural rights, because 'Natural rights is simple nonsense . . . nonsense upon stilts'. The contemporary philosopher Alasdair

> MacIntyre tells us *there are no such things as human rights*; they are similar to witches and unicorns and other figments of the imagination.[7]

Forsythe has examined the regional and global implications of human rights standards, the role of non-governmental organizations and the often unnoticed yet increasingly huge power and financial muscle of *transnational corporations*. He notes that 'Only six states have revenues larger than the nine largest TNCs. If we were to include transnational banks in this figure, the power of private for-profit enterprises would be much larger.'[8] So, for example, the Mitsubishi and Mitsui corporations have each twice as much revenue as the Netherlands, the world's seventh most prosperous nation state. Reflecting on the politics of liberalism in a realist world, he traces in contemporary geopolitics an oscillation between liberalism and neo-liberalism, between romanticism and realism. He concludes that human rights activity on any level does make a tangible difference to the contemporary world, but that there is a very long way to go.

'The various levels of action for human rights – whether global, regional, national or sub-national – were not likely to wither away because of lack of human rights violations with which to deal. Pursuing liberalism in a realist world is no simple task.'[9]

What has all this to do with theology? Not much, if theology is concerned only with abstract ideas and aesthetics without ethics. But since theology, and especially Christian theology, is committed to searching for truth and ultimate meaning in the universe, it cannot be done in isolation from these *geopolitical realities*. Behind the economic and political statistics lie equally important issues such as nutrition and health care. In the European Holocaust, six million were murdered, and in the famine in China in 1958–62, thirty million people perished. Aids currently devastates Africa. Where were human rights considerations there, and where was God's action in all of this? A theology which is done in isolation from world affairs may be a coherent and academically satisfying enterprise, but it can hardly be an adequate Christian theology.

The argument of this chapter will be that there is *an integral connection* between concern for human rights and concern for God. But it is not a simple or direct connection. God is not an interventionist God in the most literal sense, who may fix things in the world at will. But, equally, God is not entirely dependent on the cosmos. God remains creator and redeemer of the world, and may act in ways complex beyond our full understanding to encourage fulfilment in the universe along particular lines – lines consonant with God's own being and purpose as eternal compassionate love. This action may link with human action in more and in less direct ways.

The Enlightenment search for the common good, often without reference to God, may be understood by Christians as itself prompted by the divine love. This is not to suggest that agnostic thinkers were somehow anonymous Christians, but rather from a Christian perspective that all good action is a response to *the source of goodness who is God*. Enlightenment thinkers were correct in thinking that it is possible to seek for and to achieve a measure of the common good without appeal to God. But the quest need not exclude the question of God.

Nussbaum

In the search for a differentiated rationality in relation to rights we may find in the writings of Martha Nussbaum much to encourage us. In *Cultivating Humanity*,[10] Martha Nussbaum provides an exemplary retrieval of aspects of classical culture as a contribution to tackling pressing problems in the contemporary world – notably the understanding of citizenship. She identifies the dangers inherent both in modernist universalism and in postmodern particularity, and she invokes a Socratic model of rationality to steer an intelligent course between extremes. The argument is a development of her earlier *The Therapy of Desire*,[11] an examination of the theory and practice of Hellenistic ethics. In that volume, discussion of the debates between Aristotelian and Stoic ethicists led her to stress the continuing value of reason, in correction of Foucault's conclusion, based on his study of classical ethics, that reason is always the instrument of power and so is of very limited effectiveness.

Cultivating Humanity is in some ways an exegesis of Seneca's advice to cultivate humanitas. This is, as the preface indicates, a discussion of the nature of citizenship. But it is very much more than that. It is an exploration of a critical reflection on the best approaches to a multicultural society, in which there is mutual respect for all citizens. The juxtaposition of debates from ancient Greece and contemporary America provides a thread of philosophical continuity which ensures that intellectual rigour is never sacrificed to social engineering. She argues that three capacities are essential to cultivating humanity – critical self-examination, awareness that common needs and aims are realized differently in different circumstances and narrative imagination, the capacity to see the world from the standpoint of the other. It also requires 'scientific understanding'. To be a citizen of the world is to be aware of cultural difference.

How is Socratic self-examination possible? Argument, especially about matters of justice, may strengthen democracy. Progress can be made through a reflection that seeks the common good.[12] The Stoics argued that critical argument should lead to intellectual strength and freedom.[13] (We might think that philosophy departments are scarcely always paradigms of citizenship!) Socratic education is for all, must be suitable to the pupil's context, concerned for a variety of norms, and requires books that do not become authorities. The realities of power and politics do not make reason redundant; they make critical reflection even more imperative.

In a chapter on narrative imagination she underscores the value of literature as a vehicle of the compassionate imagination. After charting the role of tragedy in encouraging us to identify with suffering, she notes the coincidence of the rise of the modern novel with the rise of modern democracy. 'In reading a realist novel with active participation, readers do all that tragic spectators do, and something more. They embrace the ordinary.'[14] She recalls again the tradition of the Stoics. 'Marcus Aurelius made a further claim on behalf of the narrative imagination: he argued that it contributes to undoing retributive anger.'[15] She identifies the danger of some forms of multiculturalism. 'The goal of producing world citizens is profoundly opposed to the spirit of identity politics, which holds that one's primary affiliation is with one's own local group, whether religious or ethnic or based on sexuality or gender.'[16] A section on the study of non-Western cultures leads to reflection on the aims and limits of cross-cultural teaching. Students should become aware of their own ignorance, of other world cultures and to a great extent of their own.

Nussbaum turns to African–American studies. Particularly effective is her account of her own lack of meaningful contact with black people through her life and teaching career. 'I see few black faces. I find things out mostly by teaching and imagining.' This is a severe challenge in 'an America nominally integrated but still consumed by bigotry'.[17] The citizenship theme is in turn developed into the realm of women's studies. This was to be taken up soon in a further book.[18] Feminist thought leads on logically to other areas in the study of human sexuality. Nussbaum highlights academic suspicion of the subject from her own experience. A delicate and difficult task, it should nevertheless be a central part of the curriculum. What of the role of religion in the search for citizenship? She maintains that love of the neighbour is a central value in all major American religions. 'These religions call us to a critical examination of our own selfishness and narrowness, urging more inclusive sympathy.'[19] The 'new' liberal education will not be for an elite but for all humanity.

The passion for justice has been eloquently expressed by Duncan Forrester in many of his own writings, notably *Christian Justice* and *On Human Worth*. One might illustrate the catalytic effect of emancipatory theology from any of its dimensions – feminist theology, black theology, Hispanic or Asian theology, or where the voice of theology is particularly not just in critique of unjust cultures, but in the theory and practice of the Christian Church itself. The Church must put her own house in order, in relation to issues of race, gender and other issues, if it is to be effective in a wide society. The Church must confront the often excruciatingly painful task of examining its own employment practices before it speaks of justice and equality for workers in other spheres.

I shall illustrate my argument from issues in which Duncan and Margaret Forrester have taken a firm stand – lesbian and gay issues, the place of women, India and race issues. The first of these is not an area in which the Church of Scotland has a good record. It is an area in which taking a firm stand for justice has led to much vilification – I think of Bishop Richard Holloway. Beginning from the concrete, I reproduce here a piece which I was asked recently to write for *Trinity College Bulletin*, in Glasgow University.

> I watched the Church of Scotland Assembly 2000 debate when the BBC invited me to comment for the afternoon television programme. What was new? The tone of the debate had improved slightly since the beginning of the decade, when the mere mention of gay people in Panel on Doctrine Reports led to overtly homophobic rhetoric. Discussion of the gay issue was preferable to decades of silence. Most of the speeches were on the conservative side, especially among the younger ministers. Despite the new cordiality no openly gay person felt safe enough to utter a word. It was good that a couple of speakers mentioned the deep pain and hurt that had been caused by the issue.
>
> My own view of this issue has long been liberal. Of course there can be solid arguments on either side of the debate, as indeed there was on slavery, women ministers and numerous other issues. Exploitation is not limited to either straight or gay people. Issues of sexuality are not that simple. But I believe that the conservative views held by a large section of Scottish Christians, for example by the Board of Social Responsibility, the Presbytery of Glasgow which voted by 300 to 22 against repeal in any circumstances, Cardinal Winning and Brian Souter were profoundly mistaken.
>
> It is mistaken to think that the unity to which God calls human beings is a unity of sameness. There has to be scope for otherness, for diversity, as there is diversity and dynamic relationship within the Trinity. That is what it is to be made in the image of God. It is mistaken because people are constantly hurt,

assaulted, rendered suicidal in the atmosphere of institutionalized discrimination which clearly exists in Scotland today. This debate on high principles has already produced victims, and it may well produce more.

Anti-gay sentiment appears still to be at its strongest in Europe in Scotland and in Northern Ireland, countries with strong conservative traditional cultures. At the time of the debate the prime minister was right to call the bluff of the 'Keep the Clause' campaign, when he spoke of people who hide their homophobia under the cover of child protection. Of course constructive social change cannot happen overnight, and we should not blame too quickly people who are innocently led into dubious campaigns. Perhaps there ought to be an age of consent for involvement with such bodies as the Christian Institute, and it should be set at 95. In the end, the net effect of prejudice will be to turn more people away from the church

We can at least be glad that not all church teaching has been negative. The Scottish Episcopal Church hosted in May 2000 a valuable conference of dialogue between the churches and gay and lesbian Christians. The Panel on Doctrine of the Church of Scotland (with which I had some connection), in its reports on the subject spoke of marriage as a foundational pattern in the Bible. This need not be a limiting or exclusive pattern. It stressed love, concern, faithfulness. Appreciation of marriage is without question important. But it should not diminish the worth of other relationships. The Church and Nation Committee constantly underlines the fundamental Christian concern for human rights, and for justice and equality in ALL areas of discrimination. It is said that only a small proportion of the population are involved here. The more marginalized they are, the more important for Christians to identify in solidarity with them. The God of Jesus Christ is always there for and with the outcast and the persecuted. There are some strange things in the Bible. But this need not lead us to encourage the somewhat irreverently termed 'stone a poof for the Jesus brigade'.

In the summer semester of 1999 I was teaching in Germany. In the middle of Frankfurt, there is a bronze statue of an angel. It is a formal and almost medieval statue. But the angel's neck is almost totally severed. It is a memorial to the gay holocaust, to hundreds of murdered people, priests and ministers and lay people. It is too easy for churches to repeat ancient anathemas while at the same time disowning responsibility for fomenting discrimination. 'Thou shalt not bear false witness against thy neighbour.'

There is a need to be much more humble still in our approach to others outside the church. All is not doom and gloom. The churches are slowly creeping towards communication with gay and lesbian people. It is good that people with different views within the churches are learning to work together on difficult issues. On a brighter note, we may recall that already in large areas of the world this whole controversy seems about as relevant to the common good as disputes about flying the Union flag on public buildings. Even the churches may get there in time.

Here is a human rights issue, not perhaps on an enormous scale but a kind of litmus test at the heart of our own churches, at a point of painful and often apparently irreconcilable conflict. The Christian Gospel is a gospel of creation and reconciliation, of repentance and faith. When we consider the misery inflicted on the lives of countless people over the centuries through church intransigence – however culturally conditioned – it becomes clear that a huge amount of corporate repentance is in order here. We can hardly expect this in the near future, but in the long term it would seem to be inevitable.

In return we might have a threefold dividend. We might learn new things about the worship of God, the service of our neighbours and the joy of discipleship from gay people today. We might retrieve the spiritual legacy of people in the past whose lives were often complicated by confusion and denial: as one troubled soul famously put it, 'For through the law I died to the law. It is no longer I who live, but Christ who lives in me.' More recently, we can contemplate the cost of discipleship in the life and 1998 crucifixion of Matthew Shepard. We might also be able at last to contribute to the development of a more nuanced approach to many of the social and pastoral issues which are common to all human beings in community, when the oppressive politics of ghettoization have finally been abandoned.

It is sometimes objected that human rights issues are purely Western preoccupations, not relevant outside Europe and America. Local cultural perspectives are always to be respected. It is of course true that local perspectives are to be respected, but not at any cost – respect for a mafia culture or a gun culture will clearly be mitigated by other considerations. Martha Nussbaum has brilliantly dissected these issues.

Against the objection that a search for humanitas is inevitably simply an exegesis of Western values it is striking that in her *Women and Human Development*,[20] Nussbaum concentrates almost entirely on Indian traditions and culture, and demonstrates the continuing importance of the central values of humanity in this framework. Through the examination of legal, political and religious debates, law cases and practical outcomes, she shows that issues of rights and capabilities in India manifest in depth all the ambiguities and complexities which appear in other cultures. Much of the generalizing rhetoric surrounding the status of 'Western' and 'non-Western' perspectives will simply not stand up to close rational scrutiny.

A chapter, 'In Defense of Universal Values'[21] makes a valuable case for a balance between respecting cultural particularity and maintaining common values. It interprets human rights through a comprehensive model of human capabilities. She argues against cultural relativism:

It has no bite in the modern world, where the ideas of every culture turn up inside every other, through the internet and the media ... Why should we follow local ideas, rather than the best ideas that we can find? ... Finally, normative relativism is self subverting: for, in asking us to defer to local norms, it asks us to defer to norms that in most cases are strongly non-relativistic. Most local traditions take themselves to be absolutely, or relatively true. So, in asking us to follow the local, rationality asks us not to follow relativism.[22]

Capabilities

Arguments from diversity and paternalism are equally weak. She lists central human functional capabilities, vital to the dignity and well-being of each person. These include: life, bodily health, bodily integrity, senses, imagination and thought, emotions, practical reason, relation to other species, play and control, political and material, over one's environment.[23] These include basic capabilities, internal capabilities and combined capabilities. 'Citizens of repressive nondemocratic regimes have the internal but not the combined capability to exercise thought and speech in accordance with their consciences.'[24]

Capabilities have a close relationship to human rights, to political and civil liberties and to economic and social rights. Combined capabilities are rights, and do not have the 'Western' tone of talk of rights, though rights language is still useful in drawing attention to the role of justification and the importance of liberty in argument for capabilities. This theoretical framework provides a basis for renewed attention to women's preferences and options in a world which has long systematically suppressed women.

Nussbaum turns to the role of religion in these debates. Religion may be but need not be oppressive. She will argue here for frameworks of political rather than comprehensive liberalism, avoiding the tendency to exclude transcendence which is often a feature of secular liberal positions. The argument is illustrated from legal and religious argument in Indian court cases. Families are important to women, but the concept should not be allowed to become coercive. 'My approach, by contrast, begins by focusing on the capabilities and liberties of each person, and does not assume that any one affiliative group is prior or central in promoting these capabilities.'[25] 'The fact is that justice and friendship are good allies: women who have dignity and self-respect can help to fashion types of community that are no less loving, and often quite a lot more loving, than those they have known before.'[26]

136

'Women in much of the world lose out by being women.'[27] The world community has been slow to address the problems of women, because it has lacked a consensus that sex-based inequality is an urgent issue of political justice. A capabilities approach 'can fairly claim to make a distinctive contribution to the practical pursuit of gender justice'.[28]

Nussbaum's work seems to me to be an outstanding model of the way forward in untangling complex issues of the relationships of religion, culture and human rights. She demonstrates that these issues must be faced rationally at different levels, the ethical, the political, the cultural and the religious, and the connections must then be carefully drawn out. She provides, at a high level of intellectual distinction, both theoretical frameworks for understanding and practical programmes for achieving justice and human dignity. Her chosen target, the development of women, is both of major significance in itself and of great value as a paradigm case to illuminate related though different issues of culture, religion and justice – for example poverty, sexuality and race. Her work is a standing provocation to the theologian to show that theology can make an equally significant contribution to the quest for human capability.

Nussbaum's work provides an effective response to the problems of relativism and the charge that rights talk is always Western. As has been noted (Chris Brown in *Universal Human Rights?*,[29] 'Part of this turn involves the use of classical notions of the "virtues" to construct the kind of account of what it is to be human that would not be vulnerable to the charge of cultural imperialism. The virtues as espoused by Aristotle and other Greek thinkers are frames of mind which orient one towards characteristic human experiences.') It is clear that concepts of human rights, like all concepts, are always open to further debate and modification. But it is all too easy for autocratic rulers to attack them in order to preserve their own coercive ideologies, in any part of the world.

Theology may well wish to assert other concepts which are central to human flourishing – we have mentioned generosity. But rights may be an integral part of the realization of the purpose of a generous God for humanity. Human rights are sometimes a hard thing for Christian communities to come to terms with. We have seen the churches plead for immunity from the European Convention on Human Rights. What of the Crown Rights of the Redeemer? But that argument will work only when the churches' justice can be seen to be more just than secular justice. We must see to it that a Christian construal of human rights is more humane than other constructions. Only then will we be in a position to do what we are called to do, to witness to the love of God in and before the world.

God, Transcendence and Human Flourishing

Religion is not exhausted by morality. Christians are not more moral than others. If we were to reach a position in which all the goals of personal and social justice were achieved, faith would still have a central role to play in Christian life. Faith, Christian and other, is concerned with transcendence. A belief in transcendence will not in itself make for humane praxis or human flourishing. The world is full of religious bigots who have an unshakeable faith in divine transcendence, in Christian cases linked to the figure of Jesus Christ, and there are other bigots who do not believe in divine transcendence. Metaphysical and logical categories may be morally neutral. But they are essential for creating the frameworks by which we think about and act towards the world in which we live.

Taking account of transcendence is *necessary* to the Christian understanding of the world as a gift, which comes from God and which belongs to God. How in a transcultural context can we develop a critical theology of transcendence? This dilemma is fascinatingly articulated by Charles Taylor in his essay, *A Catholic Modernity*,[30] and in his response to comments on that paper.

The argument goes like this. Redemption happens through incarnation, the weaving of God's life into human lives, but these human lives are different. Complementarity and identity will both be part of our ultimate oneness. Our great historical temptation has been to forget the *complementarity*, to go straight for the sameness, making as many people as possible into 'good Catholics' – and in the process failing catholicity. He tries to look at the Enlightenment as Matteo Ricci looked at Chinese civilization in the sixteenth century. 'The view I'd like to defend, if I can put it in a nutshell, is that in modern, secularist culture there are mingled both authentic developments of the gospel, of an incarnational mode of life, and also a closing off to God that negates the gospel.'[31] The problem is in the project of *Christendom*, the attempt to marry the faith with a form of culture and a mode of society.

But there are problems:

> The first danger that threatens an exclusive humanism, which wipes out the transcendent beyond life, is that it provokes as reaction an immanent negation of life. The point of things isn't exhausted by life. Suffering and death help us to affirm something that matters beyond life. We may lose '*the crucial nuance*'.

> The Christian conscience experiences a mixture of humility and unease: the humility in realising that the break with Christendom was necessary for this great extension of gospel-inspired actions; the unease in the sense that the denial of transcendence places this action under threat.[32]

There is a revolt against the modern affirmation of life in Nietzsche. This is a turn to violence, which may perhaps only be escaped by a turn to transcendence. We make very high demands for universal solidarity today, but how do we manage it? *Self-worth has limitations.* Philanthropy may turn to coercion, unless there is unconditional love of the beneficiaries.[33] Christian spirituality points in faith to a way out 'either as a love or compassion that is unconditional – or as one based on what you are most profoundly – a being in the image of God.' 'Our being in the image of God is also our standing among others in the stream of love, which is that facet of God's life we try to grasp, very inadequately, in speaking of the Trinity.'[34]

Taylor responds in a later chapter to reflections given upon his lecture. He speaks of the insufficiency of human flourishing as the unique focus of our lives. But he appreciates also the affirmation of ordinary life, the new forms of inwardness and the 'rights culture'.

Much modern philosophy has been 'monological'. But the goods discovered in community, 'together-goods', are important.[35] It is important to strive for *complementarity*, and not to be content with incommensurability, as in Foucault's 'completely solo operation'. In a rights culture, the good of solidarity may be neglected.

In a Christian contribution to understanding of transcendence, the Christological matrix of love, peace and justice, of vulnerability and generosity, leads us to construe goodness in the created order as the goodness of self-giving, self-affirming love, and evil as its negation and denial. Seeing human beings through the image of God in Jesus Christ we may see occasions for self-giving love in human relations as pointers to transcendence.

Transcendence is *not* characterized as *difference* from human love, but as its *source*, inspiration and ground. As human beings experience this sense of the givenness of what is good in their lives and in the lives of fellow human beings, they affirm the active presence of the transcendent God. They do this in correlating rationality and experience with the tradition and narratives of the Christian community. They offer this construal as a contribution to a wider, transcultural understanding of transcendence. They believe that it faithfully conveys what is at the heart of ultimate reality.

A critical transcultural theology of transcendence will affirm the presence of the Christian God in such a way as always to acknowledge other understandings of transcendence, and to respect these as far as they share in *rejection of violence*, coercion and domination. It will insist that the transcendence of God has nothing to do with violence and coercion. It will encourage a generous and pluriform manifestation of human community, unfettered by prescribed forms of religious conformity. It will see this freedom as a gift of the free grace of God.

How are we to recognize the dimension of transcendence and respond to it appropriately? Sometimes it may be at crisis points in the lives of individuals and societies that openness to transcendence occurs. Yet there is much value in the biblical metaphor of the still small voice. We like our religious notions and practices to manifest certainty and decisiveness. Yet we know from historical appearances that such apparently unambiguous occasions and events are often deceptive. The presence of God is not in our power to command. It is always there, in the ways in which God through the various religious traditions has promised to be present, for Christians as the presence of self-giving, self-affirming love in our world. A vision which is not strident, dominating or controlling may still be an *immensely persistent*, persuasive and effective vision for the future of human flourishing. Such a vision may be an effective means of delivering basic rights, understood as the standards the God of self-giving love promises to all his creatures. For it will not be deflected by unusual events or by unexpected obstacles. It will expect just to continue to be there.

I end with a brief comment from what I regard as a classic of judicious analysis of human rights issues in a particular case, Cornel West's *Race Matters*.[36] It was said of America, but it applies in different tones to all our cultures. 'We simply cannot enter the twenty-first century at each other's throats, even as we acknowledge the weighty forces of racism, patriarchy, economic inequality, homophobia and ecological abuse on our necks … None of us alone can save the nation or world. But each of us can make a positive difference if we commit ourselves to do so.'[37]

Notes

1 Peter Jones, *Rights* (Basingstoke: Macmillan, 1994), p. 227.
2 Alan Gewirth, *Human Rights* (Chicago, IL: Chicago University Press, 1982).
3 David P. Forsythe, *Human Rights in International Relations* (Cambridge: Cambridge University Press, 2000).

4 Isaiah Berlin, *Two Concepts of Liberty* (Oxford: Oxford University Press, 1958).

5 Conor Gearty and Adam Tomkins (eds), *Understanding Human Rights* (London: Pinter, 1999).

6 Alan Falconer, *Understanding Human Rights* (Dublin: Irish School of Ecumenics, 1980).

7 Forsythe, *Human Rights in International Relations*, p. 28.

8 *Ibid.*, p. 191.

9 *Ibid.*, p. 236.

10 Martha Nussbaum, *Cultivating Humanity* (Cambridge, MA: Harvard University Press, 1997).

11 Martha Nussbaum, *The Therapy of Desire* (Princeton, NJ: Princeton University Press, 1994).

12 Nussbaum, *Cultivating Humanity*, p. 25.

13 *Ibid.*, p. 29.

14 *Ibid.*, p. 95.

15 *Ibid.*, p. 97.

16 *Ibid.*, p. 110.

17 *Ibid.*, p. 185.

18 Martha Nussbaum, *Women and Human Development* (Cambridge: Cambridge University Press, 2000).

19 *Ibid.*, p. 293.

20 Nussbaum, *Women and Human Development*.

21 Martha Nussbaum, 'In defense of universal values', *Women and Human Development*, Ch. 1.

22 *Ibid.*, p. 49.

23 *Ibid.*, p. 80.

24 *Ibid.*, p. 85.

25 *Ibid.*, p. 276.

26 *Ibid.*, p. 290.

27 *Ibid.*, p. 298.

28 *Ibid.*, p. 303.

29 Chris Brown, 'Human rights and human dignity: an analysis of human rights culture and critics', in R. Patman (ed.), *Universal Human Rights?* (Basingstoke: Macmillan, 2000).

30 Charles Taylor, *A Catholic Modernity* (New York: Oxford University Press, 1999).

31 *Ibid.*, p. 16.

32 *Ibid.*, p. 26.

33 *Ibid.*, p. 33.

34 *Ibid.*, p. 35.

35 *Ibid.*, p. 113.

36 Cornel West, *Race Matters* (New York: Vintage Books, 1994).

37 *Ibid.*, p. 159.

Chapter 9

From Kant to Fukuyama and Beyond: Some Reflections

ANN LOADES

My initial introduction to 'public theology' came about many years ago more or less by accident as I engaged with Immanuel Kant's assessment of various projects in theodicy prompted by Leibniz' magisterial work towards the beginning of the eighteenth century. Insofar as views of the course of events and their goal or 'end' are modes of dealing with aspects of human experiences of suffering, theodicy and 'ends of history' theses are intertwined. This is evident even in the 1992 best-seller by Francis Fukuyama, *The End of History and the Last Man*,[1] if we attend to the gruesome image to be found in its concluding pages. There he writes of a wagon train heading across country. Some wagons get stuck in ruts or stay bivouacked; some may wander around for a time; some are attacked by Indians, set aflame and abandoned – but most will eventually arrive into town. Fukuyama's book represents the kind of 'grand narrative' which philosophers have largely given up on,[2] not least for their 'totalizing' indifference to the smaller stories which constitute serious challenges to the 'Big Story'. So whilst Fukuyama's 'wagon train' image is meant to sustain his optimistic overall picture, I referred to it as 'gruesome' because of its 'bandwagon operetta' quality, its absence of a sense of terror, so acutely identified by Lutz Niethammer.[3] The Indians attacking the wagon train became those defeated by the alliance of 'liberal democracy', capitalism and the market, fuelled by the successes of science and technology, which has given such scope to the men beset by desire for 'recognition' who are Fukuyama's heroes. 1970 saw the publication of Dee Brown's *Bury my Heart at Wounded Knee: An Indian History of the American West*,[4] about the 'end' of Indian civilization a century before.[5] One of the most heart-rending parts of Dee Brown's book is his account of the 'Ghost-dancers' (pp. 431f), those who danced so that the Messiah would not pass them by, wearing the

143

Ghost-dance shirts which no bullets could penetrate, a belief which ended in the slaughter at Wounded Knee at Christmas 1890. These Indians danced, having met ghosts of other Indians when they were out and about searching for a Messiah, Indians who gave them meat, bread and horses, and who treated them like brothers. They danced for the return of their paradise of knee-high grass, new soil which would bury all the white men, running water, trees and herds of buffalo and wild horses. Comparable stories could be multiplied, and a public theology should not endorse a framework which means that such stories are not recognized for the terror of their memory and present reality. Not the least of our difficulties is to address the extent to which we are still committed to perpetrating the miseries we would prefer to associate with the regimes which have fallen – the wagons which did not make it into town. The possible contribution of theology to public life in our time is a matter to which I will return. At this point, however, I make some comments on Kant.

Kant, I suggest, is not to blame for the 'operetta-like' view of the course of things, if we take seriously the theology he wrote towards the end of his life, theology so largely ignored by theologians, though not by North American writers of political philosophy.[6] In the UK the most significant re-evaluation of Kant's importance for public theology has arguably been achieved by an expert on Goethe, Nicholas Boyle, a Roman Catholic liberal humanist, on whose fine book I shall comment at the end of this essay.[7] Of Kant, somewhat briefly, it should be recalled that he lived out his life in a cosmopolitan seaport, with soldiers quartered all over it, and with multidimensional Christianity much in evidence to add to organized Lutheranism (including Quakers, Mennonites, Socinians, Herrnhuters, Huguenots and Calvinists), with Roman Catholic Poland in the hinterland. Koenigsberg was in and out of war zones and occupation from the mid-century Seven Years' War through to the era of the French Revolutionary wars. Kant lived through the partitions of Poland, but died before the trauma of Prussian defeat at Jena and Auerstadt, and Hegel's seeing the Emperor Napoleon as 'world-soul', though, as Niethammer observes (*Posthistoire*, p. 63), the world-soul changed horses at the latest after Waterloo! The times produced the Berlin Institute of Military Sciences for young officers of infantry and cavalry regiments, and men such as Kiesewetter, Scharnhorst and Clausewitz, and, after the war, the constitutional and civil reforms of the Stein-Hardenberg period, profoundly influenced by Kant's insistence on 'respect' for others, now given institutional expression.

Kant's essays in political philosophy in the mid-1780s argued for relationships between states which would secure even to the smallest both security and justice without the endless expenditure of preparations for war. So, contrary to what is sometimes supposed, Kant was no mere 'formalist', since he manifestly paid attention to factors of many kinds which functioned as obstacles to the achievement of human dignity. He was well aware that it is by no means self-evident that reason can be brought to bear on human affairs, any more than it is self-evident that human beings can live in accordance with self-discerned and self-imposed moral principles. He knew in his own person the distresses of the thoughtful and of the hopelessness to which that can lead. Blaming others for problems and dreaming of paradise were alike deeply damaging, if human beings wanted to shift themselves from moral passivity and the confusions of self-interest. Respect for the neighbour, and thereby glorification of the deity, were integral to what in his view was the most distinctive human advantage – the capacity in the present to face up to the unknown and unknowable future. Kant's emphasis on the divine transcendence, unknowability and ineffability forced attention as it were to knowable neighbours, foreigners and strangers, and made him extremely cautious about what we would now call 'grand narratives', not least about the future. Such caution did not prevent him from proposing political objectives, such as in his 1795 essay on 'perpetual peace', which would for him be the 'end of history'. Stripped of its theological referents, determination to secure 'peace' in one's own self-perceived interests, and this to be achieved by force in twentieth and twenty-first-century Western style at no matter what the cost to others, without attention to the unconditional demands of conscience, would be intolerable for Kant.[8] He would, however, have to concede that divine transcendence can be so stressed as to be readily construed as divine 'absence' from a world stripped bare of signs and symbols of divine presence, as in the city-spaces of the liberal and rational state, and he is to a degree responsible for this state of affairs.

That said, we can read his project on 'perpetual peace' as within a framework of divine reference, however uncomfortable we may be with Kant's apophaticism so far as the divine is concerned. For him, everyone is interdependent in their need for common legislation for security, and for the sheer rational vitality such security requires for its achievement. In a league of free and independent republics, the principles of right, he insists, are capable of some measure of implementation. He does not, of course, think that human beings can finally secure their own fulfilment, and the temper of his position is nicely caught by Professor Moltmann's comments on post-historic philosophers and their expectations of the 'end of history'. He writes that 'it is illogical to assume that the institutions, organizations and bureaucracies which historical people create are not themselves historical. It is illusory to maintain that the conditions which venturesome beings create in order to secure themselves against their own hazards could not be hazardous conditions.'[9] We might add that ecclesiastical institutions too can have their operetta-like qualities, at once trivializing suffering, and denying that the story could be told differently, or that the journey could be organized otherwise.[10]

Kant's open-ended eschatological temper is expressed in his profound sense that we are subject to divine scrutiny, and that that scrutiny will be concerned with our efforts towards impartiality and self-effacement – qualities wholly at odds with the self- aggrandizement of Fukuyama's 'last men'. He relies, of course, only on what Karl Jaspers used to refer to as 'ciphers of transcendence', provoked by a biblical passion for truthfulness and its performance, and, unsurprisingly, Kant's deity appears in his texts as a Frederician monarch, as 'holy lawgiver' (creator), 'good governor' (preserver) and, above all, as 'just judge', and it is to the divine in that latter anthropomorphic guise that Kant relates himself in his last theological essays. There it is abundantly clear that Kant is well aware of the way in which feelings and thoughts may destroy valued relationships, of the communality of impulses to evil, and our complicity in indifference to social wrongs. For him, divine judgement, dissolving pretence without possibility of mistake, depends in the last analysis on trust in the divine goodness, free of coercion, and the bare possibility of final approbation. Here is exhibited a sense of 'accountability' undreamt of by contemporary managerial culture, but a dimension we might well need for a public theology in our time. It is divine, and not human, recognition which matters.

It is of course all too easy to criticize him for what we think is missing from the picture, such as Derrida's understanding of forgiveness as the exceptional and extraordinary 'impossible' interruption of 'the ordinary course of historical impossibility', described in 'dry and implacable formality, without mercy: forgiveness forgives only the unforgivable'.[11] Yet Derrida is also one of the most recent of those who have reflected on the significance of Kant's proposals for 'perpetual peace' in our time. Derrida himself proposes 'cities of refuge' as an immediate response to crime, violence and persecution, as a necessary expression of Kant's 'cosmopolitan hospitality' and which he rightly identifies as having its roots both in some Greek philosophy and in Pauline Christianity.[12] If we look for signs of redemption in our world, and work out its consequences in residence, work, housing and health, such cities might well remind us of its reality. To this we may add that, despite major differences in philosophical temperament, Derrida can at this point be aligned with Michael Dummett's argument to the effect that goods and capital should be able to move freely across the globe, and people also. We have moral duties towards citizens 'of the universal society of human beings'[13] and must work out the practical policies which need to be implemented to deal with Europe's 'currents of panic, cruelty and hatred; a strong sense of obtuse selfishness, oblivious to its likely consequences' (Dummett, *On Immigration and Refugees*, pp. 152–3). Michael Dummett, Roman Catholic, and former Oxford Professor of Logic, has together with his wife, Ann, campaigned for the just treatment of immigrants and refugees in Britain and Europe for over thirty years – a major contribution to public theology, in my view.

Derrida's profound distaste for Fukuyama's complacency about the achieved 'end of history' has much to do with his sensitivity to the way in which alternative narratives of immigrants, guest-workers and others who do not 'fit' his magisterial paradigm are simply unheard. He also echoes Kant in knowing that the language of apocalypse is the language of acute distress, and that it is dangerous, since it may precipitate appalling measures of coercion on a scale of which Kant never dreamed.[14] Like Kant, he fears coercive Christianity, with state and superstate betraying a non-coercive, unforeseeable, unanticipatable messianism which precisely as such presents us with urgent tasks which are the manifestations of hope.[15] On this view, Fukuyama's vision of the present world as the best that could be hoped for is not only stifling in its apparent reality, as electronically consummated 'history',[16] but itself the source of violence. Apart from the self-preoccupations of 'Westernized' societies with unemployment and homelessness, the indebtedness of poorer nations, interethnic wars in the heart of Europe itself, the problems represented by international drug cartels, all manifest signs of deep disturbance which cannot simply be swept away as indications of the 'wagons' which did not and will not make it into town.

Contrast Chomsky with Fukuyama, and they seem at first to be entirely at odds, since whereas Fukuyama has a one-dimensional view of economic power in its international capitalist-market form as ultimately beneficial, at least in the areas of the world in which it has presently taken root (including East Asia as well as parts of Europe), Chomsky has a one-dimensional conception of power as violence.[17] One-dimensionality itself represents a problem, as I have already indicated. That apart, they differ in that Chomsky would utterly resist Fukuyama's view of the benignity of market economics allied to Western 'democracy' (itself problematic, if it seriously is meant to indicate significant political participation on the part of citizens). One could hardly disagree, as Jowitt readily acknowledges, that there is evidence of American support for murderous tyrannies, the imposition on one and all of economic policies which it is supposed will 'make over' the world in terms of the ideal-ized image of its benefits, interventions to support 'authoritarian, corrupt and cruel government' and the use of military force in violation of international law, much of which the USA had itself written. Readers of Chomsky find Britain hanging on to American coat-tails all along. So reading Chomsky is in one sense an antidote to Fukuyama, but their critics insist that they are at one in making a quite fundamental mistake, in not acknowledging that what we are now seeing is not just 'more of the same'. Chomsky's mistake is to think only of the continuation of the rapacious policies manifest in the 'Cold War', which now proceed in much the same way, but with ever more economic and military power at the disposal of some governments, though at least he faces the world's terrors. The crucial point to make in respect of both Chomsky and Fukuyama, however, if their critics are right, is that we are in a new situation, not a continuation of either the situation which results in Chomsky's denunciation in Cold War terms, or Fukuyama's confidence, if not complacency.

For Jowitt is as uneasy as Dummett about the adequacy of our present institutions to deal with what he calls new forms of violence which is dispersed, random, and frightening, in what he calls 'a violently weak world, a Genesis-like world "unnamed and unbounded"'. He writes that we are rather 'at a point and in a time when boundaries give way to frontiers, when well-delineated, predictable, familiar practices, institutions and ways of life give way to ill-defined, diffuse, anxiety-producing and violent reali-ties'. Jowitt rightly is concerned for the regeneration of a 'core polity', with the social and cultural preconditions of a democracy, one which is integrally related to 'corresponding reconfigurations in the units of political authority, membership and action'. Those polities which are foundering, we may add, are responsible for the new age of what Edith Wyschogrod has so eloquently identified as 'man-made mass death'.[18] As she points out, for Christianity, the whole of humankind became of social significance, and that beyond death. Although Kant's hope was 'intra-mundane', with hope in the bare possibility of divine approbation for one's best efforts in co-operation with others – precisely for the sake of that possibility, no one could ever justify the 'communities of terror' which expunge the human memories, speech, traditions and loyalties which, if they can be defended and maintained, may enable us to resist the unprecedented possibility of human extinction. We need to find tactics to enable us to resist the political realities of multiple nation states and acknowledge without qualification the sheer vulnerability and fragility of all those others for whom we are accountable, hearing their speech and placing resources at their disposal. What Fukuyama fails to take seriously enough is the integral relationship of the possibility of man-made mass death with transnational economic structures, the so-called 'global market', which is small comfort for those who place too much trust in cosmopolitanism, perhaps, unless it is institutionally expressed in terms of humanitarian citizenship. The writers of a leader in *The Independent* (5 February 1995) themselves drew on the language of apocalypse in urging governments to think of ways of controlling the global market to minimize its social wreckage, lest it come to resemble 'the hooded figure of death during the great plagues, roaming the world and striking communities at random, unknowable and unbeatable, and set above us all'. It is as though only such language is adequate to help us interpret our predicament, though it is a language from which hope for the reformation of our institutions is absent. The importance of Jowitt's plea for the reconfiguration of 'core polity' given 'the disorientation, disorganisation and distintegration of state power' is given added point by a reading of Hans Magnus Enzensberger's essays.[19] On the one hand, it appears to be the case that the one thing that is worse than being exploited by multinationals is not being exploited by them, in the sense that being run by politcal gangsters is even worse: 'in New York as well as in Zaire, in the industrial cities as well as in the poorest countries, more and more people are being permanently excluded from the economic system because it no longer pays to exploit them' (Enzensberger, *Civil War*, pp. 35–6). On the other hand, civil institutions as they exist seem to be incapable of dealing with the xenophobic horrors, arsonists, hijackers and hostage-takers given instant media recognition, the immediacy which dissolves historical narrative and sequence, providing a parody of 'soul-making', we might add. Who needs or desires divine scrutiny if you can have an instant audience of millions? Beyond immediate interpersonal decencies which are the responsibility of everyone, and which create interpersonal bonds, Enzensberger insists that the first priority of government must be to deal with 'the barbarity of the everyday', and move towards the setting of priorities, assessed for their workability by those as free as they can be from self-deception (*Civil War*, p. 68). Beyond that he offers little, except by implication suggesting that the very exercise of the determination to find just solutions may regenerate politics, which is the most he offers by way of hope.

It looks as if little can be expected from the 'elites' who assent to the 'superior rationality of the market', positing an ideal of self 'which is a radically individuated subject of choice unencumbered by desires or attachments', in a polity in which the survival of society is the goal and calculating utilitarianism its procedure.[20] For those who want 'recognition', consumption indeed is not sufficiently meaningful, for 'one can only have so many houses and cars and wives before one loses count',[21] and, as the sense of identity provided by localism and regionalism wanes, 'people find themselves retreating into the microscopic world of their families which they carry around with them from place to place like lawn furniture',[22] presumably licking their wounds as they go, since the making and breaking of relationships is unlikely to be without emotional cost even to a bare 'subject of choice'. It is no wonder that these elites were so loathed by Christopher Lasch for their contribution to the destabilization of society as they looked to the global market for marriage and friendship as well as for employment and entertainment, opting out of public services and with serious interests in minimizing government, living without limits and without hope.[23] There are simply no substitutes for the local communities and societies in which people help one another and learn to take responsibility for one another, finding common cause with Enzensberger, and, in a very different idiom, with John Caputo, and his plea for a return to the world which is 'the matrix of meaning' for us, the whole 'theatre of all giving birth and dying, growing ill and growing well, sleeping and waking, succeeding and failing, maturing and aging'. This is our world, he urges, and not the technological world 'in which we are systematically divested of our humanity and robbed of our worth',[24] and, we might add, of a sense of joy and of a vision of a world we might want to live in. It will certainly be important to pay attention to governments who are inventive enough to minimize harms and risks to persons in the course of rapid social change precisely in the interests of the sustainable life-world in which we find ourselves – despair at these possibilities is premature.[25] As for *philotimia* – the urge to be thought superior – a performance or even a rereading of Euripedes' *Iphigenia at Aulis* might be salutary. Even Iphigenia is in the grip of it, whilst her father, Agamemnon, is a murderous liar, and Achilles, her promised husband, himself leads the sacrificial procession which takes her to her death. People want and need scope for achievement, but they do not have to be mad, bad and dangerous to know.

It is not to the point here to rehearse the admirable discussions of Fukuyama's *The End of History*,[26] whilst Fukuyama himself has contributed to identifying some of the elements of a renewed vision in books beyond *The End of History*, books which have received far less attention. His 1995 book on *Trust*[27] was concerned with the interplay between habits of trust learned or not in communities and the needs of an economically competitive world. *The Great Disruption* of 1999[28] draws upon it, as, for instance, in the observation that trust 'arises when people share norms of honesty and reciprocity and hence are able to cooperate with one another and is damaged by excessive selfishness or opportunism' (p. 51), which indeed needs repeating in the kinds of contexts where trust is destroyed, as arguably, in the world of those driven by the desire to be thought superior. He continues to suppose 'history' to be progressive and directional, with liberal democracy as 'the only viable alternative for technologically advanced societies', but with social order 'ebbing and flowing over the space of multiple generations'; so at least his vision is now not so one-dimensional as it first appeared to be. Moreover, he adds that there is nothing that guarantees that 'there will be upturns in the cycle'. His only reason for hope, he says, is our 'very powerful innate human capacities for reconstituting social order', essential for the process of history.[29] In his terms, therefore, it would be unthinkable that the trajectory of 'history' could result in the final disruption of social order. At least he allows for the importance of political order, however. It can create norms through legislation; it can create the conditions for 'peaceful market exchange'; and, rightly, it produces social order through 'leadership and charisma', needing not simply such virtues as honesty, promise keeping and reciprocity, the 'small' virtues needed for social order, but courage, daring, statesmanship and political creativity. His main example here is noteworthy. It is that of George Washington, modest in office, abjuring honorific titles, stepping down after two terms in office, all of which 'set important precedents for the behavior of subsequent democratically elected US presidents' (*The Great Disruption*, p. 235). Unfortunately, he does not venture to tell us how this instance of a man, born and nurtured in a very different age, has been an actual, as distinct from a notional, setter of precedent in the twentieth century, for instance. Fukuyama also acknowledges the importance of religious traditions in increasing the 'radius of trust' in human societies, extending that radius to the whole of humankind. 'The aspiration towards moral universalism may be unrealized by any actual religion, but it is nonetheless an inextricable part of the moral universe created by religion' (*The Great Disruption*, p. 237). It is not as though he believes in the truth claims of religious traditions, since these are a source of conflict, and he merely describes what he sees, which is that people may turn to religion to rebuild communities, given the absence of community and the transience of social ties, the absence of ritual in societies 'stripped bare of ceremony'. Religion can thus be taken seriously by 'modern, rational, skeptical people', much as they 'celebrate their national independence, dress up in ethnic garb, or read the classics of their own cultural tradition' (*The Great Disruption*, pp. 278–9). Quite what might happen if people began to believe religious doctrines is almost beyond speculation, except that we might think with him that religion is more likely to be a source of conflict than of a cosmopolitanism deeply secured in mutual respect and tolerance where that can be achieved. Neither every religion nor every practice associated with religion can be endorsed.

The British have of course had a recent experience of 'public theology' in alliance with liberal democracy and not-so-peaceful market exchange during the period of Mrs Thatcher's prime ministership. The world heard the nineteenth-century prayer attributed to St Francis rehearsed on the steps of No. 10 Downing Street: 'Where there is discord, may we bring harmony; where there is error, may we bring truth; where there is doubt, may we bring faith; and where there is despair, may we bring hope'.[30] And there was the important speech at Cardiff on 16 April 1979: 'If you've got a message, preach it! The Old Testament prophets didn't go out on to the highways saying "Brothers, I want consensus." They said "This is my faith and my vision! This is what I passionately believe." And they preached it. We have a message. Go out, preach it, practise it, fight for it – and the day will be ours' (Campbell, *Margaret Thatcher*, p. 438). And it was in response to the lived experience of that period of prime ministership that Nicholas Boyle's book appeared, a book written not by a professional politician or professor of government, but by an expert in German literature and intellectual history, and precisely as such able to take a wider rather than a myopically Anglophone view of the state we are in, and what might be done about it.

Boyle is liberal in the sense that he thinks that human beings are capable of change and of change for the better, and that they are ingenious and effective problem-solvers, a much-needed confidence. So far with Fukuyama, we might say, applauding his insight that with the collapse of some major tyrannies something large-scale and fundamental had indeed happened and that things might not be the same again.[31] And Boyle agrees that religious and personal identity 'is no longer dependent on the development of that form of political identity which is provided by the interaction of national states and empires, for the economic and political process is now global and singular' (*Who Are We Now?*, p. 117). Within that framework, however, there are contradictions which may well drive future change. For the British experience has provided a salutary example of the conflict between an obsolescent form of nationalism and the cosmopolitan basis of economics, together with a rhetoric of freedom from government and the honouring of choice (to have what I want) coupled with 'the definition of ever more activities as economic, and introducing ever more detailed accounting procedures for them' (Boyle, p. 118), pulverizing different kinds of institutions intermediate between government and particular persons in the process. It might appear that opportunities are limitless, at least if what we want is anything money can buy, and if we have money, though in fact money cannot buy everything, and in fact opportunities do have limits. We are learning to attend to some of those limits, no matter what human ambitions there are, since the world simply cannot provide for all that people might conceivably fancy or be persuaded that they fancy. We need not insatiable souls, but new modes of mature asceticism, marked by the capacity to say 'no' both to the pretensions of government and to limitless ambition and greed. Both we and the world are finite. 'There is one world and it is not endless and we have to work out among ourselves how we are to live in it together or we shall die in it separately' (Boyle, p. 119). The recovery of confidence in political institutions adequate to the new cosmopolitanism, and, we might add, the recovery of confidence in ecclesiastical ones, is something that has to be achieved, as no one except ourselves can take responsibility for them. In the meantime, and crucially, we need to recover a sense of ourselves as producers (not just consumers) in a timescale which does not simply rely upon our confidence in the future, and our mutual trust in one another, but also in our sense of obligation, gratitude, service, honour one to another in our relationships (Boyle, pp. 40–1). A sense of a meaningful future remains important, however, and Boyle draws on and endorses Kant's vision of the future, to the effect that states should so bind themselves into treaty relationships that war between them would be unimaginable, that this would require genuine democracy, and that the likely alternative was 'the "perpetual peace" of the cemetery'. And Kant, moreover, understood that 'all our knowledge is in the end dependent on things as they are in themselves, that is, as they are created and given to us, in a manner – or by a power – which is necessarily beyond our knowing' (Boyle, pp. 177–8).

Of all the commentators, Boyle alone can make something central of theology for his vision,[32] though this, I suggest, is because he belongs to a religious tradition which has more to offer than simply a Kantian–Protestant version of Christian freedom reduced to what Fukuyama refers to as an 'inner condition of the spirit, and not an external condition of the body'.[33] In the first place, he, like Anderson,[34] sees the emancipation of women as a significant gain in human society, even though much remains to be given institutional expression, with genuine sexual reciprocity between the sexes still to be imagined. When Fukuyama writes about 'the special role of women', he seems to find it difficult to avoid seeing women (especially single mothers battling to rear children) as problematic if they are not primarily responsible for children in stable relationships. Admittedly, more recently he has noted the connections between the kind of lifestyle which has become more widespread than ever before – the 'casual access to multiple women' enjoyed by 'powerful, wealthy, high-status men throughout history' which has allegedly been one of the chief motives 'for seeking power, wealth, and high status in the first place' and the difference between that lifestyle and one which has fathers intensively involved in the nurture and education of their children. In between lie those who have simply 'a more distant presence as protector and disciplinarian' or who function as 'the largely absent provider of a paycheck'.[35] Boyle, by contrast, works not simply descriptively, but normatively, and this is because he has a theological perspective which enables him to take our sheer bodiliness utterly seriously. He can thus be generous rather than grudging about the importance of the realization that with women present in economic life 'the recognition that the most important things we produce are not things at all but our own kind would then determine our entire social life'[36] were we to acknowledge the significance of their presence. Thus the last thing that would benefit the human community would be the obliteration of women's distinctiveness and the possibility of a more humane world in which we would rejoin Caputo's 'matrix of meaning', we might add. Bodiliness, and the bodiliness of the faithful, 'sexually generated, destined to die, and sustained in life by their participation in the economic nexus' have something to do with 'the natural and risen body of the incarnate Lord', the one and the other having become or becoming the Mystical Body (Boyle, p. 226), and material conditions and the character of human aspirations cannot then be as trivial as our prevailing culture might seem to propose. The authority of ecclesiastical institutions in the future, therefore, may have much less to do with their international presence in politics, though that should not be disregarded as a source of constructive engagement with power-brokers, than with their capacity to make temporary and local sense of events (Boyle, p. 92), of the narratives of particular women and men in a graced world of shared meaning.

Christian confidence in fulfilment depends, ultimately, on the conviction that beyond human beings and their best efforts lies a generously and readily available grace beyond mere justice, a conviction to which in a minimal form even Kant subscribed. If indeed there are available to us resources to enable us and to approve us, a public theology for our time might well attempt to make that clear, by restoring the language of grace to public life, a grace which will be a 'tough grace' for all concerned. For the grace of working together for the transformation of the world in which we share will require the grace of forgiveness for ineradicable wrongs, the grace of enduring apparently intractable differences, the grace of respect for the insights of others into human and divine possibilities we have not glimpsed and cannot glimpse unless we engage with one another in all humility, and not in competitive and judgemental terms. Above all, perhaps, at this time, human beings need the grace of courage to begin the tasks before them, and not to be reduced to lethargy by supposing that 'it's all done and dusted' and nothing more is required of them.

Notes

1 Francis Fukuyama, *The End of History and the Last Man* (New York: Free Press, 1992).
2 John D. Caputo, *On Religion* (London: Routledge, 2001), pp. 65–6.
3 Lutz Niethammer, *Posthistoire: Has History Come to an End?* (London: Verso, 1992), p. 91.
4 Dee Brown, *Bury my Heart at Wounded Knee: An Indian History of the American West* (London: Vintage, 1971).
5 See also Noam Chomsky, *World Orders, Old and New* (London: Pluto Press, 1994), p. 31.
6 See Hans Urs von Balthasar, *Apocalypse der deutschen Seele*, 1 (Salzburg-Leipzig: Verlag Anton Pustet, 1937), drawn to my attention by the late Professor Donald MacKinnon; and some of the essays in Timothy Burns (ed.), *After History?: Francis Fukuyama and his Critics* (London: Rowman & Littlefield, 1994).
7 Nicholas Boyle, *Who Are We Now? Christian Humanism in the Global Market from Hegel to Heaney* (Edinburgh: T&T Clark, 1998).
8 See the resistance to coercion expressed in his 1791 essay on the failure of theodicy and in his 1794 essay on eschatology in Allen W. Wood and George di Giovanni (eds), *Religion and Rational Theology* (Cambridge: Cambridge University Press, 1996); on Kissinger's inimitable blend of Kantian idiom with political 'realism', see Peter W. Dickson, *Kissinger and the Meaning of History* (Cambridge: Cambridge University Press, 1978), and Chomsky, *World Orders*.
9 Jürgen Moltmann, *The Coming of God: Christian Eschatology* (London: SCM Press, 1996), p. 226. I am grateful to Professor Richard Bauckham for having drawn my attention to Moltmann's discussion of Fukuyama.

10 See the cautions in Gabriel Josipovici, *The Book of God* (New Haven, CT: Yale University Press, 1988), pp. 257–75; Joseph O'Leary, 'Theology on the brink of modernism', *Boundary*, 2(13) (1985): 138–54.

11 Jacques Derrida, *On Cosmopolitanism and Forgiveness* (London: Routlege, 2001), p. 32.

12 *Ibid.*, pp. 19–23.

13 Michael Dummett, *On Immigration and Refugees* (London: Routledge, 2001), pp. 48–50.

14 Jacques Derrida, *Specters of Marx: The State of the Debt, the Work of Mourning and the New International* (London: Routledge, 1995), pp. 56–74; Christopher Norris, 'Versions of Apocalypse: Kant, Derrida, Foucault', in Malcolm Bull (ed.), *Apocalypse Theory and the End of the World* (Oxford: Blackwell, 1995), pp. 227–49; and see Ernst Bloch, *The Principle of Hope*, 2 (Oxford: Blackwell, 1986), pp. 496–502; Richard H. Roberts, *Hope and its Hieroglyph: A Critical Decipherment of Ernst Bloch's Principle of Hope* (Atlanta, GA: Scholars Press, 1990).

15 John D. Caputo, *The Prayers and Tears of Jacques Derrida: Religion without Religion* (Bloomington, IN: Indiana University Press, 1997). Derrida is also deeply suspicious of the 'Christian politics' of Jan Patocka, *Heretical Essays in the Philosophy of History* (Chicago, IL: Open Court, 1996), and its implications for Arabs, Jews, guest-workers, etc., since he resists 'totalization' in all its forms.

16 Michael Cornfield, 'What is historic about television?', *Journal of Communication*, 44(1) (1994): 106–16.

17 Ken Jowitt, 'Our republic of fear: Chomsky's denunciation of America's foreign and economic policy', *Times Literary Supplement* (10 February 1995): 3–4.

18 Edith Wyschogrod, *Spirit in Ashes: Hegel, Heidegger, and Man-Made Mass Death* (New Haven, CT: Yale University Press, 1985); and Edith Wyschogrod, 'Man-made mass death. Shifting concepts of community', *Journal of the American Academy of Religion*, 58(2) (1990): 165–76.

19 Hans Magnus Enzensberger, *Civil War* (London: Granta, 1994).

20 Alan M. Suggate, 'Personal responsibility: Hayek and Havel in Christian perspective', *Religion, State and Society*, 20(3–4) (1992): 303–19.

21 Fukuyama, *The End of History*, p. 316.

22 *Ibid.*, p. 325.

23 Christopher Lasch, *The Revolt of the Elites and the Betrayal of Democracy* (New York: W. W. Norton, 1995); Alan Ryan, 'The middling sort', *London Review of Books* (25 May 1995): 13–14; Kenneth Anderson, 'Heartless world revisited: Christopher Lasch's parting polemic against the new class', *Times Literary Supplement* (22 September 1995): 3–4.

24 John D. Caputo, *The Mystical Element in Heidegger's Thought* (Athens, OH: Ohio University Press, 1978) p. 263; see also Gianni Vattimo, 'The end of (h)istory', in Ingeborg Hoesterey (ed.), *Zeitgeist in Babel: The Postmodernist Controversy* (Bloomington, IN: Indiana University Press, 1991), pp. 132–41, on *'pietas'* as

'the attitude of devoted attention that we adopt towards the values marked by morality and finitude', p.138.

25 Kenneth Dyson, 'European states and the Euro', *The British Academy Review* (July–Dec. 2000), pp. 18–20.

26 In addition to the works already cited, see Perry Anderson, *A Zone of Engagement* (London: Verso, 1992), pp. 279–375, alone in picking up the importance of the fact that both Niethammer's book and the essay of Fukuyama's which developed into *The End of History* were published within a couple of months of one another in 1989; and Christopher Bertram and Andrew Chitty (eds), *Has History Ended? Fukuyama, Marx and Modernity* (Aldershot: Avebury, 1994).

27 Francis Fukuyama, *Trust: The Social Virtues and the Creation of Prosperity* (London: Hamish Hamilton, 1995).

28 Francis Fukuyama, *The Great Disruption: Human Nature and the Reconstitution of Social Order* (London: Profile, 1999).

29 *Ibid.*, p. 282.

30 John Campbell, *Margaret Thatcher. Vol. 1: The Grocer's Daughter* (London: Cape, 2000), p. 446.

31 Boyle, *Who Are We Now?*, p. 70.

32 See, by contrast, the anti-theology of Walter Benjamin, discussed in Niethammer, *Posthistoire*, pp. 104–34, mostly on the 'blown-away angel'.

33 Fukuyama, *The End of History*, p. 196.

34 Anderson, *Zone of Engagement*, pp. 356–7.

35 Fukuyama, *The Great Disruption*, pp. 121, 101.

36 Boyle, *Who Are We Now?*, p. 58.

Chapter 10

Pluralism, Religion and Justification in Liberal Societies

RAYMOND PLANT

The aim of this chapter is to focus on the relationship between liberalism, pluralism and the role of religion in modern Western societies. To put the theme of the chapter initially in crude and broad terms: what I want to discuss is the question of how far the justification of the institutions and practices of a liberal society has to depend upon ideal or perfectionist principles and, if it does, how such principles may or may not secure the allegiance of those whose primary moral ideals are rooted in a life of religious worship and discipleship. Is it the case that the thicker and richer the justification for a liberal political order is, the less authority it will have over religious members of such a society? If the central ideal invoked in the justification of liberalism is, for example, a commitment to individual autonomy, how does that secure the allegiance of religious people whose primary moral framework may not acknowledge the centrality of that value?

This is a crucial issue in relation to public policy in that matters of what have come to be called lifestyle and perhaps, most particularly, sexual lifestyle are dealt with in a liberal society more and more in terms of individual choice and autonomy and equal rights in respect of the exercise of that autonomy. It is certainly the case, however, that many religious members of liberal societies do not want to concede this way of thinking about such matters and still want to link questions of sex, and most specifically issues about homosexuality, to particular and religiously founded conceptions of the good. Why should an individual believer, or for that matter a religious community, be convinced that the primary value at stake in this argument has to be seen in terms of individual autonomy? If part of the project of liberalism is to put the right before the good, what are the compelling reasons, if any, for someone with a rich and detailed conception of the good which shapes her life to be prepared to subordinate what that conception of the good might entail in terms, for example, of an account of human sexuality, to a general account of autonomy and equal rights, which detaches that conception of autonomy from any particular moral framework other than mutual non-interference?

However, before pursuing these questions in more detail I want to look first at the question of why it might be thought that liberalism needs a thick ideal regarding justification. Is it not possible to provide a secure defence of liberal institutions that does not commit us to the establishment of a particular moral ideal such as individual autonomy as foundational for liberalism? Surely, it might be argued, there are defences of liberalism that would make the maintenance of liberal institutions more compatible with deeply held first-order moral convictions such as those embedded in the lives of members of faith-communities. If this is not so, it can be argued, then liberalism is on very insecure grounds because, if the ultimate justification of liberal institutions is based upon a value or set of values which are not the primary values of significant moral communities in such a society, then what allegiance can be owed to liberal values and the institutions and policies that flow from them by members of such moral communities? Political structures have to grow out of what Hegel called the ethical life (*Sittlichkeit*) of society, and if the values underpinning such structures are not in fact rooted in that ethical life as it is lived in significant moral communities then such liberalism will be rootless and insecure. There are ways in which this question can be approached which do not, on the face of it, involve the idea that liberalism requires strong and perfectionist ideals and which indeed take as their starting point the ways of life of particular communities within a modern society. These two strategies are what John Rawls, the most important liberal philosopher of the post-war world, calls modus vivendi arguments and ideas about an overlapping consensus.

It seems clear that modern liberal thought has to recognize two very salient things. The first is what Rawls calls the fact of pluralism. This is the claim that, as a matter of fact, in modern Western societies people differ about their conceptions of the good. They also differ about what Rawls calls the comprehensive doctrines within which such conceptions of the good are embedded – that is to say that they differ over basic metaphysical and religious beliefs. Of course, other people in turn do not adhere, explicitly at least, to any sort of comprehensive doctrine – they may just have a set of particular moral attitudes and outlooks which are not grounded in any specific metaphysical or religious beliefs, even comprehensive beliefs of a wholly secular sort. This fact of pluralism poses an initial problem for liberal political thought, namely how is it possible to devise a justification for liberal institutions when people differ over comprehensive doctrines?

What will not do at this stage is to say that liberalism has no positive content of its own whether ideal or non-ideal and that it is just a kind of *coping* mechanism. It is just a way of dealing with pluralism. This will not do because, if liberalism is to be defended, it has to be recognized that it is not the only possible way of dealing with pluralism. There are other ways, too, which since the twentieth century are not far to seek. There are forms of Fascist totalitarianism which sought not to cope with pluralism but to overcome it and obliterate it. This theme can, for example, be seen in Hitler's *Table Talk* and in Mussolini's *The Doctrine of Fascism*, which is a root-and-branch critique of liberal individualism. So to rest the moral security of liberalism on the basis that it is a proven way of coping with pluralism is to render it morally very weak in the face of such threats which are unlikely to have disappeared from the world for good. Equally, it will not do to become overly sceptical about morality when facing up to the justification of liberalism. It is not that liberalism is somehow justified by moral scepticism, because it is obvious that there would be a dual problem if it were. First of all, how can a political doctrine such as liberalism be rooted in a commitment to moral scepticism because that scepticism would undermine the basis of any moral basis for liberalism. Secondly if, *per impossibile*, it were possible to root a positive argument for liberalism in moral scepticism, that scepticism would not be a feasible basis for liberalism that those belonging to strongly belief-based religious communities could accept. There is a difference between an acceptance of the fact of pluralism and moral scepticism. An attempt to found liberalism on moral scepticism would undermine its own project from the beginning and destroy the allegiance of religious communities who would not accept that scepticism. So liberalism cannot be founded on what has been called the fundamentalism of doubt – that is to say, fundamental doubt about basic moral issues. It has, however, to recognize that there is a plurality of views about these basic moral issues which are not doubtful to the people who hold those views. This is the central problem for liberalism: how to build a justification for liberal institutions in the context of pluralism and a justification which will be rich and compelling enough to make liberalism more than a way of coping while at the same time not being so rich that it overrides, subordinates and weakens the allegiance of those who hold to one or other of the plurality of strong moral outlooks characteristic of liberalism.

One way of looking at this, which is derived from John Rawls and has been elaborated much more by John Gray in *Two Faces of Liberalism*,[1] is what Rawls initially called a modus vivendi argument. In his work, *Political Liberalism*,[2] Rawls situates his account of modus vivendi in the context of regimes of toleration that emerged gradually and as a result of the decimating effects of the wars of religion in Europe immediately following the Reformation. Political, economic and moral exhaustion led to the development of a politics of mutual toleration of opposing views, a willingness to live and let live, or what Rawls calls a 'modus vivendi'. A modus vivendi regime is based ultimately not on grounds of general moral principle, but on deliberation and prudential calculation. The parties to a modus vivendi do not have to accept the value or truth of the other person's point of view. They do not have to accept general philosophical arguments in favour of mutual toleration. Rather, a modus vivendi is based upon the idea that, in the context in which there has been strife as the result of commitments to incommensurable moral values and comprehensive religious doctrines, it will dawn upon the protagonists of these opposing views that neither side is going to prevail and that articles of peace have to be drawn up. The approach is rooted in prudence in a calculation of the limits of the power of the groups that each side represents and the recognition that neither side is going to prevail. This does not lead to the adherence of the parties to a set of moral and political principles of an ideal sort which, as it were, transcend their particular differences, as for example an adherence to a philosophically based doctrine of toleration might. Rather, mutual tolerance is founded on the idea of prudential calculation rather than a Millian idea that we need mutual toleration in order to arrive at deeper and richer conceptions of the truth. Each side might think that it knows what the truth is and the practice of toleration for them is not grounded in some such general doctrine or principle of toleration. Theirs is a toleration of difference arising out of a recognition of the limits of power and mutual vulnerability. It is Hobbesian rather than Millian in inspiration. It may, of course, be possible to believe that while a modus vivendi may be brought into being by prudential calculation, it may over time transform itself into a more principled doctrine in which toleration becomes accepted on the basis of some sort of independent principle rather than from prudential calculation from within different and incompatible doctrines and outlooks. Take the case of Northern Ireland, for example. The Good Friday Agreement might be thought of as a modus vivendi agreement in the initial sense as born out of prudence against a background of the limits of power. It is unlikely that the main protagonists had come to see the justice and value of their opponents' points of view and committed themselves to an agreement based upon such a positive outlook.

Nevertheless, over time, it may well be that a prudential modus vivendi will provide the background for a more positive and principled commitment to a more liberal and tolerant political order.

If one wished to look at a modus vivendi justification for liberalism in a positive light, it would be worth stressing that it allows each group in the plurality of groups making up such a society to maintain the integrity of its belief system so long as their claims, even if they are of a monistic sort – namely that ideally society should be ordered according to the principles of that group – constrained by a recognition of the demands of prudence. That is the only principle on which they have to be agreed. There is no requirement that beliefs are made subordinate by some more ideal liberal principle, such as the principle of autonomy or of equality. Over time, co-existence between such groups based on prudential grounds might grow into something more, but that would be a matter for historical evolution not of some kind of antecedent moral and philosophical commitment to ideal principles. Such ideals may emerge but there is no guarantee of that. If they do emerge, however, it will be as the result of a process of evolution of ideas and practices within groups rather than some kind of independent commitment to a framework of moral principle antecedently constraining the behaviour of such groups.

On the face of it, this might look to be a good political justification of liberalism and one that makes no metaphysical or ideal claims which could weaken the allegiance of groups, within the plurality of groups, to such ideal principles, if they were to be regarded as fundamental to liberalism. This benign picture, however, leads to very considerable doubts. The first doubt, which has been well articulated by Rawls[3] and Larmore,[4] is that, since a modus vivendi is not in fact based upon an agreement of principle but rather on considerations of prudence, it will be unstable. This is because a modus vivendi is arrived at as the result of groups recognizing that they do not have the power to get their own way. As participants in the modus vivendi, they have not abandoned their ambitions for their belief system and in particular the ambition that such beliefs should shape the agenda of public policy; rather, members of such groups have reasoned that they will not have the power to attain this goal in prevailing circumstances. However, the whole point is that such circumstances might change. A particular group based upon some particular comprehensive religious doctrine may become more powerful, whether numerically or in other ways. In such circumstances, they will no longer have prudential reasons for constraining their behaviour and their campaigning. Because, as it were, the modus vivendi position has not required them to internalize liberal principles, such an increase in power may give them every incentive to break the terms of a modus vivendi agreement. It might be argued that this is what has happened with the 'Moral Majority' in the USA. Religious groupings do not feel constrained by an attachment to modus vivendi arrangements when their power increases. The counter-argument to this is that, as I argued earlier, it is quite possible that modus vivendi arrangements will lead to a greater sense of respect and tolerance for the other person's point of view. There is no necessity about this, however, and I think that it has to be conceded that the alternative is just as likely to happen when power increases.

It is also argued by critics that a modus vivendi will be very difficult to sustain in hard cases of public policy and therefore that something more substantial in the way of agreement on principle is necessary in such circumstances. Take, for example, the case of abortion or gay rights. It is inevitable that these are going to be major issues in public policy and they are also issues over which those who adhere to comprehensive metaphysical and religious doctrines may well have very strong views. A liberal polity is likely to protect the woman's right to choose in the case of abortion, and equal rights say regarding the age of consent, or marriage rights in the case of lesbians and gays. Indeed, this may well extend to equal rights of access to IVF treatment and rights of adoption. Religious groups may well object to this and will not conceptualize the issue in terms of rights and equality at all. A polity based upon a modus vivendi would be likely to require such groups to treat their moral and metaphysical objections to such practices as matters of private belief such that, while within their own religious community such behaviour may be the subject of censure and discipline, nevertheless these beliefs should not affect public policy. Here, in the view of critics, lies the weakness of a modus vivendi arrangement. The religious believer will not want to treat her religious convictions as matters of private belief and will have no reason of principle at all so to do, since the modus vivendi has not required some kind of principled attachment to ideas such as rights and equality. The only reason for constraining belief rests on prudence, and the considerations that dictate a prudential approach to questions may change with a possible increase in power on the part of the group.

So, it might be argued, a modus vivendi approach, despite its undoubted attractions in the sense of not making much in the way of demands in terms of assent to liberal principles, nevertheless will not do. The reason lies in precisely what looks, superficially, to be its strength, namely its lack of demand in terms of principle. As we have seen, this is likely to be a fatal flaw

164

unless very favourable circumstances lead a modus vivendi to develop into a more principled set of arrangements as the result of learning mutual respect and the positive value of toleration, but this still concedes the point, namely that there has to be an agreement of principle, however that is arrived at, and that there is no certainty that a modus vivendi will in fact lead to that. So we need to look elsewhere.

John Rawls has provided an alternative perspective which is well worth exploring, namely the idea of an overlapping consensus. Like the modus vivendi approach, Rawls's position here stresses that the idea of an overlapping consensus has to be seen as a political and not a metaphysical doctrine. He shares with the advocates of the modus vivendi the view that there are major dangers in liberalism itself being seen as a comprehensive and ideal or perfectionist doctrine. That is to say, it is a position with a thick moral content of its own focused on ideals like autonomy, equality and rights which are rooted in a comprehensive moral doctrine. This would make political liberalism one of the contending comprehensive doctrines in a pluralist society and therefore would make liberalism part of the problem of pluralism, not its solution. At the same time he accepts, indeed he is the author of the view, that a modus vivendi position demands far too little in the way of principle. So, how to develop a conception of political liberalism which can provide a principled basis for a liberal political order which can command the allegiance of groups within a society marked by what Rawls repeatedly calls the fact of pluralism, while at the same time not rooting that principle or set of principles in its own comprehensive moral and metaphysical doctrine?

Rawls's much discussed answer lies in the idea of an overlapping consensus. The idea here is that the institutions of a liberal society and debates on public policy within those institutions should depend upon an overlapping consensus between the plurality of groups that make up a late modern democratic society. His suggestion is that adherents to comprehensive doctrines such as religious believers may recognize that, while they hold their beliefs to be true, it is nevertheless perfectly reasonable for other people to disagree with them. In these circumstances they will be led to accept that such beliefs cannot be the sole foundation for public institutions and public policy. The reasons for action which are wholly internal to a belief system cannot form the basis of public reason if it is accepted that it is reasonable for other people to disagree with those reasons for action. Hence the job of public reason is to arrive through deliberation at a set of principles and policies which do not rely on any specific comprehensive doctrine but which can be agreed upon via an overlapping consensus between those who adhere to reasonably comprehensive doctrines. That is to say, those who, while accepting those doctrines, regard it as reasonable to disagree with them. This is how Rawls describes this political conception of a liberal polity:

> in such a consensus each of the comprehensive philosophical, religious and moral doctrines accepts justice as fairness in its own way; that is, each comprehensive doctrine from within its own point of view, is led to accept the public reasons of justice specified by justice as fairness. We might say that they recognise its concepts, principles and virtues as theorems, as it were, at which their several views coincide. But this does not make these points of coincidence any less moral or reduce them to mere means. For, in general, these concepts, principles and virtues are accepted by each as belonging to a more comprehensive philosophical, religious, or moral doctrine.[5]

So the doctrine of the overlapping consensus in Rawls's view avoids the basic instability of the modus vivendi or the Hobbesian solution while also avoiding making liberalism itself a thick comprehensive doctrine, as, in Rawls's view, Kant's commitment to autonomy and Mill's commitment to individuality involve. Hence, is it possible to regard this as the solution to the problem with which we started, of how to secure the allegiance and commitment of individuals and groups maintaining strong comprehensive doctrines to the principles of a liberal order or justice as fairness as Rawls calls it? Rawls's theory can only work if it does not surreptitiously invoke thick moral principles of its own which would be embodied in comprehensive doctrines. There are some doubts, it must be said, on that score.

The first relates to Rawls's characterization of the parties to the agreement by the overlapping consensus in the context of pluralism. He argues on this point as follows: 'The basic intuitive idea is that in virtue of what we might call their moral powers, and the powers of reason, thought and judgement connected with these powers, we say that persons are free. And in virtue of having these powers to a requisite degree to be fully cooperating members of society, we say that persons are equal.'[6]

Now hereby hangs a problem, in that the characterization of the parties to the project of arriving at justice as fairness by means of the overlapping consensus already invokes two distinct moral categories, the detailed interpretation of which might be disputed within comprehensive doctrines. Not only that, however, because Rawls has placed at the start of his argument two basic liberal principles or values, namely liberty and equality. He makes it clear that these are to act as constraints on the achievement of the overlapping consensus, as when he argues as follows:

The fair terms of social cooperation are conceived as agreed to by those engaged in it, that is by free and equal persons as citizens who are born into the society in which they lead their lives. But their agreement, like any other valid agreement, must be entered into under appropriate conditions. In particular, these conditions must situate free and equal persons fairly and must not allow some persons greater bargaining advantages than others. Further, threats of force and coercion, deception and fraud, and so on, must be excluded.[7]

So Rawls is giving priority to two basic liberal principles as constraints that can act on what can be negotiated as part of an overlapping consensus. Therefore there is an antecedent commitment to two liberal principles before, as it were, the process of arriving at consensus gets under way. This could be defended in one of two ways. The first would be to say that these two principles are part of a true comprehensive doctrine which should constrain the emergence of the overlapping consensus. This, however, is not a position open to Rawls to take if he is to defend the political rather than metaphysical nature of his liberalism. The second alternative would be to say that Rawls is not trying to produce any sort of foundationalist account for a liberal society but rather to think through the consequences of what are in fact central principles of existing liberal and democratic societies, namely liberty and equality. These are not to be considered as part of a metaphysical theory of liberalism but as implicit in the moral and political practices of a liberal society. It is, of course, most consistent with Rawls's view to take this latter reading, but, at the same time, it then rather fails to address the question with which we started, namely why those with comprehensive doctrines which do not necessarily put liberty or equality into a significant place in their hierarchy of values should feel allegiance to a political order which does. In the same way as Rawls's *A Theory of Justice* put the right before the good, so justice as fairness and the idea of the overlapping consensus put liberty and equality as prior constraints on the sort of agreement about justice as fairness that might arise out of an overlapping consensus. The point about comprehensive doctrines, even reasonable ones in Rawls's sense, is that they are very likely to give a conception of the good a higher role than the right, a conception of virtue a more central place than individual liberty and procedural equality.

In addition, it can also be argued that Rawls quite explicitly at one point in his argument appeals to his conception of justice as a comprehensive doctrine when trying to deal exactly with the point with which I started this essay, when he argues as follows in his chapter on 'The Idea of an Overlapping Consensus' in *Political Liberalism*:

167

> Nevertheless, in affirming a political conception of justice we may eventually have to assert at least certain aspects of our own comprehensive (by no means necessarily fully comprehensive), religious or philosophical doctrine. This happens whenever someone insists, for example, that certain questions are so fundamental that to ensure their being rightly settled entails civil strife. The religious salvation of those holding a particular religion, or indeed the salvation of a whole people, may be said to depend on it. At this point we may have no alternative but to deny this and to assert the kind of thing that we hoped to avoid. But the aspects of our view that we assert should not go beyond what is necessary for the political aim of consensus.[8]

Now the case that Rawls cites may seem a rather desperate one – civil strife – calling for desperate measures, namely the assertion of at least part of a comprehensive doctrine and it might be argued that Rawls's inconsistency is justifiable at this point. It is, however, far from clear that Rawls's problem here is not more general. Those who hold comprehensive religious doctrines, the integrity of which entails some kind of attempt to reshape the public realm and public policy, will be required by the principles of justice as fairness to treat these beliefs as private beliefs. Now is there any way of ultimately justifying this constraint other than either the exercise of Hobbesian power (the consensus requires this and therefore your beliefs have to be treated as private) or metaphysical liberalism (that your comprehensive beliefs are not compatible with the central moral status of liberty, autonomy or equality or whatever, and therefore you must hold your beliefs as private beliefs)? In the first case the consensus is maintained, but not on grounds of a principle acceptable to those within such a comprehensive doctrine; in the second case there is an argument of principle but it is not in terms of a principle or set of principles that those people would regard as salient. It does not look as though the overlapping consensus strategy will be able to address the problem without moving to one or other end of the spectrum between a modus vivendi and a metaphysical theory – precisely what it wishes to avoid.

There are other problems too which are perhaps worth adverting to in the context of a book of essays on theology. The first is to go back to what Rawls calls reasonable comprehensive doctrines because it is these doctrines which will contribute to the overlapping consensus. So how does Rawls describe such doctrines? In *Political Liberalism* Rawls argues as follows:

> The doctrine any reasonable person affirms is but one reasonable doctrine among others. In affirming it, a person, of course, believes it to be true, or else reasonable as the case may be. This is not in general unreasonable to affirm any one

of a number of reasonable comprehensive doctrines ... Beyond this, reasonable persons will think it unreasonable to use political power, should they possess it, to repress comprehensive views that are not unreasonable though different from their own.[9]

This point is not, however, as benign as it seems from the standpoint of an adherent to a comprehensive doctrine. Rawls wants to distinguish between a reasonable person who holds a comprehensive doctrine in the way described and a sceptic, since scepticism cannot be the foundation of justice as fairness and a liberal polity. However, in the case of religious beliefs particularly, is it in fact possible to distinguish between holding religious beliefs in this reasonable way and scepticism? To elucidate this point we need to look at other work, since Rawls does not discuss this point to any great degree. The issue of the relationship between belief and the individual has been well discussed by Thomas Nagel and Brian Barry and in a way that bears upon the issue of the possible role of comprehensive doctrines in relation to public policy in a liberal society. Nagel argues the case for what he calls 'epistemological restraint'. The claim is that it is perfectly consistent for an individual to accept the truth of some religious doctrine while still accepting that it would be wrong to make it the basis of public policy in a society in which some would reject it. Nagel thinks that the basis for this claim is what he calls epistemological restraint and that this in turn depends crucially upon a distinction between public and private. He argues as follows: 'We accept a kind of epistemological division between the private and public domain: in certain contexts I am constrained to consider my beliefs merely as beliefs rather than as truths, however convinced I may be that they are true, and that I know it. This is not the same thing as scepticism.'[10]

According to Nagel, this distinction between public and private assessment of beliefs and their implications is partly a matter of the nature of the evidence, and partly a matter of morality. He argues that: 'the distinction between what is needed to justify belief and what is needed to justify the employment of political power depends upon a higher standard of objectivity which is ethically based.' This ethical dimension is linked to the idea that, in the public realm, political deliberation depends upon the idea of arriving at a judgement on a public or communal basis: 'it must be possible to present to others the basis of your own beliefs so that once you have done so, they have what you have and can arrive at a judgement on the same basis.' This is very close to Rawls's idea of public reason. Nagel, however, wants to go deeper into the question of whether or not this implies the same thing as scepticism towards one's deepest convictions. He draws a crucial distinction between an internal attitude towards one's beliefs and an external or impersonal one – a distinction which does a lot to illuminate Rawls's idea of holding a comprehensive view in a reasonable manner which includes that it is reasonable for others to disagree with you. Nagel makes the point as follows: 'The idea is that when we look at certain of our convictions from outside, however justified they may be from within, the appeal to that truth must be seen merely as an appeal to our beliefs and should be treated as such unless those beliefs can be shown to be justifiable from an impersonal standpoint.'[11]

So epistemological restraint constrains the sorts of beliefs that can enter the public domain and it is also different from scepticism. This last point is vital in respect of Rawls because it is no part of his project to require that people should hold their beliefs sceptically, indeed it would be highly illiberal for Rawls to seek to dictate the terms on which a person should hold his or her beliefs. However, it is not at all clear that the doctrine of epistemological restraint can in fact be differentiated from scepticism. The central point here has been well made by Brian Barry: 'A partisan of epistemological restraint would suggest that I might be absolutely convinced of the veridical nature of this revelation while nevertheless admitting that others could reasonably reject my evidence. But is this really plausible? If I concede that I have no way of convincing others, should that not also dent my own certainty?'[12]

If Barry's criticism is correct, as I think that it is, and if something like Nagel's view underpins Rawls's idea of reasonableness in holding comprehensive doctrines, then it is hard not to accept that Rawls is requiring people to adopt beliefs in a sceptical and detached way. If this is a condition of a comprehensive doctrine being drawn into the overlapping consensus then either this requires an exercise of power and his theory veers back to the Hobbesian position and a modus vivendi or such an approach is rooted in moral principle, in which case liberalism becomes a comprehensive doctrine as a way of requiring beliefs salient to the public realm being held in one way rather than another.

It therefore has to be doubted whether Rawls's theory, ingenious and humane as it is, can settle the question with which we started, and if that is so and given the drawbacks of the modus vivendi approach, it is perhaps necessary to see whether there might not be a more productive position to be found in treating liberalism as a kind of comprehensive doctrine and arguing the question of the relationship between liberalism and allegiance from that point of view. The problem with this in terms of the question with which we started is obvious, namely if liberal values such as liberty and equality are to be seen as embedded in a comprehensive doctrine, what is it that can give liberalism moral and political priority in a world of competing comprehensive doctrines? Posed in that way, I do not think there can be an adequate answer to the question, but there is perhaps a different approach that can be taken, which I can only really sketch in this context, although there are ways in which the project I shall outline has been taken further. The project is to see whether there is not some kind of moral and political space for reasoning about the nature of goods which have to be presupposed as goods by any comprehensive doctrine that can be intelligible. That is to say, are there any general or generic goods, perhaps corresponding to basic needs, which would have to be acknowledged as preconditions of any comprehensive doctrine, even if adherents of those doctrines may not explicitly recognize those goods in the moral framework of the comprehensive doctrine? Before going further, let me take an analogy. It might be argued, for example, that truth-telling has to be recognized as a general precondition of any language since, if people did not tend to tell the truth, how could language be transmitted from one generation to another? Truth must be a basic value in speaking even if in particular articulated moral codes and comprehensive doctrines it was not recognized explicitly. It still has to be presupposed in order to make sense of teaching and learning language in general and of the teaching and learning of the language of this moral code in particular. So are there any general preconditions for the exercise of moral belief, however divergent these beliefs may turn out to be, and if there are, could this not provide a basis for thinking about a common life in the context of pluralism and incommensurable moral beliefs? In a way, this approach reverses the direction of Rawls's approach where, through the overlapping consensus idea, the aim has been to construct a common set of values as a result of the plurality of reasonably comprehensive doctrines. The approach that I shall explore starts at the other end. Are there any goods which have to be recognized as generic goods by any moral code, whatever it may turn out to be?

The philosopher who has most pursued this line of enquiry is Alan Gewirth, in a range of extraordinarily rigorous writings and, in particular, *Reason and Morality*[13] and *The Community of Rights*.[14] Gewirth focuses on a very simple point, namely that, whatever the diversity of goods may be, any moral doctrine is going to want the adherents to that doctrine to pursue those goods. That is to say, any moral code or doctrine has to find a place for the idea of action, otherwise the idea of goods which we do not want to pursue sounds too paradoxical to be a moral code. So Gewirth now asks, are there any general goods which are preconditions of action, such as whatever particular goods specific actions are directed towards realizing (in the same way as truth is a precondition of making sense of speaking and learning a language)? He argues that there are indeed basic or generic conditions of action and agency – by agency here is meant only the pursuit of a moral ideal or set of ideals whatever it or they may turn out to be. Another way of putting this point, in a more familiar way, perhaps, although it is not exactly congruent with Gewirth's view, is to ask whether there are any basic needs that have to be satisfied before an individual can act in accordance with her moral beliefs whatever they may turn out to be. This is the position I have tried to explore in a number of publications since 1980.[15]

This way of posing the problem also makes a possible link with some updated theories of natural law, because after all we are really talking about whether there are any goods that belong to human nature as such, irrespective of what specific goods an individual might wish to pursue as a member of a particular moral community.

I shall pursue the philosophical idiom in which Gewirth makes this argument, when he claims that there are two basic goods which have to be seen as the presuppositions of any sort of action. They are freedom and well-being. It is important to keep in mind that Gewirth is not advocating these as basic goods from within a liberal moral framework, but rather as preconditions of any moral framework which either requires or encourages people to act on the precepts of that moral position. So how does he get to freedom and well-being as basic goods, and can they be specified any further without having to introduce into the argument resources drawn from within a particular moral framework?

Gewirth argues that in moral contexts the salient features of action are their voluntariness and their intentionality: 'By an action's being voluntary or free I mean that its performance is under the agent's control in that he unforcedly chooses to act as he does, knowing the relevant proximate circumstances of his action. By an action's being purposive or intentional I mean that the agent acts for some end or purpose that constitutes his reason for acting; this purpose may consist in the action itself or in something to be achieved by the action.'[16]

These are the generic features of action and to them correspond generic goods and, in particular, freedom and well-being. Now before we go on to analyse that transition in the argument we need to stop and look at a pretty obvious objection to the point made in the above quotation. The critic will say that the emphasis on free action as a precondition of morality betrays already that Gewirth is smuggling in a liberal principle in his account of the generic features of action and a principle which may not be a feature of all moral codes within which action takes place. This means that Gewirth's argument takes us back to seeing liberalism as a presupposed comprehensive and perfectionist doctrine rather than as a set of principles that can arbitrate between such doctrines. Gewirth, however, rejects this and his reasons for doing so are not particularly complex. He argues that, of course, it is possible for moral precepts to urge conformity to various social roles or institutions and indeed may even assume that such conformity is already being exhibited in the behaviour of the person to whom the precepts are addressed. However, he argues that the whole point of having the precepts must be to encourage and reinforce the keeping of the precepts in question and to ward off potential disobedience. Hence he argues: 'Thus the precepts assume that alternative behaviour may be open to the persons addressed so that, to this extent, their behaviour is under their control ... In any case inaction, when it is intentionally engaged in by persons who dispositionally control their behaviour, is a form of action.'[17]

Hence, for Gewirth, voluntariness or freedom is a necessary or generic feature of moral action, whatever the moral code may be within which an individual acts, since it is only possible to make sense of the role of the precepts of that moral code on the assumption that the agent has some degree of voluntary control over behaviour. This does not mean that freedom is elevated to be an explicit moral principle within a particular comprehensive or religious doctrine any more than truth, despite its being a generic condition of language. Nor does it mean that this sense of freedom is brought into play from a comprehensive moral doctrine of liberalism. It does mean that one cannot make sense of a basic human capacity, namely *to act*, without such a generic feature of action.

If this is so, and if there are generic goods relating to these two generic features of action, then Gewirth has made a major step towards solving the problem with which we started. If liberalism as a perfectionist doctrine demands too much of adherents of other comprehensive doctrines to be a stable foundation for a liberal polity and if modus vivendi and overlapping consensus strategies do not work, then focusing attention on the types of goods that have to be in place to meet the generic features of action which have to be presupposed by any moral or religious code can be seen as a significant alternative. So how do the generic goods of agency and action relate to these two generic features, namely freedom and well-being?

The answer in a rather telescoped form, which is all that I can do here, goes as follows. First of all, there are negative and positive aspects of freedom, as we begin to unpack what is meant by freedom as a necessary condition of action. The negative aspects will be freedom from coercion of various sorts: assault, interference, rape, etc., all the typical negative freedoms which liberals approve of but which for Gewirth are not rooted in a liberal comprehensive doctrine. It will, however, also include aspects of positive freedom, resources and opportunities to make such negative freedoms effective, and these will include physical integrity, food, clothing and shelter – the whole range of goods which are the physical and psychological preconditions of purposive action. This will include among psychological features a sense of mental equilibrium and confidence in the attainment of goals. Since these goods are necessary conditions of action (or, in other language, basic needs), they will at least be valued instrumentally by any agent who reflects on what are the preconditions necessary for attaining the particular moral goals that she happens to have.

There is, of course, a great deal more elaboration that has to take place before these general and rather thin ideas can become relevant resources for the justification of public policy. If, however, the general approach is right, as I think that it is, then it means that there has to be some common framework of values between different moral communities in society and, therefore, a basis for discussion and mutual deliberation. This, it seems to me, is a major gain and one that does not make the goods in question part of one of the sets of contested comprehensive doctrines in contention in the pluralistic space provided by a liberal society. The goods are rather preconditions of those doctrines. Equally, this common ground is not built up out of an overlapping consensus which may have to smuggle liberal principles into the argument for it to work; nor does the argument rest on claims of prudence. It does, however, have to be accepted that in order to get from a thin set of basic needs, or basic generic goods of agency, there has to be a process of dialogue to make an account of what will satisfy these needs or characterize these goods, but that is a political rather than a philosophical task. This may seem to be a small gain, but given a lot of loose talk about the degree of moral diversity and incommensurability within a late modern society, to engage in the task of identifying a set of necessary generic conditions for moral codes or comprehensive doctrines, whether these conditions are seen as needs or goods of agency, is a positive gain for humanity.

Notes

1 John Gray, *Two Faces of Liberalism* (Oxford: Polity Press, 2000).
2 John Rawls, *Political Liberalism* (New York: Columbia University Press, 1993).
3 See detailed references to Rawls's work below.
4 Charles Larmore, *The Morals of Modernity* (Cambridge: Cambridge University Press, 1996).
5 John Rawls, 'Justice as fairness: political not metaphysical', *Philosophy and Public Affairs*, 14(3) (1985): 247.
6 *Ibid.*, p. 233.
7 *Ibid.*, p. 235.
8 John Rawls, *Political Liberalism*, p. 152.
9 *Ibid.*, p. 60.
10 Thomas Nagel, 'Moral conflict and political legitimacy', *Philosophy and Public Affairs*, 16 (1987): 227.
11 Thomas Nagel, 'Moral conflict and political legitimacy', p. 230.
12 Brian Barry, *Justice as Impartiality* (Oxford: Clarendon Press, 1995), p. 179.
13 Alan Gewirth, *Reason and Morality* (Chicago, IL: Chicago University Press, 1978).
14 Alan Gewirth, *The Community of Rights* (Chicago, IL: Chicago University Press, 1996).
15 See particularly Raymond Plant's chapters in Raymond Plant, Harry Lesser and Peter Taylor-Gooby, *Political Philosophy and Social Welfare* (London: Routledge & Kegan Paul, 1980).
16 Alan Gewirth, *Reason and Morality*, p. 27.
17 *Ibid.*, p. 28.

Part III

Changing Contexts – Globalization's Impact

Chapter 11

Public Theology and Political Economy in a Globalizing Era[1]

MAX L. STACKHOUSE

The Issue

Globalization is, in some senses, new, and is changing our ideas of what is genuinely public. Of course, some people think of 'public' as governmental and globalization as the international spread of capitalism under Western political auspices. These views, however, are too narrow, and current political and economic changes are derivative of other dynamics. The larger reality is that *the whole world is becoming one place*, an inclusive field of spaces, peoples and activities. To grasp the meaning of this requires a viewpoint that transcends the world itself, one that is neither new nor distinctively produced by Western capitalism. Indeed, it is the other way around: a universalistic view that relativizes particular contexts has slowly produced what is now before us. The Hebrew prophets knew long ago of a single created realm where all peoples lived under a divine law and could live toward a divine end. Parallel cosmological ideas were present, to some degree, in Taoist, Hindu, Buddhist and Western pagan thought, although usually without the minority notion of a Creator God as the source and norm of the reality they studied and honoured. Thus, only some have had a sense of a reality beyond the way things were. Even the view that modified the global sensibilities in the West – the idea of one humanity in one world, which the one true, triune God created, commanded and commissioned – is old and in principle universal, even if it is not acknowledged everywhere. It points to a reality more universal, more globally encompassing than any naturalistic *kosmos* or *oikoumene* could be. In brief, God is in globalization; and that is why theology must be public and interested in global issues.[2]

The 'ization' part of 'globalization', however, suggests not only that the whole can be conceived as a single reality, a mathematical unity, an

179

ontological whole, a metaphysical entity with a purpose, a cosmopolitan universe or a divine reality that transcends the earth itself, but that an historical process is taking place whereby some different whole comes into being. Not the repeated return to origins, but a turn to something new. The 'already' and 'old', indeed, the *kosmos* and *oikoumene* themselves, are incomplete, flawed, unfinished or distorted (even if indispensable to existence and sufficiently ordered to exist). Thus, a 'not yet', something 'new', is required, and that too must be rooted in God. When the two terms are joined, we find that the result points to a possible systemic alteration of what already is, in a manner and degree that brings a *novum* that has not been before. The New Testament conveys just such views with an idea of 'the world' as something that is created by God and thus good, but which is fallen and thus is something to which we are not to conform. Yet, 'the world' is also something that God so loved that it is being redeemed, and those who know God are sent into it not to conform to it, but to aid in its process of redemption and transformation, even as it groans in travail toward a new creation and a new civilization, the Reign of God which shall be in a New Jerusalem.

Those who receive the vision of this promised reign of God are to employ every moral means to make it actual. This cluster of convictions is central; and, where strongest, the intentional restructuring of the world, selves and society by planning, technology and social transformation became a moral duty.[3] That is a second reason why a public theology is required as we consider globalization, for this cluster of convictions stands deep behind the contemporary dynamics of globalization. In our understandings of creation and redemption, we can see God in globalization. Indeed, at the World Missionary Conference of 1910, the great scholar of Indian religions, J. N. Farquhar, said: 'We have entered a new era ... The nations have become one city; we buy each other's goods, ... we think each other's thoughts, ... we begin to hear the music of humanity.' He failed to see, however, how the power generated by such motifs could also be distorted by sin into colonialism and imperialism, and how much the reaction against these could also spur reactionary movements. Mixing peoples, cultures and religions offended those who attached sacred meaning to their own 'blood and soil'. And the technologies that had made the new internationalism possible could generate both new possibilities of destructive weaponry and new methods of creative manufacture, which in turn generated uprooted workers. The 'music of humanity', of which Farquhar spoke, was soon disrupted by a cacophony of military marches accompanied by the percussion of bombs in history's shortest century, 1914–89. Yet, the forecast turned out to be partly true: the twin enemies of democracy, human rights, economic progress and the universal faith – the pagan right and the secular left – were defeated by struggles to contain them as history became increasingly planetary. Now, no culture can be entirely self-contained and no state can be fully sovereign, while religion is in resurgence everywhere. This is the new shape of globalization.

What we are seeing was anticipated by the radical Dutch theologian, Arendt van Leeuwen (who was later discredited in many circles because of his turn toward Marxism). In *Christianity in World History*,[4] his best work, he saw the gradual adoption of democracy, technological means of production and human rights by the East and the South as evidence of the spread, not of a secular or neo-pagan West, but of socially incarnated theological themes, of which many exporters and enthusiastic importers of these ideas were unaware. These developments are, he said, inconceivable without the background beliefs of Christian theology, which would eventually have to be acknowledged by those who adopted them.[5] Globalization, in other words, is a by-product of a kind of pre-evangelization, increasingly being adopted by much of the world in practice.

The context in which we now think, work, pray and seek to carry out our convictions is a comprehending context, built out of this history. It includes many specific locales and subcultures with a dynamic pluralism like that of the early Church. Life, as Robertson has said, is now 'glocal', simultaneously global and local, ecumenical and particular, catholic and congregational, in part because we live in a period of the 'compression of the world', which is not only multipolar politically (with temporary hegemonies which others co-operate to restrain), multicultural, but increasingly linked technologically, economically, morally and in terms of the flows of information and population migrations – although some, to be sure, are still left out.[6]

What are we to think about such a situation theologically? A team of eighteen scholars at the Center of Theological Inquiry at Princeton – Protestant and Catholic, men and women, some more liberal and some more conservative, all with roots or extended involvements in the world's societies or cultures – have been seeking to answer that question.[7] Of course, each scholar has brought his or her own stamp to this effort, but as co-ordinator of the project, I have my own view of the whole, one based on a 'public theological' exploration into four areas much neglected in contemporary thought:

1. A perspectival shift from 'orders of creation' to dynamic *Spheres* of relative sovereignty.

2. A theological analysis of global *Powers* – Principalities, Authorities, Thrones and Dominions.
3. A comparative investigation of how *Religion Shapes Civilizations*.
4. A recovery of covenantal thought as a mode of *Public Theology* for global civil society.

The Spheres

The idea that we live in various 'spheres of life', each having its own sense of justice and its own set of purposes, is rooted in the older medieval notion of the 'estates', as modulated by Reformation notions of the 'orders of creation'. These traditions held that, from the beginning, God established certain 'forms' in which humans are to live – generally stated as familial, political, economic and religious. After all, people are sexual, social, material and spiritual by nature, and each area of life may become distorted if not channelled into divinely predetermined patterns. This onto-theocratic view has parallels in the classical Hindu texts, the *Artha Shastra* (adapted also by Buddhism) and in other classical traditions, such as the 'rectified relationships' of Confucianism, and the interlock of familial order, political authority and religious duties in Islam (all of which saw economics under the control of all three areas). The variant shape of each view left distinctive legacies in the cultural genetic codes of all societies formed in it, whether all now affirm these traditions or not.[8] Indeed, those who struggle against them find themselves defined by that against which they contend.

The Western version of this ontocratic view was fatefully challenged by Christians on theological grounds which also generated new ranges of human association. Movements for the independency of religion from familial, political and cultural control opened the way as well to the formation of social spheres that could also be independent of the traditional threefold pattern.[9] In the past century, the idea was developed, in different ways, by both theologians and sociologists of religion.[10] The idea of 'spheres' implies that, while some areas of life may be rooted in creation, others may be rooted in the functional requirements of human living in complex societies. These demand the formation of viable institutions that cannot be controlled by family, regime or traditional religion. These spheres also change in number and contours in history, and they expand or contract in role and importance depending on the wider dynamics of a society. The classic theological traditions did not clearly see that economics, or, for that matter, culture, science and technology, are spheres distinct from family, regime or religion.

Most important for our topic is the fact that the corporation was developed, for it became the home for other activities besides the traditional three 'orders'. The formation of the corporation is decisive. It is seldom recognized, however, that the root of the Western corporation is the monastery, which was outside the family, state and the traditional religio-cultural matrix of daily life. As Berman has demonstrated, the monastery in a long history won the right to own property and engage in trade for its sustenance without being subject to inheritance laws or to control by king (or even bishop, in many circumstances). The idea is also later applied to the university, the hospital and the independent towns where a citizenry had their own compacts for government but no prince. Protestants, in fact, abolished the monasteries, and applied the legal notion of the *persona ficta*, the corporative body that could be voluntarily joined or left, and be self-governing and self-sustaining by its capacity to create wealth to aid the commonwealth. Later this body was coupled with theological ideas of stewardship and trusteeship. The legal history of the corporation is the repository of this part of what is now the world's religiously shaped economic history.[11]

Other areas were affected. When 'art troupes' were incorporated, dance, music, painting and theatre moved out from family-centred village, court-centred salon, and from worship-centred temple, to the commercial stage (or museum). Then 'culture' becomes 'independent' – a sphere governed by standards other than those of family lineage, political interests or traditional religion.[12] And when production and distribution shifted from household, palace and temple to factory, market and transport firms, economic activity became independent of the family's purse, the king's coffers and the priest's treasury. Similarly, education developed various sciences that cannot simply be faithful to the quest for truth if it remains only an instrument of familial lore, state ideology or religious orthodoxy. And, as many cultures have seen, if an economy is only run by the family, relationships of love and loyalty become calculative; if it is only run by the state, economics becomes the means of political manipulation and economic prudence is distorted; and if it is only run by a religious group, faith becomes commercialized and greed is sanctified.

Of course, the status of family, regime and religion remains important, for people must be physically, politically, materially and spiritually formed. But the development of new spheres cannot be explained only as 'secular developments' – as if some intrinsic logic of history brought them into being. Rather they are products of 'providential development' – a kind of grace that operates beyond the common grace of creation. It develops within the world distorted by sin, but nevertheless provides for the cultivation of residual possibilities that exist in fallen humanity. This grace is especially given to those who are graced to know and follow the Lord of history as well as the divinely ordained orders of creation. Indeed, those who are so graced have a duty to offer them to the world. Understanding such matters not only helps us interpret social history; they are of great importance for public theology, for they help us redefine the publics that religion helps generate. In many areas, Christians have spoken out on matters of family, political and religious life; but the spheres of culture, technology and the corporation are seldom treated, certainly not positively.

I sketch such developments in our religious past because they illustrate the fact that in a complex, global environment, economic and cultural activities need their own institutional base. It also shows that institutional spheres are strange to some cultures, and demand both altered legal arrangements and new personal habits that are disturbing when they are introduced as a foreign novelty.[13] Moreover, it can be argued that something like a corporate mode of organization is potentially critical to the development of civil society in ways seldom recognized by ideologies of individualistic capitalism or of collectivistic class analysis.[14] Indeed, one can argue that they had to be developed because humans are not only sexual, political and religious creatures, they are also economic and cultural creatures, and that these spheres too need differentiated institutional homes, for each area of life has its own logic and needs its own spheres for the various gifts and potentialities of humanity to be most gracefully cultivated. Some, but only some, theologies recognized this and fomented such historically decisive developments. The ones that have are the ones that recognized that there are compelling Powers at work in the dynamics of nature and history and that these Powers need social frameworks for their stability and guidance.

The Powers

The social sciences are marvellous companions to the deeper and wider thought that public theology demands.[15] They must be preserved and developed further, even if they finally fail. And they do often fail for this reason: they cannot fully grasp, constrain, guide or bring into civilized order the Powers that are real in life, and which the Bible calls 'principalities', 'authorities', 'regencies' (the best translation of *thronos*, I think) or 'dominions' on their own terms. Understanding these can help us engage in critical analysis, and thus to protest against or to encourage resistance to the powers that be when they become unconstrained and unguided. But the social sciences

184

finally only analyse and oppose; they do not reintegrate and propose. That is because they do not believe that we live in a world of vital, intelligible, spiritual forces that were created to be obedient to divine laws and servants of divine purposes, but who have rebelled against these norms and become celebrants of their own potencies. Instead, they can recognize the 'social forces' of the world in a critical way, but they do not recognize that they are also 'demonic' in the sense that they can possess people and cultures, and are in need not only of fundamental conversion. The loss of a theological vocabulary to deal with such phenomena impoverishes our capacity to grasp social reality. (The primal religions, folk Catholicism and the neo-Evangelical and Pentecostal movements do deal with them, and often call for the spiritual reordering of life, although usually in terms seeming superstitious to modern thought. Still, they do so better than post-religious views, which is why many modern people are making a preferential option for these movements.)[16]

In most cultures and subcultures, people seem to live in a world of enchanted powers – a world populated by spirits that can be invoked, demons that must be exorcized or charms and curses that may be used. Elaborate systems develop around these concerns, and every religion has adherents who use even their faith in such ways, even if the 'high' literary clergy discourage it. To be sure, some 'super-personal forces of good and evil'[17] are identified in other terms by the modern social sciences. They speak of 'complexes' or 'stereotypes', of 'totems' and 'taboos', or of 'isms' and 'ideologies'. They come to dominate persons or peoples who do not know quite what they are or how they came to be dominant. Ordinary people also use terms from various religious traditions to express uncontrolled dynamics in their lives. 'Fate', 'fortune', 'karma', 'kismet', etc., suggest cosmic forces that seem to determine behaviour. Today, genetics, social location and economic interests are favoured explanations of the powers that make us do what we do. All tell us that we have no choice but to live out what these powers dictate. Concerns about the powers vary from person to person, culture to culture and epoch to epoch; but they are always present. Social analysis must face the issues they pose; but only a theological view can touch the depths needed.

The Principalities

In our time of globalization, a number of primal powers have become decisive for how we live, seeking to break down the barriers of 'estates', 'orders' or 'spheres'. For instance, 'Eros', the symbol of sensuality and sexual desire, is very personal and of intimate potency, but also a more pervasive power, often celebrated when it is outside family life. No family, no society could live without it for more than a generation. Yet, persons and cultures can become obsessed with it. It can command lives far beyond its own sphere, for it can prompt the betrayal of familial loyalties and social duty, seduce political authority, become an economic resource and simulate religious ecstasy.

Similarly, every society has to cope with the threats of violence within and from without. Indeed, organized force is required to hold those threats in check, and people skilled in the arts of war have long been necessary. But if it becomes independent of social control, obsessed by its own importance, blinded to the limits of its roles and tempted to think that it can rule life or save humanity, it becomes fed by a lust for power, and tends to deploy death and destruction. They generate a fanaticism that in turn renders the terrorism in our time – often unleashing unfettered reactions that become a terror too. This kind of power, as the ancients knew, is 'Mars', the idolatrous form of skilled violence to which rulers have built temples and monuments of great glory. It may be always necessary to have political rule capable of exercising coercive force, and Mars may save us from some perils; but it imperils us also. It needs institutional constraint beyond the power of any single regime or state.

'Mammon', too, distorts greatly. Money is a convenient means of calculating cost, value and gain. It may take all sorts of symbolic forms, from coinage, to paper, to electronic signals, and these symbols are important in life, now transportable by electronic signals around the world. It is better to have some reasonable access to these symbols than not – people die for lack of it, and people with more of it are freed from the calculations of subsistence to live for larger purposes. Yet, like Mars and Eros, money can easily become an idol. It becomes Mammon when it is taken as the means of salvation, the source of security or the purpose of life. The worship of 'the almighty buck' needs disciplined institutions of accountability. Yet, they can no longer be controlled by any nation state. In most societies, it is religion that holds these Powers together and under constraint. Dispatch with religion, or subordinate religion to any one of these Powers, and each of these goes its own way, no longer drawn into the disciplined solidarity that restrains and guides the Powers that we identify as the primal Principalities. Indeed, political science, psychology, economics and cultural studies have all developed sophisticated ways of explaining religion – even explaining it away, as really something else. But reality is the other way around. These Principalities are driven largely by unacknowledged moral and spiritual forces that have lost contact with their deepest roots. Thus, our social analysis in all the various fields has abandoned a theological dimension that has been banished from academia, or becomes dominated by forms of ideological fundamentalism that cannot grasp the depth of their own fields.

The Authorities

In our time, in our global environment, it is not only these perennial powers that are a potential problem. The cultivated, classic professions are among the most honoured and compelling Authorities in contemporary life. They are: Education (especially as guided by science), Law, Medicine and increasingly Technology, both as it has created the media and as it can be used to alter fundamentally the biosphere and genetic codes. These are among the most dramatic globalizing realities of our times. The experts for our world, especially when things go wrong, have increasingly become the professors and teachers, judges and lawyers, doctors and nurses, technologists and engineers. To these we must add the more recently 'professionalized' area of management, creating 'Regencies' in every sphere of the common life by the engineering of human relations for effective organizational accomplishment.[18] Each of these is driven by a distinctive 'spirit'. As mentioned above, they are not formed in the very structure of creation; but were formed providentially in history. They are not necessary to the minimal existence of society; but they are necessary for a viable complex society that is globally interactive. Moreover, they were formed and stamped by theologically framed history, although many practitioners of these fields today are largely unaware of it. The wider availability of education, much of it non-religious, some of it decidedly anti-religious, puts professionals in these spheres at points of high authority in the culture, but only rarely do they identify any connection between what they do and the history of the root doctrines that defined these vocations, even if many professionals have high standards of integrity and are personally religious. A major question is raised: can we expect generation after generation of specialists to sustain and refine the moral and spiritual bases of their fields if they do not have in mind any sense of rootage in divine law and purpose? Doubtful!

The Dominions

Both the ancient, perennial Principalities and the historic, cultivated Authorities are Powers that were rooted in theological developments that we identify with the common grace of creation or with the historic grace of providence. But they have often shed that influence, and become highly ambiguous in their relationship to God and to the service of humanity. Yet, the only power that has a chance of shaping, constraining, reforming and guiding these Powers is religion. And the decisive promise is in that kind of religion that represents in the context of contemporary life the genuine capacity to order these Powers morally and spiritually. Only this would allow us to know where and how to enter into these realities enough to transform them from the inside as well as constrain them from the outside.

But, of course, the question arises: which religion? The question is globally fateful and forces us again to take a new kind of look at the profound contributions and challenges of the great world religions. Christianity as a religion and, even more, as a theology and ethic that self-consciously clarifies the truth and justice of this religion's God, cannot fail to recognize that it is in simultaneous contention and co-operation with the world religions. The religions shape the Principalities everywhere, they support or challenge the Authorities and Regencies of every society and of international life. Wherever they have done so, they formed enduring 'Dominions' (realms where a Lord reigns). The great religions has each given a distinctive socio-cultural shape to the spheres wherein the Powers operate. They have provided the spiritual and moral architecture around which all these Powers were organized and by which they found their purpose defined.

These Powers can press us toward chaos and a shattering of meaning (as much postmodern argument has it) or they can be guided toward a new world civilization – if, that is, they have a guide that transcends and can morally alter them. This leads to the critical question: who shall have Dominion? And what kind of Dominion shall it be? If Christ (or Krishna, or Buddha or Allah) is not the Lord, will we not structure our global society according to some understanding of another Lord? Issues that have been debated for a generation about 'inclusivism, exclusivism or pluralism', suddenly take on dramatic meaning.[19] A 'clash of civilizations' based on religious differences, as Huntington suggests, may not be inevitable;[20] but the question of how we can and should form the moral architecture of a comprehending civilization is.[21] And it is, at least in part, a theological issue.

Hinduism, Buddhism, Confucianism, Islam, as well as, of course, Christianity have already, in varying degrees and with varying degrees of effectiveness, long engaged the Principalities and Authorities and developed theories of the various other Dominions. We have to ask what kinds of civilizations they lead to (in principle and in fact) and what kinds of justice, cultural and intellectual vitality and prosperity they foster. Yet to pose these questions can be explosive, and much study of religions is 'non-theological' and 'non-evaluative'. Indeed, the academic study of 'religion' – not unlike much popular opinion – wants the religions to be viewed as if they are all of equal worth and a matter of personal background or choice. However, this perspective hides the fact that each religion judges the kinds of persons the others tend to produce and how they live in marriage, politics, culture, economics and professional life – in short, how they make distinctive impacts on civilization. The question that this raises is whether we can identify any more valid or less valid forms of religious belief and practice specifically both as they reflect the true divine reality and as they shape the Spheres and Powers of the common life. People will make these judgements. Can they be made wisely?

Christians think that it has been revealed in time and life, as well as in the structure and dynamics of creation, what the character of a true and just lordship that establishes dominion, but is not dominating, really is. This reality draws us into covenanted patterns of discipline and purpose and transforms our hearts, minds and human relationships. The issue is whether Christ's Lordship can today not only draw the Powers, these Principalities, Authorities and Regencies, into a common domain of disciplined service to God and humanity, but the Dominions too?

A Covenantal Proposal

The idea of covenant is among the central concepts of the biblical tradition, and has long been understood to be the paradigmatic, providential way of structuring the institutions of the common life in accord with God's will, law and purposes while simultaneously pointing all in covenanted life toward redemptive possibilities. That connection needs to be recovered and recast for our contemporary situation.[22]

There are, of course, different forms of covenant, implied already in the different terms in the Hebrew – *bnai berit* and *baalei berit*, for example – and in the ways they are translated and adapted into other cultural-linguistic contexts: *diatheke* and sometimes *syntheke* or even *mysterion* (Greek), *testamentum*, *compactum*, *sacramentum* or *foedus* (Latin), in the New Testament and early Christian writings, and later in social, political and legal thought as pact, compact, federation, confederation, *Bund* (German; 'bond' in English), *alliance* (French), and thus league, agreement and promise, to name the most frequent usages in Western languages. Only when we attend to the frequency and social overtones of these terms do we begin to see how pervasive and thick with implications the idea can be. All these terms refer to a voluntary bonding of persons, peoples or groups that otherwise would remain in isolation or conflict into a matrix of peace, justice, mutual obligation and care. Indeed, in every genuine covenant, six elements are present: the Divine is disclosed in the midst of history; promises are made; community is formed; duties and rights are accepted; freedom and justice are made constitutional; a vision of a new, holy future for civilization is opened for all involved.

Covenant has sometimes been interpreted in tribalistic or nationalistic ways. But under Christ's dominion, it not only contrasts with those, but with two other models that have become decisive in the West, and find parallels around the world. One is the hierarchical-suzerainty model, the other is the individualistic-contractual one. Both have elements that potentially overlap with the covenant idea; but finally they diverge. Covenantalism and its chief socio-historic form, federalism, resist on one side a power pyramid characterized by demanded solidarity and on the other side an individualism that forms all relationships according to calculations of mutual advantage.

In this new global context, we may prayerfully call for a rebirth of the 'confederation' model of covenant, one that usually became only a temporary league of convenience to defend the autonomy and sovereignty of its members. At a deeper level, however, the promise of confederation has been recognized as a promising possibility for complex civilizations since, at least, Althusius, who preserved the deep sense of the duties of and to the commonwealth as a 'consociality' of overlapping 'consocialities' under God and for humanity's well-being. In many ways, this puts a world of possibilities and choices before each person and local group; yet what distinguishes this confederated matrix from patterns of life wherein one of the units can directly control the individual or particular group in any of these areas of life? They must work through the communities of which persons are a part. Paul Tillich rightly grasped this point when he argued against both heteronomy and a sovereign autonomy in favour of a genuine and spirit-filled theonomy.

If the global trends continue, and are embraced by the people, we can say not only will the covenantal model of life find a new arena of incarnation that has implications for the emerging global civil society, but that globalization, understood in its more complex meanings, could be 'for good' – both lasting and for human well-being. It could promote a highly pluralistic global civilization with increased prospect for peace with justice. In the final analysis,

190

however, it is unlikely to happen unless it finds its focus in Christ as Lord, for Christ is the one who has, and can, renew the covenant between God and humanity, and point souls and societies towards a New Jerusalem. At least, that is the core argument of my next project on this general topic, beyond the scope of this chapter.

Notes

1 This chapter is in part developed out of a set of conversations based on previous, related papers that took place in India, Japan and China. See 'Public theology and civil society in a globalising era', *Bangalore Theological Forum*, 32(1) (June, 2000): 46–72, and (in Japanese) *Seigaquin Journal of Theology* (forthcoming). Several motifs also appear in my book with Bao Limin (in Chinese), *A Dialogical Approach to the Value of Modernity* (Shanghai, PRC: Scholars Press, 2001).

2 There are, today, at least three competing definitions of 'public theology'. One is essentially confessional in nature. That is, it understands each faith as highly particular and basically not accessible to any who do not believe it. Yet it attempts to address public issues – abortion, war and peace, etc. This position demands a place at the table of public discourse in spite of the presumption of incommensurability at its base, simply because it holds that every other public position is also confessional. A second view, the dogmatic posture, is closer to a party platform or manifesto. It works out a doctrine or ethic on its own presuppositions, combines these with selected reading of the issues before public life, and offers a social–ethical doctrine. Although it knows that its deepest views are not universally shared, it proclaims these dogmas in public forums as it seeks to influence public consciousness and public policy in a desired direction. The third and most comprehending view, for it can include key aspects of the above stances, claims that the most profound presumptions of the faith are, and can be shown to be, as reasonable, as ethical, and as viable for authentic, warranted commitment as any other known religion or philosophy and, indeed, indispensable to other modes of public discourse. This apologetic mode is, on the whole the strongest form of public theology, is willing to engage in dialogue and debate with other faith positions and is doubtful about the intellectual or moral integrity of any position or discipline that does not take theology into account.

3 See, e.g., D. F. Noble, *The Religion of Technology: The Divinity of Man and the Spirit of Invention* (New York: Knopf, 1998).

4 Arendt van Leeuwen, *Christianity in World History* (New York: Scribners, 1965).

5 Van Leeuwen did anticipate the fact that these ideas could be taken in the direction of a more comprehensive secular ideology that would play the role

of religion. See his *The Critique of Heaven and the Critique of Earth*, 2 Vols (Cambridge: Basil Blackwell, 1970). He did not see the ways in which other religions would themselves undergo reformations and draw on revised internal themes to employ in understanding these phenomena. See, e.g., Peter Berger and Hsin-Huang Hsiao (eds), *In Search of an East Asian Development Model* (New Brunswick, NJ: Transaction Books, 1988). Nor did he see the ways in which particular cultures would attempt to adopt economic techniques and material technologies without having their basic character altered, and wake up to find themselves in the midst of the shock of divided and alienating identities. See C. Fred. Alford, *Think No Evil: Korean Values in the Age of Globalisation* (Ithaca, NY: Cornell University Press, 1999).

6 I am again indebted to Roland Robertson, 'Glocalization: time–space and homogeneity–heterogeneity', in M. Featherstone *et al.* (eds), *Global Modernities*, (London: Sage, 1995). As to how many are left out, we are in the midst of an enormous debate. The best evidence suggests that lower percentages of the world population are in poverty than at almost any moment in the past, although the discrepancies between the very rich and the middle and lower classes are greater in areas where the social system is most closed to economic change and trade, family patterns involve low levels of fidelity (and thus the rapid spread of Aids), politics is led by one-party governments (which give economic monopolies to favourites) and traditions of forming independent corporations are not favoured by law or culture. An excellent summary is in 'Globalisation and its critics: a survey', *The Economist* (29 Sept. 2001): 3–30.

7 The following section is from my *God and Globalisation* (Harrisburg, PA: Trinity Press International, 2000, 2001, 2002), which consists of three volumes of essays by (in Vol. 1) Roland Robertson, Yersu Kim, William Schweiker, Donald Shriver, Mary Stewart, van Leeuwen, David Tracy; (in Vol. 2) John Witte, Allen Verhey, Ronald Cole-Turner, Jürgen Moltmann, Peter Paris, Don Browning; (in Vol. 3) John Mbiti, Kosuke Koyama, Thomas Thangaraj, Lamin Sanneh, Sze-Kar Wan, Diane Obenchain and Scott Thomas. I am writing a fourth and final volume which will focus on a Christian theological treatment of the whole set.

8 See the essays, for example, by Thomas Thangaraj, John Mbiti, Sze-Kar Wan, Lamin Sanneh and Diane Obenchain in *God and Globalisation, Vol. 3: Christ and the Dominions of Civilization.*

9 It is impossible here to trace the developments on this point from the medieval monastery to the Reformation, and between the Reformation and the theologies of our times, but they are thick with implications for globalization, and have been indicated in *On Moral Business: Classical and Contemporary Resources for Ethics and Economic Life*, ed. M. L. Stackhouse, D. McCann, S. Roels *et al.* (Grand Rapids, MI: Eerdmans, 1995); and my *Covenant and Commitments: Faith, Family, and Economic Life* (Louisville, KY: Westminster, 1997).

192

10 This idea is shared by the father of modern jurisprudence, Althusius, conservative Calvinist Abraham Kuyper, liberal Lutheran Ernst Troeltsch, 'Unitarian' social theorist Max Weber, Reformed neo-Orthodox theologian Emil Brunner and a number of sociologists and political philosophers who write about 'civil society'.

11 See, especially, Harold J. Berman, *Law and Revolution: The Formation of the Western Legal Tradition* (Cambridge, MA: Harvard University Press, 1983). The most extensive research on this development was done rather early by Otto von Gierke, in his massive *Genossenschaftsrecht* (1868–80), portions of which have been translated into English by Ernest Barker (Cambridge: Cambridge University Press, 1934). It is striking that the sharpest critics of the corporation seem to know little of this history.

12 When, for example, a 'traditional folk dance' is performed on stage by a selected troupe to celebrate a cultural heritage for tourists, as in the Edinburgh Festival, the differentiation of spheres is well established.

13 Francis Fukuyama's *Trust: The Social Virtues and the Creation of Wealth* (New York: Free Press, 1995). On the basis of the comparative analysis of ten cultures, Fukuyama argues that some religious and ethical orientations tend to stamp the persons in a society with a capacity to trust those not a member of one's own familial, ethnic or national group, and that these persons find it easier to form and sustain voluntary organizations, including corporations, and thus advance economically, faster than others. We can see the implications of his work beyond the Euro-American and East Asian countries he studied if we examine the difficulties Russia has had after the fall of the USSR. Technology was highly developed, but without a legal and social base for independent institutional formation, it was only a 'mafioso capitalism' that was able to get started for some time – compared, for example, to Catholic Poland or Reformed Hungary, where the Church and other organizations distinct from the state had preserved the habits of trust and independency that allowed corporations to form, enabling a more rapid adjustment to new conditions.

14 This view has been set forth most vigorously by the Peruvian economist, Hernando De Soto. The distrust of independent spheres of life by patriarchal, priestly and political authority has often conspired to prevent the development of these other spheres.

15 On this point, John Milbank, *Theology and Social Theory: Beyond Secular Reason* (Oxford: Basil Blackwell, 1990) not only presents a distorted view of what many social theorists have held, but offers devastating advice when he calls for us to forsake the dialogue between theology and the social sciences in favour of a 'pure' theology of 'Radical Orthodoxy'. This form of pre-modernism gives us no guidance whatsoever for the global future, and is neither radical nor orthodox. It could better be named 'reactionary heterodoxy'.

16 See, especially, David Martin, *Tongues of Fire: The Explosion of Protestantism in Latin America* (Cambridge, MA: Blackwell, 1990). Cf. Robert W. Fogel, *The*

Fourth Great Awakening and the Future of Egalitarianism (Chicago, IL: Chicago University Press, 2000).

17 The term is Walter Rauschenbush's, *A Theology for the Social Gospel* (Cleveland, OH: Pilgrim Press, 1918).

18 See Lee Hardy, *The Fabric of This World* (Grand Rapids, MI: Eerdmans, 1990), and William F. May, *Beleaguered Rulers: The Public Obligation of the Professional* (Louisville, KY: Westminster Press, 2000).

19 For a summary of the debate over these issues, see Paul Knitter, *No Other Name? A Critical Survey of Christian Attitudes toward the World Religions* (Maryknoll, NY: Orbis Books, 1985); and the wider bibliography of materials related to this question in S. Immanuel David (ed.), *Christianity and the Encounter with Other Religions* (Bangalore: UTC Publications, 1988).

20 Samuel P. Huntington, *The Clash of Civilizations and the Remaking of World Order* (New York: Simon & Schuster, 1996). That, however, was before his most recent book: Lawrence E. Harrison and Samuel P. Huntington (eds), *Culture Matters: How Values Shape Human Progress* (London: HarperCollins, 2001).

21 These questions are debated by a number of contributors to this study. Key background resources for this are: Stanley Samartha, *Living Faiths and Ultimate Goals* (Geneva: World Council of Churches, 1974); Knitter, *No Other Name?*; and Mark Heim, *Salvations: Truth and Difference in Religion* (Maryknoll, NY: Orbis Books, 1995).

22 The virtual explosion of materials on covenant can be represented by Daniel Elazar's *The Covenant Tradition in Politics*, 4 vols (New Brunswick, NJ: Transaction Publishers, 1995–9), and Robert Jackson, *The Global Covenant: Human Conduct in a World of States* (New York: Oxford University Press, 2000),

Chapter 12

Globalization:
An Economist's Perspective

C. T. KURIEN

Introduction

During the last two decades of the twentieth century, globalization as a social phenomenon has come to occupy a prominent position both in popular discussions and academic discourses. There is today a vast body of literature dealing with the subject. Whether this proliferation has led to a clearer understanding of the phenomenon is a different issue. It is possible that the diverse views expressed on the subject are rather like the blind men's attempt to describe the elephant – partial versions acceptable to some extent, but which certainly do not lead to an accurate perception of the animal. I have always been impressed that John G. Saxe, who converted the Indian fable of the elephant and the blind men into English verse, claimed that those six men of Indostan who went to see the elephant were 'to learning much inclined'. Hence it may not have been surprising that when they met for a colloquium after conducting their empirical enquiry 'they disputed loud and long, each in his own opinion exceeding stiff and strong'! There is another aspect relating to the fable that has not received the attention it deserves. The blind men's folly was perceived by the narrator who had seen the animal 'as a whole', and there are many who would claim to have that whole picture of the animal and hence can understand the blind men's blunder. But there are other animals that no one has seen, or can see, as a whole. Globalization is one such animal. Hence there can be no distinction between blind men and other men among those who set out to see that animal. The best they can do is to grope, 'seeing' the animal only in part. Any discussion and interpretation of globalization must, therefore, be prefaced by an acknowledgement of that inbuilt limitation.

In the case of globalization there is an additional factor to be taken note of. As a social phenomenon it holds together some opposing tendencies. The

United Nations Development Programme's (UNDP) *Human Development Report 1999* expresses it thus:

> Globalization, as a dominant force in the twentieth century's last decade, is shaping a new era of interaction among nations, economies and people. It is increasing the contacts between people across national boundaries – in economy, in technology, in culture and in governance. But it is also fragmenting production processes, labour markets, political entities and societies. So, while globalization has positive, innovative, dynamic aspects, it also has negative, disruptive and marginalizing aspects.

The same issue has been expressed more picturesquely by a writer who says 'Globalization is everything and its opposite'. He adds:

> It can be incredibly empowering and incredibly coercive. It can democratize opportunity and democratize panic. It makes whales bigger and minnows stronger. It leaves you behind faster and faster and it catches up to you faster and faster ... It enables us to reach into the world as never before and it enables the world to reach into us as never before.[1]

There is much truth in that depiction of the contradictory essence of globalization. But the statement also suffers from a misspecification of 'us'. For a better understanding of the phenomenon of globalization it is important to note that its contradictory essence also polarizes its impact. It empowers some of us, but enslaves others. It enriches some, but impoverishes others. A probe into the inherently differential impact of globalization is necessary to make sense of it and to indicate how to respond to it. Such an exposition is the thrust of this chapter.

Globalization as an ongoing process is, in one sense, not a recent phenomenon. It is not easy to trace precisely its early origins. But many of its strands can be seen to go back into antiquity. The movement of people across vast stretches of land and even across waters separating land is much older than the relatively recent recognition that the planet earth is global in shape. Trade between peoples of faraway places preceded the formation of nations and hence belongs to an age prior to the emergence of inter*national* trade.[2] The movement of capital in search of profit across national boundaries is an essential attribute of capitalism and hence must be considered as old as capitalism itself. In terms of the movement of people, goods and capital crossing national states as well as in terms of technological innovations facilitating it, the nineteenth century and the early part of the twentieth century can be claimed to have been a great era of globalization.[3] The momentum of that process was interrupted, and to some extent reversed, during the short period between the First and Second World Wars, but was revived again by the middle of the twentieth century. In a very meaningful sense, then, globalization is an old ongoing process, not a smooth, linear process, to be sure, but one whose antecedents can be traced back to the very early stages of human history, and which seems to have a propensity to be revived and resumed after periods of slowing down or even temporary termination. To say this is not to deny the distinct features of the present phase of globalization, but to insist that they must be sought out and explicated.

Let me touch upon two features which in popular discussion appear to be distinguishing manifestations of contemporary globalization. The first, of course, are the spectacular technological innovations of the recent decades in the information-communication area which have come to be known as the ICT revolution. It has been revolutionary in the sense that in a brief span of time it has transformed many aspects of daily life – correspondence, office work, trade and commerce, education, travel, administration and many more. It is seen as a powerful factor in contemporary globalization because a series of connected innovations have compressed space and time and have recombined the two into a new category symbolized by the 'new global village'. The second manifestation of present-day globalization that has received much attention – for it is so palpable – is closely related to the ICT revolution, an emerging and homogenizing culture that tends to impact individuals and societies in all parts of the world. While it may be debated whether this is a welcome thing or not, as a statement of fact few will question it.

Economic Globalization: Market Processes

Without minimizing the importance of the above two and many other factors in and manifestations of contemporary globalization I shall, in this presentation, concentrate on what may be designated *economic globalization*. Admittedly it is a partial view, but I would insist that it is a main part of the animal, and not just its tail end! In dealing with economic globalization and its associated political manifestations, my attempt will be to show how asymmetries of power emerge from the normal functioning of the economic system, how they get magnified over time and how these differentials in power then become the underlying parameters for the transformation of the system itself. The essence of my argument is that, while contemporary globalization has distinguishing features of its own, it is basically a manifestation of the capitalist economic order which emerged in Britain a few

197

centuries ago, spread fairly soon into Europe and then to other parts of the world, in some parts as something of a replication of that order and in other parts as its domination over other forms of economic arrangements. In brief, my argument is that what I have referred to as economic globalization is the ongoing multifaceted engagement of the capitalist economic system in different parts of the globe. I have dealt with this theme in my writings of the 1990s, especially in *Global Capitalism and the Indian Economy* (New Delhi: Orient Longman, 1994).

An entry into the exposition can be made through an understanding of market processes.[4] Money and market are among the oldest of human institutions, and I believe among the most useful as means of human interaction, although I am aware that there are those who hold the view that they are innately evil institutions. Money and market both precede the capitalist system, but under capitalism they undergo a great transformation, as Karl Polanyi has eloquently stated in his *magnum opus*.[5] Adam Smith linked market to the human propensity 'to barter, truck and exchange one thing for another', while Karl Marx maintained that exchange of one thing for another (to be distinguished from transfer of things from one person, or group of persons to another) did not exist within primordial human organizations, the family, the tribe, etc., but arose between them at a later stage of human evolution, a position that Polanyi also endorsed and documented. But there is general agreement that the first institutional manifestation of exchange was barter, the transaction of one good for another without any medium of exchange. Two parties will go into barter only if both of them perceive it to be advantageous, but even their differential power can influence the nature of the transaction. If, for instance, the good one offers is easily perishable while the other party comes with a good that is durable, the latter will certainly be able to exercise greater power in the bargaining process. A more pronounced case is where for one party the transaction is a matter of survival whereas the other party has enough resources not only to survive, but to stay away from any transaction. In many traditional agrarian societies, those who do not have any land or other resources, and have only their labour power to offer in exchange for things that they need for survival, can be forced by those who have land and resources to surrender their labour power in exchange on very unfavourable terms. This case, however, is not confined to traditional societies.

The situation can be generalized to say that exchange as an activity and market as its institutional manifestation are premised on power, resource power, that is. When exchange comes to be mediated through money, the problem becomes more accentuated, for money is, in one sense, the most condensed form of resource power, and those who have command over money will, in general, be in a position to determine the terms of transaction. Consider two cases that illustrate this condition. When a person who has only his skills, physical or mental, to offer for transaction confronts another who is looking for those skills, but has plenty of money at his disposal, the latter will be able to 'beat down' the former using any one of the many options that money power confers. For the second case think of a country which has only bananas or cocoa to offer in the international market, but the buyer has an abundance of the almighty dollar. It is not difficult to see how the transaction is likely to turn out.

To those who think of these examples as special and rare cases it may come as a surprise to learn that, on the contrary, these represent what is touted as 'free trade' and 'free market'. A 'free market' is one left to its own operational principles without any external interventions and 'free trade' is the transaction that takes place under such conditions. And that is precisely what contemporary economic globalization actively propagates and its supporters ardently advocate. But, of course, the case for such 'free trade' is put forward as a case for trade without the intervention of the state. The underlying logic, however, is that as parties to a transaction, *any* transaction, enter into it out of their own free will, it must be left entirely to those parties. The assumption is that the two parties are 'equal' – a concept of equality that chooses to overlook asymmetries in resource power and the larger issue that equality has many attributes to it. It must also be clear that free market and free trade of this kind are ideological doctrines of those who have and wield power, but couched in the terminologies of liberty and equality.

When transactions come to be generally mediated through money, another change also takes place – the emergence of those who mediate transactions, traders or merchants. If transactions are beneficial, mediating transactions, buying from those who wish to sell and selling to those who wish to buy, is also beneficial. The mediators facilitate trade by storing up goods and by disseminating information, two conditions required to generalize trade. But the emergence and domination of merchants bring with it an additional set of problems. For one, those who hold stock can withhold stock, those who disseminate information can distort information. Both these measures can be used, and are frequently used, to command control *over* markets and to derive advantage from it. This is not surprising because, unlike parties in a transaction whose interest is in the sale or purchase of a good, the merchant's interest is not in the parties

199

or in the goods but in the transaction itself and he should be expected to do whatever he can to turn it to his advantage, monetary advantage. One practical way of achieving it is by eliminating competition. Others may be trying to achieve the same result and the outcome cannot be easily predicted or influenced. What needs to be noted, however, is that, contrary to the claim that the 'free market' is a competitive market, the reality is that it is a process that deliberately and desperately tries to diminish, if not destroy competition. The fact is that the so-called 'free market' and 'free trade' that are considered to be the basic tenets of contemporary globalization are virtually and essentially controlled markets, ironically enough by invisible hands, most of the time.

Production, Finance and Property

Starting from barter, the exposition has moved into the realm of mediated transactions and its impact on trade and markets. A related analysis must be made about the realm of production also. Initially production is for the use of those immediately involved in that process. Surplus, if any, is stored or shared. But once trade is established, that surplus can be sold to those who need the good, in return either for other goods or for money. In turn it paves the way for production for sale and not for use at all. The producer, too, becomes an intermediary, both in the sense that he produces not for himself, and in the more significant sense that his purpose can be achieved only by becoming a trader as well. Just as the merchant is not interested in the parties to a transaction or the goods being transacted but in the act itself, the producer, too, becomes more directly interested in the production-for-sale activity than on the goods produced or on those who may finally use it. The producer is no longer producing for himself or for any consumer, but 'for the market'. The role of the market in a whole range of economic activities becomes more dominant, simultaneously generating more agents interested in dominating the market.

Further avenues where a similar process of intermediation emerges and becomes powerful may also be noted. Those who come to have a surplus beyond their needs may initially deal directly with those who do not have enough for the time being. But as surpluses become increasingly monetized, intermediaries willing to accept deposits from those who have surplus and to make credit available to those who need it will surface and will soon get institutionalized, as banks and a market for credit with its own features will emerge. In turn, credit will become another powerful entity in the increasingly intermeshing economic system and those who control credit will become another centre of power.

Another sphere where the regime of market got established – historically much later, but with a much greater acceleration once it was started – was property and ownership. For a long period, property was primarily land and, as Polanyi forcefully points out, substantially remained outside the operations of the market. But once legal provisions were made instituting claims to shares of ownership, markets and intermediation fed on each other, generating a cumulative augmentation. An essential feature of contemporary globalization, details of which I shall provide later, is the rapid spread of this market, the market for finance, to practically all parts of the world, including countries such as China and Vietnam where its entry was politically prohibited till almost two decades ago. A peculiarity of this market is its perpetual motion, facilitated by the ICT revolution. Finance is moving in and out of markets all over the world, minute by minute, second by second. It is the true symbol of globalization.

Globalization, even economic globalization, is much more than markets and marketization. And yet, it seems to me that a feel for the nature of markets as they really are and the intermeshing of a wide range and variety of economic activities that they bring about is absolutely necessary to make an appraisal of globalization. Taking the cue from Adam Smith's reference to the 'invisible hand' in the context of the working of markets, latterday economists have perfected a logical model of markets that shows how smoothly and effectively they would function in the absence of external interventions. But that model rests heavily on assumptions far removed from conditions in real life: it also totally ignores the role of intermediaries, sticking to the notion of the market as a relationship directly between buyers who represent demand and sellers who represent supply. Eulogizing claims about 'the market economy' are based on such contrived logic. My exposition also has been only at the realm of logic so far. If it has led to a version of markets closer to real life, it is because I have not resorted to arbitrary assumptions.[6]

Before I move on from the real-life logic of the functioning of markets, I would make two related observations. The first is that markets mediated by money have an inbuilt propensity to spread. Karl Marx referred to the tendency of this form of exchange and markets and stated that it 'breaks through all local and personal bonds inseparable from direct barter ... and develops a whole network of social relations spontaneous in their growth and entirely beyond the control of the actors'.[7] To move to the ends of the world is, therefore, quite normal for money, markets and finance.

However, and this is the second observation, as an historical process the spread of markets and the reaching of capital have been far from automatic. Rulers frequently provided protection for the movement of merchants (who, in turn, gave money to the rulers to strengthen their position and to facilitate their conquests); for a medium of exchange to become generally acceptable as money an authoritative guarantee was necessary which was also provided by those in power. Thus economic changes and political processes were always interacting and state and market emerged as social institutions fairly simultaneously. At a subsequent period, the development of banking and of joint stock companies based on the principles of the sharing of ownership and limited liability required legal sanctions, and these were provided by the state. And, of course, military powers almost always preceded or stood by extension of markets and movements of capital to foreign territories. Equally important to note is that practically every one of these changes has also faced opposition, organized opposition in many instances, which also shaped the actual course of events.

The scale has, no doubt, changed but contemporary globalization also has all these ingredients – messy markets, domestic and global, spreading under various forms of sponsorship and domination (retreating from some spheres as well); agents, small and large, who have their own agenda; capital, in the form of finance, constantly on the move; governments and political forces aiding and abetting as well as fighting and limiting; and ordinary people in many parts of the globe not knowing how to make sense of all this flux and change. They are naïve who give this phenomenon wholehearted endorsement or total opposition.

History of Globalization

From the exposition of the logic of globalizing markets, I move to a quick tour of the history of the globalization phenomenon of the past few decades. I have already referred to the rapid economic globalization of the nineteenth century and the early part of the twentieth century, which was halted and reversed after the First World War when nations of the world concentrated more on domestic economic policies, frequently erecting strong tariff walls to ward off international influences. After the Second World War, the globalizing tendencies revived, clearly under the economic, political and military leadership of the United States of America. US policy was aimed at rebuilding Japan, rehabilitating Europe and winning over nations of the world, including the many that were freed from colonial domination, in the Cold War against the Soviet Union. The global domination that the USA was coming to have was used to promote American business concerns in other parts of the world. Instead of exporting goods manufactured in America, American companies found it to their advantage to set up production units in different parts of the world which necessitated movement of capital to these places. There was, thus, a spread of American companies and capital to other countries and of American economic influence in the domestic economies of such countries. This initiated a new international division of labour and some major changes in global production and trade patterns. First, the application of technologies developed during the war to manufacturing led to an increase in production, and the United States became the market for a great share of the increase, supplying its currency, which had emerged as the world's lead currency. Second, the pattern of manufacturing changed: consumer durables like the motor car came to have their parts (said to be over 4,000) produced in different countries of the world and assembled wherever the final product was to be sold. Ford's Escort, it was shown, had its parts produced in fifteen different countries. This also meant that the character of international trade changed too, with a substantial proportion of goods moving across national boundaries being transfers between departments of huge transnational corporations. Such movements of goods and the ability of these corporations to set their prices (the phenomenon of 'transfer prices') came to have an impact on the value and stability of many national currencies. In turn, national currencies themselves entered into global trading, far exceeding the value of goods and services transacted. Finally, when several transnational corporations, of the USA, of European countries, of Japan, made their shares available to citizens of other countries and thus became multinational corporations (MNCs), many share markets became global, and, aided by the new communication technology, swift movement of shares across the globe and of currencies chasing these shares became standard patterns. The contours of the global economy as we know it today had emerged.[8]

Once again it is important to emphasize that the global economy has not been moving smoothly along a new course with predictable indicators. The decades of the 1950s and 1960s were upbeat. These decades have come to be known as 'the golden age' of capitalism. Between 1950 and 1973, the gross domestic product of sixteen leading capitalist countries increased at an annual average compound growth of 4.9 per cent, compared to just 1.9 per cent between 1913 and 1950. Under the General Agreement on Tariffs and Trade (GATT) there was steady movement towards freer trade. There was no major currency crisis, partly because the International Monetary Fund's

(IMF) regulations were generally accepted, but also because the dollar, the world's lead currency and reserve currency, was convertible into gold.

The 1970s, by contrast, turned out to be turbulent. By the end of the 1960s, the USA had already become a debtor nation and the growth of Japan and West Germany had brought in the yen and the mark as currencies to be reckoned with. Under pressure, the USA delinked the dollar from gold in 1971. Then came the first oil shock of 1973, which enabled the oil-producing and exporting countries (OPEC), including the countries of West Asia, to become significant players in the global economy. The success that private banks in the West had in persuading them to hold their surpluses as dollars (instead of utilizing them to help the development of Third World countries as was initially agreed upon) was to become one of the causes of the 'debt crisis' of the 1980s. But before the end of the decade the world had to face the second oil crisis of 1979.

Most commentators consider the three decades from 1950 to 1980 as just the prelude to contemporary economic globalization identifying the 1980s as the beginning of its real thrust. The decade demonstrated the diversity of the impact of globalization. Many countries in Latin America and Africa had begun to experience foreign exchange crisis as their exports had suffered greatly because their export goods were being driven out of global markets by new substitutes or by intense competition. But their import requirements were increasing. Private global banks were ready to lend them hard currencies, especially dollars, and so the 1980s became an era of increased and hectic movement of private capital globally. The fact that their export position did not improve, but interest payments had to be made, drove many of the borrowers into debt traps. The decade also came to be noted for the official support given to the free-market ideologies by President Ronald Reagan of the United States and Prime Minister Margaret Thatcher of Britain. Of the decade *The Economist* noted early in the 1990s:

> Twenty years from now economists will think of the 1980s not as the decade of the international debt crisis, nor of the dollar's boom and bust, still less of Reaganomics and 'monetarism'. All these mattered, but none of them marked decisive change in the forces that drive the world economy. Yet, the 1980s did witness such a change. During these years many of the boundaries between national financial markets dissolved, and a truly global capital market began to emerge. It is for this that the past decade will be remembered.[9]

The spectacular event related to the capital market was the US stock market crash of 1987, signalling frequent financial volatility across the globe.

But not everything was negative. The 1980s was also the decade of the great 'East Asian Miracle'. South Korea, Taiwan, Hong Kong and Singapore boomed and the prosperity was shared by Thailand and Indonesia as well. But the biggest triumph of global capital was possibly the decision of China which had hitherto followed an autarchic economic policy (with substantial internal reforms favouring market operations since 1978) to open up to foreign investment in 1987. The fall of socialist regimes in Eastern Europe in the late 1980s and the collapse of the Soviet Union early in the 1990s, thus leading to the emergence of a 'unipolar' world, became another factor accelerating globalization.

At the beginning of the 1990s the global mood was one of pessimism. The annual report of a leading UN agency dealing with trade and development described the situation as follows:

> The world economy has been suffering its most severe recession since the Second World War. Production has fallen in the United States and flattened in Japan. Western Europe is stagnating ... Growth has picked up in Latin America, but remains slow there and in other developing regions, other than parts of Asia. Central and Eastern Europe are suffering a precipitous fall in living standards: the transition process is proving much more painful than anticipated. Overall, signs of improvement are scant.[10]

The events of the decade are too well known to need detailed discussion. They include the catastrophe Russia faced following forced marketization; a sudden financial crisis in Mexico which till then was certified to be the ideal development paradigm under globalization; the equally unnerving collapse of the East Asian Miracle; the failure of some major hedge funds, a private initiative of several billion dollars mobilized with guarantees against risk provided by two American economists who had been awarded the Nobel Prize for their contributions towards the understanding of financial markets; record level unemployment in many European countries; financial scams and corruption in several countries of the world with their political fallout. The Japanese economy slumped almost throughout the decade. The United States managed to effect a fairly sustained economic recovery especially its IT-related 'new economy', which appeared to offer a new technology-directed avenue for economic growth. In 2000, the final year of the decade, thanks to America's good performance the world economy enjoyed a spectacular growth of almost 5 per cent – its fastest for sixteen years.

But *The Economist*, commenting on the phenomenon early in 2001, the first year of the new decade and of the twenty-first century, said: 'This year it looks much less buoyant. America and Japan, the two biggest economies accounting for 46 per cent of world output, are both teetering on the brink of recession', and states that should this happen it would be the first time since 1974 that the two biggest economies simultaneously come under recession.[11] With the tumbling of the stock markets in the USA and its spread practically throughout the world, the indications, by the middle of the year are that recession will spread and become global, because in the new global economy recession is carried more through stock markets than through trade.

Changes in the Global Economy

UNDP's *Human Development Report 1999* gives the following statistical information that may convey some idea of the manner in which the global economy has changed during the past two or three decades:

- Foreign direct investment topped $400 billion in 1997, seven times the level in real terms in the 1970s. Portfolio and other short-term capital flows grew substantially, totalling $2 trillion in gross terms, almost three times those in the 1980s.
- The daily turnover in foreign exchange markets increased from around $10–20 billion in the 1970s to $1.5 trillion in 1998.
- Between 1983 and 1993, cross-border sales and purchases of US Treasury bonds increased from $30 billion a year to $500 billion.
- International bank lending grew from $265 billion in 1975 to $4.2 trillion in 1994.

But these global figures hide as much, if not more, than what they reveal. Consider the distribution of foreign investment. In the mid-1990s, over 60 per cent of the annual flow of foreign investment went into developed countries. The same kind of concentration was noted in the flow of investment into the developing countries, the Asia–Pacific region claiming some 70 per cent, China alone accounting for 40 per cent. In contrast, Africa remained almost completely marginalized. Of the $84 billion that flowed into developing countries in 1994, sub-Saharan Africa received just $1.8 billion, the same as New Zealand. The message: foreign investment is meant for the strong, not for the weak.

This unevenness beneath the surface is indeed *the* main feature of contemporary globalization, unevenness in opportunities, incomes and power – a fact amply documented by UN publications. For instance, though the ratio of global trade to GDP has been rising impressively, it has been falling for forty-four countries with more than a billion people. The least developed countries with 10 per cent of the world's people have only 0.3 per cent of the world's trade, half their share of two decades ago. In the mid-1990s it was noted that the terms of trade for the least developed countries had declined a cumulative 50 per cent over the previous twenty-five years. Developing countries lose about $60 billion a year from agricultural subsidies and barriers to textile exports in industrial nations, a feature that has continued even after the World Trade Organization (WTO) was set up to guarantee more open trade policies.

The disparities are more glaringly seen in terms of income distributions and poverty profiles. Globally, the second half of the twentieth century was a period of rising incomes, as the global GDP increased from about $3 trillion at the end of the Second World War to $30 trillion in the mid-1990s. In spite of a substantial increase in global population, there was also a threefold increase in per capita incomes. However, towards the end of the decade (and century), 20 per cent of the global population living in the highest income countries had 86 per cent of world GDP, while the bottom fifth had just 1 per cent. Of course, income distribution globally has always been unequal, but the increase in inequality has been phenomenal in the twentieth century, particularly during its closing decades of globalization. The income gap between the top 20 per cent and the bottom 20 per cent is estimated to have been 7 to 1 in 1870, increasing to 11 to 1 in 1913. By 1960 the gap had increased to 30 to 1, by 1990 to 60 to 1 and in 1997 to a whopping 74 to 1. It was also estimated that some 1.3 billion people were living on incomes of less than $1 a day.[12]

UNDP's *Human Development Report 1997* on Human Development to Eradicate Poverty, reflecting on this factual material said: 'A rising tide of wealth is supposed to lift all boats. But some are more seaworthy than others. The yachts and ocean liners are indeed rising in response to new opportunities, but the rafts and rowboats are taking on water – and some are sinking fast.' The vessels, of course, are of different seaworthiness. But it is important to note, too, that the bigger ones that control the sea have the power to create ripples and waves that cause the smaller ones to go under.

Of these big ones, special mention should be made of the MNCs (TNCs). It has been noted already that the rise to dominance of the MNCs has been an aspect of globalization. There are now over 40,000 of them (referred to as parent firms), with some 250,000 foreign affiliates. Together they play a major role in the contemporary global economy. Not all of them are big by any standards, but the big ones are very big indeed. In 1997 the annual sales of General Motors, one of the largest MNCs, exceeded the GDP of Norway, and there are another dozen or so (Ford Motor, Mitsubishi, Royal Dutch/Shell Group, Exxon, Wal Mart stores among them) whose sales exceeded the GDP of countries such as Greece, Malaysia, Israel, Colombia and the Philippines. In the early 1990s, the global sales generated by MNCs, valued at $5.2 trillion, slightly exceeded the worldwide export of goods and services. Indeed, a third of worldwide exports consisted of intra-firm movement of the MNCs, and the prices of these goods and services were set by the MNCs themselves for internal purposes and for customs declarations. Further, the top 100 MNCs accounted for one-sixth of the world foreign direct investment (FDI) stock. In terms of control over capital and of markets and in terms of the volume of transactions and in many other ways, the MNCs are the new and major players in the contemporary global economy. They also represent the strength of the organized non-governmental sector of the global economy.

The resources that they command and their strategic role can be put to effective use in the development of the global economy. In particular, their potential for technological innovation and technology transfer can be of immense benefit. Some MNCs, in fact, play a positive and constructive role. But in general what happens is not what is claimed to be possible, but what is seen to be advantageous, profitable. As against the claim that MNCs bring capital and technology to developing countries, a UN report frankly admits that what usually happens is MNCs 'relocating assets that were no longer of use at home to neighbouring developing host countries'.[13] In many instances they do not even do that. Their attention is increasingly turning from production to acquiring existing and competing production units, thereby ensuring a larger market share, a practice that is widespread even in developing countries. The UN report points out that, in 1993, investment outlays for mergers and acquisitions by foreign firms in the United States accounted for nearly 90 per cent of total investment outlays.[14] It has also been documented that, when MNCs in fact set up production units in a country, very often they show a high propensity to import their requirements from outside, thereby offsetting any advantage the country may have come to have by the capital investment. Global firms that have no sense of public accountability where they function and no commitment to the long-term development of these locations are, however, emerging as key players in the global economy. The liberalization that the rules of the new regime insists on is the freedom of these players to enter and exit when they wish to. And in search of profits they go in and go out of countries on terms that they are able to set.

A widely prevalent view is that national governments, particularly the ones in developing countries, are helpless against these powerful agents. It reflects the nature of power relationships on the one hand, but on the other, the position that, with the rule of the market getting established in international economic relationships as well as in domestic economic matters, the state must withdraw substantially from the economic realm. Implicit in the latter is the notion of a free, self-regulating market that brings about economic efficiency and results in growth and welfare and whose operations should, therefore, be not interfered with. I have dealt with the hollowness of this ideological assertion. Whether the state should withdraw from some avenues where it is active is a contextual empirical question. But it may be recalled that Adam Smith himself had assigned some irreducible economic functions to the state.[15] Hence the relationship between MNCs and states or governments is a tactical question of power relationships, that of economic power or power of capital that the MNCs represent and political power that the state or national governments represent.

There need be no doubt that the MNCs rely heavily on political authority and the legal provisions that emanate from it. As global players it is, indeed, to their advantage to have many and diverse centres of political power or states in different parts of the world. MNCs now derive their profits to a large extent because of the differences in currencies, interest rates, tariff structures, labour laws, insolvency provisions and so on that different countries have. National governments, in turn, can derive advantages from MNCs. To what extent they succeed in doing it is a matter of political positions, the economic strength of the government concerned and many other strategic consid-erations. And there are many patterns that can be observed. The Chinese government has so far succeeded in getting the MNCs to fall in line with its designs. At the other extreme, there are governments that have practically surrendered to MNC power and strategy.

There are also governments who have used their global clout to promote the interests of *their* MNCs, successive governments of the United States since the Second World War being the best examples. I have referred to the early history of this relationship. Another chapter was witnessed during the Uruguay Round of negotiations (1986–94) which led to the winding up of GATT and the setting up of the WTO. During these negotiations, especially the early stages, the US government found ways to allow American MNCs not only to enter through the back door into a forum of representatives of governments from member countries of the United Nations, but also to determine the agenda of the negotiations.

Another aspect of the close collaboration between American economic interests represented by the MNCs and American political interest has recently been featured by Thomas Friedman in his influential book on globalization already referred to (*The Lexus and the Olive Tree*). Friedman is a great admirer of globalization and of America's leading role in that ongoing process at present. But he is also eager to see this process – the combined effect of capitalism and democracy, according to him – reach out to human beings in all nooks and corners of the world. Writing with such missionary and ecumenical zeal, he corrects those who hold the view that it will happen automatically through the working of the free market. He thinks of America as 'the ultimate benign hegemon and reluctant enforcer' of globalization. The major conclusion of the book is worth quoting: 'The hidden hand of the market will never work without a hidden fist ... And the hidden fist that keeps the world safe for Silicon Valley's technologies to flourish is called the U.S. Army, Air Force, Navy and Marine Corps.'[16] With such affirmations of the intertwining of economic, political and military power in what is now called globalization, those who suspect that it is the new name for imperialism deserve to be forgiven if they are wrong.

The defining aspect of globalization, however, is not the relationship between MNCs and governments at the national or global level. Rather, it is the relationship, at all levels, between human beings and capital, their own creation. That relationship began to take a distinct shape as the domination of people by capital a few centuries ago which soon came to be viewed as part of the natural order. Late in the twentieth century that domination became pronounced and aggressive, parading as globalization. But capital spinning around the world is only partial globalization. And when aggressive capital roameth about the globe seeking whom it may devour, it is demonic globalization that needs to be steadfastly resisted.

Authentic globalization has to be people-centred. Its aim has to be to enable human beings separated by space and by many other factors to dwell together in unity. It begins when people in their different localities and situations enter into a determined search for the common good. It gets strengthened when they tune all their institutions, from the family to the state, to uphold the dignity and rights of human beings everywhere. It involves conscious efforts to get capital, and the market as its vehicle, to become subordinated to human purposes and welfare. It calls for a renewing of the mind and a re-orienting of action. The task is not easy, but that is the global agenda for the twenty-first century.

Acknowledgement

Duncan Forrester and I were colleagues in the Madras Christian College in the 1960s and have kept up our friendship even after we were geographically distanced. In writing this piece in his honour I recall the great stimulus I used to get discussing social and theological issues with him.

Notes

1 Thomas L. Friedman, *The Lexus and the Olive Tree* (New York: Anchor Books, 2000), p. 406.

2 It may be recalled that Karl Polanyi points out that long-distance trade emerged earlier than local markets did. See Karl Polanyi, *The Great Transformation* (Boston, MA: Beacon Press, 1957), Ch 5.

3 A recent publication dealing with this theme is Kevin H. O'Rourke and Jeffrey G. Williams, *Globalisation and History: The Evolution of a Nineteenth Century Atlantic Economy* (Cambridge, MA: MIT Press, 1999).

4 The treatment here is rather terse. A more detailed discussion can be seen in C. T. Kurien, *The Economy: An Interpretative Introduction* (New Delhi and London: Sage, 1992).

5 Karl Polanyi, *The Great Transformation*.

6 A more adequate treatment can be seen in C. T. Kurien, *On Markets in Economic Theory and Policy* (Calcutta: Orient Longman, 1993), and C. T. Kurien, *Rethinking Economics: Reflections Based on a Study of the Indian Economy* (New Delhi and London: Sage, 1996).

7 Karl Marx, *Capital*, Vol. 1 (Moscow: Progress Publishers, 1971), p. 114.

8 Peter Drucker was one of the earliest to recognize the changing character of the world economy, including international trade, in the 1980s. Writing in the late 1980s, Drucker referred to the inter-country trade of the eighteenth century, which subsequently formed the basis of economic theories of international trade, as complementary trade. It changed to competitive trade in the mid-nineteenth century. Drucker calls contemporary trade adversarial. 'Complementary trade', he says, 'seeks to establish a partnership. Competitive trade aims at creating a customer. Adversarial trade aims at dominating an industry. Complementary trade is courtship. Competitive trade is fighting a battle. Adversarial trade aims at winning the war by destroying the enemy's army and its capacity to fight.' *The New Realities* (Oxford: Heinemann, 1989), p. 123.

9 *Economist*, 19 September, 1992.

10 United Nations Conference on Trade and Development (UNCTAD), *Trade and Development Report, 1992*.

11 *Economist*, 24 March, 2001.

12 Within countries similar patterns can also be observed. India threw open its economy to private foreign capital in 1991. The record of the past decade shows that growth has gone up to about 6 per cent per annum (compared with 5 per cent in the 1980s, but less than 4 per cent during the previous decades). But this growth itself is very uneven among the sectors of the economy, the performance of agriculture and allied sectors being poor, that of the industrial sector sluggish, but the service sector picking up rapidly and now accounting for over 50 per cent of GDP. By all accounts, the chief beneficiaries have been those who already had resource power to take advantage of increasing market activities. Millions of workers from occupations such as weaving and traditional crafts have been thrown out. The condition of marginal farmers and agricultural labourers, as also of casual workers everywhere, has become more vulnerable. Official estimates seem to indicate that there is a slight reduction of those below the poverty line (bare subsistence level as determined in the early 1960s) to around 26 per cent of the population (only over 250 million people!) but international estimates show 45 per cent of the population at less than $1 a day.

   According to Thomas Friedman, even in the United States the incomes of the poorest fifth of working families dropped by 21 per cent between 1979 and 1995, while the incomes of the richest fifth jumped by 30 per cent during the same period. And in 1998 America had 170 billionaires compared with thirteen in 1982.

13 UNCTAD, *World Investment Report 1995*.

14 Peter Drucker has said: 'Ninety per cent or more of the transnational economy's financial transactions do not serve what economists would consider an economic function. They serve purely financial functions. These money flows have their own rationale of course. But they are in large part political rationalities, anticipation of government decisions as to central bank interest rates or foreign exchange rates, taxes, government deficits and government borrowing, or political risk assessment.' Drucker, *The New Realities*, p. 121.

15 Apart from protecting the citizens against external aggression and maintaining law and order, Smith wanted the state to maintain public institutions and works that private individuals or group of individuals would not find profitable to undertake.

16 Thomas L. Friedman, *The Lexus and The Olive Tree*, p. 466. To be fair, it must be conceded that, according to Friedman, it is the combined operations of McDonalds and American military power that promote globalization.

Chapter 13

Farmed Salmon and the Sacramental Feast: How Christian Worship Resists Global Capitalism

MICHAEL S. NORTHCOTT

One of the joys of living in Scotland is going to watch the salmon leaping up the waterfalls amidst the pine forests, rolling hills and lush glens as they migrate from their ocean spawning grounds to the upper reaches of Scotland's rivers. The struggle between fish and the downward force of the water always seems an unequal one. The fish stand up out of the water in the dark swirling eddies at the bottom of the fall, whose water is a rich deep brown from the peat it has travelled over for many miles, and throw themselves upwards, their brown scales and fins set in relief against the vertical rush of the peaty-white water. Often a fish will leap part of the way up only to get thrown down again, but eventually these strong and determined fish make it up and their lithe majestic bodies can be seen weaving their way through rocks and rapids above the falls heading for calmer waters and pools further upstream, where, in the warmer months, they feed on Scotland's massive population of midges, and whence they and their ancestors have been travelling back and forth to the sea for thousands of years. The migration of the salmon involves an arduous trip of thousands of miles for every individual of the species. Young fish do this trip by instinct alone, following, through the internal wiring of genetic memory, the route their forebears have taken from sea to river and back again.

In other parts of Scotland today it is possible to see salmon living and dying in very different conditions. The sea lochs of the west coast of Scotland are among the grandest scenery the British Isles has to offer. Forming deep fissures between peat and heather-covered islands and peninsulas of glaciated granite, these lochs have been a haven for shellfish and migrant birds, and for fishing and crofting communities, for centuries past. But if you travel around these lochs today you will see cages moored in the deep water, with associated floats, tanks and ropes, and the occasional boat plying around the loch checking on life below. The cages are filled with farmed salmon. The wild majestic king of fish has been reduced in these Scottish sea lochs, and in Alaskan and Norwegian fjords, to the status of an intensively reared farm animal. Each cage contains more than a thousand individual salmon and, in order for them to survive in these unnatural conditions, the cages have to be regularly laced with a cocktail of chemicals, including organophosphate nerve agents and other pesticides and fungicides. These chemicals are essential to reduce the fungal and other infections to which the caged fish are prone, and they are used to control the millions of sea lice which infest the caged salmon, and against which they have no defence in these cramped conditions.

Farmed salmon has become a regular and relatively cheap meal, served in a variety of guises – smoked salmon, salmon steaks, 'ready meals' of 'salmon crumble' or 'salmon chops with garlic and chives' – in supermarkets and restaurants throughout the British Isles. Farmed salmon is distinguishable on the plate from wild salmon by an excess of a milky white liquid, which appears during cooking and by the artificial deep pink, which characterizes the flesh and is induced by colourants added to the fish pellets on which the salmon are fed. As for the palate, the differences are more subtle but nonetheless discernible to those who know their salmon.

Twenty-five years ago, salmon farming was seen as an effective way of reviving the depressed economic fortunes of many West Highland coastal communities. But cheap salmon and the income it has generated come at an ecological price. Scotland's sea lochs and connected river catchments are now polluted with the chemical wash from the salmon cages, and, as traditional salmon fishermen predicted, wild salmon are now at risk from this west coast rush for the red gold of salmon flesh. Their numbers have been reducing dramatically in many countries due to a range of factors including pollution and overfishing in both oceans and rivers, but salmon farming is seen as the most likely cause of this decline by many fisheries scientists. So, for example, a recent report from the World Wildlife Fund found that

> salmon aquaculture results in erosion of the natural gene pool through inter-breeding with escapees, resulting in a competitive disadvantage to the wild stock. Diseases and sea lice transferred from caged salmon to wild salmon are a severe hazard to juveniles in countries where salmon farming is predominant. In countries with major salmon aquaculture industries (Norway, Scotland, Ireland,

Canada and the United States), which impact upon nearly two-thirds of the salmon rivers in the Atlantic salmon's range, salmon aquaculture now constitutes a major threat to wild salmon stocks ... if not *the* major threat.[1]

Salmon are a wild and beautiful creature whose complex migration patterns and behaviour bespeaks of the richness, complexity and otherness of the living species with which we share God's creation. The fisherman who nets a wild salmon from his rod experiences a rich sense of satisfaction, often approaching awe, at the majesty of the species. The practice of fishing by rod and line has come under scrutiny in the USA recently, and to a lesser extent in the UK, as a consequence of lobbying from animal welfare organizations. However, catching salmon in this way, for food and for sport, demonstrates and sustains a much more profound relationship between humanity and wild salmon than fish farming. Fly-fishing requires patience and dexterity, and few can have seen an angler casting for salmon in the Tweed or the Tay and not have been moved by the beauty and grace of the motion of the line as it swirls onto water, or by the sight of a large salmon lying on the bank, evidence of a healthy river, a strong independent species and a successful day's fishing. The philosopher Albert Borgmann identifies fly-fishing as one of a number of 'focal practices' which bring depth and presence to the relation of a person to material existence, to places and nature and ecosystems.[2] Fly-fishing, like other focal practices such as cooking food, is not about efficiency, but its opposite; it is an end and not just a means. Technologies such as those mobilized in aquaculture subvert such focal practices and distort the relation of persons to places and other species. The salmon farmer uses and perceives salmon and the waters in which he farms them simply as a resource to be maximized and harvested: the salmon farm is an industrial production system, no more sensitive to the environment and to the species deployed than a battery chicken farm.

Salmon aquaculture is a parable of the industrial agriculture which has come to dominate food production in the Western, and much of the non-Western world, in the last fifty years. It is also a parable of globalization and its effects on local ecosystems and their human and non-human inhabitants. Salmon production in Scotland has gone from a relatively small-scale industry, producing 12,000 tonnes of fish in 1988, to a major industrial production system which produced 137,000 tonnes of farmed salmon in 2000.[3] This increase in production has had significant effects on the surrounding marine environment. The quantity of waste – all of it untreated and dumped into some of the most pristine and beautiful waters in Europe – produced by this

industry is almost double the sewage produced by the total human population of Scotland.[4] Catches of shellfish have been badly affected, while algal
blooms have begun to appear in the ocean as a consequence of untreated
waste. But the local impacts of this increasingly global industry are of little
concern to the small number of transnational food companies which now
own most of the production capacity in Scotland, and who have increased
production more than tenfold in ten years with little increase in employment
in the industry.

In a colloquium dedicated to the public theology of Duncan Forrester,
this parable of the salmon farm may seem unduly particularistic. However,
its particularism resonates significantly with Forrester's own concern to incorporate the stories of real people and communities in his writings, and with
his work in the Centre for Theology and Public Issues. Forrester exemplifies
a style of public theology that is designed to generate dialogue between these
stories of ordinary people and local communities, and the policy-makers and
opinion formers of Scottish society. The intention of this dialogue is to 'influence the influencers' and to infiltrate the establishment with the concerns
of those to whom the establishment may be deaf, including prisoners, pros-
titutes and the poor. This partnership between theologians, policy-makers,
academics and the wider public is seen by Forrester as a particular incarnation
of the distinctive relationship between Church and state which has existed
in Scotland since the Reformation. In his recent book, *Truthful Action*, he
suggests that Scots theologians at the Reformation committed the Church
in Scotland to a radical vision of a Christian society in which Church and
state were sharply distinguished in a way that they were not in England and
Germany, and that enabled the development of a Christian commonwealth
in Scotland in which Church and state were partners, albeit operating in their
own delimited spheres.[5] The result was a more radical form of church polity
than that which occurred elsewhere in Reformation Europe.[6] In the light of
this understanding of a Reformed commonwealth, the task of public theology
in Scotland is to retrieve this radical heritage. This retrieval is evidenced in
the national influence of church leaders and theologians, and in particular
in Will Storrar's authoring of the Church and Nation Report to the General
Assembly in 1989 which set out a constitutional vision for Scottish self-
government,[7] and Storrar and Kenyon Wright's roles in drawing intellectuals
and public figures to work for a new Parliament in the various coalitions of
churches, political and non-governmental organizations, which campaigned
for self-government in Scotland for more than ten years. Forrester discerns
in the subsequent establishment of the Scottish Parliament the first glimpse

of a retrieved radical Reformed orthodoxy, symbolized by the 'singing of the hundredth psalm to the Calvinist Genevan "plain tune"' at the inauguration of the Parliament by the British monarch.[8]

The theological vision of Scottish self-government as outlined in the 1989 Church and Nation report to the General Assembly was that it would be less absolutist in its expression of executive power than the English government with its ancient doctrine of the sovereignty of the Crown-in-Parliament. A Scottish Assembly would recognize the inherent limitations on governmental sovereignty as recognized by the Scottish Reformers, and the shared duties of people and parliamentarians under the law and sovereignty of God.[9] In significant ways, the constitution and procedures of the new Scottish Parliament may be said to have given effect in principle to these ideas. The Parliament is less oppositional both in physical shape and in its procedures than the Westminster Parliament. It is, at least in theory, less tied to defence of the Executive, and more able through its innovative Committee structure, rigorously to examine and critique the organs, policies and actions of government, and it is much more open than the Westminster Parliament to listening, receiving and responding to the petitions and opinions of citizens. However, when two Parliamentary committees, responding to a public petition to the Parliament on salmon farming initiated by shell fishermen, called on the Scottish Executive to initiate an inquiry into salmon farming, and government's role in promoting and regulating it, the Minister for Rural Affairs and the Environment, Ross Finnie, refused to allow an investigation.[10] Finnie is both a Liberal Democrat Member of the Scottish Parliament, and also a prominent member of the Church of Scotland. He was a member for some years of its Church and Nation Committee, that committee which seeks to express the mind of the Church to the General Assembly, and through the Assembly to the Scottish people, on matters of public policy and social concern. Finnie is then a significant representative of the partnership between Church and civic groups, parliamentary and executive institutions, which the Scottish Constitutional Convention envisaged as the new form of governance in a devolved Scotland. It is disappointing, then, that in the case of salmon farming the radical vision that Storrar, Wright and others advanced for the Scottish Parliament is less than evident in the words and actions of the relevant minister.

To those who are familiar with the extent of the corporate takeover of modern Britain, it is of no particular surprise that in the UK at the present time a government minister, whether in Scotland or England, is unwilling to enable proper public scrutiny of the activities of a major segment of the food industry. The corporatization of Britain's food production and retailing system has proceeded with the full support of both Conservative and New Labour administrations in the last twenty years, and directors and heads of food corporations have been prominent members of Conservative and Labour governments.[11] British politics north and south of the border is increasingly characterized by the transferral of the responsibilities of the state to provide public services, and to regulate those essential services – such as food production – which it does not provide to global and local corporations and international institutions such as the World Trade Organization and the European Commission. The Scottish Parliament has shown itself no more resistant to this dominant trend than the Westminster Parliament.

Forrester's own public theology reflects of course an approach fashioned before the inauguration of the Scottish Parliament. He has sought to infiltrate theological ideas into the public realm by means of dialogue and debate with policy-makers, opinion formers and civil servants, and in particular through the conferences and publications of the Centre for Theology and Public Issues which he founded fifteen years ago. This process of infiltration is character-ized by Forrester as the mobilization of fragments of truth 'quarried from the mine' of Christian doctrinal vision and ecclesial practice: 'a theologian', he suggests, 'should not be ashamed of offering initially no more than "frag-ments" of insight into public debate in the conditions of postmodernity' for 'a fragment of truth reveals that to which most people have allowed themselves to be blinded'.[12]

What fragment of truth might a Christian offer to a food company which sells great quantities of farmed salmon, such as Northern Foods which owns the large hypermarket chain Asda, and whose chairman, Lord Haskins, has been appointed by the British government to oversee an 'independent inquiry' into the future of agriculture and rural Britain? The parable of Naboth's vineyard springs to mind, as the impacts of the centralization and corporatization of food production in north Britain can be seen on every field (Scotland has no vineyards though global warming is bringing them closer to the border) and in every farming community in the land. But Forrester does not commend such a confessional approach to truth-telling for, he tells us, postmoderns are 'suspicious of grand theories and theologies'.[13] Rather, his aim is to bend the ear of the Powers in such a way as they may hear an element of Christian truth quarried, but necessarily detached from, the realms of Christian faith and practice. The idea of fragments as the core of a public theology carries with it the clear implication that theologians have no business to tell the story of the Gospel in the public square in a secular or postmodern society.[14] But this chariness does not seem to prevent Muslims, or pagans or deep ecologists from proclaiming their beliefs and ritual practices in public. Ritualized displays of dissent at global gatherings such as the G8 summit in Genoa or the EU summit in Gothenburg form a significant part of the dissenting actions of other groups whose confession involves public resistance to globalization, and the insidious dissolution of public services and public scrutiny of corporate activities around the world. Why then should Christians detach their truth fragments from their rituals, narratives and communities?

While reading *Truthful Action* I returned to an earlier, and now classic, statement concerning the social witness of the Christian in the world from that wonderful representative of the radical reformed tradition of the Mennonite Church in the USA, John Howard Yoder.[15] In his seminal essay, 'The Original Revolution', Yoder suggests that the religious sacralization of the existing order, such as existed in the various post-Reformation common-wealths of Europe, and which finds a new incarnation in daily prayers at the Scottish Parliament, was radically rejected by Jesus in his day and so cannot be an option for the disciples of Jesus in our own:

> If religion is to sanction the order that exists it must defend that order even against criticism of the prophetic word, even at the cost of the life or liberty of a prophet. The critic-from-within-the-establishment, the house prophet, will, if he stays inside when the crunch comes, be with Herod after all.[16]

Yoder rejects the idea that Christian social witness involves trying to gain a public hearing for particular truths culled from the Christian tradition, but distanced from the narratives of God's way with God's people, and from the community of the body of Christ in which these truths are embodied. According to Yoder this was not the way of Jesus Christ or the first Christians, and nor is it the way of radical Reformed churches such as the Mennonites. For Jesus, Yoder says, 'infiltrating the establishment' was not even a temptation.[17] But nor did Jesus choose withdrawal in the life of the rural village or religious sect. Instead the *original* revolution that Jesus inaugurated involved the gathering of a people 'around His word and His will. Jesus created around Himself a society like no other society mankind has ever seen'.[18] This new society had three characteristics according to Yoder: it was a voluntary society, it was mixed racially, religiously and economically, and its members pursued 'a new way of life'.[19] This new way of life involved the followers of Jesus in new practices that exemplified not withdrawal from worldly things such as money or the state but an alternative way of living in the world:

219

> He gave them a new way to deal with offenders – by forgiving them. He gave them a new way to deal with violence – by suffering. He gave them a new way to deal with money – by sharing. He gave them a new way to deal with problems of leadership – by drawing upon the gift of every member, even the most humble. He gave them a new way to deal with a corrupt society – by building a new order, not smashing the old. He gave them a new pattern of relationships between man and woman, between parent and child, between master and slave, in which was made concrete a radical new vision of what it means to be a human person. He gave them a new attitude toward the state and toward the 'enemy nation'.[20]

The anarchists who smashed banks and shops in Genoa or Gothenburg, Quebec or Seattle, are the Zealots of anti-globalization in our own day. Opposition to farmed salmon would for them involve direct action against the cages in the lochs, and against the homes and even the lives of those who tend the salmon farms, and of the corporate directors and shareholders who own them. But Jesus was as opposed to the Zealot option as he was to infiltrating the establishment. The politics of Jesus was the politics of the suffering servant named in Isaiah 42 who 'will not call out or lift his voice high, or make himself heard in the open street'. Nor will he resort to violence to 'break a bruised reed or snuff out a smouldering wick'. Instead he will 'make justice shine on every race' (Isaiah 42:3–4). And having commended this as his own way, Jesus also explains to his disciples that it is to be their way also: 'You know that in the world, rulers lord it over their subjects ... but it shall not be so with you. Among you whoever wants to be great must be your servant ... like the Son of Man; he did not come to be served but to serve, and to give up his life as a ransom for many' (Matt 20:25ff).

For Yoder these words of Jesus mean that Christians are not called to try to change the course of history through the politics of violent confrontation, but rather to witness to the alternative outcome of history that the Lordship of Christ has already established. Viewed in this light, social ethics involves following the way of Jesus Christ to the cross, a way which was triumphant only because the 'dominion of God has made use of the apparent historical failure of Jesus as a mover of men'.[21] For Yoder, then, the witness of Christians in those matters pertaining to the morality or immorality of the Powers involves 'participation in the character of God's struggle with a rebellious world, which early Quakerism referred to as "the war of the lamb"' and this approach 'has the peculiar disadvantage, or advantage, of being meaningful only if Christ be who Christians claim him to be, the Master'.[22] The central social responsibility of Christians in Yoder's account is the creation of communities of Christians whose primary purpose is to follow Christ and to witness to Christ's Lordship. In words that have echoed down the last thirty years in Christian social ethics through the Sojourners Community and the writings of Jim Wallis, and in the influential work of Stanley Hauerwas, Yoder suggests 'the very existence of such a group is itself a deep social change'. 'If it lives faithfully, it is also the most powerful tool of social change.'[23] However, this approach does not lead to sectarian withdrawal from the public domain, for the Church is not a *religious* group called together to practise particular rituals, but a public gathering, gathered to do the business of Jesus, and as Yoder puts it 'to find what it means here and now to put into practice this different quality of life which is God's promise to them and to the world and their promise to God and service to the world'.[24]

A core feature of Yoder's social ethics which demonstrates its public, as opposed to sectarian, character concerns the recognition of the role of the 'Powers' in human relationships and institutions, and their ambiguous status as created but fallen. Drawing on the work of Hendrik Berkhof and G. B. Caird amongst others, Yoder expounds the language of the Powers in the New Testament in terms of the social life and experience of humanity, and not just the demonic and angelic realm. In Galatians 4:3, Colossians 2:20 and Ephesians 2:2, St Paul identifies the 'elemental spirits of the universe' as those Powers which keep men and women in slavery and subjection to their rules, and under their tutelage, 'following the course of this world' and 'the ruler of the power of the air' (Eph 2:2). Living under the sway of the Powers characterizes the state of sin which made the Ephesians 'children of wrath' before they were made alive together with Christ (Eph 2:3–4).[25] These Powers are not just fallen angelic or demonic Powers as many liberal Protestant and Catholic exegetes have claimed, nor simply evidence of the infection of the mythic three-tier universe in the thought world of first-century Jews and Christians. Rather they are understood by St Paul, as interpreted by Yoder, Berkhof and, more recently, Walter Wink, as a way of naming the institutional and social forms which characterize all kinds of human community.[26] The Powers include states, classes, nationalisms, tribes, democratic systems and bureaucracies, religious institutions and symbol systems, ideologies, and moral codes and customs, and, for Wink, economic organizations including corporations and markets as well. The Powers are part of God's creative ordering of the cosmos in that they stand above and beyond individual humans as those ordering institutions and ideologies that are an inescapable part of human existence. Though part of God's good creation they are fallen, and prevent persons from realizing a truly free and loving existence because 'they have absolutized themselves and they demand from the individual

221

and society an unconditional loyalty'.[27] The enslavement of humanity to the fallen Powers finds divine response in the Crucifixion in which God 'disarmed the principalities and Powers and made a public example of them, triumphing over them' (Col 2:15). According to Yoder it is in witnessing to this triumph of Christ over the Powers that the Church finds its true identity and mission, not by conforming to them, nor by disregarding them as of no spiritual significance:

> The very existence of the church, in which Gentiles and Jews, who heretofore walked according to the *stocheia* (elemental spirits) of the world, live together in Christ's fellowship, is itself a proclamation, a sign, a token to the Powers that their unbroken dominion has come to an end.[28]

Critical witness to the Powers arises first and foremost not from statements of Christian truth about justice or community but from the alternative form of community life which is the Church:

> All resistance and every attack against the gods of this age will be unfruitful, unless the church herself is resistance and attack, unless she demonstrates in her life and fellowship how men can live freed from the Powers. We can only preach the manifold wisdom of God to Mammon if our life displays that we are joyfully freed from its clutches. To reject nationalism we must begin by no longer recognizing in our own bosoms any difference between peoples. We shall only resist social injustice and the disintegration of community if justice and mercy prevail in our own common life and social differences have lost their power to divide.[29]

The prioritization of the quality of the community life of the Church in Yoder's social ethics does not then involve a *withdrawal* from the world, nor a *sectarian* option, as critics of Yoder, and also Hauerwas, frequently claim. For the language of the Powers is the public face of Yoder's ecclesial ethics, and of St Paul's:

> For Paul, as interpreted by Berkhof, the very existence of the church is her primary task. It is in itself a proclamation of the Lordship of Christ to the Powers from whose dominion the church has begun to be liberated. The church does not attack the Powers; this Christ has done. The church concentrates upon not being seduced by them. By her existence she demonstrates that their rebellion has been vanquished.[30]

The Church which comprehends both the fallenness and yet the providential understanding of the character of the Powers does not treat of the social structures of the world as if they are completely outside the purposes of

222

God, and to be avoided by Christians through a process of withdrawal from worldly political engagement or social responsibility. Often the Church is called to conscientious objection to the enslavement of the Powers. But at other times the Church is called to be the 'conscience and the servant within human society'. The heart of the matter is to do this without letting the world set the agenda:

> the church must be sufficiently experienced to be able to discern when and where and how God is using the Powers, whether this be thanks to the faithful testimony of the church, or in spite of her infidelity. Either way, she is called to contribute to the creation of structures more worthy of man.[31]

The temptation in this task of social discernment is that Christians identify elements, or fragments, of Christian truth that are isolated from this larger narrative of the triumph of Christ over the Powers to which the Church is called to give witness.[32] Having so identified a principle such as justice or equality, to make common cause with others in dialogue with the Powers, the tendency is to leave aside the primary spiritual *and* social work of proclaiming the Lordship of Christ over the Powers in worship and common life, and the distinctive social practices these sustain.

For Yoder, public theology takes as its foundation the recognition that Jesus Christ is Lord both of the human community and of the Church community, of persons and the Powers that reign over their lives and the cosmos:

> The fact that the rest of the world does not yet see or know or acknowledge that destiny to which it is called is not a reason for us to posit or broker some wider or thinner vision, some lower common denominator or halfway meeting point, in order to make the world's divine destination more acceptable or accessible. The challenge to the faith community should not be to dilute or filter or translate its witness, so that the 'public' community can handle it without believing, but so to purify and clarify and exemplify it that the world can perceive it to be good news without having to learn a foreign language.[33]

But this does not mean that Christians can neglect the Powers. On the contrary, the Powers that dominate the public realm are seen as part of God's design for creation and human society and intended for the good of all, though they have become at the same time the oppressors of all.[34] According to Yoder, this dual understanding of the nature of the Powers runs prophetically counter to the univocity of the concept of power which is a core mythical feature of modernity, and to the related concept of empowerment of the weak, and so putatively powerless, which is seen by liberation theologians and others as the key to turning the tables on power.[35] Corporations which encounter the physical limits of the globe and nation states which cannot hold the centre against tribalism are both instances where the apparent strength of power is in fact revealed as bondage, as un-freedom, as weakness: 'That power is weak and weakness strong is no poetic paradox: it is a fact of life. What recent ecumenical thought calls "the epistemological privilege of the poor", what comparable Roman Catholic texts call God's "preferential option for the poor", what Tolstoy meant much earlier when he said that the oppressed are the bearers of the meaning of history, is not poetry but serious social science.'[36]

For Yoder, then, public theology takes as its fundamental point of reference the cross of Jesus Christ, in which the weakness of the cross was stronger than the strength of the powerful: 'that suffering is powerful, and that weakness wins, is true not only in heaven but on earth. That is a statement about the destiny not only of the faith community but also of all creation.'[37] Yoder, however, does not then conclude that it is impossible for Christians to identify features of human social life from their own practices toward which society as a whole may be directed. On the contrary, he identifies five sample 'civil imperatives' which may be found in the social vision of the first Christians including 'egalitarianism as implied by baptism into one body; socialism as implied in the Eucharist; forgiveness; the open meeting, and the universality of giftedness'.[38] Now these civil imperatives look rather close to some of the 'fragments' identified by Duncan Forrester in his own work in recent years, including forgiveness in relation to penal policy, and equality in relation to economic policy, so perhaps Yoder's criticism of thinness, or my own of fragments, is in the end only a matter of semantics.[39] However, for Yoder Christian witness to these markers takes the form of what he calls 'body politics'.[40] Christians for Yoder are called to embody these markers in practices in the life of the body of Christ. When they announce them to the world as elements of God's design for human sociality they do so by referring to their embodiment in the servanthood of Christ and his crucifixion by the Powers, and their ecclesial embodiment in Christian practices such as baptism, confession, table fellowship and open meetings. By so doing Christians oppose the distinction between religion and politics which is so widespread in the modern world, and in modern Christian social ethics.[41] Far from Christian rituals being of no significance for political practices and policy-making, the distinctive forms of Christian communal behaviour are the means by which Christians witness to the larger body politic against collective evils, including the corporate despoiling of local ecologies in the greedy pursuit of profit.

The particular form of body politics that bears most strongly on the issue of salmon farming is table fellowship, or Eucharist. The practice of the Eucharist was central to the life of Christians from earliest times, and was so central to the life of the Apostles in Jerusalem after Pentecost that many of them gave up eating and drinking in their own homes in order to dwell together and form what Yoder calls a new 'community of consumption'.[42] In breaking bread together the first Christians expressed an economic sharing across racial and economic divides which subverted the existing Powers, both in the form of Jewish religious institutions and laws, and Roman imperial law and practice. As Yoder puts it, 'the Lord's Supper provides ritual leverage for the condemnation of economic segregation', although Christians in subsequent eras have often failed to realize the radical implications of eucharistic worship for Christian economic life.[43]

The formation of the economic life of the people of God around eucharistic fellowship is of particular significance to salmon farming, and to the global and local food economy, which is manifest in the connections between the distinctive meal of Eucharist and all other human acts of eating and drinking. Instead of regarding Eucharist as a 'religious' meal, and meals in the home, or shared meals at church, as non-religious, we might view all actions involving the production, sale, preparation, cooking and consumption of food as significant for the Christian witness to the Powers which direct the global food economy.[44] The following words, used in some contemporary liturgies, when bread (and wine) are first taken by the celebrant, make clear the connection between eucharistic eating and drinking and the daily production of food:

> Blessed are you Lord God of All Creation. Through your goodness we have this bread to offer which earth has given and human hands have made. It will become for us the bread of life.
>
> Blessed be God for ever.

Bread and wine were and are paradigmatic foods in the Middle East and these words point to one of the core meanings of the Eucharist as symbol of the abundance of God's redeemed creation, and of the role of good earth and good work in realizing that abundance in the form of food to sustain the human community. Eucharistic feasting calls to mind, and sanctifies, other acts of human work on the land, of human food production, of human eating and feasting. The body and blood of Christ represent in the liturgical present

God's life in Jesus who in his death and resurrection redeemed humankind and moved the whole creation towards that future shalom when 'the lion shall eat straw and the nursing child shall play over the hole of the asp' (Isa 11:7b–8a).

And there is a third meaning of Eucharist which is significant for these deliberations. Christians speak of 'celebrating the Eucharist' but too often their ritual feasts feel less than celebratory: solemn assemblies are far more characteristic of the practice of the Lord's Supper, especially in Scotland, than celebration and partying. It may be this very solemnity that prevents Christians from making the connections between Eucharist and food consumption and the food economy. Jesus by contrast often seems to have enjoyed himself when he ate and drank with his disciples, and even with outcasts and sinners. As Walter Wink comments, 'Maybe Jesus was not just making a point when he ate with tax collectors and sinners. Maybe they were more fun to be with than the religious authorities! Maybe he was identified as "a glutton and a drunkard" (Matt 11:19) not just because he was seeking the outcasts where they were, but because he enjoyed having a good time.'[45] If Christians in Scotland are to make the connections between the food economy and worship we will need to recover in our eucharistic practice a sense of enjoyment in worship, and in particular of the joy and grace of eucharistic celebration. We will need to recover the eucharist as the central determinative act of Christian worship in all our churches Sunday by Sunday. And we will need to recover the connections between the Eucharistic feast and the enjoyment of food in Christian homes.

The practice of enjoying meals together and in common is increasingly threatened in some Western countries. In our own street in Edinburgh I am assured by my children that we are peculiar in the amount of time we devote to the regular preparation of shared family meals. Many time-poor families have now resorted to the television, the microwave and the supermarket as purveyor of individualized acts of leisure and food consumption which are inexorably destroying family fellowship over the dinner table, and corroding social ecology. Christian celebration of table fellowship involves daily as well as weekly acts of resistance to the privatization and individuation of consumption that is characteristic of the global food economy.[46] But these acts of resistance are not hair-shirt acts of self-denial. On the contrary, taking time to prepare and eat good food together is a central source of human enjoyment, though this is perhaps more evident in some non-Western contexts now than in the fast food culture we increasingly inhabit in the West.[47]

Taking time is in itself significant, as the Powers which direct global capitalism engage in what Nicholas Boyle calls their 'endless endeavour to make us all work more for less'.[48] Fly-fishing for wild salmon requires patience and skill and takes time, as does preparing a collective celebration, whether the Sunday Eucharist, or table fellowship in the home. The salmon farm, like the microwaved dinner, is designed to 'save' time. But of course it may have the opposite effect as more often means less: an individual frozen and microwaveable 'salmon crumble' is not actually a cheap meal, as compared say to an oven-baked potato or risotto. And the time it takes to earn the money to buy the labour-saving meal, and the labour-saving device in which to cook it, is time lost for contemplation, family interaction or community celebration.[49]

Taking time to celebrate the breaking of bread together, both in church and in the home, may then be seen as forms of resistance in the global food economy and this resistance goes beyond ritual symbolism to call into question fundamental features of the Powers which, in the form of capitalist ideology and corporate practices, advance the globalized food economy. Christians break bread in recognition that the death and resurrection of Christ represent the defeat of the Powers and that the peace of creation and the reign of God are already breaking in as they meet together around the Lord's Table. This determinative act of worship of the creator, with all its echoes in other acts related to eating and food production, already anticipates the praise of all peoples that the Psalmists declared would be offered to God at the end of all things. Such anticipatory actions are the seed ground of faith that globalization can be recovered from monopolization by corporate power, that unregulated free markets are not part of a natural pattern of human evolution and that the trouncing of the Powers is not just a past or a future event but one that is constantly breaking into our present reality, and especially so when we break the bread which is Christ's body and drink the wine of his new life.

Notes

1 WWF and Atlantic Salmon Federation, *The Status of Wild Atlantic Salmon: A River by River Assessment* (London: WWF, 2001), p. 10. See also *Statistical Bulletin: Scottish Salmon and Sea Trout Catches 1998* (Edinburgh: Scottish Executive, Rural Affairs Department and Fisheries Research Department, 1999).

2 Albert Borgmann, *Crossing the Postmodern Divide* (Chicago, IL: University of Chicago Press, 1992).

3 Friends of the Earth Scotland, *Salmon Farming: The One That Got Away* (Edinburgh: Friends of the Earth, 2000).

4 *Ibid.*

5 Duncan B. Forrester, 'Reformed radical orthodoxy: can it be retrieved?', in Forrester, *Truthful Action: Explorations in Practical Theology* (Edinburgh: T&T Clark, 2000), pp. 161–84.

6 *Ibid.*, p. 169.

7 'Church and Nation Committee, 1989 Report on the Government of Scotland', in Jock Stein (ed.), *Scottish Self-Government: Some Christian Viewpoints* (Edinburgh: Handsel Press, 1989), pp. 14–24.

8 Forrester, *Truthful Action*, p. 183.

9 '1989 Report on the Government of Scotland', pp. 17–23.

10 Letter to Minister for Rural Development, Ross Finnie, dated 8 Feb. 2001, signed by Andy Kerr MSP (on behalf of the Transport and Environment Committee) and Alex Johnstone MSP (on behalf of the Rural Development Committee). See also James Freeman, 'Salmon farming inquiry rejected', *Glasgow Herald*, 2 May 2001.

11 For a full account of the corporatization of food production and retail in Britain, see further George Monbiot, *Captive State: The Corporate Takeover of Britain* (London: Macmillan, 2000), and for an account of its impacts on rural Britain, see further Graham Harvey, *The Killing of the Countryside* (London: Jonathan Cape, 1997). For a theological perspective, see Michael S. Northcott, 'Behold I have set the land before you (Deut. 1.8): Christian ethics, GM foods, and the culture of modern farming', in Celia Deane Drummond (ed.), *Reordering Nature: Theology, Society and the New Genetics* (London: T&T Clark, 2003).

12 Forrester, 'The public theology of a servant people', in *Truthful Action*, p. 154.

13 *Ibid.*, p. 152.

14 *Ibid.*, p. 152.

15 Though see Stanley Hauerwas's ironically entitled essay 'On why *The Politics of Jesus* is not a classic', in his *A Better Hope: Resources for a Church Confronting Capitalism, Democracy, and Postmodernity* (Grand Rapids, MI: Brazos Press, 2000), pp. 129–38.

16 John Howard Yoder, 'The original revolution', in *The Original Revolution: Essays in Christian Pacifism* (Scottdale, PA: Herald Press, 1971), p. 21.

17 *Ibid.*

18 *Ibid.*, p. 28.

19 *Ibid.*, pp. 28–9.

20 *Ibid.*, p. 29.

21 Yoder, *The Original Revolution*, p. 242.

22 *Ibid.*

23 *Ibid.*, p. 31.

24 *Ibid.*, p. 29.

25 *Ibid.*, pp. 142–3.
26 See further, Hendrik Berkhof, *Christ and the Powers* (Scottdale, PA: Herald Press, 1961), and Walter Wink's Powers trilogy and in particular his *Engaging the Powers: Discernment and Resistance in a World of Domination* (Minneapolis, MN: Fortress Press, 1992).
27 J. H. Yoder, *The Politics of Jesus* (Grand Rapids, MI: Eerdmans, 1972), p. 146.
28 Berkhof, *Christ and the Powers*, pp. 41–2, cited in Yoder, *Politics of Jesus*, pp. 150–1.
29 Yoder, *Politics of Jesus*, pp. 150–1.
30 *Ibid.*
31 *Ibid.*, p. 158.
32 Yoder shows how J. H. Oldham in his contribution to the first assembly of the post-war ecumenical movement in Amsterdam in 1948 argued that the primary social task of the Church was the practice of the common life of Christians (Oldham, 'A responsible society', in *The Church and the Disorder of Society*, Vol. 3 in the Amsterdam Assembly Series *Man's Disorder and God's Design* (New York: Harper, 1948), but also how subsequent assemblies of the World Council of Churches moved toward studies of specific social problems in which the specifically Christian point of view receded and an attempt was made to discover a 'basis for social cooperation between Christians and non-Christians' which was 'something other than a specifically Christian standard. We cannot be sure that in all this process of study the central importance of the Christian community as a new humanity was kept in view, not only as a verbal affirmation, but also as an instrument of social change' (Yoder, *Politics of Jesus*, pp. 155–6).
33 John Howard Yoder, 'The paradigmatic public role of God's people', in his *For the Nations: Essays Public and Evangelical* (Grand Rapids, MI: Eerdmans, 1997), p. 24.
34 *Ibid.*, p. 35.
35 See, for example, Duncan Forrester's account of empowerment in his essay 'Power and pastoral care', in Forrester, *Truthful Action*, pp. 73–89.
36 Yoder, 'The paradigmatic public role of God's people', p. 35.
37 *Ibid.*
38 *Ibid.*, p. 33.
39 On forgiveness and its relevance to penal policy, see Duncan B. Forrester, 'Priorities for social theology today', in Michael Northcott (ed.), *Vision and Prophecy: The Tasks of Social Theology Today* (Edinburgh: Centre for Theology and Public Issues, 1991), pp. 29–31 and on equality and its relevance to welfare and taxation policies, see Forrester, *On Human Worth: A Christian Vindication of Equality* (London: SCM Press, 2001).
40 See further John Howard Yoder, *Body Politics: Five Practices of the Christian Community before the Watching World* (Nashville, TN: Discipleship Resources, 1992).

41 *Ibid.*, pp. 73ff.

42 *Ibid.*, p. 18.

43 *Ibid.*

44 The involvement of local congregations in the sale of 'fairly traded' goods such as Traidcraft tea, coffee, chocolate and other foodstuffs is one example of this witness.

45 Walter Wink, *Engaging the Powers*, p. 321.

46 One of the greatest contrasts between life in a postmodern consumerist Britain, and life in 'pre-modern' or 'early modern' communities, concerns the degree of fun, of sheer enjoyment and pleasure, that people take in each others' company, and in particular in communal acts of eating. I well remember in Malaysia visiting villages during the month of Ramadan in which vast woks of rice and fish were being prepared by whole groups of people as they prepared to break their fast together at sundown. And there was a similar infectious pleasure in food even in Kuala Lumpur around the many street stalls where special foods were prepared for sale in the streets as evening during Ramadan approached.

47 As Britain increasingly embraces a fast food and microwave dinner culture, a poor substitute for a richer food culture has emerged in the form of the growing number of television programmes in which professional cooks or wine bibbers prepare and enjoy good food and drink on screen, while their viewers are mostly watching and eating alone.

48 N. Boyle, *Who Are We Now? Christian Humanism in the Global Market from Hegel to Healey* (Edinburgh: T&T Clark, 1998), p. 316.

49 Anthropologists have long observed that so-called primitive societies have far more free time for social interaction and enjoyment than advanced industrial societies. Marshall Sahlins speaks of the 'original affluence' of the hunter-gatherer societies he describes in his *Stone Age Economics* (Chicago, IL: Aldine, 1972), pp. 42ff.

Chapter 14

Living Without Dreams:
Is There a Spirituality for Justice
in a Globalized World?

MARY C. GREY

Introduction

In 1990, at the Ecumenical Forum of European Christian Women's Conference in York, a group of women from the former East Germany surprised many of us by performing a mime for the Assembly. We had imagined them euphoric at the fall of Communism and alleged liberation of the country. Instead of this, we watched them walking in a circle, symbolizing the loss of dreams. Now they were once more in the wilderness like the children of Israel. But with one key difference – without a vision of the Promised Land. The socialist dream was dead – only the alluring arms of Western capitalism beckoned.

Ten years later, at a gathering at the Boldern Academy in the mountains outside Zurich, Switzerland, the consequences of not only political change but the war in Bosnia and Kosovo, and consequent remapping of the Balkan countries, emerged clearly, as groups of young women testified as to what this loss of dreaming meant for them.[1] Deepening spirals of poverty, complete vanishing of hope and lives defined by the struggle to survive from day to day – all this sums up what they were saying.

This loss of dreaming is directly associated with the economic, political and social consequences of globalization. *Globalization* is a concept tossed around with a multitude of meanings. Cultural globalization may be welcomed by many, but many meanings are ambiguous. In the desert of Rajasthan a few months ago, we stumbled across a villager with a Nike shirt and one in a Manchester United sweatshirt. McDonald's, as you all know, has taken over the world. Bizarre cultural surprises are to be anticipated. As Polly Toynbee wrote:

A traveller across the desert wastes of the Sahara arrives at last at Timbuktu, where the first denizen he meets is wearing a Texan baseball cap. Pilgrims in the Himalayas in search of the ultimate wilderness in the furthest kingdom find Everest strewn with rubbish, in tins, plastic bags, coca-cola bottles and all the remnants of the modern global picnicker. Explorers of the Arctic complain that empty plastic bottles of washing up liquid are embedded in the ice. Tony Giddens opened his Reith lectures with the tale of an anthropologist trekking to a remote corner of Cambodia for a field study – only to find her first night's entertainment was not traditional local pastimes, but a viewing of *Basic Instinct* on video. The film, at this point, had not even reached the cinemas in London.[2]

My argument is not directed against *all* aspects of a global culture in a negative manner. Liberation theology, the Ecumenical Movement, WCC, the World Parliament, the Beijing Congress, Interreligious Dialogue, Jubilee 2000 and the global women's movement are all examples of international solidarity which can work towards achieving peace and justice. It is the way that unregulated global capitalism knowingly works for the wealth of a few and sacrifices the well-being of the majority that is the focus here. One quotation sums this up. This is how the US policy planner George Kennan saw the challenge of the post-Second World War era back in 1948:

We (that is, America) have 50% of the world's wealth but only 6.3% of its population ... In this situation we cannot fail to be the object of envy and resentment ... Our real task in the coming period is to devise a pattern of relationships which will allow us to maintain this position of disparity. *We should cease to talk about the raising of living standards, human rights and democratisation.* The day is not far off when we are going to have to deal in straight power concepts. The less we are then hampered by idealistic slogans, the better.[3] [My italics]

It could be George Bush speaking – but this was 1948. There it is, in its most naked and brutal form – the context where an American and Western European-created economic system of unregulated markets operates *intentionally* for the increasing wealth of a few, and for the increasing desperate poverty of multitudes, of whom the largest proportion struggle for survival in the countries of the southern hemisphere. The point is both that it is global and deliberate. It is well known how these policies affect poor communities. Here is a comment from the Indira Gandhi Institute of Development and Research, the Reserve Bank of India, in a mid-year review of 1994–5:

Deregulation has freed Indian industries to decide what to produce, how to produce, how much to produce and where to produce ... [The authors go on to say that the paradigm of growth has not changed since Nehru's day – except that the actors have changed: the market has replaced the state. They comment:] Suffice it to say here that, *by definition, globalisation-led growth cannot be expected to pivot itself in the constituency of the poor*; especially when top ten percent of India's 90 million offer an immediate and lucrative market.[4] [My italics]

The feature of globalization that is directly relevant to this chapter is, according to David Korten, that globalization creates a common consumer culture unifying all people in a shared quest for material gratification, where relationships both individual and corporate are defined entirely by the market, and where there are no loyalties to place or community.[5]

Perhaps the worst feature of all, writes the ecofeminist Vandana Shiva, in the midst of all the *epiphanies of darkness* of the current situation, is the fact that

> With globalisation, life itself has emerged as the ultimate commodity. Planet Earth is being replaced by Life Inc. in the world of free trade and deregulated commerce. Through patents and genetic engineering, new colonies are being carved out.[6]

There has been a loss of diversity as to what 'life' means, since all life has shrunk to the business model of life:

> Implicit is that business is the greatest possible model of life; far superior to governments, nationalities, cultures etc. There is no talk of differentiated and diverse cultures of people, of ethnicity or gender, of animals and land, of national or international regulations or indeed that there is any genuine limitation to this frontier of capital exchange. This 'globe' of which they speak is an utter abstraction with no accountability to anything but economics.[7]

And in the shrinking of what life has come to mean, somehow we have stopped dreaming. Or rather, society has become a bad dream, a global theme park, from which we cannot wake up. There is no space to escape to. In this commodification of life, where money is the idol, Aristotle's logic has been reversed. At the beginning of the *Nicomachean Ethics*, he remarks that 'wealth is evidently not the good we are seeking; for it is merely useful for the sake of something else'.[8] But now, means have become ends: it is money itself that is desired, yearned for, dreamed of, money for which we have sold our collective soul.

It is an addiction that in psychic and in psycho-spiritual terms has hijacked our imaginations, cheapened and vulgarized our aspirations of fulfilment, and the degree of mutuality and intimacy we could hope to attain in relationship. It has substituted yearning for the infinite and experience of the sacred, for an insatiable, endless grasping for some new consumer good. For the economic system absolutely depends on us never being satisfied with the new car, TV, shoes or dress, and will drip feed us with insatiable desires for the next brand. It is the corporate addiction of our consumer society, writes Bruce Wilshire, in *A Wild Hunger*, 'which fails to acknowledge the total capacities of body-selves who need responsible agency and meaning in life and who long to circulate back and forth across the boundary between wilderness and civilisation'.[9]

Thomas Berry calls this a 'deep cultural pathology ... When the power of ecstasy is subverted into destructive channels, then, as in the Roman world, we are in a disastrous situation.'[10]

So, if our dreaming, imaginative, ecstatic capacities have been stultified, what has theology to say about this?

Where is the Theological Response?

Sadly, we are faced with a theological and spiritual vacuum. In 1999 in the conference, 'Proclaiming the Gospel in a World of Global Capitalism', many speakers denounced global capitalism in trenchant terms. Indeed, it was a precondition of being invited to speak! Ian Linden identified the lack of engagement with economic thought and context as a weakness of liberation theology. Alastair Kee challenged Jon Sobrino with the thesis that liberation theology has merely interpreted the world of the poor and not transformed it, that it was conservative rather than radical and is not facing up to the new global economic situation. As far as I know, his challenge has not been answered.[11] I want here to explore why, in all the well-meaning attempts to form and live a prophetic spirituality of justice, these efforts – individual and communal – seem largely ineffective, even unnoticed, in the face of the changed global context.

What have we considered to be key features of such a spirituality for justice? The first feature would seem to be resistance and protest.[12] From peace protests, vigils, marches, solidarity with political prisoners, non-violent *satyagrahas*,[13] to ecumenical worship crying out for justice, a spirituality of resistance has reached out with networks of global solidarity, encounters beyond the boundaries of narrowly defined identity and beyond the boundaries of sacred/secular. It must remain a key dimension in any spirituality of justice. Apartheid would never have been toppled without such a spirituality. The spirituality emerging from the Peace Camps of the early 1980s, from green circles, from Women Church, from a range of justice and peace movements has offered many – unhappy with institutional limitations – an authentic way to belong to the Christian Church. But it has not toppled the killing systems – or even ruffled their neo-colonial feathers.

But is it not true that authentic biblical prophetic spiritualities of resistance always go hand in hand, yes, with critique, analysis and condemnation of the injustices of the context, but also with vision and imagination of alternatives, God's alternatives, God's dreams, together with a lament for what is lost, for withering of land and community alike? It is precisely vision and imagination that we are missing here. As George Monbiot wryly remarked after the riots and looting that are now regularly following WTO meetings like Davos, Cologne and Prague, 'we know what we are against, but we are not very good at saying what we are for'.[14] Any alternatives to global capitalism seem anodyne and without transformative power.

But this is precisely the problem that globalization sets before us. The dreams that Isaiah, for example, put before the people in exile, the dream of the Kingdom of God that Jesus proclaimed, was one where poor people are central, where the marginalized have a respected place, where ecological limits of the earth are respected. As one contemporary equivalent I cite Horace Dammers's Life Style movement, *Life Style: A Parable of Sharing*.[15] Attempting to live a different kind of lifestyle – simply, sustainable, compassionate, less consumerism and so on, has long been a vital part of spiritualities of justice. (And the Life Style movement does have a prophetic voice.) But the problem is that to suggest to people that a culture of austerity and simplicity is what is needed, does not work in a culture where everyone is convinced that consumption and the acquisition of money and possessions make us happy. To suggest that asylum-seekers and environmental refugees should be welcomed brings out the most unpleasant forms of ethnic clannishness – because identity now depends, it seems, on exclusion of the non-consumers and the non-spenders.

How to break out of this impasse is the question. In pondering this for the last few years, I do not have solutions but a few clues. First, this is a deeply *spiritual* crisis of values – though its expressions are economic. A spiritual crisis needs a spiritual answer and this is what is missing. The cosmologist Brian Swimme mourned the fact that young people in ancient tribes were taken by their elders to caves to be initiated into the mysteries of the universe. If today's caves are the darkened rooms in front of the TV, where initiation into the titillation of the advertisements grinds on inexorably through the evening, it is not Plato's caves of ignorance that need to be returned to, but deep wellsprings of spiritual inspiration. Vincent Rossi, an Orthodox priest, also writes in the context of the environmental crisis, that its roots are spiritual.

> The crisis we face is not primarily an ecological crisis; it is rather first a theological or metaphysical crisis … a crisis in the way we think about the world … I now believe that our environmental crisis is first of all a tropological crisis, … a crisis of the imaginative morality and moral vision, of the heart first and the mind second. It is primarily a crisis in the way we feel.[16]

This is not to say that protest and resistance must not always remain an important dimension of spirituality: but the roots of such a spirituality must be watered and sustained by what is longed for. '*Mine, O Lord, O give my roots rain*', as the poet Hopkins cried.[17]

Since the responses theologians tend to give – with a few exceptions – are more and more nuanced analyses and criticisms, without recovering the dream, *What are we for … ?* remains the question. But, seeing that protest arises from widely disparate sources, a clue lies here for the kind of dream sought. The dream that eludes must appeal across boundaries. If liberation theology divided people into oppressors or victims, then the search is for a language that does not polarize in this way. Leaving the oppression for the land of freedom – the Exodus motif – can no longer function as sole inspiration when there is no space to go to, where oppressions are multiple and interrelated. History frequently obliterates the struggles of women to maintain home and community amidst the death-dealing systems. 'This above all: to choose not to be a victim', was how Margaret Attwood ended her novel *Surfacing*.[18] 'Victimhood' takes away the responsibility and agency of people as they struggle to cope with multiple oppressions. It masks the immense determination to survive, and the cherished belief in the preciousness of life expressed by poor people. As Jon Sobrino wrote in the aftermath of the earthquake in El Salvador:

> in the midst of this tragedy, life carried on regardless: people in long lines, walking or in old jalopies, with bundles on their heads and children grasping their hands – this is the most fundamental expression of life and of the desire to live. Life bursts forth from the best of what we are and have. Poor people, often extremely poor and with precious little education, put everything they are and have in the service of life, and often they do so because they have little else left.[19]

But this 'dream of a common language'[20] or 'a common language for the dream' still begs the question of content. As I said, the dream of the messianic feast where all are welcome (asylum-seekers and mentally disabled included) has ceased to appeal to all but a few. A culture of austerity enabling this has been ruled out by the universal seduction of wealth-seeking.

Is a clue not given here by Sobrino's witness that life is more than the commodified reductionism of the economic model? In the struggle to hang onto life, community, celebration and festivity and hope demonstrated by poor communities of the south and richer communities of the north in solidarity with them, can a beginning be found?

Musing again for the intimations of a common language for the dream, the apathy of the British elections and the anger of the protesters against the WTO suggest at least the weariness with spin-doctoring, suppression of truth and longing for an honest approach to public life. I thought of the Islamic poet Rumi, writing of being awoken from sleep:

> Why, when God's world is so big, did you fall asleep in a prison of all places?[21]

The idea that the seductions of global capitalism have cast us into a corporate (*sic*!) sleep suggests that the awakening needed from the bad dream is an awakening into truth. This is where the figure of Mahatma Gandhi, *the great-souled-one*, comes into his own: as he wrote in his prophetic document, *Hind Swaraj*:

> Those who are intoxicated by modern civilisation are not likely to write against it. Their care will be to find out facts and arguments in support of it, and this they do unconsciously, believing it to be true. A man while he is dreaming, believes in his dream; he is undeceived only when he is awakened from his sleep.[22]

How then to awaken from the prison of sleep, from the power of the bad dream? In what follows I want to explore the interrelatedness of Gandhian spirituality with the ideas of truth, freedom and spirit – all in the context of the recovery of dreaming.

Gandhi and the Search for Truth

Why return to this deeply controversial figure? Bitterly rejected by the Dalits as having excluded them from the Indian constitution, widely considered to have been left behind by the forces of progress, his ideas on the village-republics both idealized and archaic, his views on women ambiguous, how can I defend this move? Even *The Times of India*, in a recent article in his honour, on the anniversary of his death, titled it 'The Dismantling of the Mahatma'.[23]

I begin with a personal story. For the last fourteen years I have worked with an organization, *Wells for India*, in drought-afflicted desert areas of

Rajasthan (NW India).[24] Our partners are Gandhians and it is their vision that has convinced me of Gandhi's relevance. The story of Laxmi and Shashi Tyagi, leaders of *Gravis* (village self-help organization), brought by a former Gandhian Prime Minster, Mr Desai, to try to cope with the famine in Bihar, and then arriving in Rajasthan to respond to the water crisis, is particularly striking. The initial attempts of the Tyagis to build and deepen wells and deepen village ponds had focused on the poorest and most vulnerable sector of the villages. But this had brought the fury of the Rajputs down on them, with the disastrous consequence that their field centre was completely burnt down, destroying all records and personal belongings.[25] But the Tyagis, even though they were also stoned and attacked by the angry mob, refused to give way to revenge, and even argued with the police not to prosecute their attackers. 'We do not blame you,' they said, 'You were not given a chance – you had no proper education.'[26] This is a living-out of the Gandhian belief in the innate goodness of the human person. If some one is given a real chance to move out of the prison of both poverty and evildoing, so the theory goes, they will take it. In this case it worked. The upper caste people have become some of their greatest supporters. The Tyagis now have fifteen field centres in the Thar desert – in the worst-hit area of drought – where they have set up Hedcon, a consortium of Gandhian organizations in Rajasthan, and they continually maintain the principle of working with all people, and not merely untouchables or tribals to the exclusion of the Rajputs. Indeed, if one simply looks at the situation of women, Rajput women too suffer deeply from poverty, lack of education, caste-based patriarchy and endemic violence.[27]

The point of the story is to illustrate the contemporary influence of Gandhi on many levels. Maybe it is true that Gandhi was caught in 'the trap of his own Utopianism'.[28] It is certainly no answer to globalization to condemn all aspects of material civilization. 'I cannot recall a single good point in connection with machinery', he says *(Hind Swaraj*, p. 96), ignoring even the ship on which he was sailing. What I see in the praxis and inspiration of *Gravis* are the valuing of poor communities in a wider vision of the power of truth, reconciliation and non-violence. Non-violence is particularly outstanding in the use made of the Gandhian action of *satyagraha* (mentioned earlier). These protests are regularly held, with such disparate goals as resistance to the Indian atomic bomb experiments (these are contiguous with *Gravis* projects and villages where they are active), a massive protest that the government had failed the people in the drought context and, more recently, to protest against the police's failure to act on the report of the rape of a young Rajput woman – because the perpetrators were a powerful landlord family.

It is the coincidence with the Christian vision of the Kingdom of God that is striking. It is not that the spirituality of resistance mentioned earlier is outmoded, but that it becomes *a mysticism of resistance*. This is a mysticism far removed from simply a personal union with God. As I argued in *Prophecy and Mysticism*, mysticism is a communally owned stance of standing for truth in everyday life.[29] Since everyday life is submerged in the reality of globalization, so mysticism can be experienced as a communally owned political stance. Ethics is recoupled with economics. Here is how Dorothee Sölle described it in an earlier text. The context is a demonstration for peace:

> It was a slap on the face after years of peace work in the hope of liberation, years in which we had invested time, strength, money ... I had to give a speech and did not know what to say. Many of us demonstrators were soaked by water cannons and were hunted through the streets by the police and did not know what to say. 'Why have you forsaken us, God? Why did you not show us your face? Why did you not prepare "a table in the presence of our foes" ... ?' I cannot remember what I said in that dark night, but one text was 'The truth will make us free', an invocation to God so that the truth may not be forever buried in lies ... The God to whom this prayer was addressed was as grieved as we were, small like us, with no bank accounts and bombs in the background, exactly like us.[30]

Again, a Gandhian-like appeal for the power of truth. The same spirit emerges from Arundhati Roy's powerful text, *The Cost of Living*, written as a protest against the Narmada Dam scheme. Again a mystical appeal to other kinds of truth, other kinds of dreams, rings out:

> To love. To be loved. To never forget your own significance. To never get used to the unspeakable violence and the vulgar disparity of life around you. To seek joy in the saddest places. To pursue beauty to its lair. To never simplify what is complicated or complicate what is simple. To respect strength, never power. To try to understand. To never look away. And never, never forget.[31]

Arundhati Roy is no Gandhian, but, like Sölle, there is a conviction that the realistic facing of the power of truth is the only starting point. As Bhikhu Parekh argued, in 'Is Gandhi still relevant?', a new theory of revolution is needed. *Satyagraha*, he writes, defines this revolution:

> it presupposed a deeper sense of shared humanity to give meaning and energy to its sense of justice. The sense of humanity consisted in the recognition of the fundamental ontological fact that humanity was indivisible, that human beings grew and fell together, and that in degrading and brutalising others, they degraded and brutalised themselves.[32]

239

The *satyagrahi* – enlightened one – like the Buddhist *bodhisattva*, takes upon himself or herself the burden of corporate evil and sustains this by the power of suffering love. The power that *satyagraha* relies on is soul-force rather than brute force, the power of persuasion rather than coercion, as Gandhi's numerous hunger strikes demonstrate. The *satyagrahi*'s endurance of prison sentences is also witness to this power of self-sacrifice.[33]

In the stress on the power of truth lies the hope of the recovery of dreaming. Gandhi's ideas of truth emerged from the early text *Hind Swaraj*, written on the ship taking him back to India after his South African experiences.[34] Although they underwent a considerable evolution, from the beginning they included social as well as personal transformation. Important for the argument here is that *swaraj* is linked with the idea of freedom as the inherent possession of human beings. Freedom means the 'capacity to' or 'power to' act – but always out of the interiorization of obligations to others. (In feminist theory this would be seen as 'the self-in-relation'.) It is also linked with the notion of village self-sufficiency, with *satya* (truth) and *ahimsa* (non-violence). Hence the interlinked idea of freedom and truth. Swaraj is also linked with *moksha*, enlightenment. But for Gandhi this is a corporate idea involving the enlightenment of all, historically grounded, and in the concrete struggle of the poor for humanity. 'I cannot find God apart from humanity', he continually said.[35]

But this would develop into a much richer notion of God as truth:

Where there is God there is truth, and where there is truth, there is God.[36]

But truth is a goal to be embodied historically: it is not an archetype or a revelation of truth as a final *telos*. Truth is attainable in every heart, it is discoverable in the great religions, and is reflected in the moral order of justice governing the universe.[37] Finally Gandhi moves to what is known as 'the great reversal'. He told the story himself to some atheistic conscientious objectors in Switzerland 1931:

But deep down in me I say God may be love, but God is truth. If it is possible for the human being to give the fullest description of God, for myself I have come to the conclusion that God is truth. But two years ago I went a step further and said Truth is God ... and I came to that conclusion after a relentless search after Truth which began so many years ago ... I have never found a double meaning in connection with Truth and not even atheists have denied the necessity or power of Truth. In their passion for discovering Truth, they have not hesitated even to deny the existence of God – for their own point of view rightly. And it

240

was because of their reasoning that I saw I was not going to say 'God is Truth': but 'Truth is God'.[38]

Here Gandhi united four ideas – truth as reality, as ultimate concern (to use Tillich's phrase), as Being and as justice. It is to be lived out as *ahimsa*, or 'redemptive self-suffering love'; or as *satyagraha*, 'truth force' or 'soul-force'. And the arena in which the drama is lived out is political, economic, social, spiritual and religious.

All of this forms the background to Gandhi's idea of a 'transformed kingdom of human relationship' which he named Ramrajya.[39] This society of mutual love and concern was a global vision. Feminist theology prefers to name this the *kin-dom* of just relationships – to remove links with imperialism and to affirm that we are sisters and brothers in the new creation.

Gandhi's vision ended tragically in his own lifetime – but then, so did Christ's. The India he longed for became tragically divided, and the fruits of this division, that he had so vehemently opposed, still provoke hatred and violent deaths. I recall Gandhi's emphasis as one foundation for spirituality in the context of globalization because it offers truth in a context of the absence of it, subsumes freedom to truth ('the truth will set you free'), rejects all forms of violence, including the violence of seductions of consumerism, and because the belief in peoples' participation in structures of society responds to the current apathy as to government, the 'it doesn't matter whether I vote or not' attitude expressed by so many young people in Britain in May 2001.

And it is the congruence of these ideas with a Christian theology of the Spirit that I see to be the contribution carrying over into the new millennium, a conviction that it is the power of the Spirit to reconnect personal life with public and reawaken a people become apathetic and disillusioned with public life and church life alike. This I offer in conclusion.

Recovering the Dream

Convinced of the power of truth to motivate us to a widened vision of freedom, how does this lead to the recovery of dreaming? As Yeats wrote:

> For it is dreams
> That lift us to the flowing, changing world
> That the heart longs for. What is love itself
> Even though it be the lightest of light love,
> But dreams that hurry from beyond the world.[40]

241

Since the dying Jesus prayed that his followers would be consecrated in truth, and that the Spirit would lead into all truth, then it is in the power of the Spirit that the hope for the recovery of dreaming, imagination and vision lies. Secondly, I have argued that freedom and truth are integrally intertwined but that, contrary to contemporary idolatry of money, the priority of truth awakens visions of a different moral order and include the dreams of rejected categories of people. The economist Amartya Sen bases his ideas of development on a widened concept of freedom, including well-being, and the proper functioning, or the fulfilment of capabilities.[41] Like Gandhi, he sees freedom as attainable, yes, by public policy, but also by the effective use of participatory capabilities of ordinary people. Together with the philosopher Martha Nussbaum, he sees this as lying within a vision of *flourishing* – the old Aristotelian notion of *eudaimonia* (see also its use by Grace Jantzen in her book, *Becoming Divine*).[42] I see in this the coalescing of the Christian notion of flourishing of the *kin-dom* of right relationships and the Gandhian notion of the dignity of the most vulnerable person. The point of this is to present a vision of flourishing ranging from the most basic of human needs, to possibilities for relationship, exercise of human rights and living life to the full.[43] For Nussbaum this includes religion as a vital element.[44]

All this inspires confidence that a renewed theology of the Spirit can reawaken the power of dreaming. I use *spirit* in the widened sense, in the way Moltmann does, as 'the power of life and space for living', and as splicing a way through the false dichotomies, *God – or freedom?*[45] Spirit is understood as vitality, as energy, as the great awakener to widened visions of truth. I wrote earlier of the Spirit's power to discover cracks in culture to give birth to alternative cultural expressions, appealing to the disenchanted, as well as to the disenfranchised.[46]

Spirit reawakens the power of dreaming as first, the breath of Life, the Spirit of creativity since the dawn of creation. From those few words at the beginning of the Bible, 'A mighty wind that swept over the surface of the waters' (Gen 1:2, NEB), we are given the sense of elemental, creative, form-less energy, the energy of connection breathing life into all creatures. The breath of life emerges from chaos, formless void. The sense that the Spirit is the energy of connection links God's spirit/human spirit in a rich way. God's presence may be experienced in a hidden form in human courage, persever-ance, refusal to give way to despair. The late John Taylor saw the Spirit as the spirit of mutuality (in my terms, relation and connection), the life-force drawing people together.[47] Taylor calls these experiences *annunciations*. I call them *epiphanies* of the Spirit whose field force, the field force of mutuality, is wider than all established religions.

The Spirit as mutuality, drawing us into relationships of just relation, is a key directional impulse today, where our problems cluster around broken relation, trivial relation, the cheapening of sexual relation by the absence of commitment. Feminist theologian, Nancy M. Victorin Vangerud, in her book *The Raging Hearth*, has developed a theology of spirit as 'mutual recognition', transforming political, church and household monotheism.[48]

This links with the ancient meaning of the Spirit as the *depth dimension of God*. The Spirit as depth challenges a culture which lives to superficiality, to virtual reality instead of embodied relationships and urges on the WTO protesters who know they want an alternative world, but as yet cannot articulate its content. The Spirit is also active in the waiting, the openness, the attentiveness, the *waiting-on-God* stance of prophetic people like Simone Weil;[49] the 'I said to my soul, be still, wait without hope', stance of Eliot.[50] Linked with what the Buddhists call *sunyata* – emptiness, or no-thing, paying attention requires listening, hearing into speech, reaching out across the silences. This in turn links with the Spirit as leading us into the unknown. Rooted in Jewish and Christian history, the urging of the prophetic Spirit of hope has created and is creating the force field of witness, of solidarity, of prophetic community. The Spirit of truth cracks open not only new possibilities but also cracks open the false assumptions, the notions of personhood that sell humanity short, that cheapen and devalue relationships.

Through this movement into uncharted territory, the Spirit urges the formation of community across boundaries. The Spirit is a great *boundary-crosser* – as became clear, for example, with the Jubilee 2000 campaign, the coalitions of the Kairos movement, the global networking against trafficking in women. Many of these themes come together in another ancient meaning for the Spirit as *vinculum amoris, vinculum caritatis*. The Spirit as bond of charity and love is as much an inspiration for the recovering heart of public life as for encouraging a new body/soul/mind/heart *integration*. Resisting the splits and dualisms of history that set men over against women, mind as superior to body, human beings as superior to animals and so on, the Spirit prompts an integration promoting the flourishing of us all.

Since the power of globalization is all-encompassing, the Spirit operates not with the power of coercion and dominance, but with power as empowerment; the power of compassion, love, empathy, insight, integration; with relational power – fragile though it may be – the empowerment and energy that arises when we get structures of relationships and institutions functioning for the good. Here I think feminist theological thinking has gone further than Gandhi. The two Dutch words *macht* and *kracht* sum this up. '*Macht*' is *macho* power, the power of might and armies. '*Kracht*' is energy, the power of being vitalized and empowered, and can have a relational meaning.

My final dimension, a special one for our times, is the symbol of the Spirit as '*The Wild Bird who heals*'.[51] The Spirit calling us to protect the wildernesses and the creatures who live there. The Spirit as the green face of God, the 'Wild Bird who heals' emerges, signalling the end of theologies of stewardships of creation, to ignite full-blown biocentric theology and practice. As Mark Wallace says:

> If we allow the Spirit's biophilic insurgency to redefine us as pilgrims and sojourners rather than wardens and stewards, our legacy to posterity might well be healing and life-giving, and not destructive of the hopes of future generations.[52]

The image of the wild bird is owed to Mark Wallace, although the themes of wildness, chaotic creativity and embodiment are at home with ecofeminism, and ecological theology alike. He discovered in the Rothschild Canticles of the Middle Ages the image of the Spirit as

> giant encircling dove, whose wings enfold Father and Son and whose large talons and tail provide points of intersection for all those figures. In the canticles the Spirit is represented less like the domesticated birds or pigeons of traditional Church art and more like the mountain raptors of the mountain wildernesses. The Spirit-Bird in the Canticles spins and twirls the other two members of the Godhead into amorous and novel combinations and permutations. As the Canticles progress, each life-form within the Trinity loses its separate identity in a blur of erotic passion and movement and colour.[53]

Thus, the Wild Bird is not a feeble addition to the vertical Father/Son relation, but is the dynamic symbolic – and passionate – unity of all life forms. In this biophilic revelation of spirit the density of much of former theological inspiration moves forward. The prophetic spirit as the green face of God speaks forth (the meaning of *pro-phetes*) a language linking human and non-human, revealing the false logic on which this split is built. As Spirit of truth, the Wild Bird leads us into a truth that builds just practices, enabling flourishing for all life forms.

Thus the power, the *Kracht* of the Spirit's energy, is the power of being revitalized by being put in touch once again with the truth of sustaining forces of life. Disney World, the metaphor for the culture spawned by global capitalism, I have argued, is the world of addiction – to money/power/

wealth/alcohol/drugs/sex. One cause for the emergence of addictive culture is through the many disconnections from earth's resources and rhythms, whether this be through urban or rural poverty, pollution or extravagant lifestyle. Thus, the symbol of the Spirit as 'the Wild Bird who heals' responds to the contemporary pathology this chapter addresses. In the call to protect the wildernesses and the creatures who live there, imaginations are awakened, as a deeply satisfying connection is recovered. John Muir – one of the early founders of the ecology movement – wrote:

> In God's wildness lies the hope of the world – the great fresh unblighted, unredeemed wilderness. The galling harness of civilisation drops off, and the wounds ere we are aware.[54]

Muir saw fragments of the Spirit's presence wherever he travelled and he developed an entire wilderness pneumatology.[55] In these days of threatened wilderness, of increasing desertification, to sink into uncritical presence of the Spirit in wildness is self-indulgence. But to call for – as the ecofeminist Sharon Betcher does – a pneumatology of sanctuary is transforming practice. She suggests that, just as the churches recovered the mediaeval practice of sanctuary to try to protect refugees escaping over the border from Mexico to the USA, so we should see the Spirit as the Spirit of sanctuary, protecting and healing the wetlands, the grasslands, the deserts and all the indigenous creatures, both human and non-human.[56] In the praxis of a pneumatology of sanctuary, she says, the Spirit *takes place*.

So, we have come full circle. Beginning with emptiness, the vanishing of the dream in the all-prevailing bad dream, the imagination captive to and hijacked by the fantasies of consumerism, the Gandhian privileging of truth offered an opening to a wider notion of freedom and flourishing. It created hope that 'the common language for the dream' could be reawakened, transcending the polarization of the world into victim/oppressor. Exploring spirit language gives new content to what flourishing might mean. If disconnection with the earth leads to addiction, reconnecting with wildness/wilderness is a part of the way forward, not in self-indulgence (exploit nature again!), but as earthing the dream of new creation. We look to the Spirit as Wild Bird who heals for a re-enchantment of the world. Not for Magic Kingdoms but for embodied kinships of women, men, children and earth creatures in a reimagined and transformed world of sustainable earth communities of healing and hope. 'You don't want me to dance; too bad, I'll dance anyhow', says one of Eli Wiesel's characters,[57] expressing the tenacious hold on life, desire and joy of ecofeminist hope and sheer irrepressibility of the Spirit. As Hildegarde of Bingen put it:

> The Spirit is life, movement, colour, radiance, restorative stillness in the din. She pours the juice of contrition into hardened hearts. Her power makes dry twigs and withered souls green again with the juice of life. She purifies, absolves, strengthens, heals, gathers the perplexed, seeks the lost. She plays the music in the soul, being herself the melody of praise and joy. She awakens mighty hope, blowing everywhere the winds of renewal in creation.[58]

Waking or sleeping, we dance to this dream and are sustained by its power. As Shakespeare's Caliban cried:

> Be not afeard; the isle is full of noises,
> Sounds and sweet airs; that give delight and hurt not.
> Sometimes a thousand twangling instruments
> Will hum about mine ears; and sometimes voices
> That, if I then had waked after long sleep,
> Will make me sleep again; and then, in dreaming,
> The clouds methought would open and show riches
> Ready to drop on me, that, when I waked,
> I cried to dream again.[59]

Notes

1 This was the Summer Academy, Boldern, Switzerland, 1999: the theme, 'A Cow for Martha – a Computer for Hilary: Women's Visions of Economics and Spirituality'.

2 Polly Toynbee, 'Who's afraid of global culture?', in Anthony Giddens and Will Hutton (eds), *On the Edge: Living with Global Capitalism* (London: Jonathan Cape, 2000), pp. 191–2.

3 Cited in C. R. Hensman, 'We either transform the global order or perish', *In God's Image*, 19(3) (September 2000): 38.

4 Cited in L. C. Jain, 'Gandhi and Antyodya', in Anthony Copley and George Paxton (eds), *Gandhi and the Contemporary World* (Chennai: Indo-British Historical Society, 1997), p. 117.

5 David Korten, *When Corporations Rule the World* (London: Earthscan, 1995), p. 131.

6 Vandana Shiva, 'The world on the edge', in Giddens and Hutton, *On the Edge*, pp. 112–19; quotation, p. 118.

7 Heather Eaton, 'Ecofeminism and Globalisation', *Feminist Theology*, 24 (2000): 21–43; quotation, p. 43.

8 Aristotle, *Nicomachean Ethics* (Oxford: Oxford University Press, 1980), Book 1, section 5, p. 7.

9 Bruce Wilshire, *A Wild Hunger: The Primal Roots of Modern Addiction* (Lanham, MD: Rowman & Littlefield, 1998).

10 Cited in *ibid.*, p. 25. The source is personal to the author.

11 For the papers from this conference, see *Political Theology*, 3 (November 2000).

12 See M. Grey, *The Outrageous Pursuit of Hope* (London: Darton, Longman & Todd, 2000).

13 *Satyagraha*, a Gandhian term, is a peaceful non-violent demonstration. It is still a powerful tool across a range of groups, Gandhian, women's movements and NGOs.

14 The source is a *Guardian* column, 2001 – precise date not discoverable.

15 Horace Dammers, *Life Style: A Parable of Sharing* (Charlbury: Jon Carpenter Publishing, 2001).

16 Vincent Rossi; 'Liturgising the world', *Ecotheology*, 3 (July 1997): 61–84; quotation, p. 63.

17 Gerard Manley Hopkins, 'Justus quidem tu es, Domine', in *Poems and Prose* (Harmondsworth: Penguin, 1953), p. 67.

18 Margaret Attwood, *Surfacing* (London: Virago, 1979), p. 191.

19 Jon Sobrino, 'The human family in the face of disaster', *The Tablet* (3 February 2001): 140.

20 This is the title of Adrienne Rich's collection of poems (New York: W. & W. Norton, 1978).

21 Cited in Dorothee Sölle, *The Silent Cry: Mysticism and Resistance* (Augsburg, MN: Fortress Press, 2001), pp. 29–30.

22 Gandhi, *Hind Swaraj*, cited by Rex Ambler, 'Gandhi against modernity', in Copley and Paxton, *Gandhi and the Contemporary World*, p. 125.

23 'Let's face it: Gandhi and his philosophy are all but forgotten in the country of his birth. Gujarat ranks third in crimes against Dalits, Harijans, Adivasis and women; and organised attacks against Christians and Muslims have brought shame to the State whose most famous son taught the world tolerance and brotherhood.

Gandhian institutions have fallen onto the wrong hands ... No tribal leader or harijan leader of stature has emerged in institutions like Sabamarti Ashram, ... Lack of a leadership instinct among these traditionally disadvantaged groups and the iron-fisted hold of Brahmins and Patels over these institutions is responsible for the very people for whom Gandhiji lived and died continuing to rot at the bottom of the social ladder.' 'The dismantling of the Mahatma', *The Sunday Times of India* (3 October 1999).

24 *Wells for India* was founded in 1987 by my husband, Dr Nicholas Grey, Dr Ramsahai Purohit and myself, in response to the drought of that year.

25 This incident is recounted by William Dalrymple, *The Age of Kali* (London: HarperCollins, 1998), pp. 111–21.

26 The source here is my personal communication with the Tyagis.

27 At the moment of writing, the news has reached us of the rape of an 18-year-old Rajput woman from the Baap district. Living alone with her baby because of the migration of her husband to seek work, she was raped on her way to the pond to seek water.

28 Ambler, 'Gandhi against modernity', p. 126.

29 See M. Grey, *Prophecy and Mysticism: The Heart of the Postmodern Church* (Edinburgh: T&T Clark, 1997). Also Dorothee Sölle, *The Silent Cry*, especially Ch. 9.

30 Dorothee Sölle, 'Liberating our God-talk: from authoritarian otherness to mystical otherness', in Ursula King (ed.), *Liberating Women: New Theological Directions* (Bristol: Bristol University, 1991), pp. 45–6.

31 Arundhati Roy, *The Cost of Living* (New York: The Modern Library, 1999), pp. 104–5.

32 Bhikhu Parekh, 'Is Gandhi still relevant?', in Copley and Paxton, *Gandhi and the Contemporary World*, pp. 372–82; quotation, p. 376.

33 We know that this was the point that influenced Tolstoy so deeply: see 'Tolstoy and Gandhi', in Copley and Paxton, *Gandhi and the Contemporary World*, pp. 196–204.

34 I am grateful for the contributions of John Chathanatt SJ, 'Upon this foundation: Gandhian foundational bases for social transformation', in M. Grey (ed.), *Liberating the Vision* (Southampton: La Sainte Union, 1996), pp. 35–57.

35 Gandhi, in *Harijan* (29 August 1936), in *Collected Works*, 63, p. 240.

36 In *Indian Opinion* (6 December 1908), in *Collected Works*, 9, pp. 107–8; John Chathanatt, 'Upon this foundation', p. 51.

37 Chathanatt, 'Upon this foundation', p. 51.

38 *Ibid.*, p. 52.

39 See John Chathanatt, 'I will build my Ramrajya: the Gandhian goal of liberative transformation', in M. Grey, *Liberating the Vision*, pp. 58–77.

40 W. B. Yeats, 'The shadowy waters' (1906), in *Collected Poems* (New York: Macmillan, 1956).

41 Amartya Sen, *Development as Freedom* (Oxford: Oxford University Press, 1999).

42 Grace Jantzen, *Becoming Divine* (London: Routledge, 1998).

43 Martha C. Nussbaum, 'Human capabilities', in M. Nussbaum and J. Glover (eds), *Women, Culture and Development* (Oxford: Clarendon Press, 1995), pp. 83–5. They measure the quality of human life as:

- Being able to live to the end of a human life of normal length;
- Being able to have good health, to be adequately nourished, adequate shelter, opportunities for sexual satisfaction, choice in reproduction;
- Being able to avoid unnecessary and non-beneficial pain;

- Being able to use the sense, imagine, think, ... use imagination and thought in connection with experiencing and producing spirituality enriching material;
- Being able to have attachments to things and persons outside ourselves; to love those who love and care for us; to grieve at their absence ... ;
- Being able to form a concept of the good and to engage in a critical reflection on the planning of one's own life;
- Being able to live for and to others, to recognize and show concern for other human beings, to engage in various forms of social action; to be able to imagine the situation of another and to have compassion for that situation; to have the capacity for both justice and friendship;
- Being able to live with concern for and in relation to animals, plants and the world of nature;
- Being able to laugh, play and enjoy relational activity;
- Being able to live one's life and no one else's.

44 See Martha Nussbaum, *Women and Human Development* (Cambridge: Cambridge University Press, 2000).

45 Jürgen Moltmann, *The Spirit of Life: A Universal Affirmation* (London: SCM Press, 1992), trans. by Margaret Kohl.

46 See M. Grey, *The Wisdom of Fools?* (London: SPCK, 1993), Ch. 9.

47 John Taylor, *The Go-Between God* (London: Collins, 1972).

48 Nancy M. Victorin-Vangerud, *The Raging Hearth: Spirit in the Household of God* (St Louis, MO: Chalice Press, 2000).

49 Simone Weil, *Waiting on God* (London: Fontana, 1949), trans. Emma Crauford.

50 T. S. Eliot, 'East Coker', in *Poems 1909–1963* (London: Faber & Faber, 1963), pp. 23–4.

51 See Mark Wallace, *Fragments of the Spirit* (New York: Continuum, 1996).

52 *Ibid.*, p. 170.

53 Mark Wallace, 'The wounded Spirit as the basis for hope', in Dieter T. Hessel and Rosemary Radford Ruether (eds), *Christianity and Ecology* (Cambridge, MA: Harvard University Press, 2000), p. 56.

54 John Muir, *Yosemite Journals* (11 July 1890), in Linnie Marsh Wolfe (ed.), *John of the Mountains: The Unpublished Journals of John Muir* (Boston, MA: Houghton Mifflin Co., 1938), p. 317.

55 Wallace, *Fragments*, p.157.

56 See Sharon Betcher, 'Groundswell: a pneumatology of sanctuary', *Ecotheology*, 7 (1999): 22–39.

57 Eli Wiesel, *The Gates of the Forest* (New York: Schocken Books, 1996), trans. Frances Frenaye, p. 198.

58 Hildegarde of Bingen, as summed up by Elizabeth Johnson, 'Remembering creative spirit', in Joann Wolski Conn (ed.), *Women's Spirituality: Resources for Christian Development* (New York: Paulist Press, 1986, rev. edn, 1996), p. 372.

59 William Shakespeare, *The Tempest* (London and Glasgow: Blackie & Son): *The Plain Text Shakespeare*, Act III, Scene 2, p. 45.

Part IV

Emerging Concerns –
Twenty-first-century Issues
and Approaches

Chapter 15

Public Theology and Genetics

ROBIN GILL

For a number of years public theology has been a crucial concern of Duncan Forrester. Indeed it is a concern that probably unites all of the contributors to this collection. Duncan himself has made a very considerable contribution to public theology at both a practical level, especially in founding the Centre for Theology and Public Issues and in his membership of the prestigious Nuffield Council on Bioethics, and at a theoretical level in his various books on welfare and social justice. Public theology almost *is* the man.

A broad examination of public theology would probably be a mistake in a single chapter. A whole book would be much more appropriate.[1] Instead, this chapter will focus upon a single question of mutual interest to Duncan and myself: what does theology have to contribute to public debates about ethical issues arising from recent genetic science? A number of scientists would respond emphatically that theology has nothing whatsoever to contribute. Even some religious scientists may be sceptical about any public role for theology on genetic issues. They may also be dismayed by what they regard as naïve theological utterances on specific scientific issues, especially on issues such as the genetic modification of food. In contrast, there is a growing theological literature relating to genetic and medical science which claims that a godless society is ever moving in a more destructive and irreligious direction, relegating powers to itself that properly belong only to God.

At a theological level there seems to be an increasing gap between those theologians who make sharply particularist claims and those who see only relative differences between Christian and secular thought. This chapter will take two books published in 1999 to illustrate this difference, Michael Banner's *Christian Ethics and Contemporary Moral Problems*[2] and Audrey R. Chapman's *Unprecedented Choices: Religious Ethics at the Frontiers of Genetic*

Science.[3] Since both Michael Banner and Audrey Chapman are themselves involved as theologians on public bodies concerned with genetics and medical ethics, their work is directly relevant to this question about public theology. In theory, at least, they represent opposite positions on public theology, with Banner an enthusiastic Barthian and particularist and Chapman as more consensusual and sympathetic to process theology. In practice, as will be seen, their differences are not so clear-cut. This final observation will lead to a summary of my own position, namely that religious beliefs are important for motivation, commitment and depth on ethical issues even in a pluralistic society. It is when public theologians imagine that, by virtue of being theologians, they have some special capacity for moral discernment on complex issues in genetic and medical science that they can be most misleading. To save them from error they need their secular colleagues. Conversely, secular colleagues may sometimes underestimate the motivation, commitment and depth which religious belonging and beliefs (or the heritage deriving from them) can still give people when making difficult ethical choices.

Audrey Chapman

Audrey Chapman's *Unprecedented Choices* is a very welcome addition to the already distinguished series *Theology and the Sciences.* Chapman provides an informed critical discussion of both the implications of recent genetic science for religious ethics and the contribution that religious ethics have made, or might still make, for society at large as it attempts to evaluate the ethical and social implications of this science. As Director of the Program of Dialogue on Science, Ethics and Religion at the American Association for the Advancement of Science at Washington, DC, she has a decade of active engagement with religious leaders, theologians and scientists on genetic issues, attempting to establish properly informed and credible responses. However, this has left her less than sanguine about the contribution to date of religious ethicists on the crucial issues increasingly raised by genetic science.

Three substantial chapters survey, in turn, the contributions of religious ethicists first to the possibility of human genetic engineering, then to the possibility of human cloning and finally to the ongoing debate about the patenting of life. Those who have been engaged actively in the current debate will be very familiar with the issues and arguments used and Chapman adds little that is new in the first and second of these areas. Nonetheless, what she does write is clear, accurate and perceptive. Because she adopts a survey style in these chapters, rather than a thematic approach, there is a considerable amount of repetition of points, arguments and even quotations. She is also not particularly aware of parallel British and European discussions. As in the United States, a number of British religious ethicists have been discussing genetic issues over the last decade and most British government or foundation reports on genetics and ethics have included religious ethicists in their panels. An adequate survey should include more of these non-American contributions, although it would probably not add much to the actual substance of the debate. There are as yet only so many points to be made about the merits or otherwise of novel but circumscribed areas such as genetic engineering or reproductive cloning.

It is in the third area – on the patenting of life – that Chapman makes a distinctly more original contribution. She takes as her starting point the *Joint Appeal Against Human and Animal Patenting* made in May 1995 by more than eighty religious leaders. *The Appeal* opposed the patenting of human and animal life forms on the following grounds:

> We the undersigned religious leaders, oppose the patenting of human and animal life forms. We are disturbed by the US Patent Office's recent decision to patent human body parts and several genetically engineered animals. We believe that humans and animals are creations of God, not humans, and as such should not be patented as human inventions.[4]

Instructively, this is the area that has most actively concerned her work for the AAAS. Because of the legal complications in this area, debate about it has been particularly convoluted both in the United States and in Europe. Chapman offers a useful guide through this legal minefield and a clarification of the specifically ethical issues identified in the secular debate, before turning at some length to the theological issues involved. It is at this point that she offers her critique of what she sees as the simplicities of *The Joint Appeal*. She argues that there has been a long-standing tendency of religious leaders in such debates to offer rhetoric rather than properly informed argument. For example, as it stands, she believes that *The Joint Appeal* depends upon a static, pre-evolutionary understanding of creation in which life forms are firmly fixed by God. It also has an unnuanced understanding of 'ownership' that takes no account of the concept of humans as 'created co-creators' developed by the theologians Philip Hefner and Ted Peters. She is also sceptical about the legitimacy of religious leaders speaking on behalf of their faith traditions without extensive prior consultation of a strong cross-section of their members.

However, Chapman still believes in public theology and in religious ethicists seeking to influence society at large, especially on ethical issues. The two chapters that follow offer an extensive discussion first of how theologians should take more account of scientific developments and then of how they should seek to engage in public theology. At the first of these levels she believes that most theologians have still to assimilate the implications of Darwin and modern genetics properly into their understanding of creation, human distinctiveness, sin and the soul. She examines the claims of sociobiology and, like Stephen Pope, is sympathetic to a judicious assimilation even here (although she is also critical of some of the more exaggerated claims of sociobiologists such as Richard Dawkins and Edward O. Wilson). At the second level she argues repeatedly that public theology in the area of genetic science should succumb neither to the abandonment of theistic language (she is particularly critical of James Childress on this account in his highly influential medical ethics) nor to simplistic biblical or theological claims.

This last point is crucial to all of us who work as religious ethicists alongside physical and social scientists. What is the responsible way to do religious ethics on scientific issues within pluralistic, modern societies? Chapman is well aware that some secular scientists would exclude religious ethicists from any discussion that impinges upon their work. She counters this with the position taken by the National Bioethics Advisory Commission, namely that the claims of religious traditions should be taken seriously, without being regarded as determinative, because historically and currently they mould the moral views of many citizens. Once it is acknowledged that secularists themselves do not arrive at moral positions independently of culture, then there is a strong ground for not excluding any significant section of a particular culture.

An additional point might be made here to strengthen this position. It is sometimes argued that, although neither religious bodies nor their theologians can properly claim to represent society as a whole today (in the USA, of course, they never could, but at times both the Church of England and the Church of Scotland have imagined that, in England and Scotland at least, they can), secular moral philosophy might be able to make such a claim in a pluralistic society. It was, after all, one of the central hopes of the Enlightenment that the use of universal reason without the particularist claims of divine revelation might help to deliver Europe from interreligious wars. European countries fractured by the Protestant Reformation could no longer unanimously rely upon religiously derived moral precepts. Morality based solely upon universal human reasoning might instead be able to unite people morally in a way that religion no longer could. However, following the criticisms of Alasdair MacIntyre and others, it has become distinctly less plausible to make such universal claims for moral philosophy. Rivalries between different theoretical positions in moral philosophy are just as evident as those among theologians.

So, in a discussion of the public role of applied ethics, my colleague, the secular philosopher Richard Norman, has argued that 'if the resolution of moral conflicts about abortion, or euthanasia, has to wait the resolution of disputes between utilitarianism, rights-based theories and their other theoretical competitors, there is little hope of progress towards agreed answers'.[5] Instead, Norman argues more modestly that the function of the philosopher in public ethical decision-making is to be concerned with 'the clarification and articulation of the values which people actually hold'.[6] Rather than insisting upon some unified theory or set of principles, philosophy in this area 'consists in the attempt to understand and clarify, non-reductively, the plurality of ethical values and concepts'.[7]

Given such a modest understanding of the role of secular philosophy in the public arena, it is not so difficult to imagine that the theologian may have some public role as well. Yet it is at this point that Chapman's own position becomes more problematic. Her book is strongest when exposing the inadequacies of various religious positions, either because they fail properly to understand genetic science or because they make tendentious connections between theology and particular claims or prescriptions relating to genetic science. Such versions of public theology thus fail either at the cognitive or at the hermeneutical level. Yet her own positive connections are quite tentative and are seldom distinctively theological. So, although she argues that genetic patenting does raise important theological questions, she leaves these questions articulated rather than answered. And when looking for something positive to say about *The Joint Appeal*, she writes only in general (and non-theological) terms:

> Like the members of the Joint Appeal campaign, I am disturbed by the failure to have a meaningful public discussion of this issue. The courts and the patenting office are not the proper venue for making such decisions. To embark on a course of promoting commercialisation and privatisation of biology without a single meaningful public debate constitutes a violation of the implicit social contract between the government and the governed in a democratic society.[8]

And when she does address directly how it is that religious ethicists tend to differ from secular ethicists, she points to three distinct ways: religious

257

ethicists are more likely than secular ethicists to move beyond individual autonomy and consent and to emphasize wider interpersonal and social relationships; they are more committed to justice and concern for the vulnerable; and they belong to religious communities with uniquely long traditions of moral discussion and attention to moral behaviour.

I agree with all three distinct ways and see them as crucial to the role of a number of theologians, including Duncan, who work with secular bodies. Yet all of these are derivative virtues rather than the explicitly doctrinal claims usually advanced by exponents of public theology. What is more, such differences between religious and secular ethicists are, at most, relative differences. Manifestly there are secular ethicists (for example, secular communitarians) who are deeply concerned about wider interpersonal relationships and about justice for the vulnerable, as well as secular ethicists who value long traditions of moral discussion (moral philosophy itself can claim a lengthy history). There are also some religious ethicists who are distinctly individualistic in style and dismissive of religious traditions on moral issues. All that can be safely claimed here is that religious ethicists in general are more likely than their secular counterparts to enshrine these three derivative virtues. At most this is a relative rather than absolute difference between religious and secular ethicists.

But what about distinctive theologically based arguments in public theology? Chapman claims briefly that there is a greater tolerance in secular society today for such arguments (but, tellingly, she makes this claim for theistic rather than Christological arguments). Perhaps this is true in the United States (although I doubt if it is true in the secular academy in the USA), but I fear that it is not true in Britain or more widely in much of Europe. Memories of religious wars and/or religious hegemonies over here are still too recent for this to be possible. Given the latter, the religious ethicist engaged in the genetics debate within the public forum may simply have to choose: either to use explicitly religious arguments and, in the process, inform their religious communities but be ignored largely by society at large; or to represent the virtues of social concern and justice derived from their communities while largely eschewing public discussion of theological metaethics. Those from the first position often regard those from the second as faithless whereas those from the second tend to regard those from the first as sectarian. Neither label withstands much intelligent scrutiny[9] since these differing positions are as much public strategies as ontology. Yet they remain difficult to resolve and continue to have a profound affect upon religious ethics at the frontiers of genetic research.

Michael Banner

In 1993 Michael Banner was appointed to chair a government committee on farm animals, which produced *The Report of the Committee to Consider the Ethical Implications of Emerging Technologies in the Breeding of Farm Animals*,[10] and then to the F. D. Maurice Chair of Moral and Social Theology at Kings College London. In 1999, he published his first substantial collection of essays on ethical issues, *Christian Ethics and Contemporary Moral Problems*. It offers a sharp contrast to Chapman. In the opening chapter of this book, his inaugural lecture at Kings, he argues for a particularist theological approach to Christian ethics, which he terms, somewhat provocatively, 'dogmatic Christian ethics'. He argues that the only authorities for Christian ethics are the Bible and the Creeds – although, in reality, it is Karl Barth whom he treats as the authority in almost every chapter that follows. In these he considers, in turn, euthanasia, abortion, health-care rationing, the environment, biotechnology and sexuality – concluding, provocatively again, with a 'prolegomena to a dogmatic sexual ethic'. Throughout he makes his mark as a leading player in the new theological right.

For Banner:

> Where Christian ethics understands itself as dogmatic ethics – that is, as providing an account of human action as it corresponds to the reality of the action of God – it necessarily understands itself in such a way as to differentiate itself from a number of other accounts of ethics, even when those are given from the Christian side.[11]

He is highly critical of those forms of public theology which seek to find common ground between religious and secular ethicists and argues that a sharply particularist approach to Christian ethics offers a more significant dialogue partner even within a pluralist society. In turn, this leads him to defend such an approach within medical ethics:

> Christian medical ethics, in so far as it is *Christian* medical ethics, speaks on the basis of the distinctive knowledge of humankind which is given by the Word of God. It thus does not and cannot make common cause with 'bioethics', or 'biomedical ethics', as they are usually practised, for as thus practised they do not view humankind in the light of this knowledge. Christian medical ethics is, rather, obliged to begin from its own starting point, taking up the constructive task from its unique and distinctive presupposition, namely the Gospel of Jesus Christ. For it is in the light of this Gospel of the Word spoken to humankind, that humankind gains a true self-understanding.[12]

Michael Banner's sharp-edged conservatism makes him an effective critic of sloppy, liberal writing. Secular exponents of consequentialism in moral philosophy are dissected with considerable panache. In a pluralist context it becomes ever more difficult to argue for agreed moral principles of any kind and there is a real danger that measurable consequence will become the only public guide on moral issues. He successfully shows just how impoverished a stance that would be. Yet, on issues such as abortion, euthanasia and homosexuality, which he implacably opposes, he comes near to arguing that consequences should simply be ignored. Even if prudence is not all, principles alone can be terrifying.

However, it is striking that, when he comes to the area of ethics in which he has a public role himself (namely on the environment and farm animals), he allows prudence a much greater place and eschews 'black and white' solutions. He criticizes other genetic reports for being purely consequentialist – when in reality they typically combine consequentialism and deontology – while offering a mixture of consequentialism and deontology himself – a mixture that then sits uneasily with the dogmatic Christian ethics with which he concludes. For example, he cites the following paragraph from the BMA report, *Our Genetic Future*, as typifying secular consequentialism:

> Using the science of genetic modification to produce a 'master race', or to select children with particular attributes, is unacceptable. Even if parents are entirely free to reproduce as they choose, considerable social and ethical problems could arise if we eventually reach the currently remote possibility of being able to choose not just the gender but also some of the physical, emotional, and intellectual attributes of our children. If it became commonplace, for example, for parents to choose a boy as their first child, then this might well make it even harder to diminish sexual discrimination in our society.[13]

Clearly, consequentialism is present in this argument, but 'sexual discrimination' seems to be regarded deontologically as simply wrong in itself. And the conditional clause at the beginning of the second sentence suggests that parental autonomy may not be decisive here. A careful reading of the rest of the report, and of almost any other report of the BMA Medical Ethics Committee, would soon confirm that the deontological principles of justice and non-maleficence are regularly considered alongside autonomy and beneficence. What Banner tries to show is that other reports on issues in genetics rely exclusively upon a consequentialist balance between 'risks' and 'benefits' and thereby overlook the possibility that some things may be wrong in themselves. Perhaps some do, but it is difficult to find evidence of this in the sophisticated reports produced by bodies such as the BMA or the Nuffield Council on Bioethics. And even the term 'benefits' allows for other possibilities.

When in the 1980s I first started discussions with scientists involved in biotechnology, I found that some talked simply about risk analysis without any mention of beneficence. At that stage such scientists were puzzled about why ethics (let alone theology) had anything to do with their work at all. However, once it was acknowledged that biotechnology should be as concerned about whether or not it really did contribute towards beneficence, then the role of the ethicist became more obvious to the scientists themselves. Clearly this in itself raises the issues of what constitutes 'beneficence' and whether it is right that some should benefit at the risk of possible harm to other people, to animals or to the environment. Card-carrying consequentialists can doubtless avoid deontological principles even when addressing these issues, but they have to be unusually determined to do so. Most people (whether religious or not) offer a mixture of consequentialism and deontology in moral arguments.

And that is exactly what Michael Banner does himself. He cites with approval the three principles which his own report enunciates, namely a deontological principle that there are harms of a certain degree and kind which ought never to be inflicted upon animals (such as the non-therapeutic tongue amputation of calves), a more consequentialist principle that even less serious harm to animals must be weighed against the good to be achieved and a third deontological principle that harm to animals should always be minimized. He also argues against a deontological position that seeks to prevent all forms of genetic engineering on animals, arguing as follows:

> If things were black and white it would, of course, be a lot easier. If the effect of genetic engineering were invariably deleterious for an animal's welfare, or if the very use of genetic modifications expressed a contempt for animals and a disregard for their natural characteristics (as some objections to genetic engineering maintain) a system of regulation might be devised which would aim to prevent all genetic modification ... As it is, however, genetic modification cannot be regarded as a single moral entity – some genetic modification may be intrinsically objectionable as manipulative of an animal's good, some not.[14]

The Christian philosopher and radical vegetarian Stephen Clark would take a much more robust position here, rejecting all such genetic modification on deontological grounds.[15] In contrast to his univocal moral stances against

261

abortion, euthanasia and homosexual practice, Banner is more cautious on this public issue.

Yet when he turns to theology in the conclusion of this discussion, he appears to reject genetic engineering altogether and suspects that those Christians who talk about human acting as 'co-creators' may 'serve only to provide to projects which may repudiate rather than embrace the created order an air of pious respectability'.[16] He also returns to his attack upon consequentialism:

> For what this line of questioning wonders is not just whether projects, for example, of perfective (as opposed to therapeutic) genetic engineering will have a balance of good over bad consequences, but rather whether they express a fundamentally mistaken attitude towards human being in the world, an attitude which will be overcome only as we learn what it means to keep the Sabbath as a day on which humankind is called to a knowledge and love of the order which God himself knows and loves.[17]

Now of course this last theological consideration could be an argument against any scientific intervention within 'the order which God himself knows and loves'. On this basis some Christians have concluded that we must reject the whole of modern medicine and others that we must become thoroughgoing vegans. Yet most Christians, including Michael Banner, have not adopted such absolutist positions. For us, theological considerations about God's creation have not univocally resolved our ethical dilemmas about biotechnology.

So both Banner and Chapman, despite approaching genetic science from very different theological perspectives, appear to reach a very similar point. On other moral issues Banner's position is typically absolutist and particularist, but on genetics he, like Chapman, generally eschews 'black and white' solutions.

The Role of Theology in Genetics

So what do theological considerations actually do for us in this context of genetic science? Here my own position can only be summarized briefly and must wait a while for longer exposition (which I hope to do in the next few years). My suggestion is that such considerations can bring critical motivation, commitment and depth to health-care ethics and, more specifically to genetic issues. However, moral discernment in the complex and fast changing world of genetic science (and, indeed, innovations in health care more widely) is possible only if theologians are prepared to listen carefully to their colleagues in science and moral philosophy. On complex ethical issues arising from genetic and medical science neither theology nor church bodies have privileged access to moral discernment.

The philosopher William Frankena adopts a similar position, arguing that theological presuppositions do provide both a rationality and motivation for ethical enquiry but cannot in themselves resolve problems of interpretation and application in such complex and novel areas as biotechnology.[18] Having worked directly alongside Richard Norman, I have learned to respect his role as a philosopher attempting 'to understand and clarify, non-reductively, the plurality of ethical values and concepts'. Even if theologians are suspicious at times of the motivation, commitment and depth of some of their secular colleagues, they have no privileged access to moral discernment on issues such as those raised by genetic science.

Both Chapman and Banner hold that Christian ethics has a distinctive critical function within the public forum. Whether this takes the form of questioning the sufficiency of autonomy as a moral principle or of pointing towards justice and concern for the vulnerable (Chapman), or whether it entails reminding a pluralist society of the theological roots of many assumed values (Banner), there does seem to be a critical public role for the theologian. Elsewhere[19] I have argued that public theology has a threefold critical role – criticizing, deepening and widening the ethical debate in society at large. The deepening and widening aspects depend upon theistic and Christological assumptions, offering a vision for those who will hear of how things could be if all shared these assumptions and were committed to a Christian *eschaton*. Where my position differs from both Chapman and Banner is in expecting that the second and third functions can play a role in the direct work of public bodies concerned with ethics. The latter should remain sensitive to the beliefs of those who are religious within society at large, but it would be inappropriate in a pluralist context for them to adopt explicit theological beliefs themselves. Indeed, public bodies are likely to regard such explicit adoption not just as inappropriate but, given their fear of religious wars (strongly reinforced by September 11), as dangerously partisan.

On occasions, it is the role of a theologian on such bodies to remind them of a need for sensitivity towards religious minorities. Yet, ironically, it as likely to be sensitivity towards the beliefs of Jehovah's Witnesses as towards those of mainstream practising Jews, Christians or Muslims.

Within the public realm, religion also remains an important source of ethical motivation and commitment for individuals. Elsewhere again,[20] I have set out the considerable empirical evidence showing that religious belonging and stated moral attitudes and behaviour are closely connected. These connections are never absolute. Values and patterns of moral behaviour are distributed throughout the population, but some, especially those concerned with altruism and moral order, are clustered among those who are explicitly religious. Richard Norman does not discuss this, but his formulation of applied ethics does allow for it. He does not suggest that it is the function of the philosopher to inspire or engender moral values but rather to understand and clarify 'the values which people actually hold'. Presumably this includes both the values that explicitly religious people hold as well as the religiously derived values of those who are not or are no longer explicitly religious them-selves. Indeed, there is growing empirical evidence, waiting to be assimilated properly by theologians, suggesting that religious belonging and motivation has often been underestimated in health care.[21] Religious factors may yet be more significant in the public realm than is often realized. While avoiding pontificating beyond their own data, public theologians could make fuller use of this intriguing evidence.

Notes

1 For an excellent and up-to-date critical overview, see Robert Gascoigne, *The Public Forum and Christian Ethics* (Cambridge: Cambridge University Press, 2000).

2 Michael Banner, *Christian Ethics and Contemporary Moral Problems* (Cambridge: Cambridge University Press, 1999).

3 Audrey R. Chapman, *Unprecedented Choices: Religious Ethics at the Frontiers of Genetic Science* (Minneapolis, MN: Fortress Press, 1999).

4 General Board of Church and Society of the United Methodist Church, 'Joint appeal against human and animal patenting' [press conference announcement] (Washington, DC, 17 May 1995).

5 Richard Norman, 'Applied ethics: what is applied to what?', *Utilitas* (Edinburgh: Edinburgh University Press), 12(2) (July 2000): 131.

6 *Ibid.*, p. 131.

7 *Ibid.*, p. 136.

8 Chapman, *Unprecedented Choices*, p. 162.

9 See David Fergusson, *Community, Liberalism and Christian Ethics* (Cambridge: Cambridge University Press, 1998), and Nigel Biggar, in Mark Thiessen Nation and Samuel Wells (eds), *Faithfulness and Fortitude: In Conversation with the Theological Ethics of Stanley Hauerwas* (Edinburgh: T&T Clark, 2000).

10 London: HMSO, 1995.

11 Banner, *Christian Ethics*, p. 13.

12 *Ibid.*, pp. 48–9.

13 British Medical Association, *Our Genetic Future: The Science and Ethics of Genetic Technology* (Oxford: Oxford University Press, 1992), p. 209.

14 Banner, *Christian Ethics*, pp. 218–19.

15 See Stephen R. L. Clark, *Biology and Christian Ethics* (Cambridge: Cambridge University Press, 2000).

16 *Christian Ethics*, p. 224.

17 *Ibid.*

18 W. K. Frankena, 'The potential of theology for ethics', in E. E. Shelp (ed.), *Theology and Bioethics* (Dordrecht: D. Reidel Publishing, 1985), pp. 49–64.

19 See my *Moral Leadership in a Postmodern Age* (Edinburgh: T&T Clark, 1997), pp. 6f.

20 See my *Churchgoing and Christian Ethics* (Cambridge: Cambridge University Press, 1999).

21 Two large empirical studies suggesting a connection between religious attendance/belonging and health in the United States are: Harold G. Koenig *et al.*, 'Does religious attendance prolong survival? A six-year follow-up study of 3,968 older adults', *Journal of Gerontology: Medical Sciences*, 54A(7) (1999): 370–6; and Robert A. Hummer *et al.*, 'Religious involvement and US adult mortality', *Demography*, 36(2) (May 1999): 273–85. For British research, see Kenneth Howe, *Religion, Spirituality and Older People* (Centre for Policy on Ageing: 25–31 Ironmonger Row, London, EC1V 3QP, 1999).

Chapter 16

In Search of the Virtuous Patient:
An Essay in Empirical Theology

ALASTAIR CAMPBELL and TERESA SWIFT

Introduction

Medical ethics has changed dramatically over the past three decades. We have seen a total transformation of the subject area from an approach dominated by the medical profession and based on a mixture of codes and etiquette to a critical, multiprofessional and interdisciplinary endeavour. No longer is medical ethics merely about doctors' decisions and obligations. It has become a many faceted discussion of issues of concern to health professionals, patients and society generally, issues provoked by the dramatic increase in therapeutic interventions made possible by scientific discovery and technical innovation. Thus medical ethics has become, as the title of the first author's chair suggests, Ethics in Medicine. The activity of medicine and its related sciences becomes the object of critical appraisal. Philosophers, theologians, lawyers and social scientists have all joined in the new discipline, often now referred to as 'Bioethics' rather than 'Medical Ethics', to make it clear that it is much wider than professional self-regulation.

But in all this enthusiasm for the new and the controversial, some of the fundamental features of the medical encounter appear to have been missed. The ancient insight attributed to Hippocrates, 'life is short but the art is long', seems to have been lost in the excitement of the technological fix. The modesty of medicine, caught in the aphorism 'To cure sometimes, to alleviate often, to comfort always', has become submerged in the hubris of a medicine which will countenance only the scientifically certain (if such a thing truly existed). We are left with a medical ethics which focuses on decision-making, parallel to the clinical decision about diagnosis, prognosis and treatment options. On the analogy with scientific rationality, ethics becomes based on formulae, on the application of well-established, if not self-evident, principles to cases. Somewhere along the way, the possibility of medical failure and of aspects of illness and disease that cannot be remedied has been lost or discarded. The result is an impoverished medical ethics, which cannot speak to those parts of medical care in which cure is not an option.

This essay presents an alternative way of approaching the dilemmas and uncertainties of medicine. It is not attempting to substitute this approach for the many volumes of useful discussion about principles, which might guide medical decision-making. Rather it seeks to shift the direction of our gaze from the doctor to the patient and from cure to living with illness. The aim is to enrich our understanding of how the moral experiences of individuals and communities are affected by the challenges of disease and disability. It therefore raises the key question of virtue ethics – 'How shall I *live?*' – seeing this as prior to the decision-focused question, 'What shall I *do?*'

We are beginning our search for the 'virtuous patient' with the empirical rather than the theoretical, by reflecting on the results of a multinational study of patients with chronic illness. This reflection seeks to understand what virtues enabled people in irremediable situations to continue with a sense of their moral identity as agents not simply as patients. What might it mean to be a 'virtuous patient' for these groups? We shall then consider how we might understand these findings theologically and will relate them to some theoretical accounts by theologians, Karen Lebacqz and Stanley Hauerwas. We shall end with some tentative conclusions about how a theological account of the virtues of patienthood might offer a contribution to the enrichment of medical ethics. Thus this is an essay in 'empirical theology', which is also intended to be a contribution to 'public theology'.

Virtues and Chronic Illness: An Empirical Study

Over the past three years we have been project co-ordinator and project officer respectively for a study funded by the BIOMED II programme of the European Commission. The project was entitled, 'The relevance of virtue ethics to patients with chronic illness.'[1] Four chronic conditions were selected: rheumatoid arthritis, endometriosis, end-stage renal disease and mood disorder.[2]

Individual interviews were conducted with small groups of patients in each of these diagnostic groups according to an agreed interview guide, which focused on the question of 'living well' under the conditions of irremediable disease. Patients were asked to discuss not simply coping strategies, but ways in which they felt they could continue to live lives of value and fulfilment. Three centres took part in the empirical aspect of the project: Bristol (UK), Nijmegen (Netherlands) and Rome (Italy).[3] Two other centres, Copenhagen (Denmark) and Cardiff (UK), participated in the theoretical analysis, the interpretation of the findings and the preparation of educational materials for patients, carers and health professionals.[4]

The research was conducted using qualitative methods, in which small groups of patients were interviewed at depth. Patients were encouraged to tell their own story in their own words, rather than having to respond to a series of predetermined questions. The interviews were audio-recorded and transcribed. Table 1 shows the number of patients in each group, their age range and their nationality (indicated by the location of the interviews).

Table 1   Participant sample

Diagnostic group	Interview location	No. of interviews	Age range	Patient gender
Rheumatoid arthritis	Bristol	10	20–68	7F 3M
Endometriosis	Bristol	12	31–55	12F
End-stage renal disease	Nijmegen	7	55–82	2M 5F
Mood disorder	Rome	15	28–64	6M 9F

The transcripts were then given an Interpretative Phenomenological Analysis (IPA), a qualitative analytical method used to identify recurrent themes in narratives. The focus of the analysis was on 'living well through chronic illness'. The transcripts were explored for descriptions or explanations of characteristics or personal qualities that participants felt they possessed, which were salient to how they faced the challenges of their condition. Each transcript was examined individually, and significant words, phrases or explanations were noted. These were then given a code capturing the meaning of the content of the text portion. The recurrence of certain codes across interviews indicates emerging themes; codes appearing together frequently indicate an interrelation between themes.

The results of the empirical research were rich in content, some of it relevant only to the specific diagnostic group, but much of it containing central themes consistently found across all four groups. On the basis of this common

269

material, the project partners were able to construct a suggested model of how chronic illness provokes the development of virtues, enabling people to maintain a sense of personal integrity. We shall shortly describe the full range of findings and then present the model of the 'virtuous patient' suggested by the research. But first it is important to recognize that in discussing virtue and character we are referring to a person's life and experiences as a whole and the development through that life of certain virtues (or vices). The 'virtuous patient' is first and foremost a person, whose excellences of character, or virtues, relate also to his/her life prior to the onset of illness. The experiences of chronic illness can help to strengthen the virtues or it can make them more difficult to maintain and develop. It is perfectly possible for the experience of acute or of chronic illness to be largely destructive of a person's character, leading not to a sense of continued fulfilment and personal value, but to a loss of hope, meaning and personal integrity. For this reason, as we shall see below, a central part of being a virtuous patient is to maintain one's self respect.

Table 2 summarizing the research findings for all four groups of patients, illustrates how the common themes leading to a construction of a model were identified.

Table 2   Common themes leading to the construction of a model

'Positive' traits related to:	Rheumatoid arthritis	Endometriosis	Chronic renal failure	Depression	Common main themes
Self	Strength Optimism Sense of humour Acceptance Future goals Self-identity Threats to self-worth and dignity	Enduring Accepting Being self-directing Keeping a sense of purpose in one's life Putting other considerations ahead of one's illness Being cheerful and positive	Bearing–endurance–perseverance Second-nature–habituation–balancing–deciding Sense of reality Gratitude–hope Awareness of finitude Acceptance–acquiescence	Realism about the disease Acceptance Insight Self-aware-ness Refusal to surrender Sense of humour Respect for own dignity	Acceptance Sense of humour Maintain self-respect Courage / perseverance

'Positive' traits related to:	Rheumatoid arthritis	Endometriosis	Chronic renal failure	Depression	Common main themes
Self – body	Listening to your body Perspective Expectations		Vitality–being active–being able to enjoy– happiness		Understand limitation but remain active
Others	Participation in the present Responsibilities Respect from others Respect for others	Getting others to acknowledge one's illness experience Assertive Better at communicating	Sense of community– relationships with other people Faith	Capacity to develop trust and friendship Ability to maintain interests Ability to make use of social network Taking care of others Humility – acknowledging need for others	Maintain and build relationships
'Negative' traits	Intolerant of stupidity More badtempered Not as sociable Bitter Unsympathetic	More impatient More shorttempered Less sympathetic to others' problems Bad at communicating		Too strong sense of duty Self-conceit	More selfcentred (in a negative way)

Taking these findings as a summary of the ways patients themselves see the challenges to living well with chronic illness and of their responses to these challenges, we can now construct two models. The first (see Figure 1) represents the dynamic interrelationship between the threats or challenges of the illness and the continuing self, with its core values and aspirations. Three of the threats are external (threats to physical capacity, threats to self-respect and threats to social life), but there is also the important internal threat, self-centredness, which cuts one off from others and destroys communal life. By noticing this internal threat (perceived by the patients themselves), we can stress that the survival and continued flourishing of the self is not to be confused with selfishness and hostility to others.

It should be stressed that this is just one possible way of constructing a model from data provided by the interview transcripts. It may well be that, in focusing on threats to self-respect, the model is an oversimplification of how the patients themselves saw the moral challenges of their condition. For example, it could be just as valid to see two complementary sets of virtues – self-regarding and other-regarding[5] – and so to see good relationships with

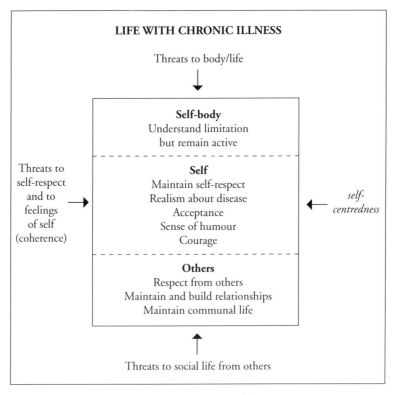

Figure 1 First model

others as of intrinsic value, not merely of instrumental value in maintaining self-respect. This will be discussed below when we consider the theological significance of the research findings. Equally, we might interpret the findings in the style of Aristotle by identifying the 'cardinal virtues' of courage, prudence, temperance and justice as these are expressed in the patients' realistic approach to their ill bodies and their endeavours to maintain good social relationships. Finally, an interpretation in terms of the theological virtues of faith, hope and love could be seen to fit the empirical data also, since the patients are clearly reflecting on all three of these in their awareness of what they need to persevere despite their illness.

We see then that the transition from the raw data of the interview transcripts to the construction of a model is undeniably biased by the theoretical stance of the interpreter. In what sense then is such model-building valid or useful? In our research project, we tried to answer this question by involving the representatives of patients in all the theoretical analysis. Thus the focus on self-respect is the feature best recognized by patients as the core value, since it is closest to their experience of what is at risk and what is crucial to 'a life worth living'. To this extent, then, the model has some authority and it has been used by the project group to help design educational materials that suggest how patients and their carers may alleviate the destructive effects of an ongoing and irremediable condition of disability and physical or mental pain.

The second model is a construct based on this central focus on the self. It takes self-respect as its core value and clusters the virtues of courage, realism, acceptance and communality around it (see Figure 2).

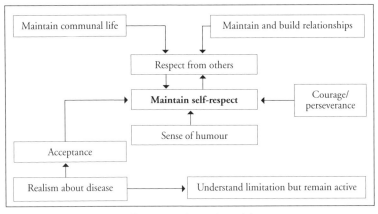

Figure 2   Second model

Theological Reflection

We turn now to the possibility of reflecting on these findings from a theological perspective. This is no easy task. The project was not designed with any theological concepts in mind and, although for some patients religious belief and faith were important parts of their ability to live well, no specific questions were asked of participants about their religious beliefs. Moreover, there is hardly any literature on this topic. While it is true that there is an increasing interest in the relevance of virtue ethics to medicine,[6] there is very little discussion of a theological account of virtues in medicine.[7] If we reduce the scope still further to my interest in the virtuous *patient* (as opposed to the virtuous *professional*) we are left with only two relatively short essays: Karen Lebacqz's chapter in Shelp's edited volume, *Virtue and Medicine*[8] and Stanley Hauerwas's chapter in *Christians among the Virtues*, entitled 'Practising patience: how Christians should be sick'.[9] I shall consider each in turn before proceeding to my own theological reflection on the findings.

Lebacqz's essay begins with four assumptions: firstly, virtue is a mean between extremes, so, for example, one can have both too much and too little patience, the virtue being a balance between them; secondly, 'virtues are not simply character traits but responses to situations',[10] and this means that they are developed as life progresses; thirdly, some, if not all virtues, are culturally relative and for this reason it is very difficult to give a general account of them; fourthly, 'virtues' are to be distinguished from 'virtue', some kind of unifying characteristic which gives coherence to any list of virtues. Lebacqz believes that a unity of the virtues is an elusive concept, but she does suggest that it might be described as 'an integrity or cohesiveness of character'.[11]

Consistently with her stress on virtue as response, Lebacqz goes on to describe the experiences associated with illness, and she finds that these may be summed up as threats to the self, which require changes in the self-concept. Part of this threat is that illness puts one in a new social role, a 'more onerous citizenship' as Susan Sontag put it,[12] and this again requires a major adjustment in the understanding of the self. Lebacqz sums up the required responses to such threats as follows: 'The "virtues" of the patient are qualities of excellence in response to the stresses of pain, discomfort, physical limitation, loss of autonomy, violation of privacy, vulnerability, and loss of self.'[13]

The latter part of Lebacqz's essay suggests that three virtues, fortitude, prudence and hope, are the relevant responses of the virtuous patient and that these must be seen in contrast with the stereotype of the virtuous patient as compliant, cheerful and uncomplaining. *Fortitude* is described partly as

274

accepting limitation, enduring that which cannot be changed and remaining 'quiet of heart', serene, but at the same time being able to rage against the situation and reassert one's autonomy. These paradoxical responses can achieve a hard-won acceptance, which is fortitude. The virtue of *prudence*, on the other hand, requires a new perception of the self, listening to the body and a realistic adjustment to its new limitations. At the same time, the caring for the self, which prudence requires, entails a new awareness of the value of things and a reaching out to others. Thus such care of the self is far removed from social isolation and self-absorption; rather it is a kind of wisdom, which brings balance to one's life. Lastly, *hope* enables people to look for 'meaning to emerge out of the chaos, pain and sense of injustice' associated with illness.[14] Lebacqz notes that frequently an enabler of hope is a sense of humour, not only because it relieves stress, but because it offers a sense of transcendence and restores courage.

Finally, Lebacqz rejects the idea that such a list of virtues should become prescriptive or that there should be any one pattern of virtue, which would fit all people confronted with illness. As we noted above, she stresses the cultural relativity of virtue and resists the idea of a unifying 'virtue'. Yet it is clear that in her account *some* notion of personal integrity, a realistic and open optimism despite the threats to self, is in fact determinative.

What then can we make of Lebacqz's analysis in relation to the research findings about patients' experience of chronic illness? There is clearly a striking similarity between much of her theoretical account and the model derived independently from our research. Perhaps this is hardly surprising, since Lebacqz has based her account on real-life and fictional accounts of people's experience of illness. But the similarities extend beyond the threats to the self, posed by illness, to the responses described by the patients. For them perseverance, acceptance, a sense of humour, a realistic assessment of the future, keeping a sense of purpose in life, listening to the body and maintaining rewarding relationships with others were all key responses. Even though the words are different in some respects, the detailed descriptions by Lebacqz of fortitude, prudence and hope are virtually identical to the virtues the patients themselves sought to exercise. Above all, like Lebacqz, the patients strenuously oppose the idea that the virtuous patient is compliant, unassertive and unrealistically cheerful.

However, despite these similarities with our models of virtue, Lebacqz does not take us much further in our theological quest for the virtuous patient. Firstly, because she resists the idea of a unity of the virtues – what we have called a 'model' of the virtuous patient – she does not offer us a vantage point for reflection on – and criticism of – our unifying concept of 'self-respect'. This is a real weakness in her essay, since a refusal to offer any normative account, for fear of cultural imposition, makes her choice of the three virtues seem wholly arbitrary. If there is no unifying rationale for the separately described virtues, why are they to be preferred over other virtues in the classical or theological repertoire of virtues, for example, justice, temperance, faith or love? One could just as easily make a case for some or all of these as for the three she has selected. In analysing our research data, on the other hand, we ordered the patients' descriptions by an overall scheme, which saw the maintenance of self-respect as normative. This could be a mistaken interpretation, but it is at least clear and consistent.

A second difficulty with the Lebacqz's essay is that, although it is written by a theologian, it is not an explicitly theological analysis. Certainly, she recognizes that her third virtue is one of the three theological ones, whilst the others are from classical sources; and she does mention transcendence and trust in God as aspects of hope in some people's experience. But there is again no underlying rationale for these references to religion and certainly no attempt to give a theological account of why certain virtues should shape a person's response to illness. We are left with an account, which is sensitive, perceptive, imaginative and close to experience, but in the last analysis theoretically and theologically unsatisfying.

We must turn therefore to our second source, Stanley Hauerwas, a writer who is uncompromising in his opposition to theologians who use the language of Athens in place of that of Jerusalem. The title of his book, co-authored with Charles Pinches, makes plain his view of current secular thought, since *Christians among the Virtues* is a deliberate echo of Walker Percy's novel, *Love among the Ruins*, and is meant to convey the poverty of present-day 'liberal political arrangements'.[15] Hauerwas has clear sympathy for the celebrated closing passage of Alasdair MacIntyre's *After Virtue*:

> if the tradition of the virtues was able to survive the horrors of the last dark ages, we are not entirely without grounds for hope. This time, however, the barbarians are not waiting beyond the frontiers; they have already been governing us for quite some time. And it is our lack of consciousness of this that constitutes part of our predicament. We are waiting not for a Godot, but for another – doubtless very different – St Benedict.[16]

When he comes to relate his account of virtue and the virtues to illness, Hauerwas is again clear, from the title of the chapter itself, that this is an explicitly Christian account: 'Practising Patience: how *Christians* should be sick' (our italics). The chapter is written in reaction to the *impatience* of contemporary society, in which we are as unwilling to be frustrated by the failures of our bodies as we are by the breakdown of our motor vehicles. We look for technological solutions, for repair of the faulty, and we cannot tolerate the fact of our vulnerability and finitude. This prevailing social attitude results in what Hauerwas calls 'the pathos of medicine in modernity':

> the practice of medicine was formed under a quite different set of presumptions than those now so widely held. This is why some physicians at least still presume that they are to care for the patient even though they cannot cure, or even alleviate to any significant extent, the patient's malady. This kind of behavior makes little sense if physicians are there for the sole purpose of repairing our bodies when they don't serve us as we like.[17]

In response to this, Hauerwas wants to reassert the importance of the term 'patient' (as opposed to the more autonomous sounding 'client') and to combine this with an advocacy for the Christian virtue of patience. By so doing, he believes Christians may help modern medicine to regain its historic functions.

What then is the nature of this virtue of patience and what makes it distinctively Christian? Hauerwas presents a theological account of this virtue, drawing on Christian tradition (Cyprian, Tertullian, Augustine and Aquinas) and on biblical sources. He relates patience first to the suffering of Christ and to Christ's advocacy of forbearance against evil (Matt 5:43–8). He then argues that such patience can only be a gift from God, made possible in human life by the presence of the Holy Spirit, for humans cannot achieve such tranquillity and forbearance unaided. Faith, hope and love combine to make such patience possible and all are gifts of the Holy Spirit, not human achievements.

When this is applied to the experience of illness, pain and death, the consequence is a somewhat paradoxical position in which Christians are wholly realistic about the evil in the world and about their own vulnerability and mortality (and so have a certain sadness and realism), yet at the same time are hopeful and positive, motivated to work for the betterment of the world, in the faith that all things are in the hands of a God that is love. Thus Christian patience in the face of illness is not false optimism, but nor is it a fatalistic despair of worldly things. Instead, being a patient enables us to achieve certain good ends, despite our fear and suffering.

Firstly, such patience helps us to 'love the great good things our bodies make possible',[18] without hating our bodies because they are the instances of

277

our death; secondly, it helps us to reach out to others in love, even though we know that such love must result in sadness and loss through their, or our, death; and, thirdly, it gives value to our time and our space, enabling us to engage in 'worthy activities' that have significance, even though they will not endure, and enabling us to share these with our children and pass on a heritage to them of memories and exemplary activities.

We can now consider whether Hauerwas's lustily theological account provides resources for reinterpretation or critique of the findings of our research. At first sight, this may not seem promising. His insistence on a revelatory religion, which gives virtues to believers not accessible to those outside the community of faith, seems to rule out a generalizable theory of virtue of the kind we were seeking in our research. But this would be to simplify his rather complex approach to the relationship between Christianity and the societies in which it is practised. In this, and in many other of his writings, Hauerwas clearly sees that the community of faith can and should in numerous ways influence the nature of the societies in which they live, even if they do not presume to convert them wholly to Christian belief. In the case of this and other accounts of religion and medicine,[19] we see an attempt to alter social attitudes to illness and disability and change the ways in which secular society organizes its social and medical institutions. Therefore, we should not abandon too quickly the possibility that Hauerwas's account of how a Christian can face illness has relevance outside the circle of faith.

In reaching this conclusion about the usefulness of Hauerwas's analysis we have been influenced by an important essay by Martha Nussbaum in which she asks the question, 'Can there be non-relative virtues?'[20] Nussbaum accepts that the problem of cultural relativity in virtue theory is a major one. However, she argues that an objective account of human good according to which non-relative virtues can be specified is in principle possible. We can achieve this, she suggests, by identifying spheres of human experience connected with our finitude and limitation as humans, spheres in which human choices are 'nonoptional and somewhat problematic'.[21] We then have to distinguish between 'thin' and 'thick' accounts of virtue. A thin account is one which identifies 'whatever it is to be stably disposed to act appropriately in that sphere'.[22] But, because there are often competing ways of describing what is required, a thick account will have to be more concrete in its specification, and thereby more open to cultural influences. Thus, illness and mortality are clearly universal areas for attention with regard to virtues, since all cultures will develop beliefs about how to act appropriately in such 'nonoptional' situations. But, if virtues like fortitude, courage, hope or patience are specified as part of this appropriate response, we shall quickly run into 'thick' questions. What is the content of such virtuous responses?

Using this terminology, we can easily see that the description of patience by Hauerwas is a 'thick' account. It makes full sense only if it is seen within its setting of Christian tradition and belief. At the same time, it shares many similarities with both the research findings and the account by Lebacqz at a 'thin' level. All three accounts are describing ways in which the sense of helplessness, loss and isolation, which comes with major and disabling illness, can be transcended. Hauerwas describes a coming to terms with the fragility of our bodily selves, a revaluation of simple things and a reaching out to others, which are matched by the fortitude, hope and prudence in Lebacqz and which find ample illustration in the descriptions by patients of their self-development through illness. It is especially important that patients see a realism about their bodies and a pressing need for social acceptance and close friendship as vital to their personal integrity. Moreover, transcendence of the sense of limitation and the rediscovery of simple things, though not often expressed in religious language, is a feature of this quest for survival of the self. The 'thin' parallels are quite striking.

But is this as far as we can go in relating Hauerwas to the research? We think not. His 'thick' account of virtue offers a standpoint from which to assess our model of virtue as located round a core of self-respect. It helps us to think more deeply about the notion of the self, which is so vital to our subjects' enduring sense of value. In a theological account of the self there is always a tension about the location of value. Christian ethics rests on the Great Commandment, to love God with heart, soul and mind and your neighbour as yourself. The richness of this injunction is easily lost, both inside and outside religious communities. Firstly, religion can often negate the self, putting self-denial or self-sacrifice above the command to love the self; secondly, a self-obsessed religion or secular culture can negate the neighbour, emptying the commandment of its insistence on agapeistic justice. Thirdly, the commandment can be secularized, removing the transcendent reference to a God whose goodness draws us close in heart, mind and soul and so frees us to love without fear. Seen in its full meaning, the survival of self in Christian context is all about the nature of love. A 'thick' account like that of Hauerwas resists a splitting of the self from both the community of other selves and from its transcendent source and goal. The loss of self is equated not with illness or death but with an impoverishment of love.

279

In *Health as Liberation* the first author has developed at greater length this understanding of how we can find health even in the midst of illness. The following passage may illustrate the point we are trying to make:

> The real ordeal of human life is not that we can suffer pain and disability and death itself. The real ordeal comes when people lose all hope, when there is no shred of meaning to be found in their suffering, and when there is no world for the self to inhabit ... Health is not to be found by grasping for advantage over others in an effort to insulate oneself against life's maladies; on the contrary, it is those who risk themselves to protect the neediest and most vulnerable that may hope to find some ways of living with their own vulnerability and finitude.[23]

This agapeistic approach to the self provides a unifying concept of virtue in which the excellence of human life is found in the receiving and giving of a love that honours, values and cares for the object of love. This applies equally to our honour and care for others and our honour and care for ourselves, since we are to love self and others equally, neither less nor more.

This, we believe, is a justified elaboration of Hauerwas's account of Christian patience in the face of illness and it allows us to consider finally the use of self-respect as a unifying or core concept for the research findings about virtue and chronic illness. We have already observed that this is bound to be a 'thicker' account than can be possible when we are trying to create a generalized account, which crosses over different beliefs and value systems. Nevertheless we think it does provide insight into why the model proved helpful to the patients themselves and also into how it might be modified and enriched.

Self-respect is, we recall, quite different from self-centredness or self-ishness. If we see it in terms of the Christian concept of agape, it is an acknowledgment of intrinsic worth, of a value, which cannot be taken away by the loss of capacity or the inability to compete in materialistic terms. Thus for these patients the self was never seen as of mere instrumental value – even when they felt frustrated by their disability and when their disturbed emotions or painful bodies were a source of great suffering for them – they sought to recover and treasure that self. But because ill people are often shunned or ignored or misunderstood, the patients were also acutely aware of the fragility of that sense of self-worth and knew that it must be fostered and strengthened by the loving attention of others who do not patronize or disable them further by their insensitivity. Self-respect is essentially relational and is much more complex than individualistic autonomy. It is defended and

280

fostered when the sick person feels truly still part of a loving community, rather than an embarrassing aberration.

We can see then that self-respect is a very rich concept and may well serve to capture much of what is aimed for in Hauerwas's exposition of the virtue of patience. But there is of course a further step urged by theologians. This is to see the self within the context of faith, in which the honour and value comes from a transcendent love, given not achieved, and hope is based in confidence in a divine and omnipresent love. There is no reason to force our general model into such a religious mould, but it is possible to take one step further. This is to suggest that the greatest restoration of self-respect comes when ill people go beyond patienthood to a new kind of agency, when in some paradoxical sense they can make their weakness into strength by being people upon whom others depend for a restoration of wisdom and serenity in their life. Thus the illness becomes a gift for others rather than a burden on the self. Many people achieve this, seeing beyond their need in order to give a new kind of love to others. It may not be religious in any conventional sense, but in the way love grows from the ashes of despair it is perhaps as close to God as any of us could hope for in this life.

How the Virtuous Patient can Rescue Medical Ethics

Finally, and very briefly, we would like to suggest that medical ethics is desperately in need of rescue by the virtuous patient. In the introduction to this chapter we mentioned the way in which such applied ethics has tended to adopt the style and even the terminology of modern medicine. While this can be valuable in some respects, since it allows practitioners to gain some understanding of the nature of their professional decisions, it carries the risk that ethics will be seen as no more than a new clinical skill. Such a view encourages inappropriate ideas of expertise and mastery, and easily leads to a continuing professional dominance of health-care decision-making.

The truth is that there is no real expertise in ethics: it has to be learned anew, as we struggle to safeguard human value in a constantly changing technological environment. Of course philosophers, lawyers and theologians can facilitate a reasoned and conceptually rich discussion of the issues and can help to develop the reflective practitioner through case-based courses at all stages of training. We are strongly in favour of this, and indeed, heavily involved in it. But it is an illusion to suppose that this is all that is needed to deal with the real anguish which accident, disease and disability bring into people's lives. Hauerwas is correct to describe the pathos of modern medicine as a mismatch between our impatient culture and the realities of our finitude.

So how may the virtuous patient rescue medical ethics from being bewitched by the magic of scientific medicine? Firstly, the virtuous patient refuses to be patronized and to be reduced to second place in the process of decision-making in medicine. As we have repeatedly said, patience is not the same as compliance. To maintain self-respect, patients have to become assertive, to insist that they are listened to and that they are willing to bear responsibility for the options they choose. This reversal of roles will not be easy in a profession that has become accustomed to 'possess' patients and to believe that they know what is best for them. But a patient-centred medical ethics and medical practice is the first requirement of any genuine approach to the ethics of medicine.

Secondly, the virtuous patient needs not just bodily restoration but a restoration of relationships. Health-care institutions are notably disempowering and depersonalizing in their treatment of the sick. The technological imperative strips people of their personal identity and puts technical intervention above sensitive communication. It has long been observed that the vast majority of complaints about health services are not about failures in competence, but failures in communication. Yet we know that on our model of the virtues of patienthood, love is the supreme value. People need to be cared *about*, not merely cared *for*. This means that the main focus of medical ethics should not be on technical competence or logical argument but on the formation of the character of professionals, so that they communicate respect and appreciation of each person in all their dealings with patients. This is not easy in the harried setting of modern health care, but if it is excluded from professional life, then one cannot imagine how medicine can hope to restore *health* to people.

Thirdly, the virtuous person has come through, and beyond, fear. That is why the best teachers of medical students and young doctors are the patients themselves, especially those who have had to learn to live with chronic illness. We wrote in the last section about the 'gift' which virtue can bring, the transforming of depression and helplessness into a discovery that in one's illness there are new insights, which can help others. We have barely begun to think in this revolutionary manner about how patients themselves may be the ones to overcome the fears of those who care for them professionally. Yet this perhaps is the main strand of public theology which can emerge from a theological appraisal of the qualities of the virtuous patient.

In his memorable poem, 'Ten Types of Hospital Visitor', Charles Causley wittily describes the horrors to which patients are subjected by visitors of various types from the one who 'destroys hope in the breasts of the sick' by 'her ferocious good will', to the one who makes them cheerful because 'he looks infinitely more decayed, ill and infirm than any patient'.

The poem ends with these lines:

The ninth visitor is life
The tenth visitor is not usually named.[24]

The virtuous patient is not afraid to name the tenth visitor. It is a great, and needed, gift of honesty to medicine and to medical ethics. It is life even in the face of death.

Acknowledgments

We are indebted to the BIOMED II Life Science and Technologies RTD Action of the European Commission for the funding which made the empirical study possible and to our partners in the project:

- Professor Henk ten Have, Department of Ethics, Philosophy and History of Medicine, Catholic University of Nijmegen, Netherlands.
- Dr Emilio Mordini, Psychoanalytic Institute for Social Research, Rome, Italy.
- Dr Søren Holm, Department of Medical Philosophy and Clinical Theory, University of Copenhagen, Denmark.
- Dr Andrew Edgar, Department of Philosophy, University of Wales, Cardiff, UK.

Notes

1 Contract Number BMH4-CT98-3112.
2 Definitions: Endometriosis – a condition where cells from the lining of the uterus occur outside the uterus, causing inflammation, scarring and pain. Rheumatoid arthritis – a systemic rheumatic disease, which can affect numerous joints in the body; causing inflammation, pain and stiffness. It can cause deformity of joints and increasing restriction of movement. Mood disorder – a group of diagnostic entities involving exaggerated mood reactions, primarily depression or mania. End-stage renal disease – a condition in which the kidneys function at less than 10 per cent of normal capacity. Survival requires dialysis or kidney transplant.

283

3 Full details of the partners in the research are appended to this chapter.
4 A full account of all the findings and of the materials produced is available from the Centre for Ethics in Medicine, University of Bristol.
5 See Gabrielle Taylor and Sybil Wolfram, 'The self-regarding and other-regarding virtues', *Philosophical Quarterly*, 18 (1968): 238–48.
6 See Warren T. Reich (ed), *Encyclopaedia of Bioethics* (New York: Free Press, 1978).
7 For a very general discussion from one theological perspective, see Gilbert Meilaender, *The Theory and Practice of Virtue* (Notre Dame, IN: University of Notre Dame Press, 1985).
8 Earl Shelp (ed.), *Virtue and Medicine* (Dordrecht: D. Reidel, 1985), pp. 275–88.
9 Stanley Hauerwas and Charles Pinches, *Christians among the Virtues* (Notre Dame, IN: University of Notre Dame Press, 1997), pp. 166–78.
10 Karen Lebacqz, in Earl Shelp, *Virtue and Medicine*, p. 276.
11 *Ibid.*
12 Susan Sontag, *Illness as Metaphor* (New York: Vintage Books, 1977), p. 3.
13 Lebacqz, in Earl Shelp, *Virtue and Medicine*, p. 278.
14 *Ibid.*, p. 284.
15 Hauerwas and Pinches, *Christians among the Ruins*, p. xi.
16 Alasdair MacIntyre, *After Virtue: A Study in Moral Theory* (London: Duckworth, 2nd edn, 1985), p. 263.
17 Hauerwas and Pinches, *Christians among the Ruins*, p. 170.
18 *Ibid.*, p. 176.
19 E.g. Stanley Hauerwas, *Suffering Presence: Theological Reflections on Medicine, the Mentally Handicapped, and the Church* (Edinburgh: T&T Clark, 1988).
20 Martha Nussbaum, 'Non-relative virtues: an Aristotelian approach', in Peter French *et al.* (eds), *Midwest Studies in Philosophy, Volume XIII: Ethical Theory: Character and Virtue* (Notre Dame, IN: University of Notre Dame Press, 1988).
21 *Ibid.*, p. 37.
22 *Ibid.*
23 Alastair V. Campbell, *Health as Liberation* (Cleveland, OH: Pilgrim Press, 1995), p. 44.
24 Charles Causley, 'Ten types of hospital visitor', in Dennis J. Enright (ed.), *Oxford Book of Contemporary Verse* (Oxford: Oxford University Press, 1980), p. 85.

Chapter 17

Punishing Christians

STANLEY HAUERWAS

How Not to Begin Thinking about Punishment

John Howard Yoder begins his contribution to a book entitled *The Death Penalty Debate* observing that 'it has not been my privilege to be vocationally involved in ministries of witness related to "corrections", nor in the social sciences which study these matters, but my conviction as to the importance of the matter has not diminished.'[1] That the question of punishment was never far from Yoder's attention is indicated by his early pamphlet entitled *The Christian and Capital Punishment*, as well as the book, *You Have It Coming: Good Punishment – The Legitimate Social Function of Punitive Behavior*, which he was preparing when he died.[2] Some may think it strange or odd that Yoder, the pacifist, took punishment so seriously; but Yoder rightly thought those committed to Christian non-violence cannot avoid providing an account – or even more important, alternative practices – of and for punishment.

I suspect one of the reasons many do not think that pacifism deserves serious consideration is not because they think war is a 'good thing'. Rather they sense that pacifism simply cannot give an account of how our daily lives depend on violent forms of behaviour. How could we live if we had no understanding of crime and/or were unwilling to punish those who engage in crime? I began to explore this kind of challenge in an essay entitled, 'McInerny Did It: or, Should a Pacifist Read Murder Mysteries?'[3] That essay was written in honour of my friend, Ralph McInerny, a philosopher and writer of murder mysteries. In this chapter which is written to honour another friend, Duncan Forrester, I will try to extend the argument I began in that essay in the hope I can convince those who think of themselves as almost pacifist to drop the 'almost'.

285

It is my hope that the focus on punishment will provide a way to explore what some, including Duncan himself, may think to be differences between us on matters concerning the responsibility of Christians to the societies in which they find themselves. Duncan has graciously expressed appreciation for the kind of questions I have been pressing against Christian accommodation to liberal social arrangements. Yet he is a good Scot. He has worked tirelessly as a representative of the Church of Scotland to help Scotland be a more just society. Contrary to what some may think I should think as a representative of Christian non-violence, I applaud Duncan for the work he has done for social reforms in Scotland. For example, he has thought hard as well as helped encourage prison reform in Scotland.[4]

The work Duncan and his colleagues have done for reform of Scottish prisons is the kind of work Yoder would encourage. For example, Yoder observes that neither Jesus nor Paul rose up against capital punishment. They did not do so because the Gospel cannot eliminate such practices 'from secular society, since, being non-coercive, the gospel cannot "rule the world" in that way. Yet, to condone the way things stand is not approval: "from the beginning it was not so" (Matt 19:8)'.[5] According to Yoder, though Jesus said this about the Mosaic provision for divorce, this is the way early Christians thought about other areas where the world was ruled by pagan powers. Yet the Christians also thought that the new level of love and forgiveness made possible by the Holy Spirit is good news for the 'real world' because such love will work as salt and light for those who are not Christians. Yoder continues:

> This should be true anywhere; even more evidently should it be the case in the Anglo-Saxon world, where a large number of citizens claim some kind of Christian sanction for society's values. If Christ is not only prophet and priest but also king, the border between church and the world cannot be impermeable to moral truth. Something of the cross-bearing, forgiving love, and dignity which Jesus' life, death, and resurrection revealed to be the normative way to be human, must be the norm for all humans, whether they know it or not. We cannot expect of anyone, not even of believers, that that norm be lived out perfectly. Yet, [there] is the calling of the followers of Jesus to testify that there is no other norm. The one strategy which will not serve that calling, which could not be done in the first century, and cannot be done in our century, is to claim to possess, and to impose on society, a body of civil rules independent of the faith of the persons called to respect them. The alternative is to work with the acceptance of the others' unbelief which is what I call 'condoning' the lesser moral level of the civil order.[6]

However, Yoder's understanding of the permeable boundaries between Church and world does not in itself suggest how Christians ought to think about punishment in general and/or, in particular, capital punishment. He observes that watching the debate between advocates and opponents of capital punishment over the years has taught him there is no one right place to begin.[7] That there is no place to begin seems to me to be right, but it is a hard lesson to learn. For our temptation is to once again roll out the various theories of punishment – rehabilitation, defence against the criminal (deterrence), retribution – and then to grade the practice of punishment against these theories of punishment.[8] The problem is not that these theories are 'wrong' (though I think they often give us a false sense that we know what we are talking about when we talk about punishment); but it is by no means clear what work the theories are meant to do. In particular, the theories give the impression that how Christians punish is but an instance of a more general practice of punishment shared by all societies. It is that presumption I want to challenge in this chapter by calling attention to the way Christians have and should punish. Of course, the strategy of beginning with general theories of punishment is often an attempt to show that capital punishment fails to be justified on grounds of this or that theory. For example, it is suggested that capital punishment cannot pass muster if we believe that rehabilitation or the protection of society is the primary purpose of punishment. You certainly cannot rehabilitate someone you have killed nor does it seem that the use of capital punishment protects society by deterring others from killing. It is often pointed out, for example, that murderers are seldom repeat offenders, unless they are professional killers, so capital punishment does little to deter. Professionals after all will not be deterred exactly because they are professionals.

One response to the attempt to defeat capital punishment by showing it does not deter is to observe that capital punishment is associated with the wrong crime. If we killed people for stock fraud, for example, there is every reason to believe that capital punishment would deter. Erect a gallows or a guillotine on Wall Street, televise the execution of those guilty of stock fraud, and I think there is every reason to believe that stock fraud would be a much less common crime. That most people today recoil against killing people for theft indicates that questions of punishment involve more than the various abstract theories of punishment suggest in and of themselves.

For example, Duncan Forrester reports that the penal policy group that took as their assignment an attempt to understand how the penal system worked and should work in Scotland began by looking at the various theories of punishment. However, he reports it soon became apparent that none of the theories or all the theories together failed to explain what actually happens in the penal system in Scotland. He observes his group increasingly became convinced 'that theories often disguise, mystify, and subtly justify what is really happening'.[9] It was only when the group began to go more deeply into the experience of being and surviving as a prisoner that theological themes began to emerge to illumine the practice of punishment. Forrester observes:

> We discovered the necessity of *hope*. We noted that although offence involves *guilt*, this is not today recognized as something with which the penal system can or should engage. And, most important of all, we noted that in the Christian tradition offence, crime and sin are met with *forgiveness* which wipes away the guilt and the memory, while our society remains highly punitive and former prisoners rarely experience real forgiveness and reconciliation at the hands of their neighbors and colleagues. We concluded that any Christian account of punishment must see it as *discipline* directed to the good of society and of the offender. Most of those working in the system or in academic criminology found the notion of forgiveness a fresh and exciting and challenging idea. In Christian theology it is of course rooted deeply in the understanding of God, and theologians would wish to affirm that it is a universal truth that God is a God who forgives.[10]

I am sure that Forrester and his colleagues are on the right track for helping us think as Christians about punishment. Too often attempts to think through the practice of punishment using the standard theories means theological considerations are absent or used to support positions determined on other grounds. I am, moreover, sure that Forrester and his colleagues are right that the *telos* of punishment must be reconciliation and forgiveness. As he observes, the absence of the hope of forgiveness means 'prisons become human warehouses and both offenders and those who operate the criminal justice system have great difficulty in seeing their experience and their work as significant and meaningful'.[11]

Yet I am equally sure that we must be careful not to let appeals to forgiveness and reconciliation hide from us the seriousness of punishment and the proper role punishment has, not only for any society but in particular in the Church. It is not enough for Christians to say 'forgiveness' if they do not exemplify in their own lives why punishment is a necessary practice if the Church is to be the Church. Appeals to forgiveness are too easy if we have not first made clear why we think it is wrong to execute people for stock fraud. After all, the Church at one time thought those convicted of heresy should be killed – a position we may find extreme, but one justified if you

288

believe that heresy is a more serious crime than murder. A murderer after all only robs us of our life; a heretic robs us of our salvation.

In order to explore the theological issues at the heart of punishment, I want to introduce Oliver O'Donovan's compelling justification of capital punishment. His account, moreover, is all the more important because it emerges in the process of his critique of John Paul II's praise in *Evangelium Vitae* for the growing tendency in our time for the limited use or abolishment of capital punishment. O'Donovan, I think, rightly fears that the Pope on this matter may have succumbed to the sentimental humanism of our time. However, before such a judgement can be sustained, I need to attend to the details of O'Donovan's analysis and critique of the Pope's position.

O'Donovan's Analysis of *Evangelium Vitae*

O'Donovan's critique involves a close reading of the passage in *Evangelium Vitae* that deals with capital punishment. That passage reads:

> This is the context in which to place the problem of the *death penalty*. On this matter there is a growing tendency, both in the Church and in civil society, to demand that it be applied in a very limited way or even that it be abolished completely. The problem must be viewed in the context of a system of penal justice ever more in line with human dignity and thus, in the end, with God's plan for man and society. The primary purpose of the punishment which society inflicts is 'to redress the disorder caused by the offense'. Public authority must redress the violation of personal and social rights by imposing on the offender an adequate punishment for the crime, as a condition for the offender to regain the exercise of his or her freedom. In this way authority also fulfills the purpose of defending public order and ensuring people's safety, while at the same time offering an incentive and help to change his or her behavior and be rehabilitated.
>
> It is clear that for these purposes to be achieved, *the nature and extent of the punishment* must be carefully evaluated and decided upon, and ought not go to the extreme of executing the offender except in cases of absolute necessity: in other words, when it would not be possible otherwise to defend society. Today, however, as a result of steady improvements in the organization of the penal system, such cases are very rare, if not practically nonexistent.
>
> In any event, the principle set forth in the new *Catechism of the Catholic Church* remains valid: 'If bloodless means are sufficient to defend human lives against an aggressor and to protect public order and the safety of persons, public authority must limit itself to such means, because they better correspond to the concrete conditions of the common good and are more in conformity to the dignity of the human person.'[12]

O'Donovan begins his criticism of the Pope's position noting that three points in particular are in need of clarification: (1) what characteristics of a society are presupposed by the 'steady improvements' to which the Pope refers? (2) What kind of situation would count as an 'absolute necessity?' And (3) why does the Pope justify capital punishment in classical retributive categories, but make the possibility for the lessening use of capital punishment turn on remedial considerations?[13] Though the first two questions of clarification are important, O'Donovan's most important challenge to the Pope's position involves the third challenge.

O'Donovan observes that in the late eighteenth and nineteenth centuries a consensus developed that retributive appropriateness was the final criterion for means of punishment.[14] Accordingly, the death penalty was required since only life could witness to the sanctity of life. O'Donovan therefore observes: the Pope simply gives no reason why we should believe that rehabilitation should count more than public safety. But even more important, the Pope does not adequately explore what is at stake in his praise for societies that have abandoned retribution as the primary purpose of punishment. In order to clarify what the Pope needs to say, O'Donovan offers an account of why retribution can never be disavowed by the public authorities.

Punishment is expressive act, according to O'Donovan, just to the extent that 'punishment must pronounce judgment on the offense, describing it, disowning it, and refounding the moral basis for the common life which the offense has challenged'.[15] Punishment, so to speak, 'gives back' the offence, not simply as vengeance, but in the sense that a true statement is made about what has happened. Retribution is the primary end of punishment which means that that is what punishment *is* in the same way that telling the truth is the primary end of making a statement. Retribution is the alternative to vengeance because vengeance is 'private' and, therefore, arbitrary.[16]

So understood, punishment is not a means to some other end – even the end of making the offender good – but rather the end of punishment is justice. To be sure, there may be secondary goods associated with punishment, but such goods should not qualify that the end of punishment is justice. As O'Donovan puts it, 'punishment is a kind of enacted language', reminding us that the equivalence of punishment to crime is a 'symbolic construct' that 'evolves as the symbolic meaning of certain acts with the context of social expectation changes'.[17] Thus it may be as Montesquieu observed that, in countries with mild laws, inhabitants are as much affected by slight penalties as inhabitants of countries with more severe laws. O'Donovan hopes that the Pope's understanding of the 'improvements in the penal system' simply means that the influence of the Christian message makes it possible for those in authority to follow Ambrose's message concerning the use of capital punishment – 'You will be excused if you use it, admired if you refrain.'[18]

Yet O'Donovan fears John Paul II may in fact come close to recommending the abolition of capital punishment in principle. For example, O'Donovan calls attention to paragraph 40 of *Evangelium Vitae* in which the Pope seems to be moving to a position that would not require capital punishment to be considered a necessary part of a humane justice system. In this paragraph the Pope, in commenting on the prohibition of murder in the Decalogue, says: 'Of course we must recognize that in the Old Testament this sense of the value of life, though already quite marked, does not yet reach the refinement found in the Sermon on the Mount. This is apparent in some aspects of the current [i.e., *then* current] penal legislation, which provided for severe forms of corporal punishment and even the death-penalty.'[19]

O'Donovan thinks this account of capital punishment breaks the link between public safety and the system of retributive justice. As a result, capital punishment becomes but an emergency provision that allegedly is no longer required in modern, economically developed and well-governed states. Accordingly, the coercive powers of the state in criminal justice are derived and justified from a just war perspective of 'legitimate defense'.[20] From O'Donovan's perspective this is a terrible mistake because:

> one should never attempt such a thing. The right of the state to impose coercive measures against wrongdoers arises not from its need to defend itself but from its office of *judgment* … For if the death penalty is never at home in ordinary penal practice, then it is never invoked for purposes germane to penology but only to shore up the institution upon which all penal practice depends, that is, the state. The idea of an 'emergency provision,' whether we meet it in John Paul or in some well-known Protestant exemplars, implies an inevitable drift towards statism; for once the power of the sword is notionally set free from the constraints of justice *in extremis*, there can be no function for the sword but to enforce the state's grip. We should hardly be surprised if the state that is refused the just use of force in ordinary operations but is promised a *carte blanche* in emergency, sets about creating one.[21]

To make capital punishment morally discontinuous from other forms of coercive punishment not only invites a loss of constraint on when states may declare their very existence is at stake, but, even more disturbing, theologically severs death from God's judgement. According to O'Donovan, all Christians have to say that death is not part of God's 'original' created order. Death is not just death, but judgement on sin. Without such a view of the linkage between judgement and death, Christ becomes but another victim of injustice rather than the one that bore our sins and suffered our death. That is why, as happy as it may be to be rid of the ordinary uses of the death penalty, we 'cannot be rid of the symbolic role that the death penalty plays in relating death to judgement. There will always be a death penalty in the mind – if, that is, we are all to learn to "die with Christ," understanding our own deaths as a kind of capital punishment.'[22]

So runs O'Donovan's justification of capital punishment. I admire O'Donovan's argument because he makes overt the moral and theological presuppositions associated with retributive accounts of punishment. Christological questions are rightly at the centre and O'Donovan rightly puts them where they should be. Moreover, O'Donovan makes clear that capital punishment cannot be separated from why and how we punish in other aspects of our lives. Accordingly, any alternative account to O'Donovan's understanding of punishment requires, if not forces, us to leave behind the sentimentalities so characteristic of compassionate responses to punishment.

The Christian Practice of Punishment

O'Donovan rightly calls into question the sentimental humanism that currently dominates discussions surrounding capital punishment in liberal social orders. Moreover, he helps us see why it is extremely unwise for Christians to identify with the call for an end to capital punishment just to the extent our understanding of punishment is confused with humanist ideologies and practices. Yet I do want capital punishment to come to an end because I think the end of punishment has been transformed by the cross and resurrection of Christ. Moreover, I think that transformation is a possibility not only for the practice of the Church but for any society and the public authorities (what is sometimes identified as the state) who have responsibilities to serve the goods in common, which include punishment.

By distinguishing 'public authorities' from the 'state' I mean to do no more than to call into question the assumption that the 'state as such' is a known entity. I assume peoples can exist with structures of authority that are not the same as 'a state', particularly when the state in modernity is identified with the locus of hegemonic power. This may seem an unimportant distinction, but too often 'the state' is simply accepted as a given in a manner that makes it impervious to the Gospel. For example, Avery Cardinal Dulles observes that, while the Church can and does punish, she is also indulgent toward offenders. He notes that 'it would be clearly inappropriate for the Church, as a spiritual society, to execute criminals, but the State is a different type of society. It cannot be expected to act as a Church.'[23]

Far be it for me to suggest that a cardinal of the Church of Rome has gone over to the Lutherans, but to claim that something called 'the state' exists that has not been transformed by Christ could be interpreted as accepting the Lutheran understanding of the distinction between the orders of creation and redemption. For example, it is quite interesting to contrast Dulles's (and O'Donovan's) understanding of the state with that of John Howard Yoder.[24] Responding to the assumption shared by many that to call for the end of capital punishment is to destroy all government, Yoder observes that for the Christian to accept the question 'but where will this lead?' is to distort the whole problem. Of course Christians know that the world does not share our faith, that the world cannot be expected to live as Christians should live, but that does not mean there is some line drawn in the sand that determines what Christians cannot ask of the societies in which we find ourselves.

The resurrection and ascension of Christ means there is no situation in which Christians think nothing can be done.

> The world can be challenged, one point at a time, to take one step in the right direction, to move up one modest notch in approximation of the righteousness of love. To challenge capital punishment no more undermine government than does the rejection of the oath (Matt 5:33–7, James 5:12) undermine truth telling; no more than does the consent of the governed destroy the authority of the state. The civil order is a fact. That it might be done away with by pushing the critique of love 'too far' is inconceivable. Thus the Christian (and any believer in democracy) will be concerned to restrain the violent, vengeful potential of the state. That potential for violence does not need our advocacy; it is already there.[25]

Of course, Dulles and O'Donovan may object that Yoder fails to understand that the issue is not whether the state does or does not exist or have a justification to sustain the legitimacy of the state. The issue is justice. Yet, just as he challenges the assumption that there is any one thing called the 'state', so Yoder questions the assumption that there is any univocal 'concept of justice, having the same meaning in all times and places, consisting in an exact logical or mathematical equivalence of offense and retribution, and that such "justice" must (or can) be either wholly respected or fundamentally rejected'.[26] There is, therefore, no culturally invariant understanding of what equivalent punishment should or does entail. The presumption that 'retributive justice' requires the murderer's life in return is not written in stone.[27]

293

For Yoder, justice is a direction, not an achievement. I take this claim to mean no more than what is emphasized in all classical accounts of justice, namely, that justice depends on the practices of a people that embodies the hard-won wisdom of the past tested by the challenges of the present in the hope of a better future.

Yoder has no reason to deny O'Donovan's account of punishment as an 'enacted language'. O'Donovan, moreover, rightly suggests that, as a language, punishment can and should evolve in which the symbolic meaning of certain acts changes, given the context of social expectation.[28] Rather, Yoder is trying to force questions about the 'context of social expectation' that Christ's cross and resurrection have made possible. For Yoder is sure that, if it is inappropriate for the Church to execute criminals, this is equally the case for the public officials of any society. If the shedding of blood is meant to expose the killer to killing in expiation in the name of justice or the cosmic order, it is Yoder's contention that Christ is the end of expiation.[29] At the very least this means Christians cannot help but challenge accounts of justice that assume the only way to restore the injustice murder names is by taking the life of the murderer.[30]

That Christ is the end of expiation does not mean, however, that Christians do not punish. Yet the Christian understanding of punishment must begin with the recognition that we are not punished for our sins, but sin is our punishment. John Howard Yoder and John Milbank are not usually considered allies, but I believe they share this understanding of sin. *In Theology and Social Theory*, Milbank observes that God does not will to punish sin, because 'punishment is not an act of a real nature upon another nature, and God always remains within his nature. Punishment is ontologically "self-inflicted", the only punishment is the deleterious effect of sin upon nature, and the torment of knowing reality only in terms of one's estrangement from it.'[31]

According to Milbank, the trial and punishment of Jesus judges all other trials and punishments just to the extent the latter cannot help but be 'alien'. It is, therefore, not adequate to say, as O'Donovan seems to do, that such 'alien punishment' is a symbolic language. The tragic necessity of such punishment cannot be a sign of God's justice if God's justice is the cross. So the only

> tolerable, and non-sinful punishment, for Christians, must be the self-punishment inherent in sin. When a person commits an evil act, he cuts himself off from social peace, and this nearly always means that he is visited with social anger. But the

aim should be to reduce this anger to a calm fury against the sin, and to offer the sinner nothing but good will, so bringing him to the point of realizing that his isolation is self-imposed.[32]

Milbank's position does not commit him to the absurd position that we know that we are being punished for our sin. Indeed, one of the most frightening realities is that we may appear to be quite happy in our unrighteousness – happiness can be a form of punishment. To suffer for our sins is a great gift that makes possible the identification as well as the appropriate penance for our sin. For that is exactly what Christian punishment is – penance that makes possible the reconciliation with God, the neighbour against whom we have sinned and even ourselves. Milbank is quite right that the effect of sin estranges us from ourselves creating a loneliness that cannot be overcome. To be punished as a Christian is to be called home so that we may be reunited with the community of forgiven sinners called Church and, thus, reconciled with our own life.

Christian punishment is properly understood to be excommunication or binding and loosing. To be confronted by our brothers and sisters because of our sin is a call to reconciliation. Not to hear the call is to condemn ourselves. To be excommunicated is not to be 'thrown out', but rather to be told that we are already 'outside'. Excommunication is a call to come home by helping us locate how we have alienated ourselves from God and those that gather to worship God. Christian punishment only makes sense against the background of the practice of holiness commensurate with the Christian desire to be a people called to witness to the One who alone is able to forgive sins.[33]

The Christian practice of punishment cannot help but resist being confined by the various theories of punishment. What Christians have to offer our non-Christian brothers and sisters is not a better theory, but a practice of punishment that can be imitated. There is always the question, however, whether what we do as Christians can be done abstracted from our worship of God from which all that we do gains its intelligibility. Yoder, for example, reminds us that prisons were once called 'penitentiaries' because they were understood as places to repent.[34] Once the background practices that make repentance the *telos* of punishment were missing, prisons could not help but become the hell-holes they are today.

Christians are rightly concerned with prison reform. Christians rightly seek to live in societies that no longer use the death penalty. But Christians, particularly Christians committed to non-violence, fail themselves and their

295

non-Christian neighbours when they act as if punishment is a problem 'out there'. What Christians must first give to the world is to be a community that can punish. Only then will the world have an example of what it might mean to be a community that punishes in a manner appropriate for a people who believe that we have been freed by the cross of Christ from the terror of death. I believe that is the kind of community Duncan Forrester has always represented and so doing became for the world the kind of 'permeable boundary' God desires.[35]

Notes

1 John Howard Yoder, 'Against the death penalty', in H. Wayne House and John Howard Yoder, *The Death Penalty Debate: Two Opposing Views of Capital Punishment* (Dallas, TX: Word, 1991), p. 107.

2 John Howard Yoder, *The Christian and Capital Punishment*, Pamphlet in the Institute of Mennonite Studies Series, No. 1 (Newton, KS: Faith and Life Press, 1961) and John Howard Yoder, *You Have It Coming: Good Punishment – The Legitimate Social Function of Punitive Behavior*. Yoder prepared and 'published' the latter book for his Internet site in 1995. I have a downloaded copy of the book which indicates that, in spite of Yoder's claim that he had not kept up in the social science literature surrounding issues of punishment, in fact he had. He was particularly interested in the work of René Girard. ('You have it coming' is also available online from Shalom Desktop Publications, 1995.)

3 This essay was originally published in *Recovering Nature: Essays in Natural Philosophy, Ethics, and Metaphysics in Honor of Ralph McInerny*, edited by John O'Callaghan and Thomas Hibbs (Notre Dame, IN: University of Notre Dame Press, 1999), pp. 163–75. It can also be found in my book, *A Better Hope: Resources for a Church Confronting Capitalism, Democracy, and Postmodernity* (Grand Rapids, MI: Brazos Books, 2000), pp. 201–10.

4 I know of this work primarily through conversations with Duncan, but he discusses the work of the penal policy group in his essay, 'Priorities for social theology today', in Michael Northcott (ed.), *Vision and Prophecy: The Tasks of Social Theology Today* (Edinburgh: Centre for Theology and Public Issues, 1991), pp. 29–31.

5 Yoder, 'Against the death penalty', p. 141.

6 *Ibid.*

7 *Ibid.*, p. 107.

8 The examples of this strategy are legion, but for a recent display of how this kind of analysis works see Avery Cardinal Dulles, 'Catholicism and capital punishment', *First Things*, 112 (April, 2001): 30–5. I am not suggesting that the various theories of punishment are not useful ways of exploring the conceptual issues

entailed in various claims about punishment. Rather I am calling into question the temptation for the theories to take on a life of their own irrespective of the thick practices that surround punishment in different historical periods and in various cultural locations.

9   Forrester, 'Priorities for social theology today', p. 30.

10 *Ibid*. I think it wrong to suggest that the Christian practice of forgiveness 'wipes out memory'. On the contrary, forgiveness makes memory possible. For an argument along these lines see my *A Better Hope: Resources for a Church Confronting Capitalism, Democracy, and Postmodernity*, pp. 139–54.

11 Forrester, 'Priorities for social theology today', p. 30.

12 I am using the text as it appears in *The Encyclicals of John Paul II*, ed. with introductions by J. Michael Miller CSB (Huntington, IN: Our Sunday Visitor, 1996), para. 56.

  John Paul II's claim that 'this is the context' to discuss capital punishment is fascinating. Paragraph 55 deals with the 'paradox' that occurs when the right to protect one's own life and the duty not to harm someone else's life cannot be reconciled in practice. John Paul II observes that the 'intrinsic value of life and the duty to love oneself not less than others are the basis of a *true right* to self-defense'. He then notes that the commandment to love the neighbour presupposes love of self as set forth in the Great Commandment. Therefore, 'no one can renounce the right to self-defense out of lack of love for life or for self. This can only be done in virtue of a heroic love which deepens and transfigures the love of self into a radical self-offering, according to the spirit of the Gospel Beatitudes. The sublime example of this self-offering is the Lord Jesus Christ.'

  I confess I find the Pope's defence of self-love as the basis for self-defence puzzling. If our self-love is to be formed by charity, what could it possibly mean to suggest that Christians have a right to self-defence? Our love for life and self only makes sense if the 'self' is shaped by the love of God found in the cross. To suggest that such a love is 'heroic' seems to accept the natural, if not sinful, self as normative.

  This is extremely important for the issue of capital punishment, for the Pope goes on to suggest that legitimate defence is not only a right but a 'grave duty' for those responsible for the common good of the family or the state. Accordingly, it happens that there is a need to render an aggressor incapable of causing harm which may even require the taking of his/her life. In such cases, the 'fatal outcome' is not murder because the loss of life is attributable to the aggressor's action. As we shall see, this justification makes the Pope's judgements about capital punishment the harder to understand.

13 Oliver O'Donovan, 'The death penalty in *Evangelium Vitae*', in Reinhard Hutter and Theodor Dieter (eds), *Ecumenical Ventures in Ethics: Protestants Engage Pope John Paul II's Moral Encyclicals*, (Grand Rapids, MI: Eerdmans, 1998), pp. 220–3.

14 O'Donovan does not explain how or why this 'consensus' developed or whether it is a development Christians should applaud. I should think the 'reformative' account of punishment was and is the justification most modern people assume justifies punishment.

15 O'Donovan, '*The death penalty in Evangelium Vitae*', p. 224.

16 I understand the distinction O'Donovan is making between retribution and vengeance, but I confess I find it a bit forced. If vengeance is the symbolic way people gesture that order is deeper than disorder, it seems appropriate that retribution serve to provide the vengeance those directly involved in a crime feel they need. That those who have someone close to them violated so often express the need to have the perpetrator of the violence killed and even to see them executed cannot be easily dismissed as 'a primitive attitude'. That a 'public authority' should perform the execution is important, but the execution remains the working out of vengeance.

Yoder in his early pamphlet, *The Christian and Capital Punishment*, maintained that vengeance shapes capital punishment. His position in this regard does not necessarily make his view of capital punishment different from O'Donovan's stress on justice because Yoder also observes that 'vengeance is happening; the necessity is that it be controlled. Thus the significance of civil order is that it *limit* vengeance to a level equivalent to the offense ... Vengeance was never God's highest intent for men's relations with one another; permitting it within the limits of justice, i.e., of equivalent injury, was never really his purpose' (p. 7). According to Yoder, what God wants to do with evil, what he wants us to do with evil, is 'to swallow it up, drown it in the bottomless sea of His crucified love' (p. 7). Yoder's account of how the civil order 'limits vengeance' has at least resemblance to O'Donovan's understanding of justice.

17 O'Donovan, 'The death penalty', p. 225.

18 *Ibid.*, p. 227.

19 *Ibid.*, p. 229.

20 I confess I am not quite sure what point O'Donovan is making by suggesting that the Pope is making a mistake when he seemingly justifies capital punishment in a just war as 'legitimate defense'. I assume he must mean that 'legitimate defense' is a 'last resort' which makes 'capital punishment' justified only if the survival of the society is at stake. But that would rob capital punishment of its 'normality'. In other words, capital punishment is not like just war if it is required by justice. That said, I think the relation between just war reflection and capital punishment has not been sufficiently spelled out either by those who support just war and capital punishment or by those who support neither. In particular, I think O'Donovan's analysis opens up the question of what 'justice' a just war is meant to serve. This is particularly important if just war is understood not as an exception to non-violence, but rather is required because justice always requires us to defend the neighbour. It is, therefore, wrong to try to rid the world of war

if war is a necessity for the realization of justice. If such is the case, then capital punishment and war are analogous but it remains a question in what ways the justice that is the end of each is similar and different.

21 O'Donovan, 'The death penalty', pp. 232–3. For O'Donovan's extended account of the importance of judgement, see his *The Desire of the Nations: Rediscovering the Roots of Political Theology* (Cambridge: Cambridge University Press, 1996), pp. 37–41, 147–51. O'Donovan explicitly criticizes Yoder's account of Matthew 18: 15–20. O'Donovan thinks Yoder, at least in 'The original revolution', gives the state a role in judgement. Unfortunately, according to O'Donovan, Yoder did not continue that line of analysis in *The Politics of Jesus*. I am not convinced. O'Donovan, I think, fails to appreciate Yoder's refusal to give a 'theory' of state action. For Yoder 'vengeance happens'; it does not need a justifying theory.

   By some 'well-known Protestant exemplars', O'Donovan means Barth. In his *Church Dogmatics*, III/4, trans. by A. T. Mackay *et al.* (Edinburgh: T&T Clark, 1961), Barth argued that capital punishment 'must be put on the far edge of what can be commanded'. According to Barth, there is a place for the killing of those 'whose existence threatens the state and its stability in such a way that a choice has to be made between their existence and that of the state' (p. 446). Barth thinks, for example, that the treasonous giving of secrets to the enemy might be grounds for capital punishment. O'Donovan quite rightly observes that Barth-like justifications put the ordinary operations of penal justice in an idealized light. Such justifications hide from us the coercive character of all punishment which draws its power over us through our mortality.

22 O'Donovan, 'The death penalty', p. 235. O'Donovan suggests that, to the extent John Paul II leaves this understanding of capital punishment behind, he becomes a modernist in spite of his otherwise attack on 'the culture of death'. O'Donovan notes that, at the heart of the 'culture of death' rests a culture of life. 'Precisely because our brief span must (it seems to us) carry the whole meaning of existence, offering all the reconciliation we can ever hope to find; precisely because death (whether Christ's or ours) is allowed no role in this reconciliation; we become greedy of life, demanding to live each moment to the full, snatching from others opportunities to live that could compete with our own, making calculated sacrifices of the "worthless" lives to enrich the "worthwhile", and so on' (p. 236).

23 Avery Cardinal Dulles, 'Catholicism and capital punishment', p. 34. Dulles, like O'Donovan, thinks that in predominately Christian societies the state can lean toward leniency as long as such leniency does not violate the demands of justice. Dulles, also like O'Donovan, thinks the state must believe in a transcendent order of justice which it has an obligation to protect. Such an order of justice is but a 'symbolic anticipation of God's perfect justice' (p. 33). Dulles quite rightly distinguishes this view of the state from the general view in our time that sees the state as but the instrument of the will of the governed in which the death penalty becomes but an expression of the collective anger of the group. When

this happens, punishment is no longer an analogue of the divine judgement on objective evil but simply the self-assertive act of vengeance. I share Dulles's view of the transformation of the state in modernity, but I wonder why he does not conclude from that change that in such social orders capital punishment should be ended exactly because the end of capital punishment has been lost. I often wonder why the same line of reasoning does not lead advocates of just war, which again is dependent on some account of justice, to call for an end to war. Liberal societies simply lack an account of justice that would make just war intelligible.

24 My suggesting that Dulles and O'Donovan may have a similar view of this matter may be mistaken. O'Donovan may well believe that the Church can and should execute criminals.

25 Yoder, 'Against the death penalty', p. 142. Yoder observes that 'anarchy' is a grammatical abstraction with no reality. There are varied forms of government – from tyranny to constitutional democracy – but given the many possibilities there is always authority. Even in cases where authority is functioning too little for the welfare and stability of the society, the reason for such dysfunctioning is never due to Christian love being too effective.

26 *Ibid.,* p. 143.

27 Yoder observes that if life for life is required by justice, then there is no reason why the mentally handicapped should be spared the death penalty. The character or 'freedom' of the murderer should not be taken into account if all that matters is that justice be served. Yoder rightly uses all the anomalies created by capital punishment – it can result in killing the innocent, it falls disproportionately on the poor and African-American, its infrequency ironically makes it more arbitrary – to call into question its use.

28 O'Donovan, 'The death penalty in *Evangelium Vitae*', p. 225.

29 Yoder, 'Against the death penalty', p. 128.

30 The refusal to kill those who kill can be seen as a kind of cruelty just to the extent such a refusal refuses to allow those that kill to determine their own self-understanding. To kill another human being can be the ultimate act of self-assertion, the claim of ultimate autonomy, and thus an act that creates an extraordinary loneliness. Murder is not an act to be shared. The refusal to kill others is the refusal to let them determine the meaning of their lives. The refusal to kill them is the refusal to let their loneliness determine who they are.

30 John Milbank, *Theology and Social Theory: Beyond Secular Reason* (Oxford: Basil Blackwell, 1990), p. 420. In an extraordinary essay on the Book of Job, Herbert Fingarette argues that 'the Book of Job shatters, by a combination of challenge and ridicule and ultimately by direct experiential demonstration, the idea that the law known to human beings reflects law rooted in the divine or ultimate nature of being, and the idea that the divine or ultimate nature of being is in its essences lawlike'. Fingarette argues that, if God were required to punish us for disobedience to God's law, then we could control God by forcing God to punish us. That is a

bargain decisively rejected in Job. See 'The meaning of law in the Book of Job', in Stanley Hauerwas and Alasdair MacIntyre (eds), *Revisions: Changing Perspectives in Moral Philosophy* (Notre Dame, IN: University of Notre Dame Press, 1983), pp. 249–86. The quotation comes from p. 269.

32 Milbank, *Theology and Social Theory*, p. 421.

33 That Christians punish means we must also have practices that make it possible to recognize sins. In other words, we need to know how to name actions such as lying, stealing, rape, adultery, killing. A fascinating question that needs exploration is the relation between what Christians call sin and what is understood as crime. Christians that commit crimes may sin; but criminals who are not Christians may not be sinners. Yet Christians no doubt have contributed to the current understanding of crime that rightly makes it difficult to distinguish between sin and crime. In social orders as fragile as those in the so-called First World, one of the few places the language of the common good works is in agreements about what constitutes crime. But to recognize a crime requires an account of the positive goods the crime injures. It is not clear liberal social orders can confidently name such goods, which makes their presumed arguments about crime increasingly arbitrary.

34 Yoder, 'Against the death penalty', p. 130.

35 I am grateful to Alex Sider and Charlie Collier for their criticisms of an earlier draft of this essay.

Chapter 18

On Whether Forgiveness has Boundaries[1]

ALAN J. TORRANCE

The grammar of the Torah and the history of the Covenant integral to it present us with the structure of what was to become the Christian ethic of unconditional love. As God was unconditionally faithful to Israel, so Israel was created to correspond to or to 'image' that faithfulness, not only in its response to Yahweh, but in its horizontal relationships. And what may be regarded as the zenith of Israel's theological reflection on God's faithfulness and its implications is found in Deutero-Isaiah, where the author perceives that Israel's election is to be fulfilled in her witness to Yahweh's all-inclusive covenant love for the Gentiles – and where Israel's witness to that inclusive faithfulness is to be so radical that a bruised reed on the edge of disintegration will not be broken or a smouldering wick quenched.

As E. P. Sanders has emphasized, Jesus was simply being true to the heart of Judaism when he suggested that the Torah is fulfilled in loving God and our neighbour as ourselves. The same can be argued to apply to Jesus' unambiguous response to the question put to him concerning the boundaries of forgiveness – forgiveness of enemies is to be unbounded and unconditional. As God forgives us unconditionally, so are we to forgive each other unconditionally. Just as it was while we were still sinners that Christ died for us (Rom 5:8), it is while our enemies remain enemies that we are both to love and to forgive them.

The injunction to forgive our enemies, however, has been widely interpreted to be a personal, spiritual injunction addressed to individuals, the assumption being that it is to be regarded, therefore, as private and not relevant for the formulation of public policy. For the purposes of this chapter, I shall start by considering some arguments in support of Miroslav Volf and Gregory Jones's contention that forgiveness does indeed belong to the business of politics. In the second part of the chapter, however, I shall proceed to consider a problem which is raised by such an approach – one, indeed, which serves to pose a dilemma for the Christian doctrine of the atonement.

Firstly, to be a Christian is to operate from a particular epistemic base. Intrinsic to this is the belief that the *telos* of humanity, the only valid form of human existence, is that form of existence realized in Jesus Christ who, as the Second Adam, defines in his person what it is to be 'human' in truth. To be human as we are intended to be – that is, to be properly functional – *is* to affirm and to forgive one's enemies unconditionally. That is the only mode of orientation toward enemies, therefore, that we can advocate, recognize and endorse as valid. Not to do so is to be inconsistent with fundamental epistemic affiliations at the heart of the Christian faith. And to the extent that that is the case, there can be no valid distinction between what we advocate at the political and personal levels – between what we preach in church and what we vote for and advocate on the political platform.

Tactical considerations aside, it is simply confused to suggest that we should not argue for what we believe God wills and endorses with respect to all forms of relationships between all peoples. What this means is that there is no political word which the Christian can speak, or act on or vote for, which does not embody the affirmation of the dignity of the enemy, and which is not simultaneously, therefore, a word of unconditional forgiveness. This applies not only to internal politics and our approach to criminal justice but to our political engagement with peoples who have endorsed the rule of war criminals committed to ethnic cleansing and genocide.

Secondly, whereas it is commonplace to rehearse the problems and risks of introducing the notion of forgiveness here, the Croatian theologian, Miroslav Volf, has highlighted in his book, *Exclusion and Embrace*, the profound political relevance of such a political orientation toward enemies. The practical significance of this courageous thesis is explored most fully in his chapter entitled simply 'Embrace'. Far from undermining justice, forgiveness *serves* justice, he argues, and is intrinsic to the creation of the just society. Far from weakening or even undermining justice and the universal rule of law, as it is often assumed to do, forgiveness serves and preserves justice.

In illustration of this he refers to two basic predicaments which charac-terize contexts of alienation and hostility. The first is the 'predicament of partiality' – the problem of the diversity of perceptions which characterize alienated parties – what he terms the 'lack of sync between the perspectives of social actors'. One party will interpret its own actions as simply seeking justice or even settling for less than justice, whereas the other party may perceive those same actions as perpetrating injustice or even taking revenge.[2] Parties at enmity with each other invariably see and interpret things from different perspectives. To put it another way, a hermeneutical problem arises leading to discrepancies in the *calculi* which two hostile parties bring to bear on the assessment of the propriety of actions. As the *intended justice* of one party is translated by the other party into *actual injustice*, 'a "just" revenge leads to a "just" counter-revenge'. The result is a 'spiral of vengeance' deriving from 'the inability of the parties locked in conflict to agree on the moral significance of their actions'.[3]

Undergirding all this is what Hannah Arendt calls the 'predicament of irreversibility'. The fact is that, by nature, we find it difficult to countenance the hard fact that evil acts cannot be undone. No one can undo what they have done. If they could, then revenge simply would not be necessary.[4] It is this predicament of irreversibility and its offence to the natural human psyche which drives people to seek revenge in the ill-conceived belief that revenge can serve to cancel a debt. Revenge, in which the penalty is gauged by the victim, becomes a substitute for reversibility. As Volf points out, this kind of restorative justice can never be satisfied and justice can never be its outcome due, first, to the fact that partiality means that revenge will never be mutually perceived to be right and appropriate but also because the evil act simply *cannot* be reversed. He concludes, 'If the predicament of partiality puts the lid on the coffin of such justice, the predicament of irreversibility screws the lid tightly down.'[5]

But why should this dilemma lead us to opt for forgiveness as opposed to a *genuine* justice, that is, a *measured*, just retribution? Clearly, a great deal requires to be said here. Space, however, allows me to make only a couple of comments.

One practical reason concerns the failure of 'justice' to deliver what it promises – to make things *iustus*, that is, 'right' (*dikaios*). Indeed, the demands of retributive justice are no less difficult to satisfy than those of revenge. How much retribution and what kind of retribution could ever be supposed to redress the injustice of an event such as the Holocaust, for example? How could the demands of retributive justice ever be 'satisfied' in the context of the murder of a child? What could it possibly mean to speak of satisfying society's, let alone, the parents' desire for justice? Justice requires that the child be allowed to live her life fully and in peace. When that has been irretrievably denied, even the ultimate retributive act, namely, the death penalty, cannot make the situation 'right'. Indeed, it arguably does little more than give the last word to the social, familial, biological and other evils that serve to create murderers.

So wherein lies the universal, intuitive appeal of retributive justice? In large measure, it reposes on a myth, what I have described elsewhere as the 'metaphor of the scales' – the view that an evil act generates an imbalance in nature which then requires, by virtue of some kind of necessity, to be redressed by an act of counterbalancing. The negativity requires to be negated, cancelled out. The attendant supposition is that the negativity of punishment negates the negativity of the original crime, thereby re-establishing a just order. It makes things 'right' again. The suffering or evil involved in punishment is thus transmuted into a 'good' because justice is 'restored' or 'satisfied'. Our whole language is pregnant with this myth and we are thereby subliminally conditioned into thinking in terms of it!

What is interesting to note here is that to say that the suffering involved in punishment is a means to an end has the effect of making all retributionists into consequentialists. To obviate this, they have to hold that the punishment (and the suffering inherent in it) is an intrinsic good. Suffice to say, the Christian faith acknowledges no such scales, no such Neoplatonist concept of balance, no such concept of law or justification or establishing of the right, struggles to endorse the view that evil was a quantifiable reality in this sense at all and can never make the suffering imposed by one human being on another an intrinsic good.

In sum, the Christian concept of righteousness challenges the idolatrous service of some kind of balance in nature which human beings can restore by the infliction of suffering. What I am also suggesting is that it is precisely such a view which means that the insatiable pursuit of the demands of justice too easily translates into the pursuit of revenge. In other words, the language that subliminally serves the pursuit of retributive justice in public policy serves simultaneously to undergird the hunger for revenge so often preyed upon by the tabloids!

However, there is a further parallel between 'just' retribution and revenge which also needs to be considered – and I should add, of course, that drawing parallels between retributive justice and revenge does not necessarily condemn retributive justice! In *The Warrior's Honor: Ethnic War and the Modern Conscience*, Michael Ignatieff points to the fact that revenge is sustained and motivated by a profoundly significant virtue, namely, that of 'keeping faith with the dead'. He writes:

The chief moral obstacle in the path of reconciliation is the desire for revenge. Now, revenge is commonly regarded as a low and unworthy emotion, and because it is regarded as such, its deep moral hold on people is rarely understood. But revenge –morally considered – is a desire to keep faith with the dead, to honor their memory by taking up their cause where they left off. Revenge keeps faith between generations; the violence it engenders is a ritual form of respect for the community's dead – therein lies its legitimacy. Reconciliation is difficult precisely because it must compete with the powerful alternative morality of violence. Political terror is tenacious because it is an ethical practice. It is a cult of the dead, a dire and absolute expression of respect.[6]

Clearly, any attempt to establish the political significance of forgiveness and thereby offer a theological reconfiguration of what is and is not 'right' must address appropriately the issues of justice which undermine the advocacy of forgiveness and drive the culture of retaliation and counter-retaliation. Two issues must be confronted: *First*, the issue of respect for the dead – the desire that those who have given their lives and the opportunities and joys that lay before them for a cause, should not have done so in vain. The *second* concerns the healing of memory. This is not to suggest that the two can be dissociated – there can be no mutual peace, reconciliation or at-one-ment if one party sees itself as having betrayed the sacrifices of its kith and kin, as having sold out relatives who may have made the ultimate sacrifice for their cause. Nor can there be atonement without the healing of memory – a healing that transcends simply the fading of memory or forgetfulness – the annihilation of memories by way of the passage of time and death.

A great deal has been written (by Jones, Volf, Hauerwas and others) on the second of these, that is, the healing of memory, and there are profound arguments to suggest that memory is healed more effectively through forgiveness than the pursuit of retribution. However, it is on the first issue, namely, the question of respect for the dead, that I wish to focus in the second part of this chapter. It is perhaps this above all else which stands as the stumbling block to the prioritization of forgiveness in the political realm. And the underlying nub of the problem concerns the following two questions: *Who are the appropriate agents of forgiveness? Who has the right to forgive whom?* Do *we* have the right to forgive evils perpetrated against others? When, for example, we speak of forgiving Serbs for atrocities they have committed, what conceivable right could we have (as Scots or English) to forgive Serbs for atrocities committed against Bosnians? Is it not Bosnians alone who can forgive? Moreover, if only Bosnians have a right to forgive, do the living have the right to forgive the perpetrators of murder or is it not those against whom

307

the atrocities have been committed who alone have the right to forgive? If the living forgive atrocities perpetrated against the dead, is that not a betrayal of respect for the dead? Is it not the usurping of a right that belongs to them and to them alone? If that is so, *then any reference to forgiveness whatsoever in the aftermath of war and conflict is going to be little more than vacuous at best, and at worst a further repudiation of the rights of those who are now dead – the illegitimate appropriation of what is theirs and theirs alone to offer.*

No one has articulated this question more poignantly or more tellingly than Simon Wiesenthal in his profoundly honest and moving book, *The Sunflower: On the Possibilities and Limits of Forgiveness.* The focus of the book concerns the events surrounding a particular work detail. Wiesenthal and his group were marched from the camp to help dispose of the waste in a local hospital. When he arrived at the hospital a nurse called him over, asked whether he was indeed a Jew and then led him through the hospital to a private room and left him there and shut the door. Before him lay a man dying of his injuries. He had been blinded and his face was entirely concealed by bandages. The patient, it turned out, was an SS soldier, only 21 years old, who had been involved in an appalling atrocity. On his deathbed, he was overcome with guilt and desperately desired that he be forgiven by a Jew so that he could die in peace. Over the following hours, the young man detailed the events in which he had been involved. In a town by the name of Dnepropetrovsk, the SS had herded nearly two hundred Jews, many of whom were children, into a building in which they had placed drums of gasoline. The doors were then locked and the SS men ordered to circle the building and throw hand grenades through the windows. They were then to stand with their rifles at the ready to shoot anyone who tried to escape. As flames licked the building and cries were heard from within it, he noticed a man with a small child in his arms standing behind the windows of the second floor. His clothes were alight and by his side stood a woman, doubtless the mother of the child. With his free hand the man covered the child's eyes as if to hide the scene from his child ... then he jumped into the street. Seconds later, she followed, only to be shot by the SS.[7]

The man insisted on confessing every detail, hiding nothing, in the desperate hope that he would receive forgiveness for all these acts from a Jew and thus find the peace he craved. Wiesenthal listened but felt utterly helpless. Finally he made up his mind and left the room without uttering a word.[8] The next day the SS man died. Wiesenthal was left haunted by the episode. Indeed, his main purpose in writing the book was to ask whether forgiveness has boundaries of this kind and to ask quite simply, therefore, whether he did the right thing. The fundamental question concerns whether Wiesenthal had the *right* to forgive the SS man. He could, of course, forgive SS men for suffering that they had caused him – but could he forgive on behalf of those who were dead, anonymous bodies who did not even know the dignity of a grave, let alone a grave with a sunflower – the prerogative of dead Nazi soldiers. His final decision was that it was not his place to offer forgiveness. Had he done so he would illegitimately have trespassed a boundary, usurped the rights of another.

How do we respond? If Wiesenthal is right, then there can be no forgiveness or advocacy of forgiveness of the most tragic and divisive events in the histories of those contexts which most require it – the Balkans, Rwanda, Northern Ireland, etc. And if there can be no forgiveness without selling out the dead, how can there ever be genuine reconciliation without selling out the dead? How can there be a reconciliation that heals the memory of atrocities and injustices perpetrated against those who are no longer here to forgive on their own behalf? The connection between Wiesenthal's dilemma and Michael Ignatieff's analysis of the spiral of vengeance should be clear – both concern a fundamental ethical dilemma regarding how we honour victims, most particularly, the dead.

This question as to who has the right to forgive was one which concerned Plato as evidenced in his discussion of the four rivers of the underworld in the *Phaedo*.[9] If someone has murdered another in a fit of passion 'and yet has lived thereafter a life of repentance', he and those like him will be cast into Tartarus. After a year, they will find themselves swept along to a point near the Acherusian Lake where 'they call to those whom they have slain or despitefully used, begging and beseeching them that they would suffer them to come forth into the lake and give them a hearing. If they can prevail, they do come forth, and find an end to their trouble; but if not, they are swept back into Tartarus, and thence into the rivers again; nor can they ever have respite from their woes until they prevail upon those whom they have injured; for such is the penalty appointed by their judges.'[10] For Plato, forgiveness would clearly remain the exclusive prerogative of the victim and would do so for all eternity.

The question I wish to raise here is whether Christian theology has any distinctive resources which address what turns out to be a twofold dilemma in that, in practice, it concerns both the *agency* and *scope* of forgiveness. The implication is not only that the right to forgive belongs exclusively to the one against whom the offence has been perpetrated but that any forgiveness offered by the victim can only relate to that *element* of the offence of which he or she was the victim. This second element is problematic since most crimes affect not only what we might term the 'primary victim' but also all those secondary victims who are victims by virtue of the fact that they care for the primary victim. Take, for example, the implications of this for a case of serious assault. The victim of the assault may forgive the perpetrator for the extent of the crime committed against her. But she is not in a position to forgive him for the suffering the crime caused her family. Similarly, her family could not justly forgive the perpetrator for the crime he committed against their daughter or sister or mother, but only for the suffering the perpetrator caused them. For either the assault victim or her family to suggest forgiveness beyond what is their right to forgive would be for them to perpetrate a further evil – namely, to offend further the rights of the victim by appropriating what belongs to her and her alone, namely, the right to forgive. Any such appropriation would, of course, be a further sin against her personhood and dignity. To take the argument still further, if the family of an assault victim forgives the dimension of the offence that is an offence against them, can they do so independently of their daughter/sister's forgiveness of the perpetrator? If they do, is that not to deny that what remains an offence against the victim continues to be an offence against them until the former offence is forgiven? Do we not have to acknowledge a further principle of solidarity which suggests that the forgiveness of every victim requires to be seen as contingent upon the forgiveness of the perpetrator by every other victim?

The issues raised here concern ultimately whether the language of forgiveness can have any currency or relevance whatsoever in the socio-political context. Unless the 'Sunflower' dilemma can be addressed, we can never be in a position to forgive the Nazi perpetrators of the Holocaust, nor those associated with the Rwandan atrocities – and Miroslav Volf has no right to forgive the evils perpetrated by the Serb *Cetniks* against his Croatian people. None of us has the right to forgive or adopt an attitude of forgiveness towards anyone for any crime which is not perpetrated exclusively against me and the scope of which is limited exclusively to me. This is not because we have never been victims or cannot identify with their plight. Rather, it is because we have never been *those particular* victims. Those who suffered in Nazi concentration camps would be in no more of a position to forgive those who suffered at the hands of the Hutus, or the Serbian *Cetniks*, than we are.

What also requires to be observed here is that the theological questions raised by this penetrate right to the very heart of the doctrine of the atonement and the scope or compass of the forgiveness which even God can offer.

When forgiveness from sin is pronounced, can this refer in any way to sin whose compass extends beyond God and which is not, therefore, exclusively sin against God? Can God forgive us for sins we commit against others or for the element of a sin against God which is also a sin against another human being? If so, on what grounds can God do so? Does this not involve a divine violation of the rights of human victims? Could it ever be right for God to forgive someone for a sin perpetrated against a child? Can God's forgiveness extend beyond that dimension of the sin which is an offence against God and God alone? And, finally, given the principle of solidarity noted above, can it ever be appropriate for one to proportion sin in this way, that is, into that dimension of an evil act which is sin against God and that which is an evil perpetrated exclusively against the human victim? If not, then one is left asking whether it is ever appropriate to speak of a just forgiveness on God's part.

Clearly, the question which this raises concerns whether reconciliation can ever be *God*'s to offer – certainly at the horizontal level. Is there reconciliation in the Kingdom of God, or is this conditional upon the forgiveness of every victim, as Plato suggests? *In sum, the question as to whether the scope of forgiveness can be such as to allow it to have socio-political significance turns out to be irreducibly bound up with the question as to whether the atonement can ever (even in eternity) liberate us from the horizontal dimension of sin.*

Proposal for a Theological Solution

The faith of the Church catholic affirms that God became incarnate as a marginalized Jew and vicariously in an act of solidarity with humanity took to himself the suffering of the sinned against – the brutality, the physical and psychological (even sexual)[11] abuse, the sadism, the torture, the humiliation and the inconceivable physical pain associated with death by crucifixion. As the One on behalf of the many, the One in whose suffering and atonement the many participate, he can say, 'In as much as you have done it unto the least of these, you have done it unto me!' The implication is that sin against a fellow human is not simply sin against that human but additionally and in parallel sin against God – suggesting two different and distinct objects and kinds of sin. Rather, the sin against that victim requires to be seen, first, as sin against God conceived as *one and the same object* as the victim. Second, it requires to be seen as *the same sin* against both. In short, the sin against the victim, Christologically and pneumatologically conceived, is identical – both as the particular act that it is and with respect to its particular object

311

– with sin against God. What the vicarious humanity of Christ seems to suggest, therefore, is that God can forgive at the horizontal as well as the vertical level.

At the heart of the Christian faith, therefore, stands not simply an 'ethic of forgiveness' generating exhortations to forgive. (As we have seen, this could only involve the advocacy of forgiveness which would necessarily have extremely limited, individualistic reference and compass.) Rather, what is presented is an ontology of forgiveness. In God crucified we have the One who alone is entitled to forgive on behalf of the victim because the victim is 'in him', and he 'in the victim'. But not only does he, in forgiving, do what he is entitled to do, he does it *as the one who does not dishonour the victim in this act*, but upholds the eternal dignity of the victim not least those who are dead. Indeed, for reasons which should hopefully be clear, God's forgiveness is not only compatible with *upholding* and *affirming* the dignity of the victim, it is intrinsic to it. This is not least because it is only God's unconditional love and forgiveness that exposes, affirms and addresses the offence for what it is, namely, an eternal offence – as Nietzsche realized.[12] The alternative to a theology of the atonement conceived along these lines is one that so localizes the offence to the victim that atonement is a natural process realized by the passage of time or, alternatively, by the perpetrator's annihilating not only his victim but all those who have any grounds for holding a grudge against him. This, in turn, leaves us asking how far we dare press 'postmodernism' on this score.

Notes

1 This forms part of an extended paper written for a Research Group on Forgiveness and Reconciliation in Politics, sponsored by the Erasmus Institute of the University of Notre Dame. The Research Group is composed of seven theologians, political scientists and historians including Miroslav Volf, Nicholas Wolterstorff, Scott Appleby and Dan Philpott.

2 The whole point of the predicament of partiality is that, as human beings, we are invariably blind to an objective, detached, neutral perception of complex historical situations. We always interpret events, see events 'from a perspective'. We can only see that perspective for what it is when we are given a new perspective – and that is not something we can give ourselves. The concept of 'natural justice' will invariably struggle to offer a way out of this predicament – it presumes that we have an ability objectively to assess and to weigh up all the relevant natural evils in a situation. It is not clear that this is possible either for individuals or society as a whole. History offers a plethora of illustrations of genuinely collective

blindness – to the evils of torture, slavery, classism, racism, patriarchy and the oppression of women. Future generations will operate with perspectives from which they will doubtless be able to assess the blindnesses which characterize our present perspectives.

3 Miroslav Volf, *Exclusion and Embrace? A Theological Exploration of Identity, Otherness and Reconciliation* (Nashville, TN: Abingdon Press, 1996), p. 121.

4 Cited in, *ibid.*

5 *Ibid.*, p. 122.

6 Michael Ignatieff, *Warrior's Honor: Ethnic War and the Modern Conscience* (New York: Henry Holt & Co., 1997), p. 188. This quotation is cited in a paper which Stanley Hauerwas originally presented in Northern Ireland with the title: 'Why time cannot and should not heal the wounds of history but time has been and can be redeemed', and published in the *Scottish Journal of Theology*, 53(1) (2000): 33ff.

7 Volf, *Exclusion and Embrace?*, pp. 42–3.

8 *Ibid.*, p. 55

9 I am grateful to my colleague, Professor Richard Bauckham, for drawing my attention to this. Cf. his discussion of this section of Plato's *Phaedo* in *The Fate of the Dead: Studies on the Jewish and Christian Apocalypses* (Leiden: Brill, 1998), p. 146. Bauckham goes on in Chapter 7 to discuss Augustine on whom this argument was clearly influential.

10 *Phaedo*, 114, A–B.

11 It is suggested that there was customary sexual abuse of prisoners prior to crucifixion.

12 For Nietzsche, 'no deed can be annihilated' – the offence associated with a crime is eternal and unalterable, it cannot be undone. For this reason, he argues, 'all punishments, too, must be eternal.' But then again 'even an eternal hell' for the guilty still could not 'put right', could not cancel out what has been done. The suffering of the father, the mother and the child as they jumped in terror to a brutal death cannot be 'undone'. *Thus Spoke Zarathustra: A Book for Everyone and No One*, trans. R. J. Hollingdale (London: Penguin, 1969), p. 162 (cited in Volf, *Exclusion and Embrace*, p. 122).

Chapter 19

Slouching Towards Jerusalem: Achieving Human Equality

TIMOTHY GORRINGE

Duncan Forrester began his academic publishing career in Britain with a book on caste, and marked his retirement with a book on equality. The theme of equality, therefore, spans his extremely productive career. In both *Caste and Christianity* and *On Human Worth*, whilst allowing for the failure of the Church in many areas, Forrester argues that the Gospel has in fact been at the heart of the advancement of equality, whether in challenging caste or in questioning meritocracy. In both books the importance of the shared table fellowship of the Eucharist is affirmed, whilst in the most recent book Forrester adds the way in which promotion within the Church was open to all, the counter-culture provided by the monastic movement and the implantation of egalitarian values brought about by reading and expounding Scripture.[1] Forrester is not an apologist who spoils his case by claiming too much, too rashly. He is modest and measured as to the Christian case. Even so, I want to ask whether there are not structural processes which may not be still more important in the realization of equality than the preaching of the Gospel, and in putting this case I begin with another debate, as to the origin of inequality.

According to social anthropologists human beings have existed as hunter-gatherers for the vast majority of their history.[2] Amongst hunter-gatherer groups there are at least some who still live in egalitarian, non-patriarchal and non-property-owning communities, and the suggestion is that this situation may have characterized the earliest days of the human race.[3] Was it a memory of this situation which led to the myth of the golden age when, as Virgil put it, 'no peasants subdued the fields; it was not lawful even to assign or divide the ground with landmarks: men sought the common gain, and the earth itself bore everything more generously at no one's bidding'

(*Georgics*, I)? This Eden, like the hunter-gatherer society, knows no agriculture. The problem with it is that hunting and food-gathering sustain less than ten people per acre. The agricultural revolution was necessary for human development and expansion, for real growth in the quality of life, but it is this revolution which begets the 'Fall' into inequality: so far, all are agreed. The puzzle is to know why stratification then arose. Two current suggestions are that 'aggrandizing' individuals subordinated others, which we can call the 'fatal flaw' theory, or that some families slowly grew worse off by a combination of factors, the 'hard luck' theory.[4] On the first view, competition occurs where abundant resources can be converted into scarcer desirable goods or services. In the context of competitive feasting, excess subsistence resources are converted into desirable resources and, as research amongst existing hunter-gatherers has indicated, 'ambitious individuals vie with one another for control over excess resources, labor, and the wealth and power that such control confers.'[5] On the second view, settled communities were organized around households whose relative position was constantly changing. Illness, failure to capitalize on new developments such as animal traction, sheer bad luck, could lead to downward mobility in which households would sink below existing norms of accumulation of property and prestige. In what are called 'transegalitarian societies', in which full equality is no longer·in place, but there is no developed social stratification either, asymmetries of power would slowly consolidate. 'Wise decision making and good luck would have played a critical role.'[6]

Neither of these theories call in question Marx's response to something like the 'hard luck' theory that 'primitive accumulation', which he read as the reality of original sin, quickly supervened. 'In actual history it is notorious that conquest, enslavement, robbery, murder, briefly force, play the great part.'[7] John Ball and Gerrard Winstanley had already suggested much the same thing.[8] Note that in this whole process ideology plays no part. The shift to agriculture was a *necessary* one, suggesting the line, 'O felix culpa'. If the 'hard luck' theory is right, then it was not violence, envy, cupidity or any other vice which was responsible for the 'Fall', no sinister bias in human nature. It happened imperceptibly, perhaps over millennia. As social complexity and the level of surplus increased, however, so did inequality. Lewis Mumford argued that it was greatly exacerbated by the rise of the city. Consequent upon the discovery of agriculture, human beings lived for millennia primarily in villages, the mother of the human race, the place where ethics were first formed.

But at some point a great elevation of the ruler and the priest took place: apparently after 3000 BC, when there was a similar expansion of human powers in many other departments. With this came vocational differentiation and specialization in every field. The early city, as distinct from the village community, is a caste-managed society, organized for the satisfaction of a dominant minority: no longer a community of humble families living by mutual aid.[9]

Here ideology, in the shape of theology, emerged with a vengeance, justifying the rule of the strong over the weak as in the Marduk myths or the Atraharsis epic.

There is a great irony in Mumford's description of villages as communities of mutual support for those who know the caste-divided villages of south India. Caste is one of the most culturally saturated, and one of the most intractable, forms of human inequality. To date there is no consensus on what exactly is meant by it, and what its origins are. Explanations based on race and Aryan conquest, on the division of labour, and on class, all face objections.[10] The most discussed account of modern times, that of Louis Dumont, seeks to understand caste through the oppositions of purity and impurity and of ritual status and secular power. Here, too, there are cogent counter examples, targeting Dumont's Achilles heel, his admission that whilst, in theory, power is subordinate to priesthood, in fact priesthood submits to power.[11] Exploiting this weakness, Declan Quigley argues that the common structure underlying caste systems is found in the constraints of kinship on the one hand and authority structures (rather confusingly called 'kingship') on the other.[12] The debate will certainly not end soon, and it is probably fair to note that such a complex phenomenon as caste is overdetermined, and that any simple grand theory will fail to account for some of the evidence. However we understand it, caste illustrates how, once in place, structures of inequality become 'principalities and powers' which govern human lives in every detail and which are hugely difficult to change. How are they to be contested? Where does 'redemption' come in relation to them?

Forrester notes the role bhakti movements, and later Ram Mohan Roy and the Brahmo Samaj, played in challenging caste. With regard to the bhakti tradition, it has given us a great and beautiful literature, and a noble theology, but it has to be said that no great movement towards equality flowed from these unless we count Sikhism as a form of bhakti movement. With that possible exception, their impact on Indian society as a whole was negligible. They offered one option of redemption amongst many and were subsumed, as Syrian Orthodox Christianity was, within the broad umbrella of Hindu social organization. The challenge from Ram Mohan Roy, drawing inspiration both from Christianity and from Enlightenment ideals of the dignity of the person, is more significant, partly because it feeds the stream of what both Indians and non-Indians spoke of as the Indian Renaissance.[13] As someone who worked in Madras, Forrester properly draws attention to the role of E. V. Ramasamy Naiker in the Dravidian movement, who confounded most Western readings of the Indian scene by avowing an explicitly atheist attack on religion, holding meetings outside temples mocking the credulity of priests and the devout alike. The role of this rationalist strain in Indian society is much underestimated, at least in 'Orientalist' writing which likes to cast India as the religious 'Other' to a sceptical Western world. The impact of Enlightenment ideals as expressed in the American Declaration of Independence, the French Revolution, Tom Paine and, not least, Marx and Engels has certainly been considerable as any consistent reading of the *Economic and Political Weekly* would show.

The palm for opposition to caste within Hinduism, however, obviously goes to Mahatma Gandhi, and he illustrates perfectly the ambiguities and weaknesses of the religious case. Gandhi lived equality. In his ashram he did the work of the sweeper. Any concessions to caste mentality provoked in him blazing opposition. Why, then, did he defend varnashramic society, society ordered along hereditary lines into traditional occupations? It was one of the questions he debated over two decades with C. F. Andrews, who never accepted Gandhi's views on caste. Gandhi wanted to distinguish between caste, which he considered a useful institution, and untouchability, which he regarded as an unmitigated evil. He wanted to purify the former and destroy the latter. 'Rid this caste of its impurities', he wrote to Andrews in 1920, 'and you will find it to be a bulwark of Hinduism and an institution whose roots are embedded deep in human nature.'[14] This was something which Andrews, with his roots in the incarnationalism and labour politics of the Christian Social Union, could not accept. To Andrews, caste was every bit as bad as white racism. 'This kind of thing appears to me every whit as bad as the religion of the "white race" which is being proclaimed in Africa today', he wrote to Gandhi.[15] Gandhi returned to the issue the following year, playing the expatriate card: 'I look at the problem as an Indian and a Hindu, you as an Englishman and a Christian. You look at it with the eyes of an observer, I as an affected and afflicted party ... That Hinduism considers it a "sin" to touch a portion of human beings because they are born in a particular environment! I am engaged as a Hindu in showing that it is not a sin and that it is a sin to consider that touch a sin. It is a bigger problem than that of gaining Indian independence but I can tackle it better if I gain the latter on the way.'[16] Gandhi's appeal to ethnic difference here is, of course, absolutely tendentious, as the disagreement with Ambedkar shows.

Why did Gandhi need to resort to such poor arguments? Part of the answer, of course, is his deep-seated opposition to the conversion of Untouchables to Christianity, but it is also clear that he was, in a sense, misled by religious idealism. He envisaged everyone returning to voluntary *shudra* status in order to re-create the true nature of Indian society.[17] He could not see that the idea of *varnas* 'had become the legitimising spirituality and ideology for the existing *Jatis*'.[18] He had himself no objection to cleaning latrines, and indeed urged everyone to do it. 'A scavenger is as worthy of his hire as a lawyer or a President', he wrote in his magazine *Harijan* in 1937. 'That according to me is Hinduism.' But what this amounted to was the consequence that 'one born a scavenger must earn his livelihood by being a scavenger, and then do what he likes.'[19] There are two problems here. First, Gandhi reads society through an intense religious idealism, which he expects everyone to live up to. He felt that if scavenging and bread labour were part of every person's duty a new outlook would develop and caste barriers disappear.[20] He saw that, in the issue of non-violence, it was unrealistic to expect everyone to live up to his ideal, but with regard to caste his idealism prevented him from seeing how structural factors, like employment in a certain trade, function to keep people poor, oppressed and effectively guarantee a much lower standard of life. In effect Gandhi endorses karma here. Writing in 1989, Abraham Ayrookuzhiel speaks of caste as the 'cultural contradiction' of Hinduism. Gandhi did not admit this contradiction. 'He romanticised the Indian cultural heritage and advocated the integration of Dalits within Hinduism. It has totally failed.'[21] Effectively, Gandhi's position is rather similar to those evangelical Christians who are only concerned with 'personal sin' and are not concerned about structures. He wanted to convert India, to change its inner attitudes, to teach respect and love without changing caste structures which corroded all such attitudes.[22] Since Independence, however, comments John Webster, 'Dalits have experienced not the widespread caste Hindu "change of heart" Gandhi had promised, but a growing "backlash" against whatever modest gain Dalits have made.'[23] Neither pious nor liberal ideologies have delivered the goods. Social realities prove remarkably intractable.

The reference to structural inequality, and the failure of idealistic attempts to dismantle inequality, leads me on to what Forrester calls the 'elaborate theological justifications for the structures of inequality in society'.[24] What were these, and how did they survive the implicit critique that Scripture as a whole mounted to them? I would like to be able to play off natural theology against the theology of revelation, but this is unfortunately not possible. Forrester notes the so-called 'household tables' texts, which urged submission on slaves and women (Eph 6:5–9; Col 3:22–5; 1 Cor 7:21–4) but there is also especially the counter-revolution announced in 1 Timothy and Titus which gave later theorists of inequality plenty to build on. Thus the monks of Angers in thirteenth-century France appealed to these texts to bring their serfs into line: 'God himself willed that, among men, some should be lords and others serfs, in such a way that the lords should be obliged to venerate and love God, and that the serfs should be obliged to love and venerate their lord, according to the Apostle's saying: Servants, be obedient to them that are your masters.'[25] This analogy of proportion: as God to the lord, so the lord to the peasant or serf – simply reproduced the hierarchy Dionysius had discerned in the heavenly sphere into the earthly. The force of this argument, derived from Scripture, cannot be underestimated. The Book of Common Prayer was saturated in this theology. 'What is thy duty towards thy neighbour?' asked the Catechism. Answer: 'To honour and obey the Queen, and all that are put in authority under her: To submit myself to all my governors, teachers, spiritual pastors and masters: To order myself lowly and reverently to all my betters … Not to covet nor desire other men's goods; but to learn and labour truly to get mine own living, and to do my duty in that state of life, unto which it shall please God to call me.' Thorold Rogers wrote of the nineteenth-century agricultural labourer in England that he was 'bowed down by centuries of oppression, hard usage and hard words, with every social force against him, the landlords in league with the farmers and the clergymen in league with both, the latter constantly preaching resignation, the two former constantly enforcing it.'[26] When the poor have complained of their lot they have been accused for centuries of the politics of envy: Tory propaganda in the 1980s was nothing new. Le Goff notes that '*Invidia*, envy, was, according to the moralists (clerics) and the confessors' manuals, the great sin of the peasants and the poor.'[27]

Aquinas characteristically appeals to both Scripture and natural theology to defend inequality. Citing Aristotle's *Politics*, he notes that there is an order amongst human beings: 'for men of outstanding intelligence naturally take command, while those who are less intelligent but of more robust physique seem intended by nature to act as servants … So it is clear that divine providence imposes an order on all things and manifests the truth of the Apostle's saying: "All things that are, are set in order by God".'[28]

Arthur Lovejoy, in his study of the idea of the 'great chain of being', can cite a sheaf of texts justifying inequality through some form of natural theology, all in some shape or form making the point which Pope made in his *Essay on Man*:

> Order is Heaven's first law; and this confest,
> Some are, and must be, greater than the rest,
> More rich, more wise. (Book IV, II)[29]

As in Marcus Agrippa's use of the body metaphor, this appeal to the natural order might work in both directions, emphasizing that all parts of society had to care for each other, as expressed in these verses in Richardson's *Pamela*:

> Wise Providence
> Does various parts for various minds dispense;
> The meanest slaves or they who hedge and ditch,
> Are useful, by their sweat, to feed the rich;
> The rich, in due return, impart their store,
> Which comfortably feeds the lab'ring poor.
> Nor let the rich the lowest slave disdain,
> He's equally a link of nature's chain;
> Labours to the same end, joins in one view,
> And both alike the will divine pursue.[30]

The idea that such a society represented 'the will divine' was, of course, famously advocated by the 'Sermon on the Mound', and represents the theology of all recent United States' administrations.

Ideology commonly denotes strain. Why is this justification of inequality needed? Is it the simple self-evidence of the egalitarian case, as Isaiah Berlin would maintain, or are there forces within society making for equality? Forrester notes Gottwald's persuasive thesis that there was an egalitarian form of community in ancient Israel which lasted for around two hundred years, until destroyed by the threat of the superior Philistine Iron Age technology.[31] The reason for the demise is significant because, according to Marc Bloch, European feudalism arrived in precisely the same way. Viking and Hungarian raids on Western Europe threw the social order into absolute confusion, in which there was no safety and no hiding place. In this situation people traded their freedom for their safety.[32] From these humble beginnings and without any ideological underpinnings to begin with, the vast structure of European feudalism, a structure of inequality which equals caste in its completeness, emerged. It did not, however, spread everywhere. Parts of Spain and, ironically, Scandinavia itself, escaped it. It was for this reason that, when a trustworthy observer like Mary Wollstonecraft visited Scandinavia at the end of the eighteenth century, she discovered that 'The Norwegians appear to me the most free community I have ever observed.'[33] The foundation of this freedom, as it had been in tribal Israel and large parts of Europe, was security of tenure for the peasant farmers who formed the bulk of the population. There was a (small) class divide in this society, and there was poverty and hardship, but not the vastly unequal pattern of landownership which Norwegian ancestors foisted on much of the rest of Europe. The result is that class is to this day in Norway not the issue it is in a country like Britain.[34] The survival of security of tenure as a guarantee of equality seems to indicate, *pace* Dahrendorf, that Rousseau had a point in linking inequality and the emergence of private property. Or, as the Diggers put it, people were free, 'before the Norman yoke'. The existence of free peasant societies provides an interesting comment on the relations of freedom and equality, and calls Dahrendorf's thesis that free societies require differentials into question, for in such societies people were not judged by the size of their holdings, and there were no hewers of wood and drawers of water, no permanent underclass. In such societies holdings could differ substantially, and poverty could lead people to seek emigration, but security of tenure grounded an independence and equality of respect which bore dramatic fruit, for example, in resistance to the Nazi invasion. If inequality is kept at bay by security of tenure then perhaps there is something to be said for Henry George's call for land reform, an idea constantly talked down, but which refuses to go away.

The survival of peasant societies is due in part to the failure to industrialize. It is significant that Norway has only one large city. With respect to the dissolution of inequality, cities play a profoundly ambivalent role, as the remark Mumford loved to quote – *Stadtluft macht frei nach Jahr und Tag* – makes clear. This referred to the opportunity to escape feudal bonds by staying in the city for a year and a day, a role replicated, to some extent, by the chance of escaping caste in the anonymity of the big Indian cities. Cities are the focus of that revolutionary role of the bourgeoisie to which Marx and Engels draw attention in the Communist Manifesto, which puts an end 'to all feudal, patriarchal, idyllic relations' and 'pitilessly tears aside the motley feudal ties that bound man to his "natural superiors"'.[35] In his book on caste, Forrester noted 'the cumulative effect of the western impact on India', which went beyond ideology to a profound disturbance of traditional village society.[36] In contemporary India, André Béteille has argued that the middle class has dropped caste for a family ideology, and it is this which now serves to reproduce inequality. The family will accumulate capital wherever and however it can and caste simply does not come in to it.[37] In his study of Dalit Christians, John Webster observes that whilst Dalits remain in the villages, they remain economically dependent on dominant castes. Only if they move to the city can they escape these bonds.[38] At the end of his analysis of the 1381 Peasants' Revolt, Rodney Hilton concludes that 'the only social force emerging from the medieval world which was capable of taking over from the aristocracy was the bourgeoisie ... the leading social force in medieval peasant movements, even the most radical, seems to have been those elements most in contact with the market, those who in suitable circumstances would become capitalist farmers.'[39] The dynamic of the city, then, and of the capitalist society which is centred there, at one and the same time increases and dissolves the structures of human inequality and does so with an almost deterministic force. We recall Frederic Jameson's remark that capitalism is at one and the same time the best and the worst thing that has ever happened to us. It is the best because of the colossal improvements in quality of life it has delivered; the worst because of the holocausts of victims, and the planetary destruction the process has produced.

These observations about societies which do not develop inequality and about the impact of urbanization on inequality at least call to mind the base and superstructure thesis, according to which ideas are epiphenomenal to the social and material base. We know that in 1998 the proportion of people living in cities finally crossed the 50 per cent mark. One could, then, construct a narrative according to which inequality is consequent upon the improvement of living conditions, and will be with us until the full gains of urbanization have been realized and everyone joins the middle class. Rather than straining towards an ideal we are, rather, slouching towards the Utopia of equality, and ideology has little to do with it. The present widening of the gap between rich and poor, both between North and South, and within the North, is just a temporary inflammation which will pass in time. One can hear Hayek applauding. In this narrative, social and economic processes are the main actors. Ideologies, as expressed in faith systems, only have walk on parts.

Before commenting on that, I want to note that another key solvent of caste and class, not taken up by Forrester as I recall, is eros, or romantic love. Denis de Rougemont proposed the famous thesis that romantic love began in Provence in the twelfth century, but the love poetry of the ancient world, from Greece to China, surely calls that into question. We are all social constructionists now, and properly suspicious of arguments from biology, but when we have made the fullest allowance for the social construction of affective relations, does there not remain a dynamic and transgressive force which challenges all cultural boundaries bound up, to say the least, with the need to procreate? Are there literate cultures without stories of 'star-crossed lovers', brought together across class, caste, ethnic or religious divides? Eros may be transitory, but in full flood it has the power to sweep away inequalities. It can, of course, at once be objected that it operates purely on an individual, or at least interpersonal level, but from the eighteenth century it became the stock-in-trade of the publishing, and in the twentieth century, of the film industry. What happens when it is taken up by an industry as important as Bollywood, becoming the staple of a diet consumed by high and low? Who can tell how deeply it may be transforming deep-seated societal attitudes, changing structures of affect? For underlying it is the most radical affirmation of equality between persons:

> My face in thine eye, thine in mine appears,
> And true plaine hearts doe in the faces rest,
> Where can we finde two better hemispheares
> Without sharpe North, without declining West?
> What ever dyes, was not mixt equally;
> If our two loves be one or, thou and I
> Love so alike, that none doe slacken, none can die.[40]

I am suggesting, then, that there are social, material, perhaps even genetic factors which challenge inequality more surely than our religious idealisms. But, of course, like Marx and Engels I am not a vulgar Marxist after all. With them I recognize the need for dialectic. This is something the 'aggrandizing' theory of the origin of inequality occludes, smacking, as it does, of that essentialism which marked the Heidelberg Catechism's assertion that 'Man is inclined by nature to hate both God and his neighbour.' In this case only individual conversion is possible. The principalities and powers cannot be engaged and overcome until the eschaton. There is, though, the alternative Irenaean view, which thinks of redemption as growing from the image to the likeness. We might then follow Juan Luis Segundo and understand 'sin' as the sediment of those instincts once necessary for survival. Thus,

> the word man designates a painfully slow process whereby the evolution of the animal kingdom gradually gives rise to a being which we are willing to call 'man' only in a certain sense and with great difficulty ... what we call moral conscience is still in gestation even today. It is still emerging from its more primitive and instinctual forms; it is still unfolding in and through the tangle of instincts and

324

determinisms which form the sure basis of hominization and which can never be totally abandoned.[41]

We need no thesis about humankind's intrinsic viciousness to understand the grip of systems of inequality. Rather we need to understand how and where the Gospel fits in the process of redemption. The process of hominization has to be a move towards equality because, as Karl Barth put it, 'The common life of men is based from the very first on their equality. Where this is called in question, their life together is also called in question, and if life means life together, then so is life itself.'[42] In the process, debate, dialogue, poetry, art, prophecy, the clash of ideologies and faith systems, play a critical, and not just an epiphenomenal, part. This was clear in the somewhat acrimonious debate around mass conversions of Dalits in the 1930s. 'Much more devastating than physical oppression', wrote J. W. Pickett in 1938, 'has been the psychological oppression inflicted by the Hindu doctrines of karma and re-birth, which have taught them that they are a degraded, worthless people suffering just retribution for sins committed in earlier lives. It is, then, a true instinct that makes the Depressed Classes respond more eagerly to the preaching of the Christian Gospel than to any direct ministry to their social and economic ills.'[43] When Ambedkar led a mass movement of Dalits out of Hinduism into Buddhism, converts took an oath 'discarding the Hindu Religion which is detrimental to the emancipation of human beings and which believes in inequality and regards human beings other than Brahmins as low born'.[44] In both cases, changing ideologies was a crucial event.

The need to take ideology seriously is also emphasized by the fact that, as we have seen, commitment to equality cannot be taken for granted. For Ralf Dahrendorf, writing in 1968, the year of the Prague Spring and the Paris *événements*, the idea that inequality originated in the advent of property was nonsense, disproved (his word) by the survival of social inequality in propertyless societies such as the Soviet Union and the Israeli kibbutzim.[45] He also dismissed the argument that inequality rests on the division of labour, the different worth ascribed to different functions within society – the argument of Marcus Agrippa to the Roman crowd which Paul picked up and modified in 1 Corinthians 12. All such arguments, he believed, rested on 'dubious' assumptions about human nature. His own defence of an open meritocracy, passionately anti-Utopian on Karl Popper's grounds that Utopias breed terror, was in terms of the rules human societies frame to govern themselves. 'Because there are norms and because sanctions are necessary to enforce conformity of human conduct, there has to be inequality of rank among men.' Inequality guarantees the continuance of an ongoing, dynamic society.[46] These two theses are different, of course. That all societies have norms and enforce them only leads us to recognize difference, the kind of just society which Iris Marion Young has more recently adumbrated. It does not necessitate an unequal society. That societies are only healthy when there is movement or even conflict is a quite different, a priori position, resting on a rather Hegelian reading of history: 'Every society honours the conformity that sustains it, i.e. sustains its ruling groups; but by the same token every society also produces within itself the resistance that brings it down.'[47] Inequality, then, is necessary for freedom, and whilst it will always be challenged, it will always also be reproduced. At the end of the Thatcher decade, the philosopher and former Labour MP for East London, Bryan Magee, could argue that 'history had passed Tawney and Crosland by'. Rising affluence had simply made the notion unnecessary and it was now possible to see that it was muddled, the product of a nervous tic by guilt-ridden middle class socialists.[48] His East End constituents, God bless 'em, loved nothing better than a toff. Such toxic arguments, bookending a particularly toxic political period, warn us that we had better take ideas seriously. This Forrester has endeavoured to do.

Building on his earlier discussion of caste, Forrester in his most recent book shows that not only Scripture, but all of the doctrines of the Creed, endorse equality. The existence of powerful theologies of inequality within the Church, however, highlights the need for careful hermeneutic criteria. In the 1928 lectures on ethics, from which I have quoted, Barth based his insistence on equality on an appeal to creation.[49] The reception of *Die Christliche Dogmatik im Entwurf*, published the previous year, and the events of the next few years, made clear to him that this was a false start. He came to see just how malleable appeal to creation, and natural theology, could be, when it was used to vindicate Aryan supremacy. He therefore concluded that the only sure ground of appeal was Christological. In place of an appeal to equality based on the doctrine of creation, he put Christ the man for God and the man for Others, who made clear to us what humanity in likeness and hope might mean. Barth would say that Isaiah Berlin's statement that equality is a moral given, the 'self-evidence' of the American Declaration of Independence, was far too abstract, as the omission of black people from the latter seems to indicate. If we learn from the history of Christ, he argues, then we can spell out what fellow humanity means in a series of determinations: being able to look the other in the eye, to speak and listen to one another and to render mutual assistance. What we learn from the history is that human beings are made for encounter and this is only possible in freedom. 'Companions are free. So are associates. So are comrades. So are fellows. So are helpmates. Only what takes place between such as these is humanity.'[50] It is the whole Gospel narrative which has priority, and which constitutes the essential hermeneutic key to reading the household texts or the Pastoral epistles, not to mention the arguments of 'natural' theology. In this sense Forrester is right, that it is above all the reading of Scripture which has kept the claim of equality alive, working like yeast despite the best efforts of the Church to render it harmless and, as C. F. Andrews claimed, vivifying cultures entirely outwith the Church. Scripture, itself, of course, embodies the clash of ideologies, and in the hermeneutic circle the doctrine of the incarnation formulated by the Church itself represents a critical commentary on the Gospel story. According to this, in taking 'flesh' God assumed all human beings – black, white, female and male, Dalit and high-born, cognitively disabled and others – into a full filial relation, and therefore into equality. Precisely in this sense, in all the ambiguity of interpretation, or reading of Scripture, it takes its place in the dialectic of historical process, witnessing to that event in which God embraced the dialectic in Godself, the Word becoming flesh, entering and generating a historical process in which fellow humanity insistently seeks recognition in what we know as 'equality'.

Notes

1 D. B. Forrester, *On Human Worth* (London: SCM Press, 2001), p. 117.

2 K. Sale, *Human Scale* (New York: Coward, McGann & Geoghegan, 1980), p. 182, citing a lecture by René Dubois.

3 The Biaka, the !Kung, the G/wi, the Hadza, in Africa, and the Western Shoshone in North America. See *Key Issues in Hunter Gatherer Research*, ed. E. S. Burch and L. J. Ellanna (Oxford: Berg, 1994), p. 219.

4 Brian Hayden represents the first theory: 'Competition, labor, and complex hunter gatherers', in Burch and Ellanna, *Key Issues in Hunter Gatherer Research*; Peter Bogucki represents the second: *The Origins of Human Society* (Oxford: Basil Blackwell, 1999).

5 Hayden, 'Competition, labor and complex hunter gatherers, p. 239.

6 Bogucki, *The Origins of Human Society*, p. 214.

7 See K. Marx, *Capital* (London: George Allen & Unwin, 1972), Vol. 1, Pt 8, Ch. 26.

8 Walsingham, a hostile witness, said that John Ball 'tried to prove ... that from the beginning all men were created equal by nature and that servitude had been introduced by the unjust and evil oppression of men against the will of God ...

327

Froissart, *Chronicles*, ed. Brereton (Harmondsworth: Penguin, 1968), p. 212. Winstanley argued that buying and selling land 'was brought in by war'; 'For the power of inclosing Land, and owning Property, was brought into Creation by your Ancestors by the Sword; which first did murther their fellow creatures, Men, and after plunder or steal away their land', 'A Declaration from the Poor Oppressed People of England', in Gerrard Winstanley, *Selected Writings* (London: Aporia, 1989), p. 26.

9 L. Mumford, *The City in History* (Harmondsworth: Penguin, 1991), p. 50.

10 D. Quigley, 'Is a theory of caste still possible?', in M. Searle-Chatterjee and U. Sharma (eds.), *Contextualising Caste* (Oxford: Basil Blackwell, 1995), p. 30.

11 L. Dumont, *Homo Hierarchicus* (Chicago, IL: University of Chicago Press, 1980), pp. 71–2.

12 Quigley, 'Is a theory of caste still possible?', p. 42.

13 Rabindranath Tagore, for example, argued that the energy for getting rid of caste derived from 'the contact of East and West' which 'has done its work and quickened the dormant life of our soul'. Cited in C. F. Andrews, *The Renaissance in India* (Edinburgh: Foreign Mission Committee of the Church of Scotland, 1912), p. 186.

14 25 May 1920, *The Collected Works of Mahatma Gandhi*, Vol. 17 (Delhi: Ministry of Information, 1958), p. 534.

15 B. Chaturvedi and M. Sykes, *Charles Freer Andrews* (Delhi: Ministry of Information, 1947), p. 156. In *The Renaissance in India* Andrews puts this query in the mouth of a Hindu friend: 'What can we think of the hauteur, the spirit of distrust, the sense of inequality with which every Christian official in this land treats every one of us?' (p. 170). 'Do you not see what is happening? Mr – is pulling down your work faster than you can build it up. Every time he calls us "niggers" it is a blow dealt to your religion; for you teach us that caste is sinful, while you Christians are building up a "white caste" of your own.' It would be sad indeed if the Church which condemns caste in the Indian Christian were to condone it in the English ... caste was originally nothing else except race exclusiveness.' *Ibid.*, p. 172.

16 29 Jan. 1921 *Works*, 19, p. 288.

17 *Harijan*, 25 March 1933. Cited in I. Jesudason, *A Gandhian Theology of Liberation* (New York: Orbis, 1984), p. 127.

18 P. Susai SJ, 'Gandhi's response to the Depressed Classes', in X. Irudayeraj SJ (ed.), *Emerging Dalit Theology* (Madras: Jesuit Theological Secretariat, 1990), p. 99.

19 Cited in B. Das and J. Massey (eds), *Dalit Solidarity* (Delhi: ISPCK, 1995), p. 81.

20 M. Chatterjee, *Gandhi's Religious Thought* (London: Macmillan, 1984), p. 39.

21 A. Ayrookuzhiel, 'The ideological nature of the emerging Dalit consciousness', in A. P. Nirmal (ed.), *Towards a Common Dalit Ideology* (Madras: Gurukul, 1989), p. 88.

22 Forrester, too, notes that Gandhi sounds 'strangely like some missionaries' and understands untouchability as primarily a religious problem. See *Caste and Christianity* (London: Curzon, 1980), p. 162.

23 J. C. B. Webster, *The Dalit Christians* (Delhi: ISPCK, 1992), p. 162.

24 Forrester, *On Human Worth*, p. 117.

25 Cited in J. Le Goff, *Medieval Civilization* (Oxford: Basil Blackwell, 1988), p. 309. Cf. Piers Plowman, Book 6, where Piers says to the knight: 'I'll sweat and toil for us both as long as I live, and gladly do any job you want. But you must promise in return to guard over holy church and protect me from the thieves and wasters who ruin the world.'

26 J. E. Thorold Rogers, *Six Centuries of Work and Wages* (London: Swan Sonnenschein 1903), p. 509.

27 Le Goff, *Medieval Civilization*, p. 307. Scripture was forced into service to obtain social submission in another way when, in 1336, the Cistercian abbot of Vale Royal in Cheshire made his peasants swear on the Bible that they and their sons after them were villeins for all eternity. Le Goff, p. 300.

28 *Summa Contra Gentiles*, Book III, Ch. 81.

29 A. Lovejoy, *The Great Chain of Being* (Cambridge, MA: Harvard University Press, 1964), pp. 206f. He cites Leibniz's Theodicy in which 'Inequality is not to be counted amongst evils' and then ventures the poor *ad hominem* argument: 'M. Jaquelot rightly asks those who would have all things equally perfect, why rocks are not crowned with leaves or why ants are not peacocks. If equality were everywhere requisite, the poor man would set up his claim to it against the rich man, the valet against his master.' Likewise in Soame Jenyns, *A Free Inquiry into the Nature and Origin of Evil* (London: R. & J. Dodsley, 1758), we read that 'The universe resembles a large and well-regulated family, in which all the officers and servants, and even the domestic animals, are subservient to each other in proper subordination; each enjoys the privileges and perquisites peculiar to his place, and at the same time contributes, by that just subordination, to the magnificence and happiness of the whole.'

30 S. Richardson, *Pamela* (Oxford: Basil Blackwell, 1929).

31 N. Gottwald, *The Tribes of Yahweh* (London: SCM Press, 1979).

32 M. Bloch, *Feudal Society* (London: Routledge & Kegan Paul, 1965), Vol. 1, p. 147ff.

33 M. Wollstonecraft, *Letters written during a Short Residence in Sweden, Norway and Denmark* (London: Cassell, 1889), p. 63.

34 Half of Scotland's nineteen million acres is owned by 608 landowners, and 10 per cent by eighteen. A. Wightman, *Who Owns Scotland* (Edinburgh: Canongate, 1996); R. Callander, *How Scotland is Owned* (Edinburgh: Canongate, 1998). In England, the top 1 per cent of the population own nearly two-thirds of the land (Royal Commission on the Distribution of Income and Wealth, Report No. 7, 1979). The Commission was abolished three months into the Thatcher

government. There is a debate about how real equality is in Norway. In a cele-brated book, *The Distant Democracy* (London: Wiley, 1977), Willy Martinussen argued that Norway was in fact characterized by widespread apathy, alienation and social inequality. These findings were challenged by W. Lafferty, *Participation and Democracy in Norway* (Oslo: University Press, 1981).

35   *Manifesto of the Communist Party* (Moscow: Progress, 1952), p. 45.
36   D. B. Forrester, *Caste and Christianity*, p. 74.
37   A. Béteille, 'Caste and family in representations of Indian society', *Anthropology Today*, 8(1) (February 1992): 13–18.
38   J. C. B. Webster, *The Dalit Christians*, p. 151.
39   R. Hilton, *Bond Men Made Free* (London: Methuen, 1973), p. 235.
40   John Donne, 'The Good Morrow', *Complete English Poems* (Harmondsworth: Penguin, 1971).
41   J. L. Segundo, *Evolution and Guilt* (Dublin: Gill & Macmillan, 1980), pp. 10–11.
42   K. Barth, *Ethics* (Edinburgh: T&T Clark, 1981), p. 245.
43   J. W. Pickett, *Christ's Way to India's Heart* (Lucknow: Lucknow Publishing House, 1938), p. 36.
44   *The Dalit Christians*, p. 157.
45   R. Dahrendorf, 'On the origin of inequality among men', in A. Béteille (ed.), *Social Inequality* (Harmondsworth: Penguin, 1969), p. 24.
46   Dahrendorf, 'The origin of inequality among men', pp. 34, 42.
47   *Ibid.*, p. 39.
48   The *Guardian*, June 1990.
49   'It is a matter of equality in the relation to God the Creator and therewith also of an equal justification of the claim to life and all that this involves.' Dependence is fundamental to our existence together as human beings. 'And as with this knowledge I meet another person, I know him as a fellow man, and it makes him my fellow man that he becomes for me the mirror of my own self knowledge as God's creature and that again I affirm him as such by my conduct. Humanity, is . . . awareness of our equality before God which no distinctions can erase.' Barth, *Ethics*, p. 245.
50   K. Barth, *Church Dogmatics* (Edinburgh: T&T Clark, 1960), Vol. III/2, p. 273.

Chapter 20

'The First will be Last, and the Last First': Practical Theology and Equality

CHRISTOPHER ROWLAND

A discerning reader of the first two volumes of *Liberation Theology UK* will notice a change of tone between the volumes. The first volume has a rather academic 'feel' with a series of theoretical discussions, while in Volume 2 there is much more personal narrative of the cause and course of liberation. The change might be taken to indicate a policy change on the part of the editors. That was not the case, as the first volume happened to contain the presentations offered at the first Sheffield liberation theology institute in 1996. In retrospect, I wish that more thought had been given to the contents of the volume, its gender balance and the character of the writing, and that we had waited rather than risked giving the impression (which was doubtless the case) that we were embarking on yet another series in which we would be merely theorizing about liberation theology rather than describing its practice. Too often liberation theology has become a topic of academic discussion rather than something practised. There is, as Denys Turner has pointed out

> performative contradiction, a lived misrelation with reality in which untruth is unmasked by the recognition of lying and yet that unmasking is disabled in the very act in which it is embodied ... our seminars [*discussing* liberation theology] turned out to be structures that embodied as their characteristic practice the routinization of the disengagement of truth from praxis: what we, in our seminar, said about liberation theology was true enough; and yet the manner of our saying it disengaged the theology from its liberating potential within the processes of academic learning as such *insofar as to do so is purely academic.* (italics in the original)[1]

It has been very easy to emulate the kind of sophistication of the systematic theologians. There is a role for this in practical theology, but to allow this to dominate the discipline would be to deprive the heart of its subject matter:

the actual practice of faith and the context in which understanding the ways of God comes about. Such perspectives have a long pedigree in Christian theology. They are already evident in, for example, the mid-sixteenth-century English writer, Gerrard Winstanley's, words, that 'tradesmen will speak by experience the things they have seen in God, and the learned clergy will be slighted'.[2] Here priority is given to that inner prompting of God peculiarly derived from the experience of poverty and vulnerability which offers a glimpse of the mind of God. Winstanley's own career as an activist persuaded him that theory and practice must be closely intertwined and the former without the latter was vain:

> Many things were revealed to me which I never read in books nor heard from the mouth of any flesh, and when I began to speak of them, some people could not bear my words and amongst these revelations this was one: that the earth shall be made a common treasury of livelihood to the whole of mankind, without respect of persons; and I heard a voice within me bade me declare it all abroad which I did obey, for I declared it by word of mouth wheresoever I came. Then I was made to write a little book called *The New Law of Righteousness* and therein declared it: yet my mind was not at rest, because nothing was acted, and thoughts ran in me, that words and writings were all nothing, and must die, for action is the life of all, and if thou dost not act, thou dost nothing. With a little time I was made obedient to the words in that particular, for I took my spade and went and broke the ground upon George Hill in Surrey thereby declaring freedom to the creation and the earth must be set free from entanglements of law and landlords, and that it shall become a common treasury to all as it was first made and given to the sons of men.[3]

We may think that Gerrard Winstanley's (of whom more later) words are an overstatement. Mere activism without reflection is misguided; but theological reflection without action runs the risk of disempowering practical theology as a discipline.

What I want to suggest in this chapter is that what is true of practical theology is also true of biblical exegesis and that the practice of faith is at least a necessary contributor to the shared quest to understand the text and may, arguably, be a necessary condition of it. At the risk of appearing to offer a proof text for what I am seeking to explore, I often recall the words of Jesus to his disciples in Matthew 10:19 ('When they deliver you up, do not be anxious how you are to speak or what you are to say; for what you are to say will be given to you in that hour') that is, in situations where they have to give testimony and find that what they have to say arises out of that context and would not come apart from it. The act of faith, cutting across

332

human predilections for planning order, predictably and safely represents the character of the divine promise. The adventure of the life of faithfulness to the way of the Lamb turns out to be the door to theological knowledge, as the human is enabled to be a channel for the divine word.

In the first part of this chapter I will focus on the issues thrown up by the question of the relationship between practical theology and biblical exegesis. Out of this, what I want to suggest is that in exploring the meaning of the biblical text a necessary component of exegesis is the narratives of those who have struggled to be obedient to Jesus Christ and have found themselves driven to espouse equality, or at least some redress of the imbalance between rich and poor and weak and strong. The meaning of the text that emerges from within lives lived in obedience to Jesus Christ and the struggles to practise equality deserve as much attention by the exegete as the detached exercise of mental struggle with the text. In the second part I consider the seventeenth-century Digger writings of Gerrard Winstanley, the latter emerging in the context of Winstanley's practice of equality in the small Digger communes which emerged at the height of the English Revolution in 1649. In the third part I suggest that Winstanley's perspectives echo an emerging ethos in pre-Constantinian Christianity that equalization of goods (wealth, power, holiness and knowledge) was considered an appropriate way of embodying Christ.

The Relationship between Practical Theology and Biblical Exegesis

For many exegetes the essential prerequisite *before* she embarks on contemporary application is understanding.[4] This was set out in an influential essay by Krister Stendahl,[5] in which he distinguished between exegesis and application. Positively, there is in this position a warning which needs to be heeded by all readers: the ongoing temptation to find in the text what suits us is enormous. Nevertheless, the distinction between pure and applied exegesis is one that has been subjected to critical scrutiny by Nicholas Lash. In two seminal passages Lash challenges what he calls the 'baton exchange' method of theological enquiry, in which the exegetes do their job and then pass their wisdom onto the systematic theologians and the ethicists.[6] More importantly, he suggests that Scripture is something to be performed, lived and acted upon and not just analysed. If we take the performance of Scripture seriously, a rather different approach to the Scriptures emerges, more imaginative, and one that sometimes sits more loosely to the letter of the text. It is more akin to some features of the methods which have emerged in the liberationist tradition and the wealth of methods of scriptural interpretation explored in earlier centuries in the life of the Church. It is an 'actualizing' of the Scripture (to use the term suggested in the Pontifical Biblical Commission's document of 1993),[7] in which understanding of the text comes in the process of living the texts. That seems to be one of the points which Lash wishes to make in suggesting that the understanding of Scripture is incomplete without attention to the performance of them. An understanding of biblical texts may particularly be vouchsafed to those who have an affinity with what that text is saying on the basis of the obedience of faith. Those who seek to engage with the address, promise, commission, praise, pardon and liberation of Scripture may best understand the biblical texts. I think that this is something of what Karl Barth was doing in *The Epistle to the Romans*. Barth[8] is right to state 'judged by what seems to me to be the principle of true exegesis, I entirely fail to see why parallels drawn from the ancient world should be of more value for our understanding of the epistle than the situation in which we ourselves actually are and to which we can therefore bear witness.' What in effect Barth does in Romans is an excellent example of the exegetical task as actualization (that is, the reading of texts in the light of new circumstances) which seeks to listen to the text and respond humbly in the context in which it is read. He describes his task as wrestling with the text, so the walls which separate the twentieth century from the first century become transparent, and the actual meaning is thereby disclosed, to paraphrase Barth's words. Getting at the meaning means being true to the spirit of the text and not just to the letter. For Barth, the divide between meaning and meaning for is pulled down in the process. Barth's work represents a sincere attempt to discover what the text has to say, which is certainly pervaded with theological learning but without the inhibitions of the norms of historical exegesis.

So, I would like to suggest that, if we seek to approach the issue of equality, we go to accounts of those who in their obedience to Christ have judged that equality in Christ is a matter of Christian discipline, to listen to their descriptions of why they have responded as they have, how these practical responses seek to interpret Scripture and to see those responses as themselves exegesis of Scripture. The answer might not be a detailed verse by verse exposition of the Bible, but it will be a letter written in flesh and blood and will, to that extent, relate to the biblical texts, which in their different ways offer reflections of practical essays in faithfulness. The narrative of the Bible can engage our narratives, individually, as in humility we allow the possibility of those biblical narratives to search out and challenge our own. The testimony of those people who have sought in obedience to Christ to embody this practice are part of the resources for the interpretation of Scripture which sits alongside the ancient parallels, the wisdom of the past interpreters and the modern exegetes.

Experience suggests that the insight into the meaning of Scripture, and what constitutes its performance, will time and time again come from those with few *formal* theological credentials but whose learning of the Christian life has equipped them with a wisdom which an interpreter needs to draw on in their exegesis of Holy Scripture. Jim McClendon in his remarkable *Systematic Theology*, which gives priority to ethics over doctrine and which draws its inspiration from the Anabaptist (or as Jim preferred to describe it, Baptist) tradition, draws attention to the writing of his Baptist forebear, Roger Williams, who wrote of those who arrogated to themselves alone, on the basis of a university education, the title 'scholar', a term he felt belonged properly to 'all believers and saints, who are frequently in the testament of Christ styled disciples or scholars of Christ Jesus … And this title is so much theirs that both men and women, believing, were called "scholars".' McClendon finds for himself in the following a model for the theological task: 'It is the command of Christ Jesus to his scholars to try all things: and the liberty of trying what a friend, yea what (an esteemed) enemy presents hath ever (in point of Christianity) proved one special means of attaining to the truth of Christ.'[9] The reference to 'try all things' may be understood in two senses: testing, to which we are all instinctively (and, in my view, too quickly) drawn, and also trying in the sense of 'essaying' beyond our horizons, natural or self-imposed, in search of the Christ who seeks us. In addition to contemporary performance of Scripture, we shall look to other ages and situations.

A recent study of Anabaptist hermeneutics suggests a historical precedent for this kind of approach.[10] Anabaptist stories offer evidence of a different tradition of Christian discipleship which was formally outlawed in England at the end of the sixteenth century. There is evidence of an approach to the interpretation of Scripture in which the whole congregation was involved. The sixteenth-century Anabaptist Pilgrim Marpeck wrote, 'I gladly submit my mind to a more clear and lucid understanding which is given by the Holy Spirit, and I would gladly submit to the least among Christ's own.' Three theological convictions undergird the hermeneutic community: 'the theologianhood of all believers', the centrality and continuity of the Church in God's purposes and the belief that the gathered Church was the main locus of the Spirit's work.

This is the context of practical theology and exegesis which is first and foremost about the practice of faith: how we set out to follow Christ, learn

335

from those moments of testimony when it is not ourselves but the Spirit at work in us, and our discernment of how we have acted when we believe we have been learning the things of God. It is a complex affair whose maintenance is going to owe as much, if not more, to understanding the practical politics of power relations or group dynamics as philosophy or social theory, to the work of Foulkes, Bion and Habermas as much as Gadamer and Ricoeur. Mention of these names signifies scores of men and women whose ideas never get into the canon of writings about exegesis and practical theology from whom I have picked up tips and methods which have helped with the engagement with Scripture over the last twenty years.

Like many others, I have struggled for many years now to find ways of linking theological expertise and practical discipleship. In workshops on interpreting the Bible, mainly in the church, I and usually one other colleague have sought to set up an arena in which participants can explore the relationship between Scripture and the contexts of the participants. It has been an exercise with its tensions and frustrations, not least for those who have come wanting to sit at the feet of a professor of the exegesis of Holy Scripture and hear from him what the text really means. What is always tricky is to employ the exegete both as a group facilitator and power-broker and also as a resource for biblical study and preaching who manages to enrich the process. There is a demand for the biblical expert to pronounce on a subject and for him to function as problem-solver rather than facilitator who can help provide the circumstances in which the text can be properly and humbly attended to and contemporary narratives can be owned, expounded and open to challenge in the light of the biblical texts. In espousing this multifaceted role, I would like to think that there is essential continuity with ancient Jewish and Christian interpreters who offered exegetical rules as a way of enabling interpretation of the Scripture to take place, rather than doing the job for people which most commentaries tend to do. Hillel's *middoth* or the rules of Richard of St Victor help the readers or hearers learn how to go about making the connections and using the text as a gateway for themselves.

In this process, the scriptural expert may enable modern readers to see the ways in which ancestors in reading such passages have been informed by them (this will include the ways in which the first readers of these texts might have understood them in their time and place, though this is not given a position of priority). Over the years I have come to see that the role of one who is trained in the contents and study of the Bible is an important but limited one. The primary task is to enable those who participate in the Bible study to have insights open to them. Depending on the context, one may look for appropriate ways of enabling people to engage with Scripture, to be attentive and open to it in order that insight may be opened up through it.[11] There are both diachronic and synchronic perspectives to the task. The diachronic is served by attending to how the text has been interpreted and other people's engagement with it; the synchronic attends to the practice of engagement, what facilitates it, what hinders it, how the power relations function in the group, etc. Then there is the ongoing task of suggesting ways in which discernment among competing interpretations can take place, though I think the tendency to short-circuit the process of exploration by sorting this out is often a way of engaging an experimental engagement. In both the diachronic and synchronic dimensions the role is to broaden horizons and guard against the tendency to make oneself and one's experience the measure of truth.

The 'professional' exegete has a role to play in this but has no prerogative on the proper effectiveness of the task. Attention to memory is a necessary complement to imagination. The recall of what has been said balances what is perceived and performed here and now. Engagement with Scripture leads to resistance to the letter of the text and sheer bewilderment as often as enlightenment. Here, too, it is less explanations or apologetics that are required than different methods whereby one may engage with the various stumbling blocks, for example, the process whereby texts which seem opaque may be opened up by the enormously fruitful exercise of historical imagination. Here, too, caution is required, however, lest historical reconstruction becomes the major criterion for proper understanding.[12]

The capacity for self-delusion, and for finding in Scripture only what we want to hear, has been the engine which has driven the convictions of modern exegesis. The origins of modern exegesis were part and parcel of an approach to authoritative texts, of which the Bible was pre-eminent. By reading the Bible in the context of ancient texts rather than as part of a tradition of interpretation within Christianity, Catholic and Protestant, a rather different perspective on these texts appeared, which made them ancient texts like others, strange and remote from modernity and of questionable value for a contemporary theology and ethics. The creation of distance between the Bible and modernity, however, has as one of its consequences that the Bible can be read in and for itself, and its meaning can be discerned without any modern issue driving interpretation. This has had two consequences: a way of dealing with partisan readings; and, in a situation where theologians in academy and society wish to be regarded as respectable by their colleagues, readings which have little correlation with the beliefs and practices of modern religious people.

Historical distance has been a way of undermining contemporary application of the text which antedates the Enlightenment. In the sixteenth century,
Protestants of all shades identified Babylon in the Book of Revelation with
Rome and the papacy. Catholic interpreters dealt with this by adopting either
a futuristic perspective (Babylon and the Beast are figures of the last times
which have not yet arrived) or an ancient historical perspective (the Beast
and Babylon are Rome of old). Were those Protestant interpreters (and their
medieval forebears in the tradition of Joachim of Fiore) deluded and guilty of
eisegesis? I think not. The image of the Beast and Babylon speaks of oppression, conformity to and worship of the Beast, and of spectacular opulence.
To juxtapose such images with Rome and the papacy in the sixteenth century
may be uncomfortable for modern exegetes but is not a misunderstanding
of the text which, as many commentators agree, offers a strong critique of
an overbearing empire and its consumption.

There is a concern that in the use of Scripture in relation to present
situations, modern preoccupations would so determine the exegesis that the
integrity of the text and its distinctive contribution would in fact be lost. That
concern reflects a widespread view that in modern academic exegesis we are
extracting from the text simply what it contains.[13] Would that the matter were
so simple. In conventional exegesis, authorial intention is a way of imposing
unity on the material. Nevertheless, the quest for intention has led to an
inevitable eisegetical activity in which the literary remains form the rudiments
of an imaginative reconstruction of the life of particular Christian communities, another story which then functions as a determining commentary on
the literal sense of the text. Characters become ciphers for different groups
seeking to expound or reject the Christian legacy. This approach is a modern
form of spiritualizing or allegorical exegesis, though of course the referent to
the hidden story is history rather than the higher truths of divinity.

Most historical criticism represents a good modern example of allegorical
exegesis.[14] While it can take its start from the text, it is often interested in
another story: the struggles behind the text; the historical Jesus; the evangelist's community; the intention of the evangelist, etc. In this the fabric of
the text and its form can easily get left behind. They become merely a kind
of window through which, with varying degrees of distortion, the situation
behind the text, that other story which allegory seeks to expose, can be laid
bare. This is a reminder that, however laudable the canons of modern exegesis
to respect the text and not co-opt it to modern concerns, this is precisely
what happens in much academic exegesis, though the modern concerns are
the historical reconstructions of a biblical studies practised in the context

of the modern academy and its non-doctrinal and objective interests. Such objectivity is more apparent than real. Historical exegesis does not offer the literal sense of the text which is an exercise in the plain sense of a text far removed from the sophisticated reconstructions which can pass as the literal meaning.

A critical exegesis will acknowledge the importance of the two poles (text and reader) and, in the interaction between the two, one will need the highest level of awareness on the part of the interpreter, of self and circumstances in the process of reading. In certain circumstances it may be necessary to acknowledge those prejudices to enable the peculiarities and strangeness or 'otherness' of the text to become fully apparent and for the text to 'speak' on its own terms, not those of the reader. Critical awareness is necessary in interpretation of any kind, so that facile assumptions and credence to a text or tradition may be avoided and attention given to the reasons why there may be resistance to a text or too ready acceptance of its contents on the part of the reader: why do we allow ourselves to be carried along by a text or a particular way of reading? Has the development of resistance to a text more to say about us? Is it necessary to resist co-opting the text in order to allow space for it or the concerns of the interpreter? Modern, post-Enlightenment readings have refused to be 'taken in' by the text or, in the case of contextual theologies, have demanded that present experience (of oppression, doubt, etc.) set the interpretative agenda. Care must be taken not to treat Scripture as the problem which the 'enlightened' interpreter can solve. Part of the process of reading means that critical self-awareness and attentiveness may result in a reversal of roles in which the interpreter becomes 'the client'. Too often the emphasis in criticism is on analysis and not enough on receptivity and 'listening'. In reading one needs to create an environment which will encourage the interpreter to explore the extent to which s/he projects onto the text or is resistant to it. There will be two dimensions to this: diachronic and synchronic. The diachronic approach will attend to the wider context of reading (habits of mind and the way the text has been interpreted). A synchronic approach is also necessary, however. There is need for attention to *where* reading is done and the effect of text on interpreter and vice versa.

Biblical scholarship in the last two hundred years has invested an enormous amount of time and energy in the pursuit of the elucidation of the text in its ancient context and the text's problems for modern sensibilities have meant that it has been the object for critical concern. The need to take seriously the modern context is long overdue. In a little noticed book, John O'Neil[15] set the biblical interpretation of the giants of biblical scholarship of the last hundred years in their historical and philosophical context. Alongside this there is need for attention to the synchronic approach to the text. By that I mean not only that kind of holistic reading which has been typical of what are loosely termed narrative approaches, but the kind of understanding of the interaction between text and reader which has taken place at different periods of history. We need to be reminded of the ideological character of our study, in particular imagining that we are 'drawing from the text simply what it contains' (to quote the words of Leslie Houlden).[16] Ideology is not something which belongs to the overtly committed readings.[17] Indeed, it is part of the insidious character of ideology that those who are in control of the way in which the text is interpreted deny that their readings are in any way ideological and instead are the product of 'scientific' methods.[18] It is a mark of a truly critical interpretation that it manifests an awareness of its own approach to the text but also the understandable constraints that this method imposes and the necessity of openness to other interpretative methods as both checks and a stimulus to change.

It is incumbent upon the interpreter to reflect on the approach taken to the text. Not only is there a question of whether the interpretation 'fits' the text, or, to put it in other terms, whether exegesis rather than eisegesis has been undertaken, but also there must be as frank an assessment as possible to locate the interpretation within the quests for meaning and significance which exist within contemporary society. A location in an academic environment demands certain canons of critical application partly in order to gain a hearing and partly to gain credibility for the enterprise. Theologians have an interest in maintaining not only the existence of their subject but also their own livelihoods. However, they also recognize that the mere use of these canons is insufficient without the wider kind of activity that involves the oscillation between different sorts of worlds, trying to make sense of them, trying to inhabit both and be heard by the inhabitants of both and trying to interpret one to the other. The canons of Christian theology cannot in the last resort be shaped by the academy. The EATWOT Conference of 1976[19] spoke of the need for an 'epistemological rupture' which makes commitment the first act followed by critical reflection on praxis amidst the reality of a suffering and unjust world. There is a legitimate question whether that kind of rupture is possible in Britain. Armchair radicals do well to explore their own interpretative interests as honestly as they can.

The attempt to be attentive to the text is not solved by academic detachment. William Blake understood better than anyone the enormous difficulty confronting a way of life pervaded by the Bible. Simply putting the Bible

340

in the hands of people does not deal with the stumbling blocks which stand in the way of understanding. It is not something which can be rectified by the provision of further knowledge about the text and its ancient context so much as the way in which the cultural values of society have so permeated the consciousness and lifestyle of interpreters, 'experts' included, that nothing less than a 'mental fight' is required to enable the adequate appreciation of the kinds of values and practices which inform exegesis and are at variance with the way of the Lamb. To set that wisdom free requires of the interpreters a variety of approaches to learn to be attentive to the divine Spirit, to enable dominant ideologies to be understood and challenged. The expert exegete's role is more about the ongoing task of finding a means of enabling that real meeting with the text rather than about telling people what the text means and being the final arbiter of true and false opinions. Indeed, Blake would have none of the idea that there was expert hermeneut to be consulted. As the Bible is a gateway to wisdom, it is up to all to make use of the gateway and enter and enjoy the garden of God in their own way and in their own time. It is the interpreter's job to provide the means of discovering, getting through the gate of perception and imagination to the life of faith.

Gerrard Winstanley: Private Property as the Fall

Nonconformity in Britain had over the centuries produced a series of interpretations of Scripture expounding equality, from John Ball in the fourteenth century to the Levellers, John and Elizabeth Lilburne, in the seventeenth.[20] By far the most extensive and systematic theology of equality is that of Gerrard Winstanley (1609–76). He was instrumental in setting up the 'Digger' colony on St George's Hill in Surrey in April 1649.[21]

What is important about Winstanley's writing is that it was done in the midst of action to grasp what he and many others believed was an opportunity for a new kind of polity and in conflict with the local gentry who opposed the legitimate claim to dig the common land. The Digger vision was to create a moneyless and propertyless society of the kind such followers believed had existed before the Fall. The Diggers held the Earth to have been originally a 'common treasury' for all to share, with the practice of buying and selling the land, which allowed some to become rich and others to starve, constituting the Fall, from the consequences of which humanity stood in need of liberation. The view of the Fall as the demonstration of covetousness in the rush to private property goes back in part at least to Josephus and Augustine.

341

In Josephus's version of the Cain and Abel story in *Jewish Antiquities*, i.60 (Augustine, *City of God*, xv. 5), Cain

> increased his substance with wealth amassed by rapine and violence; he incited to luxury and pillage all whom he met, and became their instructor in wicked practices. He put an end to the simplicity in which people lived before the invention of weights and measures: the guileless and generous existence which they had enjoyed in ignorance of these things he converted into a life of craftiness. He was the first to fix boundaries of land and to build a city ... the descendants of Cain went to depths of depravity, and, inheriting and imitating one another's vices, each ended worse than the last. (Loeb translation)

All could not enjoy true freedom until the land was held again in common. In *Truth Lifting Up Its Head* and *The New Law of Righteousness* Winstanley demonstrated a concern also to understand the roots of the economic and material struggles facing humankind in the enclosure movement which began in his day. Winstanley was concerned to expose the way in which the preoccupation with private property, the curse of Adam, reflected a fundamental flaw in human existence, individual, social and institutional, after the Fall. Those who possessed private property had gained it by oppression, murder or theft.[22] He links this social injustice with the internal struggle in each person. This struggle in individuals and society is exemplified in the story of Adam which is paradigmatic for, and at the start of, all oppression and injustice:

> this Adam appears first in every man and woman; but he sits down in the chair of magistracy, in some above others; for though this climbing power of self-love be in all, yet it rises not to its height in all; but every one that gets an authority into his hands, tyrannizes over others; as many husbands, parents, masters, magistrates, that live after the flesh, do carry themselves like oppressing Lords over such as are under them; not knowing that their wives, children, servants, subjects are their fellow creatures; and hath an equal privilege to share with them in the blessing of liberty.

And this first Adam is to be seen and known in a twofold sense:

> First, he is the wisdom and power of the flesh in every man, who indeed is the beast, and he spreads himself within Creation, man, into divers branches. As into ignorance of the creator of all things, into covetousness after objects, into pride and envy, lifting up himself above others, and seeking revenge upon all that crosses his selfish honours; and into hypocrisy, subtlety, lying imagination, self-love; from whence proceeds all unrighteous outward acting. This is the first Adam lying, ruling and dwelling within mankind. And this is he within every man and woman

which makes whole mankind, being a prisoner to him, to wonder after the beast, which is no other but self, or upon every thing whereupon self is stamped.

Secondly, the first Adam is the wisdom and power of flesh broke out and sat down in the chair of rule and dominion, in one part of mankind over another; And this is the beginner of particular interest, buying and selling the earth from one particular hand to another, saying, This is mine, upholding this particular propriety by a law of government of his own making, and thereby restraining other fellow creatures from seeking nourishment from Mother earth. So that though a man was bred up in a Land, yet he must not work for himself where he would sit down; But from Adam; that is, for such a one that had bought part of the land, or came to it by inheritance of his deceased parents, and called it his own Land: So that he that had no Land, was to work for these small wages, that called the Land theirs; and thereby some are lifted up into the chair of tyranny, and others trod under the foot-stool of misery, as if the earth were made for a few, not for all men.

For truly the common people by their labours, from the first rise of Adam, this particular interest upheld by the flesh's law to this day, they have lifted up their land-lords and others to rule in tyranny and oppression over them. And let all men say what they will, so long as such are Rulers as call the Land theirs, upholding this particular propriety of Mine and Thine; the common people shall never have their liberty, nor the Land ever freed from troubles, oppressions and complainings; by reason whereof the Creator of all things is continually provoked. O thou proud selfish governing Adam, in this Land called England! Know that the cries of the poor, whom thou layeth heavy oppressions upon is heard.

This is unrighteous Adam, that damned up the water springs of universal liberty, and brought the Creation under the curse of bondage, sorrow and tears: But when the earth becomes a common treasury as it was in the beginning, and the King of Righteousness comes to rule in every one's heart, then he kills the first Adam; for covetousness thereby is killed. A man shall have meat, and drink and clothes by his labour in freedom, and what can be desired more in the earth. Pride and envy likewise is killed thereby, for every one shall look upon each other as equal in the creation; every man indeed being a perfect creation of himself. And so this second Adam Christ, the restorer, stops or dams up the running of those stinking waters of self-interest and causes the waters of life and liberty to run plentifully in and through the Creation, making the earth one store-house, and every man and woman to live in the law of Righteousness and peace as members of one household.[23]

The interest of the economically and politically powerful is upheld by the rule of the Serpent and manifests itself in four ways: a professional ministry, royal power, the judiciary and the buying and selling of the earth. These correspond to the four beasts in the Book of Daniel: the lion with eagle's wings is kingly power; the one like a bear is the power of selfish laws; the leopard is the thieving art of buying and selling; the fourth is clergy power and the little horn coming out of it is the ecclesiastical establishment. Religion is made to offer the ideological justification for economic power, in a way which is very much akin to that described by Marx. The triumph of right-eousness comes as the result of the appropriation of the way of Christ and the overcoming of 'covetousness' so that community, called Christ or universal love, may prevail. Private ownership, inheritance and rents, the purchase and selling of land, the system of hired labourers, must all be abolished as the sign of the process of spiritual regeneration within. Only when this takes place will peace be ensured; then Christ will rise up in sons and daughters, and the earth will become a common treasury, as it was in the beginning.[24] The new heaven and earth may be something to be seen here and now,[25] once the kingly power of the old heaven and earth has passed away. The New Jerusalem is not 'to be seen only hereafter'. God's kingdom comes when God arises in his saints. The perfect society will come when there takes place 'the rising up of Christ in sons and daughters, which is Christ's second coming'.[26] Research on seventeenth-century radicalism has demonstrated that, however remarkable Winstanley's views might have been, his was not a lone voice. In the midst of political and theological struggle, a string of writers, women as well as men, put down markers for the practice of equalization of status and power as a necessary component of Christian discipleship.[27]

Equalization of Goods as a Way of Embodying Christ

Equality is not something about which the biblical writers have much to say, at least explicitly.[28] There are three references in the New Testament, two in 2 Corinthians 8:13 and one in a passage dealing with the master–slave relationship. This is a reminder that the biblical material is ambiguous, and it should cause no surprise that it has been used to justify hierarchy and subordination as well as inspired liberation and egalitarianism. Approaches to Scripture, however, in the context of a discussion of Christian ethics need to start with the evidence of the gospels and Jesus, which provide the neces-sary hermeneutical framework for considering other parts of the biblical tradition. It is easy for us to choose those parts of the Bible which suit our case, particularly in the Old Testament, where all are agreed that there are conflicting strands.[29] It is the gospels' witness to Jesus which privileges what Duncan Forrester calls 'the liberative/egalitarian trajectory' in the Bible over against others.[30] Within Jesus' circle there was a rejection of established status and power epitomized by the contrasting ethic in passages like Mark 10:42–4 and Luke 22:24–7. Solidarity with the insignificant is the character of discipleship (Matt 18:1–5). There is a message of hope for a great reversal when the first shall be last and the last first, which is not just a pipe dream but begins 'in the midst of time'.[31]

When we turn to the Hebrew Scriptures, although the issue of equality never emerges in connection with it, there is something thoroughly equalizing about the Sabbath observance. It is a reflection of the character of God, in which rich and poor, king, priest and ordinary citizen alike find themselves under the same obligation to abstain from work. In that situation there is a break in those patterns of relationships which sustain inequality, for those who are used to being served can no longer expect those who serve them to minister to their needs. There is a Sabbath for the people of God (Heb 4:9, where the image is used for God's eschatological reign of peace on earth), in which the weekly observance, like the Jubilee, marks a break in social relationships and indicates a different kind of polity in which exploitation temporarily comes to an end and beckons to that future eschatological rest where the polity will be different.

Elsewhere is a more pragmatic approach: the achievement of a degree of redress so there is no significant discrepancy between different members of society. The view of society in the laws of Exodus and Deuteronomy has been termed 'egalitarian'. That is a helpful description only in the most general sense. The laws do not countenance large disparities of wealth and status within the people of God. These are not Utopian tracts but practical exemplifications of the way in which redistributive mechanisms can effect a degree of equalization. That is an ongoing task, which requires constant attention to its effectiveness (the meaning of the notorious comment in Deut 15:11, 'the poor will never cease out of your land'). 'The poor you always have with you' is not a recipe for fatalism but for vigilance to ensure that one maintains an awareness and a level of appropriate and imaginative action to bring about redress. In Deuteronomy we find a radical challenge to the Judean state. The year of remission takes place every seven years (Deut 15:1–11). After six years of work a slave is to be released (15:12). The charging of interest is forbidden (23:20; 24:17). The harvest leftovers remain for the hungry (24:19), and laws are linked to an incessant reminder about the story of a people set free from slavery. The tithe is no longer for state but for self and the needy: the first social tax. In Leviticus there is a related though slightly different emphasis. The key verse of Levitians 25 is 'the land is mine; you are aliens and tenants' (v. 23). In the year of Jubilee (25:8–31) there is concern for kinsfolk who are down on their luck (vv. 25–8; vv. 35–8). Nevertheless, pragmatism pervades the legislation here in the casuistry found in 25:29, 47ff. The Book of Nehemiah also echoes the Jubilee tradition. People appeal to common humanity (Neh 5:5), which leads to the intervention of the enlightened ruler (Neh 5:7).[32]

In the Pauline letters the word 'equality' is actually used in the context of a significant discussion in 2 Corinthians 8:9ff, which relates directly to this issue of the sharing of goods: the collection of Pauline churches for the poor in Jerusalem and Judea. The collection occupied the last years of Paul's career.[33] It was an extraordinarily novel project and a logistically complex operation, which involved organizing a collection, which had to be taken hundreds of miles before delivery to the recipients. It has few obvious parallels in the ancient world. The collection runs like a leitmotiv throughout Paul's apostolic ministry (it is mentioned in Romans, 1 and 2 Corinthians, as well as Galatians, and there is a parallel item of mutual support noted in Philippians). Paul deals with it in a rather prosaic manner which might lead an unsuspecting reader to deem it less important within the spectrum of Pauline theology. Closer examination reveals the centrality of this activity for his theology. Paul justifies the operation Christologically: 'though Christ was rich yet, for our sake he became poor' (2 Cor 8:9), and speaks of it as an act of grace (2 Cor 8:7). The collection was to be a channel of divine aid which was both a means of alleviating misery and also a demonstration of God's character. It is spoken of in terms which are reserved elsewhere in the Pauline corpus for the proclamation of the Gospel itself (2 Cor 9:12, cf. Col 1:24).

The need is dealt with not in terms of the dependence of the needy on those who have plenty but by means of stressing mutual responsibility and the sharing of resources, albeit with attention to the different kinds of resources available to those in relationship one with another (Rom 15:27). There is no suggestion of impoverishment of one group in order to relieve another (2 Cor 8:13). Rather, it is a question of assessing need at a particular time and balancing resources so that the needs of all may be met. The materially wealthy are in fact indebted to the materially poor who share with them their spiritual resources. What Paul seems to be suggesting in these verses is the reverse of the usual understanding of indebtedness. Those who are in debt are the materially wealthy not the materially poor. Their contribution is now recognized as a bestowal of resources. The divine inheritance of those materially poor was not deemed by them to be private property but to be shared. For this reason, the Gentile Christians are in debt and have a reciprocal obligation to contribute to the Jerusalem church's material needs. The discussion in 2 Corinthians is about redistribution and equalization, though not equality. It is about redressing the balance between different groups, more in the sense of mutuality of obligation in Christ, that sharing of spiritual things by one party may be matched by the sharing of the material things which come from the other (so Rom 15:25).

There is at the heart of emerging Christianity a distinctive identity in which goods and privileges which had hitherto been the preserve of a tiny elite were opened up to people who shared one baptism in Christ. Wealth, power, holiness and knowledge ceased merely to be the prerogative of an elite but were open to all within the common life of the Christian communities.[34] The ethos of early Christianity involves the ongoing evocation of the pattern of a Christ who humbled himself, in obedience to the 'one who sent him' and in identification with the neediest and most vulnerable (Matt 8:17).[35] Those with earthly power and status and wealth renounce that status and learn a very different lifestyle (exemplified by conversion narratives such as those we find in Justin, *Apology* 1.14, and Cyprian, *First Epistle to Donatus*, 3–4). Exercising power means identifying with the Lamb that was slain, the victim of injustice, the humble king (Matt 21:7), whose story from the 'underside of history' the Christians tell week by week (Justin, *First Apology*, 61). Holiness belongs to all, not just to priests or the ritually clean: 'you are a royal priest-hood' (1 Pet 2:11). Status means sharing the lot of the lowly: the first shall be last and the last first (Matt 20:16). The ordering of things in the adult world is challenged as the ultimate embodiment of wisdom (Matt 18:1–5). It is the children, the weak, the lame and the blind who recognize Jesus in the Temple (Matt 21:15). God's wisdom is not the property of the elite but of the 'little ones' (Matt 11:25ff), and it is not sophistication, according to Paul, which will enable the Corinthians to discern the divine wisdom (1 Cor 1: 26). Early Christians found themselves being pushed beyond the boundaries of convention, not least being pushed out of the security of Jerusalem 'to the ends of the earth' (Acts 1:8), where the divine presence was now to be found (Matt 28:16ff; 18:20). There is no systematic exposition of equality in this, but an ethos of difference and a rejection of the culture of the 'principalities and powers', all of which is typical of the various forms of pre-Constantinian Christianity.

Winstanley's work reflects the way in which understanding of faith was worked out in the midst of practice. His is a classic example of practical theology. William Stringfellow could have been writing of Winstanley's 'Digger' period when he describes the heart of the Christian life as 'unpre-dictable; extemporaneous; serious but not pretentious; conscientious but not presumptuous; dynamic and never immutable; historically serious and realistic and, hence, often inconsistent; momentary or imminent and yet transcendent, commonplace, and sacramental. Winstanley was a Christian who lived politically within time, on the scene of the Fall, as an alien in Babylon, in the midst of apocalyptic reality.'[36] Winstanley and his radical follower, William Blake, were not committed to the principle of equality but to the practice of the way of Christ, which meant challenging the vested interests and the violence which is used to maintain those interests.[37]

What this requires is practice and immersion in one's context.[38] William Blake makes the point in a slightly different way. He challenged the preoccupation of the academy with abstractions and insisted that one should concentrate on 'minute particulars'. 'Every minute particular is holy', writes Blake (*Jerusalem*, 69.42). An abstraction though related to reality removes one from the reality of the complexity of those particulars and can easily obscure the demands of humans in their particularity (*Marriage of Heaven and Hell*, 11; *Jerusalem*, 91.31; cf. 31.7; 55.62). Blake objected to the rapid move to principles by discarding or transcending details, for the details were the keys to understanding: 'Minute discrimination is not accidental. All sublimity is founded on minute discrimination' (*On Reynolds*, K453). It was attention to the detail of what he saw on the streets of London that elicited Blake's response in his *Continental Prophecies*, or 'London'. So, 'he who would do good to another must do it in Minute particulars: general Good is the plea of the scoundrel, hypocrite and flatterer' (*Jerusalem*, 55.60). Winstanley and Blake both exemplify biblical exegesis with differing degrees of direct attention to textual analysis. In their differing contexts, the practice of faith informed their understanding of the Bible, whose meaning emerged for them as they followed in the way of Jesus.

Notes

1 Denys Turner, 'Liberation theology in Britain today', *Political Theology*, 2 (2000): 74.

2 Quoted in C. Rowland, *Radical Christianity* (Oxford: Polity Press, 1988), p. 110. On the biblical interpretation of radical theology in early modern England, see C. Hill, *The English Bible and the Seventeenth Century Revolution* (London: Allen Lane, 1993). Winstanley's theology is compared with that of the German Reformation radical Thomas Müntzer in A. Bradstock, *Faith in the Revolution: The Political Theologies of Müntzer and Winstanley* (London: SPCK, 1997).

3 Gerrard Winstanley, 'A watchword to the City of London', in C. Hill, *Winstanley: Law of Freedom and Other Writings* (Harmondsworth: Penguin, 1973), pp. 127–8. See also Bradstock, *Faith in the Revolution*, and Rowland, *Radical Christianity.*

4 J. Ashton: *Studying John* (Oxford: Clarendon Press, 1994), pp. 206–7.

5 K. Stendahl, 'Contemporary biblical theology', in G. A. Buttrick *et al.*, *The Interpreter's Dictionary of the Bible* (Nashville, TN: Abingdon, 1962), pp. 418–32.

6 N. Lash, *Theology on the Way to Emmaus* (London: SCM Press, 1986), and also Stephen C. Barton, 'New Testament interpretation as performance', in *Life Together: Family, Sexuality and Community in the New Testament and Today* (Edinburgh: T&T Clark, 2001), pp. 223–50.

7 J. L. Houlden, *Interpreting the Bible in the Church* (London: SPCK, 1994).

8 K. Barth, *The Epistle to the Romans* (English trans., Oxford: Clarendon Press, 1933), p. 11.

9 J. McClendon, *Systematic Theology I (Ethics)* (Nashville, TN: Abingdon, 1986), p. 46.

10 S. Murray, *Biblical Interpretation in the Anabaptist Tradition* (Kitchener, Ontario: Pandora, 2000).

11 G. West, *The Academy of the Poor* (Sheffield: Sheffield Academic Press, 1999).

12 Cf. the line taken in the Pontifical Biblical Commission's document, J. L. Houlden (ed.), *The Interpretation of the Bible in the Church* (London: SCM Press, 1995), pp. 259–60.

13 Leslie Houlden, 'Schools of thought', *Theology*, 93 (1990).

14 See also J. Barr, 'The literal, the allegorical, and modern biblical scholarship', *JSOT*, 44 (1989), pp. 3–17, and B. Childs, 'James Barr on the literal and the allegorical', *JSOT* 46 (1990), pp. 3–9.

15 J. C. O'Neill, *The Bible's Authority* (Edinburgh: T&T Clark, 1991).

16 Leslie Houlden, 'Schools of thought'.

17 See, e.g., T. Eagleton, *Criticism and Ideology* (London: Verso, 1976), and F. Jameson, *The Political Unconscious* (London: Methuen, 1988).

18 Such espousal of 'science' as a description of biblical interpretation has pervaded even the in many ways commendable summary of biblical interpretation published by the Pontifical Biblical Commission in J. L. Houlden, *The Interpretation of the Bible in the Church*.

19 See S. Torres and V. Fabella (eds), *The Emergent Gospel: Theology from the Underside of History* (Maryknoll, NY: Orbis, 1978), p. 269.

20 A. Bradstock and C. Rowland, *Radical Christian Writings: A Reader* (Oxford: Basil Blackwell, 2002).

21 G. H. Sabine (ed.), *The Works of Gerrard Winstanley* (Ithaca, NY: Cornell University Press, p. 247. See also D. W. Petegorsky, *Left-Wing Democracy in the English Civil War* (London: Gollancz, 1940); Christopher Hill, *The Religion of Gerrard Winstanley* (Oxford: Past and Present Society, 1978); T. Wilson Hayes,

Winstanley the Digger (Cambridge, MA, and London: Harvard University Press, 1979); Timothy Kenyon, *Utopian Communism and Political Thought in Early Modern England* (London: Pinter, 1989); George M. Shulman, *Radicalism and Reverence: The Political Thought of Gerrard Winstanley* (Berkeley, CA: University of California Press, 1989); C. Rowland, *Radical Christianity: A Reading of Recovery*; Andrew Bradstock, *Faith in the Revolution: The Political Theologies of Müntzer and Winstanley*; Andrew Bradstock (ed.), *Winstanley and the Diggers 1649–1999* (London and Portland, OR: Frank Cass, 2000).

22 'New Law of Righteousness' in G. H. Sabine (ed.), *The Works of Gerrard Winstanley*, pp. 158–9; and, further, Hill, *The Religion of Gerrard Winstanley*; Bradstock and Rowland, *Radical Christian Writings: A Reader*.

23 Sabine, *Collected Works*, p. 158

24 'Fire in the Bush', Hill and Law, p. 268.

25 Sabine, 153, 211, 216–19, 223, 226–7, 377, 409, 454, 462–3, 484, 495.

26 'True Levellers', Sabine, pp. 86f.

27 E. Hobby, *Virtue of Necessity: English Women's Writing 1649–88* (Ann Arbor, MI: University of Michigan, 1988), and P. Crawford, *Women and Religion in England 1500–1720* (London: Routledge, 1993).

28 R. Bauckham, 'Egalitarianism and hierarchy in the Bible', in A. N. S. Lane, *The Interpretation of the Bible* (Leicester: Apollos, 1997), pp. 259–73.

29 Duncan Forrester, *On Human Worth* (London: SCM Press, 2001), pp. 77–101.

30 *Ibid.*, p. 80–1.

31 *Ibid.*, p. 96.

32 See U. Duchrow, *Alternatives to Global Capitalism* (Utrecht: International Books with Kairos Europe, 1995); S. Ringe, *Jesus, Liberation and the Biblical Jubilee* (Philadelphia, PA: Fortress Press, 1985); J. H. Yoder, *The Politics of Jesus* (Grand Rapids, MI: Eerdmans, 1972).

33 D. Georgi, *Remembering the Poor: The History of Paul's Collection for Jerusalem* (Nashville, TN: Abingdon, 1992); H. D. Betz, *2 Corinthians 8 and 9: A commentary on the Administrative Letters of the Apostle Paul* (Philadelphia, PA: Fortress Press, 1985); D. Horrell, Paul's collection: resources for a materialist theology', *Epworth Review*, 22 (1995): 74–83.

34 G. Theissen, *A Theory of Primitive Christian Religion* (London: SCM Press, 1999), pp. 81–118.

35 K. Wengst, *Humility* (London: SCM Press, 1987).

36 William Stringfellow, *An Ethic for Christians and Other Aliens in a Strange Land* (Waco, TX: Word, 1973), especially pp. 62–4.

37 A point stressed by J. Ellul in *The Presence of the Kingdom* (London: SCM Press, 1951), pp. 39–44.

38 Kenneth Leech, *Through Our Long Exile: Contextual Theology and the Urban Experience* (London: Darton, Longman & Todd, 2001).

Chapter 21

Blessed are the Excluded

ALISTAIR KEE

The Ideology of Exclusion

The gospels are full of reversals: the last shall be first and the first last. None is more surprising than the words of Jesus to his disciples: 'blessed are you when men hate you, and when they exclude you and revile you, and cast out your name as evil, on account of the Son of man!'[1] Blessed are the excluded. Yes, 'blessed are you poor'; 'blessed are you that hunger'; 'blessed are you that weep now', but exclusion is not simply an economic category. It is a moral category which divides society into two unequal groups; it is a spiritual category which distinguishes two life choices. Blessed are the excluded: it is yet another reversal. The judges are judged. Have you been cruelly and unjustly excluded? Congratulations on a lucky escape! The film *Titanic* begins with Leonardo de Caprio gambling for two tickets for the liner's maiden voyage. What a stroke of luck – for those who lost. Blessed are those who are excluded – from a social order hurrying to destruction. The meaning of exclusion in the teaching of Jesus is a reversal of its meaning in contemporary social policy.

For a number of years Duncan Forrester and I have jointly edited the *Cambridge Series on Ideology and Religion*. Its various studies seek to combine a sympathetic treatment of religion with analytical perspectives from the social sciences. This combination can be seen in his own recent work *On Human Worth: A Christian Vindication of Equality.*[2] It contains a chapter on 'Equality and the Politics of Inclusion', in which he undertakes a sensitive and informed criticism of the literature on 'Social Exclusion'. In this present chapter I wish to approach the subject by combining a biblical paradigm and a Marxist critique of ideology.

351

An ideology is a shy creature: it does not want to be seen, to be identified, to be named. It would rather that its view of reality were simply taken for granted, without further thought. It rests content if its values and prejudices are simply assumed as too obvious to be contested. 'Exclusion' is an ideological category, but you would not think so from the literature about social exclusion. Or rather the ideology of exclusion cannot believe its luck that its values and assumptions are simply taken for granted, without any critical discussion. Any group that is described as 'excluded' cannot be allowed to get away. They must be brought into the body of mainline society. Attention is focused on their plight and their problems. Ideology chuckles behind its hand. No evaluation is required of mainline society. Its essential health and virtue are simply assumed. Its part in exclusion is never examined. The possible and potential role of the excluded in the regeneration of society is not even envisaged. The fact of their exclusion is not seen as a symptom of disorder, neither as a witness to corruption. No gospel reversal here. Blessed are those who exclude. And twice blessed are the excluders who graciously attempt to draw the victims into the kingdom of this world.

Of course, a provisional distinction can be made between those who through their own decisions put themselves outside the pale, those who do so for moral or spiritual reasons – 'on account of the Son of man' – and those who are thrust outside in spite of themselves and their desire to be part of society. Poverty itself is a particular case. There are those who have chosen poverty both to free themselves of a corrupting materialism endemic in society and to witness to an alternative set of values. But their poverty is not the poverty of the poor. Indeed, it is unfortunate that the same word is used to describe two very different situations. The poverty of those who belong to a religious order which guarantees their security, health, cultural enrichment, facilities for work and study is not the poverty of those who suffer deprivation in all of these matters, the poverty of risk, abuse, ill-health, restriction, hopelessness and despair. They have nothing and find that even the blessing of Jesus is taken away from them. As Julio de Santa Ana observes, 'blessed are the poor' soon became 'blessed are those who give to the poor'.[3] So it is with exclusion. There are those who by their own decision stand over against society, to criticize, to condemn, to witness and to challenge. This is not the experience of those whose dearest wish is to be allowed and enabled to enter that Promised Land.

This is a provisional distinction, but are the excluded not excluded – regardless? In pronouncing the poor blessed, Jesus did not have in mind simply those who had made a decision to give up wealth. Asceticism was not a Jewish tradition. So it is with exclusion. Blessed are the excluded – whether they choose exclusion or have exclusion thrust upon them. How can this be? Let us consider two specific examples of social exclusion, exclusion on the crudest basis, i.e. race.

Welcome to Uncle Tom Land

The first example comes from the USA, where exclusion was called segregation and inclusion was called integration. The Civil Rights Movement might have taken as its logo a door. The segregationists manned the door to keep it firmly closed, to exclude the negroes, as they called them. They were prepared to violate men, women, children and the Constitution itself in order to keep the door closed. On the other side were the blacks, as they called themselves, and their white supporters who pressed forward with conviction (literally) but with non-violence to secure their rightful place in American society. Described in this way, we can see the fundamental flaw and why it was that the agenda of the Revd Dr Martin Luther King Jr was rejected by many blacks, especially in the northern cities such as Detroit. The model of the door is ideological. Integration is not the answer to the problem of racial exclusion, it is the perpetuation of the ideology of white racism. This is nowhere more clearly exposed than in the thought of the Detroit pastor, the Revd Albert B. Cleage of the Shrine of the Black Madonna, the most original and creative black theologian of the twentieth century.

To understand Cleage's position we must understand his rejection of integration. He does not stop to declare himself on miscegenation. The matter is in the mind rather than the loins. Regardless of the Constitution, blacks have historically been excluded from the American way of life. Cleage does not hesitate to uncover the feet of clay of the Great Liberator. Abraham Lincoln 'freed all the slaves only because it was necessary to preserve the dominant power and supremacy of the white group of which he was leader'.[4] Ironically, America, founded ostensibly by a revolution to end injustice, has seen the white man 'willing to sacrifice the Constitution, the courts and the law, to preserve what he held sacred, the status quo'.[5] Blacks have been forced to live separately from the white mainstream. They have been in America, but not of America. The right to life, liberty and the pursuit of happiness, the right to vote and even the right to bear arms were never intended to apply to blacks. In a phrase which Cleage uses frequently, the separation is founded on 'the white man's *declaration of black inferiority*'.[6]

353

It is therefore more than ironic that black radicals should be described as separatists, should be *accused* of being separatists. The separation has always been there. How to respond to it? Integration is unacceptable to Cleage because it requires blacks to accept 'the white man's declaration of black inferiority'. Integration does not describe a coming together such as might be seen in the merging of two companies in which each contributes from its strength, each sets aside elements which do not enhance the new reality. In the case of integration there is no new reality. The old reality continues, except that a door is opened fractionally, grudgingly to permit a few selected blacks to pass into white society. In passing through this door 'into Uncle Tom Land',[7] they must first agree to black inferiority. Integration means giving up being black insofar as this is humanly possible, and accepting white values and the white way of life as the ultimate goal. Of course it cannot be achieved. The requirement cannot be met. But this only confirms the premise concerning black inferiority. 'Self-hatred was a part of the Black man's desire for integration.'[8]

Those who have been brought up to believe that white is right and white is best are devastated by exclusion. But this act of exclusion, this enforced separatism can also be experienced in a positive way. What if blacks decide that they do not want to enter that door marked 'Self-castration'? They are being told to stay where they are, but what if they *decide* to stay where they are? Once the decision has been made to stay outside, everything changes. Instead of being excluded from the American nation, it is now possible to conceive of blacks forming their own nation. No, they need not travel one mile to do so: this is not a matter of geography. They can be a Nation within the nation. They can be a Black Nation living within America, no longer begging at the door of the white nation. 'We are not Americans. We are an African people who against our will were brought to America.'[9] They can begin to affirm themselves and reject inferiority; they can look to themselves instead of turning to whites; they can unite as friends instead of being divided by their enemies.

We can sense here a dynamic, but it must have a direction. Black, yes, but being black, affirming blackness is not enough. 'Being black is a condition, not a program.'[10] Black people have suffered from separation: now they must learn from it. 'Black people must remain separate using the separateness that already exists as a basis for political power, for economic power, and for the transmission of cultural values.'[11] The affirmation of blackness must issue in black power, the power to be able to control black neighbourhoods, schools, shops, businesses. It is with the taking of power that the Black Nation will be united and enriched. It is on this reading of the situation that Cleage is so scathing of Roy Wilkins and the NAACP, but also critical of Dr Martin Luther King and the SCLC. 'Genuine black leadership cannot lead in the direction of integration.'[12] The old reality was separation, the new reality is Pan-Africanism, 'the bringing together of Black people across artificial national boundaries as one people'.[13]

This analysis is specific to blacks in America, but *mutatis mutandis* it is suggestive for any situation of exclusion/segregation and any proposed policy of inclusion/integration. The model of the door perpetuates the ideology of the excluders. A more suggestive model is a merging of two roads which issues in a single but new way forward. The excluded have their opportunity to contribute to the new and better way. Segregation in America was a tragedy, but integration has been no solution. A minority of blacks have become acceptable to white society. The price of entry has been the loss of any positive critical distance from mainline society. In their relief at being allowed through the door, they have been reluctant to criticize the values of a society founded on exclusion. The majority of blacks are still excluded, but they have not liberated themselves from what Cleage calls 'the declaration of black inferiority'. In tacitly accepting it, their alienation further guarantees their unfitness for integration. Blessed are the excluded, if it means that through the experience they find a better way. The second example comes from South Africa.

No to Integration

Apartheid is the Afrikaans word for exclusion. In theory, it excluded in both directions: the door was bolted from both sides. I recall standing in a long queue for the white counter in the main post office in Cape Town, while at that moment blacks could get served right away at the black counter. But that was the exception. Apartheid meant exclusion from the best jobs, schools, residential areas, from the most fertile farming regions. The deserted beaches reserved for blacks were on the cold Atlantic side of the Cape, while the popular beaches reserved for whites were on the warmer Indian Ocean coast. Apartheid was an ideological concept not because it meant separation, but because in reality it meant exclusion.

What greater love is there than for a leader to lay down his life for his people? Well, if there is a greater love, then perhaps it is not to lay down his life but to continue with life under the cruel conditions of imprisonment for year after year, decade after decade without knowing how long it will

355

be before the cause prevails. No one in the twentieth century was held in higher esteem throughout the world than Nelson Mandela. Subject to every form of exclusion and deprivation yet he never allowed himself to become a victim. In the end he prevailed not because he survived, but because he never treated those who abused him as enemies. He refused to be overcome by evil. But when all that is said, his analysis of apartheid was deeply flawed and the new South Africa is paying the price of failure. In this there is a curious, tragic parallel between Martin Luther King and Nelson Mandela. The African National Congress never addressed the ideology of apartheid. Its one-time president, the Nobel Peace Prize laureate Chief Albert Luthuli, used the failed model which we have discussed. 'Who will deny that thirty years of my life have been spent knocking in vain, patiently, moderately and modestly at a closed and barred door?'[14] When towards the end of the 1960s Mandela (ANC) was in prison and Sobukwe (PAC) was banned, black leadership passed to Bantu Stephen Biko. As his friend, the Anglican priest Aelred Stubbs, observed: 'Given the circumstances he faced of a strongly entrenched, powerfully armed minority on the one hand and a divided, defeated majority on the other, perhaps the political genius of Steve lay in concentrating on the creation and diffusion of *a new consciousness* rather than in the formation of a rigid *organization*.'[15]

It was for Biko to provide a new analysis of apartheid and therefore a new path forward. Cleage saw integration as an acceptance of black inferiority. Biko saw that in South Africa blacks were not innocent victims.

> The first step is to make the black man come to himself; to pump back life into his empty shell; to infuse him with pride and dignity, to remind him of his complicity in the crime of allowing himself to be misused and therefore letting evil reign supreme in the country of his birth. That is what we mean by an inward-looking process. This is the definition of 'Black Consciousness'.[16]

They had bought into the ideology of apartheid: 'the most potent weapon in the hands of the oppressor is the mind of the oppressed'.[17] They must free themselves from 'the myth of integration'.[18] Once again a black leader rejects the holy grail of liberalism. 'If by integration you understand a breakthrough into white society by blacks, an assimilation and acceptance of blacks into an already established set of norms and code of behaviour set up by and maintained by whites, then YES I am against it.'[19] Once again the model of the door is rejected in favour of a new path. 'Each group must be able to attain its style of existence without encroaching on or being thwarted by another. Out of this mutual respect for each other and complete freedom of self-determination there will obviously arise a genuine fusion of the lifestyles of the various groups. This is true integration.'[20]

Steve Biko, the man of non-violence, died under police interrogation. Nelson Mandela, the man who reluctantly turned to violence, survived. It is the ANC which has prevailed, not the way of Black Consciousness, and with its hegemony has come the bitter harvest of the new South Africa, a land in which the ideology of apartheid has neither been addressed nor defeated. Integration/inclusion is a failed model through which is perpetuated the ideology of apartheid/exclusion. The experiences of blacks in America and South Africa are not paradigms for the UK, but they are suggestive of the ideological dangers inherent in the rhetoric of exclusion/inclusion.

Sacralizing the Poor

There is one further point which might be gained from these two examples. One of the reasons why the words 'blessed are the poor' lack credibility is because the conditions of poverty, as already noted, lead to deprivation. The poor as a class do not seem to be admirable in virtue of their poverty. In the same period we have been considering a great deal that was said about the poor in Latin America. These sentiments went beyond sympathy towards the poor and conferred on them a certain moral and even spiritual status. It is significant that Gustavo Gutiérrez, who has made his life among the poor of Lima, refuses this romantic route.

> Contrary to what a certain romantic notion would hold, the world of the poor is not made up simply of victims, of solidarity and the struggle for human rights. The universe of the poor is inhabited by flesh-and-blood human beings, pervaded with the forces of life and death, of grace and sin. In that world we find indifference to others, individualism, abandoned children, people abusing people, pettiness, hearts closed to the action of the Lord. Insofar as the poor are part of human history, they are not free of the motivations found in the two cities of which St Augustine spoke: love of God and love of self.[21]

As Sobrino assures us, 'There is no question of idealizing, much less sacrilizing the poor.'[22]

We find the same lack of romanticism in Cleage. Cleage accused the white church of legitimizing naked power. He seems to offer a licence to every mindless act of violence and lawlessness, so long as it is committed by a black man. But no, Albert Cleage is more courageous than that. He does not follow along ingratiating himself to black radicals by saying Amen to every black excess. He is confident in his own Christian black nationalism, from which standpoint he can say some brave and salutary things about the rioters in Detroit. He derides the self-styled radical blacks, who announce that they go to the ghettos to learn from the ordinary people. This is an idealizing of the victims which can only arise from a false reading of the situation, and a total lack of critical perspective. 'Black people are not good because they are poor and powerless.'[23] Cleage committed his life to working with poor blacks. That experience does not lead him to a romantic idealizing of them, but rather to a clear view of why the revolution is necessary. 'Basically, oppressed masses are sick.'[24] The ideology of black inferiority has impoverished their lives, but only after it has contaminated their minds. 'Masses of people who have been oppressed, discriminated against, who have lacked opportunity, who have in every way been shut out of the mainstream of life are sick because of their oppression.'[25] There is a long road to travel to health and fulfilment. Cleage knows very well what is going on in the streets. His response is neither to condemn nor to condone – but to propose a solution.

> So we are developing a generation of monsters, little vicious individualists concerned only about themselves. You can idealize them, you can say, 'They are the vanguard of the revolution.' But they are the vanguard of no revolution. They are the vanguard of chaos. They are mad, they are evil, and they are lonesome. They are by themselves, and nobody offers them anything to believe in and to become a part of. This, then is a basic task of the Black Nation.[26]

Black people must recognize that white society has made them sick, has taught them self-hatred, has miseducated them and has led them to betray their own. 'Blessed are the poor', but not in virtue of what deprivation has done to them. Steve Biko makes the same point.

We have already seen that Biko does not regard his fellow blacks as innocent in their attitude towards apartheid, but rather complicit. (We might note here Allan Boesak's indebtedness to Biko in the title of his work *Farewell to Innocence*.) 'Blessed are the poor', but Biko had no illusions about the effects of poverty. In the townships 'we see a situation of absolute want in which black will kill black to be able to survive. This is the basis of the vandalism, murder, rape and plunder that goes on while the real sources of evil – white society – are sun-tanning on exclusive beaches or relaxing in their bourgeois homes.'[27]

'Blessed are the poor', but without romanticizing, idealizing or sacrilizing what deprivation does to people.

358

Blaming the Excluded

Enlightened by these analyses we can turn to the situation in the UK. Individuals and groups have been excluded from their societies throughout human history, but the rhetoric of social exclusion first appeared only in the 1980s. Like many terms, notably 'fascism', the fact that there is no agreement on the meaning of social exclusion has not inhibited its widespread use. It was used in the second poverty programme of the European Commission and it had the political merit of avoiding the implication that member states allowed poverty to continue within their borders. As Jos Berghman points out, '"social exclusion" would then be a more adequate and *less accusing* expression to designate to the existing problems and definitions'.[28] Stated thus we can see that the term social exclusion derives from an idealist analysis which serves ideological interests.

Ideologies are by definition idealist systems. They generate pictures and images which, far from reflecting social reality, seek to create and maintain illusions which further the interests of those who benefit from the ideology. The first article I ever published was written when I lived in Africa. 'Underdevelopment and how to maintain it'[29] described the contradictions of colonialism. The economic advancement of Africans (the excluded) was not in the interests of those who devised programmes for development. David Byrne, in his Marxist analysis of the subject, uses the same term. 'Underdevelopment seems to me to be a good term to use as a synonym for the actual processes that constitute social exclusion. The socially excluded are those parts of the population who have been actively underdeveloped.'[30] It is difficult to read the reports of the government's Social Exclusion Unit without experiencing the same contradictions, for example *Bringing Britain Together: A National Strategy for Neighbourhood Renewal*.[31] The analysis of social exclusion and the programmes devised to end it presuppose the views and values not of the excluded but of the excluders. What is at stake here can be illustrated by the two approaches to social exclusion distinguished by John Veit-Wilson. 'In the "weak" version of this discourse, the solutions lie in altering these excluded peoples' handicapping characteristics and enhancing their integration into dominant society.'[32] This is the culture of blaming the poor for their poverty. I digress for a moment to draw a parallel with the situation envisaged on *The Onion* website in a piece entitled *Vatican Rescinds 'Blessed' Status of World's Meek*.[33] According to the report, the pontiff gave the following reason for this step. 'There has always been a tacit understanding between the Church and the meek that this "blessed" status was conditional upon their inheritance of the earth, an event which seems unlikely to happen anytime in the foreseeable future.' Addressing the College of Cardinals on the matter, the pontiff continued, 'for years, the Catholic Church has made every effort to help them, but at some point, enough is enough. We are patient, but we are not saints.' Support was quick to follow. Cardinal Jean-Claude Turcotte of Montréal observed: 'Everything about the meek, from their simple garments to their quiet demeanour to their utter lack of can-do spirit, goes against Church philosophy.' We may doubt the veracity of this report, but there is no doubt that, in society at large and among politicians of the main parties, it is this 'lack of can-do spirit' which leads people to despair of helping the excluded. This is the 'weak' use of social exclusion and indeed it represents an attack on the weak. Veit-Wilson claims that by comparison the 'strong' uses of the term point to 'the role of those who are doing the excluding and therefore aim for solutions which reduce the powers of exclusion'.[34] This is suggestive so far as it goes, but, as we have seen, the terminology itself is calculated to be *less accusing* of the excluders and their power. This approach still does not provide a proper basis on which to analyse the phenomenon.

Capitalism and Exclusion

So far we have discussed idealist analyses which attribute exclusion to the inadequacies of the excluded – moral, social and psychological. When social exclusion is reduced to such sources it allows ideological interests to continue unchallenged. We must turn now to a materialist analysis which uncovers the economic causes of social exclusion. Social exclusion has been brought about by the transition to post-Fordist production. The term 'social exclusion' attempts to describe a new feature of social life. As with all major changes in the superstructure of society, this new phenomenon is an expression of fundamental changes taking place in the economic base. Under the conditions of capitalist production industrial societies were stratified into social classes. The aristocracy represented an irrelevant and quaint survival from feudal times, overtaken by the new property-owning bourgeois class of entrepreneurs. The Industrial Revolution produced not only goods and services but also the working class itself. That class was a society within a society, with its own moral and aesthetic values, its own stratifications related to labour skills, its own aspirations, its own signifiers of fulfilment. The working class, at least in Scotland, were not excluded from the life of other classes – not from the aristocracy, whom it held in contempt, neither from the middle class whose ostentation it condemned. Social stratification has been fundamentally disordered by the de-industrialization of the economy. The working class has disappeared, but so has the middle class. There has been not so much *embourgeoisement* as a homogenization of society in the economic transformation from production to consumption. The working class has not been accepted into the middle class: the post-Fordist economy has produced a much more fluid society in which individuals and families move rapidly up and down the scale of socio-economic indicators. But the unification of society brought about by this economic change has also created a new sphere, those who are excluded from economic activity, those who by being outside the market soon find themselves outside all other aspects of social life. The excluded are sometimes referred to as an underclass but this is a misapplication of a previous category. As Nelson observes, it is 'inequality without class conflict'.[35] The consciousness and solidarity of the old working class are entirely missing from their situation. This sphere of society is *déclassé*. Families within it may have belonged historically to the working class but they are now *déraciné*. They do not form a society within society, with the previously noted moral and aesthetic values. They do not possess the skills which bestowed social status within the working class. They do not generate their own aspirations or criteria of fulfilment. Their self-understanding is negatively generated by the ideology of exclusion.

In colonial times it used to be said, 'The natives are restless', as if they were to blame for being exploited. The modern equivalent is to blame social exclusion on the excluded. On a material reading of the situation social exclusion has not been caused by the excluded. It is a consequence of the economic transition to a post-Fordist, post-industrial society. As Byrne notes, 'it also directly challenges the idea that the solution to the problem of social exclusion comes with changing individuals' skills in order to make people more marketable according to the demands of market capitalism.'[36] The appearance of social exclusion in the 1980s did not simply coincide with the next phase in neo-liberal economics. It was not a coincidence but a consequence. The creation of social exclusion is inherent in a society in which the free market is allowed – encouraged – to restructure society at every level. Social exclusion cannot be ended in a society which presupposes the essential rightness of the economic system which causes it. It is for this reason that the approach of the Social Exclusion Unit displays internal contradictions. Social exclusion is the cost of supply-side economics. The only question is who is to pay the price – and whether the price is too high.

The Excluded and Salvation

We began by observing that Jesus' words, 'blessed are the excluded', represent a reversal of the social policy on exclusion. How to move forward? There is a saying in Latin America: 'The poor evangelize the Church.' How could this be so, given the deprivation of the poor and the power of the Church? It suggests a reversal no less unlikely. 'The excluded evangelize the Church.' Is it possible that those who are excluded from mainline society might yet bring salvation to their oppressors?

What makes this, as other Gospel reversals, seem incredible is the acceptance of the premises of the ideology of exclusion/inclusion. The ideology is attractive to the haves because it explains why the have-nots are responsible for their own misery. Like all ideologies of the ruling classes it justifies the ways of man to God, indeed the ways of man are presented as the way of God. It confirms the essential rightness of things as they are. It affirms the values of the powerful and how they gained control. It lauds the lifestyles of the affluent as the norm to which all should aspire. The rhetoric of exclusion/inclusion offers no standpoint from which mainline society might be challenged and changed. The door is not a path. 'Blessed are the excluded.' Society at large does not believe it. It looks to help the excluded join the majority. It cannot see anything of worth in the excluded. 'Blessed are the excluded.' Nor do the excluded believe it. The amelioration of their condition must be bought at a price. They must believe, or claim to believe, the ruling ideology that they are to blame and that they must be kitted out with those skills which will make them members of society. Didn't George Orwell write on this subject? In their deprivation the excluded are persuaded that they have nothing of value to contribute to the well-being of society at large. Before them lies a door, not a path.

What might they contribute to the society that has everything? Some have found the clue in the description of contemporary life as 'post-Fordist'. This is a postmodern term and it is tempting to fall into the romantic rhetoric of postmodern analysis and claim that the excluded must be valued as the Other, the Different. In the postmodern world there are no longer absolute moral or aesthetic standards. No lifestyle can be imposed as the norm. The näivety of this perspective is as embarrassing as it is irresponsible. In any case it does not work. From the perspective of the ideology of exclusion/inclusion the excluded are not the Other from whom we might learn but merely the Lesser at whom we take fright. They are viewed not as the Different by whom we might be enriched, but as the Deprived who are but ourselves impoverished.

Postmodern analysis finds grand narratives incredible, but easily succumbs to contemporary ideologies.

The categories of those whom Jesus called 'blessed' are secular, not religious. This befits a God who by his own admission does not hang about religious buildings in metropolitan city centres, but is more likely to be found on peripheral council estates. He is more interested in the poor who have not chosen poverty, the deprived rather than the ascetic. We should not be surprised therefore that the excluded are blessed and that it too is a secular category. They are not blessed because of their deprivation but because they are a witness to the Kingdom of God in a society which has handed over sovereignty to the market. Can the excluded save our society or will they continue to be understood as evidence of our failure to be absolutely committed to the Market? Faith in the Market is promoted by the ideology of neo-liberalism. Its *credo* contains the attributes which were formerly applied to the Christian God: it is almighty (there is no alternative), omniscient (no government intervention) and omnipresent (global).

Notes

1 Luke 6:22.
2 Duncan B. Forrester, *On Human Worth: A Christian Vindication of Equality* (London: SCM Press, 2001).
3 Julio de Santa Ana, *Good News to the Poor: The Challenge of the Poor in the History of the Church* (Geneva: WCC, 1977), p. 15.
4 Albert Cleage, *Black Christian Nationalism* (New York: William Morrow & Co., 1972), p. 163.
5 Albert Cleage, *The Black Messiah* (New York: Sheed & Ward, 1969), p. 17.
6 Cleage, *Black Christian Nationalism*, p. xxvi.
7 Cleage, *The Black Messiah*, p. 154.
8 Cleage, *Black Christian Nationalism*, p. 24.
9 *Ibid.*, p. xxx.
10 *Ibid.*, p. 197.
11 *Ibid.*, p. xxxvii.
12 *Ibid.*, p. 13.
13 *Ibid.*
14 Quoted in Nelson Mandela, 'The Rivonia Trial', in *The Struggle is My Life* (London: International Defence and Aid Fund for South Africa, 1978), p. 157.
15 Steve Biko, *I Write What I Like: A Selection of His Writings* (London: Bowerdean Press, 1978), p. 182.
16 *Ibid.*, p. 29.

17 *Ibid.*, p. 68.
18 *Ibid.*, p. 22.
19 *Ibid.*, p. 24.
20 *Ibid.*, p. 21.
21 Gustavo Gutiérrez, *We Drink from Our Own Wells* (London: SCM Press, 1984), p. 125.
22 Jon Sobrino, *The True Church and the Poor* (London: SCM Press, 1984), p. 95.
23 Cleage, *Black Christian Nationalism*, p. 139.
24 Cleage, *The Black Messiah*, p. 179.
25 *Ibid.*
26 *Ibid.*, p. 234.
27 Biko, *I Write What I Like*, p. 75.
28 Jos Berghman, 'Social exclusion in Europe: policy context and analytical framework', in Graham Room (ed.), *Beyond the Threshold: The Measurement and Analysis of Social Exclusion* (Bristol: Policy Press, 1995), p. 16.
29 Alistair Kee, 'Underdevelopment and how to maintain it', *The Record* (New York: Teacher's College, Columbia University 1968), Vol. 69, pp. 321–9.
30 David Byrne, *Social Exclusion* (Buckingham: Open University Press, 1999), p. 55.
31 Report by the Social Exclusion Unit, *Bringing Britain Together: A National Strategy for Neighbourhood Renewal* (HMSO, CM 4045, 1998).
32 John Veit-Wilson, quoted in Byrne, *Social Exclusion*, p. 4.
33 www.theonion.com/onion3323/popemeek.html
34 Veit-Wilson, in Byrne, *Social Exclusion*, p. 53.
35 John Nelson, quoted in Byrne, *Social Exclusion*, p. 53.
36 Byrne, *Social Exclusion*, p. xi.

Chapter 22

In the Centre there are no Fragments:
Teologías Desencajadas
(Reflections on Unfitting Theologies)

MARCELLA MARÍA ALTHAUS-REID

Everlastingly chained to a fragment of the Whole, man himself (*sic*) develops into nothing but a fragment; everlastingly in his ear the monotonous sound of the wheel that he turns, he never develops the harmony of his being.

Friedrich Schiller, *On the Aesthetic Education of Man*
(Oxford: Clarendon Press, 1997) p. 35

To put this more scientifically, I shall say that the reproduction of labour power requires not only the reproduction of its skills but also, at the same time, a reproduction of its submission to the rules of the established order.

Louis Althusser, 'Ideology and ideological state apparatuses',
Althusser, *Lenin and Philosophy* (London: New Left Books, 1971), p. 132

When are theological fragments only fragments, that is pieces which fell from a totality but still retain some identity linked with that original centre of belonging? What qualifies a fragment to be a mere piece estranged from a self-defining totality, as for instance, a theological totality, and not an *Otherness* in itself, belonging to a different kind of evaluative and symbolic structure? Where does prophecy find its place, in *Otherness* requiring conversion (as in the order of, for, instance, a Christian totality) or even disjunction? Confronting these questions, we need recognizing that what any 'centre' understands as 'fragments' may sometimes be only detached parts of its own legal claim. After all, quoting Lucía Etxebarria, we may say that, for totalitarian thinking, 'all novelty is an insult'[1] and that, in Christian theology, the prophetic voices of dissent can easily be seen as mere fragments of a recognized truth. Obviously, we know that the fragment belongs to the centre precisely because the central truth is still recognizible in it. That may

365

be the paradoxical case of paradigms of inculturation, which aims to find a home (of language and concepts translated into praxis) in, for instance, alien structures of theological praxis. That may be the case of theology as an exercise of translating theology. Thus, it is interesting to notice how Althusser finds in ideological fragments the whole structure of the dominating paradigms left intact even if the main ideological discourse is presented in an oblique, non-transparent (or fragmentary) way at the margins.[2] The problem is that this makes sometimes innocent theologians happy. From a Christian colonial perspective, if the natives see Jesus as one of their own, as happened in the inculturation of Christian theology, it may be regarded as successful, that is to say that people who come from different cosmological understandings have appropriated the essence of Jesus beyond the traditional cultural vestments of Jesus. Yet, is it not right to consider that Jesus is still a translated Messiah? That reminds me of a conversation I had some years ago with a young Chinese student who was considering becoming a Christian, but who was struggling to see Jesus as a man of her own Chinese community. Her argument went from seeing Jesus dressed as a Chinese, speaking Chinese and fully sharing Chinese culture to what a Chinese Jesus' praxis would be. At that point she stopped, and asked me quizzically, 'Would not then this Chinese Jesus share Confucianism instead of the Gospels with my people?' Her final argument was in a way related to the dialectics of identity and translation theology. In Christianity, these fragments of faith in which we rejoice when we see our people engaging with what we call 'popular religiosity', may be, at the end, still fragments from the religion of the empire. In them, we can recognize the point made by Althusser. The main ideological discourse in theology is there, but in a non-transparent way. Where and how can we find the authenticity of Christianity in the margins?

These questions of identity and prophecy in public theology in relation to theological margins are deeply engaged in several aspects of Duncan Forrester's reflections regarding a theology of fragments.[3] Following a hermeneutics of suspicion, we are highlighting here issues mainly pertaining to conflictual aspects of fragmentary identity and the complex characteristics of their hermeneutical behaviour. By claiming that in the centre there are no fragments, I intend to enter into a dialogue with Forrester's socio-theological project, unveiling the dimension of neocolonial dependency of concepts such as margins or fragments. In the same way that Spivak has asked in a seminal essay if the subaltern could ever speak,[4] without being subsumed in a colonial articulation of discourse, I would like to posit the question if theological fragments can ever overcome the hegemonic matrix which gave them their origin, even if in a dissenting mode. It may be that the condition for fragments to be able to speak out is for us to cease to consider them fragments, but wholeness (*integridades*) in themselves. 'Wholeness', which I am translating here from the Spanish concept of '*integridad*', refers also to that important aspect of the option of the poor. To be *íntegro* also means to be of a whole piece, respected, honest and speaking truth to power. *Íntegra* is the person who stands independently and rebellious to confront a social, economic or theological order which is imposing and powerful. *Integridades* are not fragments; instead they represent the different.

In considering these reflections, it may also be important to follow a fragmentary way of reflection. After all, the discussions of recent years on *écriture féminine* as presented by philosophers such as Hélène Cixous challenge us to fit what we say with the style in which we write. The structures of writing theology and their logic and order, dictated from Western androcentric and hierarchical patterns, show the first difficulty we may be facing in the theological discourse today. Theology as a discourse may sometimes be working in structurally sinful ways. It may be difficult to think in terms of a more authentic theology of fragments unless our style of writing is allowed to contradict old patterns. When dealing with the challenge of alternative thinking in the midst of totalitarian globalization processes, we should remember that nothing different can come from the old patterns of theological praxis.

Fragments Reflections

On Integrity

To mention here a framework of analysis such as post-colonialism is appropriate when we remember that the current globalization of capitalism has its historical precedents, precisely linked to the creation of colonial and neocolonial empires, and the struggle of people to remain *íntegra*, that is, not as a fragment of the political given, but in search of people's own identity. Capitalism, in two of its previous historical processes, included the *Conquista* of the Americas and the complex consequences of the invasion. One of these consequences was the beginning of the creation of a colonial world model. Therefore, it is important for us to consider that our theological reflections on globalization processes should have a sense of continuity with this past. In a way, we are called to gather different traditions of the Church to inform our reflections. For instance, there is the tradition of oppression which did not allow dialogue except on its own terms. Similarly, there are the traditions of a rebellious people; of their Christian nonconformity and of a policy of silencing which was broken in many ways by anonymous people.

By that I mean that any reflections on margins and theological fragments need a neocolonial framework of analysis, lest we forget that the identity of our theological reflections is closely dependent on modes of interpretation which, far from detached or neutral, are economically determined. That includes the production of theological praxis in global capitalism, and also the effective production of society (patriarchal Western models). The theologian is a worker and theology is a product of work. I stand in a faculty of divinity as a worker amongst workers, together with the servitors and the cleaners. My theological praxis shares a matrix of increasing exploitation and uniformity common to these and other workers of the world. A theologian does more than consume concepts and traditions: she engages with forms of production, in this case, her theological praxis, in the limitations and constraints of the present globalization processes as with everybody else. How then can a theologian engage with the *integridades* at the margins, if she is not even aware of the conditions of production of her own work?

As I would like to cast suspicion on the independent identity of theologians and theological fragments alike, I would also like to introduce into this hermeneutical circle more conflictual, dialogical elements, such as the possibility of subversion in theological fragments which come from the underside of theological history. For that we need to localize instead of globalize our discourse. 'The poor' (as in the option for the poor) has worked sometimes as a big blanket category in which people (women, for instance) are easily subsumed. That is, by the way, the modus operandi of ideology. People get subsumed by ideas. People become things, and ideas, paraphrasing Marx, become people.[5]

Duncan Forrester's theology of fragments is a theology struggling with the processes of the objectification of people, and searching for a strategy of transformation. His is a theology searching at the margins for the different and the transformative which is already (using a post-colonial metaphor) 'speaking back to the Empire'. But real transformation in a world which hears that there is no alternative to the market is subversive and produces nasty responses, because rebellions have more in common with Genoa 2001 than with romantic tales of people's rights. Such subversion, lying in what Forrester calls 'fragments of truth', makes of fragments, theological aliens, or unfitting truths not well received. I welcome that. That prophetic, dissenting role presents theological fragments as if they belonged – using Forrester's own metaphor – to another theological quarry. They may belong to another sacred mountain, or, to use a biblically inspired metaphor, to another Sinai, in dissent from an imperial North Atlantic understanding of God and truth. That might make subversive fragments difficult to fit. They are fragments belonging to what, in another place, I have described as 'Indecent theologies',[6] that is, unfitting theologies which do not conform towards any centralized line of intellectual exchange, linked to the evaluative powers which determine current values and the totalitarian symbolic structures of the market. I have said that theologians should stand as workers amongst workers. Therefore the authorized frame of exchanges of the market society and its contradictions may have become so common that they affect whole communities, including churches and faculties of divinity alike, in such a way that only a structural revision, that is, a revision of the conditions of production and construction of theological praxis, can help us to move forward.

Unfittingness

This indecency of unfitting theologies may be seen as the characteristic of models of fragmentary theology independent from the expectations of the centre. They may be in conflict with neocolonialism and its patriarchal order, and they may refuse to accommodate to such expectations. These theologies of fragments may have as their main and only characteristic their 'unfittingness' or reluctance to perform the part of a 'popular theology' or theology at the margins, if by that is meant the game of adaptation to which neocolonial centres of knowledge submit different understandings in their politics of re-presentation and theological translation. For in many instances, in a cruel twist of power, the so-called theologies from the margins have been manipulated to support or justify the ideologies of the centre by simply restoring given understandings in an exercise of cultural translations.

However, there is more to unfitting theologies than just not fitting into the jigsaw. I have used the Spanish word, *desencajada* for unfitting, because it is more appealing to the theological imagination than its English counterpart. *Teologías desencajadas*, apart from not fitting in certain structures, are also distressed theologies, for *desencajado* means out of harmony, fearful or wild. *Desencajadas* are the faces of the *Other*; the faces of the poor, expressing anguish and suffering because, in the middle of oppression, people cannot disguise their feelings and thoughts. So should it be with theologies from the margins if they are honest, showing dissent and also their own vulnerability in the midst of suffering. *Desencajado* is the state in which these theological fragments are when they realize that there are no desirable possibilities to reconcile themselves with a neocolonial or global theological praxis, even if that cast them in a real periphery location. They are called to honest subversion.

On Memory and Traditions

For honest theological subversion, the gathering of different and honest theological traditions has an important role to play. There is already a theology of integrity in the margin where race, sex and gender and class elements are intimately related. Honouring the tradition of popular historians from my continent, one task is to make visible the invisible story of resistance of common people in opposition to the centre. Therefore, instead of searching into the well-known theology of resistance from De las Casas to Montesinos, I would like to reflect on the theology of subversive fragments as it comes from unknown women in dissent during the colonial times of the British Empire. In honouring these reflections, we are reminded that there is an integrity at the margins of theology clamouring for its own space. These testimonies are seldom part of any tradition of the Church. The main structures of the Church and theology alike have never taken any of these memories from the margin as their own tradition.

Therefore, honouring the theological style of liberationist reflection, I would like to share a story which is part of this unacknowledged tradition of the Church, and as such, a real, *íntegro* fragment. This story is taken from an issue of the *Women's Missionary Magazine* published in 1913. Church magazines during the time of the colonial missions show us sometimes what the real praxis of the living theology of the times was. We can trust their testimonies more than theological treatises published then because in them we find theology in action with less abstract theory and with fewer lies, too. The context of this story is related to us in some way, because expansive capitalism, in the form of colonization, had many a common cause with globalization. This is a story of a Purdah Party, and a group of women who went to it. It is a story which has something to tell us about theological fragments and fragmented people, too.

Fragments from Ajmeer: A Theology

On 6 September 1913, a Purdah Party was held at Ajmeer. The article from the *Women's Missionary Magazine* reports that one hundred Indian

370

women were present. The article is old and the theology is strongly colonial, but the women were neither old nor colonial. Moreover, their theological insights grow fresher all the time. The article, through its numerous sexist and racist statements, punctuates the reading by asking how the heathen could be reached when they were so dark, so corrupt and so many, while the missionaries (who were characterized by the opposite virtues) were so white, so pure and so few. This is a symbolic scene of encounter between a theology represented by the few at the centre and the masses at the margin who need to be reached. It is a familiar representation also for some of us in the area of political theology.

The appeal for money to sustain the enterprise was an important part of the article. The expansion of capitalism, achieved in part by the useful tool of Christianity, was obtained at a high cost. It required what Foucault would call a complex set of docile bodies in place, in addition to policies of land allocation and the putting in place of new arrangements for transport and international trade. Nowadays, when religion is not so crucial for market expansion, we tend to forget how politically and strategically important the Church was at the time – though some view this transition with feelings of nostalgia and regret.

The article from the church magazine goes through the usual banalities of Christian women's clubs. There were competitions on the recalling of proverbs and the naming of flowers. Indeed, the competition on the making of buttonholes threatened to collapse because nobody knew what they were, until the *Mem Sahib* taught them to make one. These are images of an emerging pattern of globalization. In this case, a market was created which required the production of new styles in ladies' clothes under European influences. But there were also colonial influences on the social function of food, notably in the tea party. While European types of food were introduced into India, some Indian food in turn was introduced into Europe. In this we see the effects of the globalization of products and styles of consumption similar to the McDonald phenomenon of our world today. Europe was eating tomatoes, and cocoa, while tea parties with afternoon dainties were introduced in Ajmeer. The introduction of sugar into European food radically transformed diets and lifestyles – not to mention the effect on children's teeth.

However, this story is not only about women making garlands and drinking tea. Surprisingly these women created a discussion space for what Duncan Forrester has called theological fragments, but a theology in the dissenting mode or, to put it another way, an 'out of (colonial) tune

371

theology'.The point is that some of the Indian women were asked to speak to the assembly. All of them shared stories of powerful women, whose power was to be found in social and/or religious dissenting. I would like to mention these women by name: Gulab Devi, Begum Fulsum and Ms Metha. Gulab Devi presented a paper on someone who refused to marry unless she could choose her own husband, and how she succeeded in doing so. Begum Fulsum remembered Nur Jahan, who was such an influential woman during Emperor Jaganhir's life that her face appeared on the local coins. She commented on Jahan's administrative talents, encouraging women to think about high administrative work as part of women's natural talents. After them came Ms Dhanjishah Metha, a Parsee. She gave a provocative paper in which she claimed that Persian women have traditionally been not only physically strong but also trained in the military arts. They went to battle, and some exercised their muscles by carrying cows up twenty steps. 'Practice makes perfect', was Ms Metha's reply to doubts about women's strength. She ended by saying that in studying science, art and medicine, Persian women could easily compete with any European woman or man. Concerning Christian philanthropy, she claimed that in Persia, as in Europe, there is a tradition of ladies of wealth and philanthropic instinct, who have given money for hospitals, schools and charitable institutions in general. What we call today development projects, after all, were not such a novelty when brought by Christians to her country. In a way, all the women, and especially Ms Metha, were talking back forcefully and theologically to the empire, specifically to the Christian Empire, from a dissenting perspective which, interestingly, dissented both from foreign missionary customs but also from the patriarchal structures of their own cultures.

What is important here is to rescue these women's fragmentary theology as one way of reclaiming a subversive identity which could sustain a very different kind of theology, a theology which would probably be irreconcilable with official theology. Therefore, while the writer of the article keeps asking the readers the question, 'How can we reach these women?', a more significant question emerges. How can these women reach the readers? This is an important issue for political theology today. How can subversive fragments reach (central) theology? What kind of power could these theological fragments have? How might these fragments reach the centre in order to produce an implosion? Obviously, subversive fragments have been talking to the centre throughout history. Why have they had so little impact? Why have they remained dispersed, disempowered, marginalized and forgotten?

Forgetting Ms Metha

Reading the speeches, and especially the words of Ms Metha, arouses feelings of indignation. The very essence of colonial theology, past and present, is exposed as the art of forgetting Ms Metha. There is here a whole hermeneutical circle based on ignoring people's voices. These women were articulate and had a voice which did not need a theological exercise of translation. They even knew the empowerment exercise of the theology of stories, in their sharing of their own and those of their communities. And they did this long before Hispanics in the United States started their *Mujerista* theology, and long before womanist and feminist liberation theology. They started thinking in public theology terms long before political theology, too. These women opened up the space for theological fragments in dissent and conflict to claim their place, but because Christianity and patriarchy were as incompatible as the Gospel under the empire expansion, they did not stand a chance. They could talk, but they could not act on what they said, because theology has always required some line of compatibility amongst the parts (fragments) and the defined whole. It was Marx who announced that the conflicts between the parts which form a whole are not only unavoidable but desirable. Only the presence of fragmentation in totalitarian praxis puts, paraphrasing Heraclitus, the presence of the limitations of the finite in the context of totality. When theological fragments have that quality, they seem also to manifest the instability or impermanence of theological conceptualizations. In other words, they draw the line between different ideological alliances and their sacralization systems. However, theological fragments are not revolutionary guarantees per se, since a fragment acknowledges necessarily a belonging to some totality. But sometimes, as Ms Metha and the ladies who spoke at the Purdah Party in Ajmeer seem to prove, the fragments are not loose pieces but whole structures of praxis in themselves. The structures of the *Other* are not what colonial thinking may call 'fragments' if in them there is a desire to establish that anything outside *Sameness* must be an adherence of some kind. That is the theological problem. Instability and impermanence, which fragments announce, are either rejected or assigned to oblivion. Popular theologies can fall into that mechanism if cultural theologies forget the economic base (in which sexual thought is based) which affects theological thinking. However, unfitting theological elements are precious things because they carry with them the possibility of breakthroughs. There were incompatible fragments present in the beginning of liberation theologies, which gave them enough elements for the substantial departure of particular alliances of ideology

373

and theology. Only those of us who have somehow witnessed the liberation movement in Latin America know how deeply provocative, against the grid and dissenting was liberation theology. There were many Ms Methas there too. Therefore, ignored or persecuted, liberationists proved in their time that their theology did not belong to the core theology of state.

Incompatibility

Liberation theologies have been *teologías desencajadas* made by people who were also *desencajada*, that is, keeping strong integrity in the midst of their vulnerability and powerlessness. As with the women in Ajmeer, I have elsewhere discussed how the continuation of that radical stand of liberation theologies lies precisely in that movement of identification and encouragement of new incompatible fragments which allows us to act and reflect theologically in a different, alternative way. For instance, sexuality and poverty are incompatible fragments which cannot be assimilated with any form of static theologies (and static in the double sense of immobility and also of their relation to *state* types of theology). Race analysis is also an incompatible fragment. Traditions and the ordering role of Western-based systematic theologies do not accommodate fragments easily. The Christological debate in feminist theologies has also shown us what cannot be integrated because it does not fit easily, for example the 'texts of terrors' read by women in their Bibles.

Developmentalism and Political Theology: No love affair there

In the same way that in the midst of the current expansion of capitalism in the world, developmentalism struggles to eliminate the contradictions of the system by a moral work against poverty, some forms of political theologies have been tempted into moralizing about what should be changed in order to have a society of peace and justice. The theology of cancelling the external debt is an example of this: well motivated but short-sighted and short-circuited. The difference is once again to be found in the identity of the fragments we are talking about here: basically, whether we want to encourage theologically subversive fragments to stand up in opposition or to integrate with the structure which gave them the name of fragments in the first instance. The problem in this case is that, in the particular structure of totalitarianism, no alternative thinking can recognize diversity without committing suicide.

In the theology and globalization discourses we consider that the theologian has basically two options: we could easily follow a moral, developmental discourse on the lines of improvement, for instance, asking the World Bank to listen to the poor, or we could indecently bare our bums as protestors against the power of the corporations to destroy life, as in Seattle. As George Monbiot has said, when intelligence is banned from public life, baring our buttocks at George Bush and the power of the corporations is one of the few things left for thinking people to do.[7] I could not have put it more clearly in my own *Indecent* theological proposals. We are doing political theology in times of desperation. Baring our bums in public has become a gesture of thinking people and perhaps of thinking theologians too. We need a political theology much more disruptive in thinking but also in writing. Or in not writing, but joining rebellious people. A political theology, the aim of which is to destabilize the status quo, and to destabilisze itself.

Localizing the Unfitting Fragments: Some Methodological Reflections

We are reflecting on popular rebellions such as that of the women in Ajhmeer or what Prime Minister Tony Blair has called 'the travelling anarchist circus' of the anti-capitalist movement. We are still following Marx in that double possibility of rupture or regression which is part of the dynamic between fragments and the whole to which they conform. But we must not forget that Marx's method of study was one of abstraction, that is, a method based on approximations to the problem which he wanted to study, carefully selecting the key elements which required intensive investigation. For instance, Marx abstracted the dyadic class struggle for his own particular investigation of capital. Today we would call this a 'localization' method, and should probably start by asking first which specific aspect of the current expansion of capitalism we would want or need to investigate, and second which are the essential and non-essential elements which need to be differentiated. If we say that our interests are, for instance, the current processes of social exclusion, then it is important to clarify that we will be dealing with some selected aspects of this reality, theologically framed according to our perspective and location in relation to them. For instance, I would like to know what kind of theology of subversive fragments could make an effective difference, or paraphrasing Marx, how theological concepts in political theology may anticipate actions. From my own perspective, I can see our theological effectiveness only if it has been preceded by a careful analysis of the theological conditions of production. As the materialist theologian which I have always been, I firmly believe that, although it is true that economics does not mechanically determine our thinking, it nevertheless affects them. Our theological thinking is affected by

375

economics especially structurally, that is, in the patterns of institutions such as the Church and the academy, and, of course, our affective relationships too. No matter what our good intentions are in the debate about globalization and social exclusion, we can never avoid the fact that our theology is done by us through different relations of the production of globalization, and that this is happening even against our will. It is with our theological production that we have entered and become fully participants in the economic structure of society. Without a serious analysis of those conditions, we might be tempted to forget that our theological reflections are very much rooted in the present capitalist structures of society. To be more specific, they are based on legal and political superstructures which condition our socio-political and spiritual processes. We are talking here about institutions, and faculties of divinity in Britain, which participate also in processes of inclusion and exclusion. What we include is as important as what we exclude.

The preceding globalization processes (the ones which culminated in the creation of colonial empires, the last one covering the period between 1870 and 1914) differ from the current one in the point of exclusion. As Manuel Castells has pointed out, the present expansion of capitalism creates exclusion by inclusion.[8] That is to say, capitalism is able to include any element which helps its mythical ineluctable growth by the use of the media and technologies of communication. According to Carlos Zaldívar, any new discovery or enterprise in global capitalism is welcomed by the same logic that can leave anybody and anything aside when they no longer serve its purpose.[9] However, the first global acts of capitalism had theological opponents; there were alien fragments, such as Ms Metha in Ajmeer challenging a patriarchal colonial Christianity – and that was no mean achievement.

To have followed the example of the theological fragments of the women from Ajmeer, including that of Ms Metha, could have changed the history of theology and of political theology. They stood in contradiction to the official patriarchal theological core understanding of the time, and that could have had, amongst other things, a serious influence on a theology which equated women with nature and subordination. The environmental catastrophe in which we are living, rooted as it is in Christian patriarchal conceptions of domination over nature, and a female (subordinate) construction of nature, may not have developed. Instead of that, a different understanding of sexuality and nature could have emerged. Unfortunately, colonial and neocolonial theology is the art of forgetting and of reconciling differences in particular ways. It is a regressive and not a disruptive art. How could we identify the alien theological fragments in the scene today? How are we to see what

Luther called the obvious message of God for our times? Laughing at Ms Metha in 1913 was easy; laughing at Seattle or Genoa may be easy too. The *teologías desencajadas*, indecent or improper, may be laughing stocks at times, but they are still able to help us focus on pragmatic questions such as who revolts, and who dares to get crushed in the revolt? One cannot forget that the objectives of revolt are constitutive parts of any radical public theology. Investigating the structural conditions of production of theological thought in, for instance, British universities, can teach us why our political theologies are unfortunately not laughing stocks, but serious things that people do not take seriously at all. How that space for theological thinking is constituted, and what is censored or legitimized in it, is part of the crucial theological questioning we must do. Consider what I have said about the theologian as a worker. After all, many of us sharing our reflections for this colloquium in homage to Duncan Forrester are reflecting and writing in what Marx might have called our rate of exploitation. That is, thinking and writing in the hours which follow work, understanding work as the long hours of teaching and ever-increasing administrative duties which exceed the normal working day and go unpaid and unrecognized. This increasing administrative load includes unfortunately some research which has ceased to be research, for it should be considered a result of exploitation, demanded for institutional financial purposes instead of being born of genuine praxis and concern. The words of Schiller have become a reality for the theologian who feels 'Everlastingly chained to a fragment of the Whole', a fragment in the sense of an appendix to the monotonous sound of the market wheel that she turns, never developing the harmony of her being.

Last Fragment: The Empty Cathedral

> Se trata, pues, siempre, de la censura como institución de Estado, que dispone de la fuerza pública y que se ejerce en actos públicos. Las comisiones se nombran, se conocen, se centralizan. Los expertos de las universidades, especialmente de teología, han jugado siempre, en esto, un papel esencial (…) Pero, ¿Cómo negarlo? Hay cosas que no se pueden decir en la universidad, ni fuera de ella. Hay ciertas maneras de decir las cosas, que ni son legítimas ni están autorizadas.[10]

Jacques Derrida's essay, *Transfert ex Cathedra, Le Langage et les Institutions Philosophiques* is the basis for some of the analysis that, together with Marx's approximations, I would like to consider now for the study of the dynamic of theological fragments as breakthrough strategies for an alternative political and economic system. The point of consideration is the location of the theologizing activity, which in Britain is provided by the university community. That is the location of production. This is our Purdah Party, and there are many Ms Methas amongst us. How that space works, legitimizes and facilitates or, on the contrary, de-authorizes or censors, theological praxis is therefore an important issue. These are our conditions of production. How theologians locate themselves in that structure and how they support it or dissent from it is also important. It was Alistair Kee who made a remark to José Míguez-Bonino about the role of the university in Britain as having taken the place that in, for instance, Latin America, is still occupied by the community. There is a community nurturing in most cases the work of the Latin American theologians but, in Britain, the university has a strong censorship role on community engagement. A faculty of divinity may censor any engagement with a community through the allocation of hours of work and duties to be carried out outside working hours, in the rate of exploitation denounced by Marx. This includes, for instance, research, when done for the economic benefit of the university, using the timescale and the output (publication) of the sort that is valuable for the university. Theological research is invalidated within certain given evaluatory premises. It is no wonder that Freirean processes have seldom prospered in Britain, since they cannot be evaluated in the current financial terms. Other censorships have resulted from the policies of short, unstable contracts which have forced teachers to move from place to place searching for jobs or promotion (equivalent to salary increases in the present circumstances), thus disconnecting themselves from any long-term engagement with a geographical community. Everything plays a role in these structures of sin, and a system of promotions which are obtainable through the pursuit not of community work, but of more administrative work and publications, makes clear which values a theologian should expect to be respected. And, of course, race and gender, are sites of injustice and suffering even amongst our own colleagues. Some of our more privileged fellow theologians can speak about the poor in terms of global generalizations, while at the same time showing little or no solidarity with their comrades. There are black British theologians who no longer attend 'white conferences'. There are women excluded by many injustices in our theological communities. There is an exclusion of people fitting the competitiveness of the market. This is a form of censorship too, if we consider the black theologians who are never appointed to teach or the women whose reflections are allowed to make as much impact on the system as those of Ms Metha.

Censorship of people is also a way of thinking. As a verb, it is associated with numbers, as Derrida reminds us: *Cencere* relates to counting or to computing.[11] It is a word for accountants, for financial audit and for a kind of administrative thinking which may be defined as finding the right place for everything within a certain order. How curious, by the way, that we are now able to equate censorship with administrative demands, a framework which provides us with a quasi-technological role of prioritizing order over content or adjusting content to a given order. This is one of our sites of theological production in the context of doing theology: censorship of people by a teaching system that is very discriminatory according to race and sexuality, and discourages community involvement. Censorship is providing us with a value system which is not resisted enough, and history may judge us harshly for this.

Are we facing other forms of censorship, for instance in the theological research we do? The point is that for any faculty of divinity to have such a structure means not necessarily the banning or censoring of what is to be researched or taught, but rather the prohibiting of certain books or issues from being discussed. However, censorship also works simply by failing to provide the necessary conditions for developing any alternative praxis. For example, how can we reflect theologically (and, especially, ethically) on issues of exclusion from a structural location which is itself part of a matrix of social exclusion? How can we reflect theologically (and, especially, ethically) on issues of exclusion when the poor are excluded from becoming students, when Third World students are excluded not only by ridiculously high fees, but by the insistence on accepting only Western patterns of argument, evaluation and assessment? How can we reflect theologically (and, especially, ethically) on issues of exclusion when complex webs of exclusion based on race and sexuality exist amongst teachers? And, finally, how can we discuss exclusion when we exclude any discussion on the university's own structures of exclusion, including the exclusion of research and theological praxis which cannot be demonstrated to be cost-effective for the system? What kind of efficacious public theology can we develop then, in this almost unchallenged context? Only if our first theological challenge is directed to our own context, the one which provides for us the conditions for our theological production, may we find an opportunity. It is easy to forget that the first challenges of liberation theologies were always structural. For example, the Basic Communities in Latin America and the challenge to apartheid in South Africa were first of all political challenges; theology was a second act because structural changes are also needed to liberate theology from its many captivities. The lack of resistance against the domestication of universities that we are suffering is notable. Our projects are directed to attract money, to increase profit. These are the values of the market. We do the theology of the market since we are, as Derrida says, happy to speak without doing, and happy to speak truth without contributing to a serious breakdown of the public paradigms.[12]

The theological fragments which are potentially revolutionary are not welcome in our structures. Duncan Forrester's theology has been, and still is, one which would like transformative strategies to be seen to be in place. For theological fragments are not to be integrated into the system, but simply followed as if they were a prophetic part of 'the travelling anarchist circus', as lone voices in the wilderness of the logic of the market. The ambiguity of intellectuals is always something people fear because they smell the scent of easy betrayal. The challenge to the conditions of theological production, including the structures of the present university system in our country, is the first chapter of any theology of exclusion. It is a strategic, if also costly, ambition of honest theologians who know that in the present moment the need is for alternatives, not adaptation. We may ponder sometimes on the lack of collective resistance that we theologians are presenting to the increasing McDonaldization of higher education. As reports appear on performance-related pay, measuring academic success in the very terms of commercial output, we theologians can surely claim to be doing theology in the belly of the beast. In reality, we are back to Althusser's materialist ideology, because the order under which we are increasingly producing theology ensures, as Althusser would say, the subjection to the ruling ideology of the market, and also the mastery of its practice.[13] In our theology we may be denouncing social exclusion and the steady deterioration of life under the expansion of capitalism, but the underlying reality is our reproduction of submission to a university system which is seriously undermining any possibility of alternative praxis in theology. Ideologies are not speeches, but practices. Social exclusion is a real thing that happens to real people. When imposed statistics and evaluative control methods start to interpellate us as proper, just and creative facilitators, then there is little difference between being answerable to an increasingly totalitarian regime or to a totalitarian God. In both cases, a system of confession, guilt and punishment may be required. For Freire, who followed Althusser in this, it was the teacher who needed to be interpellated first, in order to mirror a combination of action and reflection to the students. It is the theologian who is the subject of market interpellation by structures beyond her control.

Until we confront this ideological manipulation that we are facing, there will be no possibility of doing any serious public theology, at least in the sense of effectiveness. Such a practice requires structural agency too in the conditions of learning and teaching, from where theological reflection should arise. To do a public theology under these conditions means to interrupt and intervene with alternative practices. It is for this reason that I started this chapter by speaking of *teologías desencajadas*, because they can never willingly fit or adapt themselves to elements of capitalist expansion. There are theological fragments which carry with them the possibilities of disrupting and working their way through a transformation of our current system, and we could start, following Marx's method of approximation, by making a list of dispersed fragments of reflection and practice which stubbornly refuse to be *included* because they want to *be*. There is resistance. There are more Porto Alegres to come, more Genoas, but public theologians need to find their own Genoa, too, and their own 'travelling anarchist circus' to join. The agents of transformation may be found today, as Amin has suggested, only in a radical heterodoxy.[14] Today integration threatens the theologian, and especially the political theologian, through developmentalism masquerading as realism, the false realism of the claim that 'there is no alternative' with its moral illusions of bettering capitalism. These are difficult times. We cannot improve theology and Church praxis in order to resist and reorganize an anti-capitalist theological movement. This would not work. However, the good thing is that there are people in the streets protesting and celebrating a loose alliance of interests against globalization. There is the liberation theology of Europe, singing songs and dancing while showing bums to the G8. There are challenges from action from people who are not fragments at the margins but, on the contrary, integrities in dissent. Would theology ever show its bum to power, and to its participation in unjust structures of production? Can a Church which is not able to conscientize itself in respect of a simple issue such as gender expect to transform itself into a community based on different ways of relating and organization?

The history of the Church and of theology is made up of a mixture of betrayals and liberative gestures, and answers to these questions are not easy to predict. However, we are living under different social and economic configurations which require us to conceive of a new agenda for doing theology and being Church. The first task, however, needs to be what Amin calls 'the reconstruction of the social power of the popular classes'.[15] In theological terms, it means a serious disruption and redistribution of power, and of strategic institutional thinking. The task of public theology is precisely strategic, by providing a space for the people who are integrities in dissent at the margins to engage in a network of thinking and sharing experiences. As Joshua called on the people to choose between two ways, so public theology needs to choose to be with the dissenters or with the developmentalists, to discern fragments from fragments, in order to find that alternative Utopia which still eludes us.

Notes

1 Lucía Etxebarria, *La Letra Futura. El Dedo en la Llaga: Cuestiones sobre Arte, Literatura, Creación y Crítica* (Barcelona: Destino, 2001), p. 81.

2 See, for instance, Althusser's analysis of how ruling ideologies represent themselves in rituals forever interpellating individuals, in his paper, 'Idealogy and ideological state apparatuses', *Lenin and Philosophy* (London: New Left Books, 1971), p. 181.

3 Cf. Duncan B. Forrester, *On Human Worth* (London: SCM Press, 2001), especially Ch. 8, 'Equality and the politics of inclusion'.

4 G. Spivak, 'Can the subaltern speak?', in C. Nelson and L. Grossberg (eds), *Marxism and the Interpretation of Culture* (Urbana, IL: University of Illinois Press, 1988).

5 For further analysis on this point, see for example my article, '¿Bién sonados? The future of mystical connections in liberation theology', *Political Theology*, 3 (November 2000): 46–7.

6 Cf. my book, *Indecent Theology: Theological Perversions on Sex, Gender and Politics* (London: Routledge, 2000).

7 See George Monbiot's article, 'Stealing Europe', *Guardian* (20 June 2001), p. 15.

8 For this point, see Manuel Castells, 'Information technology and global capitalism', in Will Hutton and Anthony Giddens (eds.), *On the Edge: Living in Global Capitalism* (London: Jonathan Cape, 2000).

9 Carlos Alonso Zaldívar, *Al Contrario: Sobre Liderazgo, Globalisación e Injerencia* (Madrid: Espasa, 2001), p. 118.

10 'This is concerned, as usual, with censorship as a state institution. The state has the public force at its disposition and exercises it in public acts. Commissions are nominated, known and centralized. The university experts, especially in the faculties of theology, had always a special role to play in this ... But, how can we deny this? There are things that cannot be said in the university or outside the university. There are certain ways to speak about certain things which are neither legitimate nor authorized.' Jacques Derrida, 'Cátedra Vacante: Censura, Maestría y Magistralidad', in Derrida, *El Lengueje y las Instituciones Filosóficas* (Barcelona: Paidós, 1995), p. 92 (my translation).

11 *Ibid.*, p. 93.
12 *Ibid.*, p. 89.
13 Althusser, 'Ideology and ideological state apparatuses', p. 132.
14 Samir Amin, *Capitalism in the Age of Globalisation* (London: Zed Books, 2000), p. 77.
15 Amin, *Capitalism in the Age of Globalization*, p. 152.

Chapter 23

Public Theology
in an Age of Voter Apathy

ELAINE GRAHAM

Introduction

On the weekend after the 2001 British General Election, most newspapers
gave prominence to pictures of Tony and Cherie Blair and their children
posing happily outside No. 10 Downing Street. There was good reason to
celebrate; the government had been re-elected for a second term, a feat not
achieved by any other Labour administration in the party's history. What is
more, a Commons majority of 167 represented another 'landslide' victory
for the party, an unprecedented pattern of success.[1]

Closer analysis of the inside contents of these same newspapers, however,
told a slightly different story, suggesting that the outcome of Campaign 2001
might have been something of a hollow victory. The so-called 'landslide'
could hardly be said to represent a popular mandate, given that only 59
per cent of the electorate had bothered to vote, the lowest turnout since
1918. Labour's own share of the vote stood at 40.7 per cent.[2] No wonder
commentators referred to the result as an 'Apathetic Landslide'.[3] A particular
cause for concern in many quarters was the lack of interest amongst younger
people: less than four in ten of those aged 18 to 25 cast their vote. And, in
some inner-city constituencies ('old' Labour's traditional heartland), little
more than one-third of those registered to vote actually did so.[4]

Opinion is divided, however, as to the significance that can really be
attached to so-called 'voter apathy'. Some analysts identify specific factors
about Campaign 2001 that failed to generate enthusiasm, and argue that,
despite low turnout on this particular occasion, the electorate's commitment
to the political system is undiminished. Others, however, trace emergent
patterns throughout the West which suggest an unprecedented and widespread loss of faith in public institutions: not only a disaffection with the

organs of the state (Parliament, legal system, civil service) but also a with-drawal from voluntary and community activity, including trade unions, community associations and organized religion. The implications of this, they argue, are serious for the health of participatory democracy.

Even though a more considered examination of 'voter apathy' which follows in this chapter sketches a quite complex and subtle picture, such research still raises important questions not only for political debate in general but for the discipline of public theology in particular. On one level, the increasing fragility of many civic institutions may confirm fears about 'the withering of public hope',[5] a symptom of the fragmentation of moral discourse that has preoccupied public theology and social ethics since Alasdair MacIntyre's *After Virtue*. Yet whilst public trust in the institutions of participatory democracy may rest to a large extent on moral agreements concerning *procedural* norms by which matters such as human rights, democ-racy, freedom and the rule of law may be debated, it also requires us to think about the *iterative* processes by which individuals connect to the wider social order. It concerns not only what kinds of values need to inform the public domain, but also the very infrastructure through which the fabric of the state, public institutions and civil society is maintained. But in changing contexts, increasingly one of rapid globalization, it is not simply a matter of defending 'politics as usual', but looking at how institutions facilitate the common good and respond to the challenge of social exclusion.

Such developments have an impact on the discourse of public theology, not only because Christian churches have traditionally been actively engaged in politics at many levels – from practical service delivery through to moral debate – but also because any contraction of the public domain could radi-cally affect the kinds of contributions deemed acceptable or legitimate. Amidst such problems, however, new opportunities emerge, not least in the shape of New Labour's encouragement of faith-communities' participation in urban regeneration and welfare services, and the insistent question of the role of organized religion in relation to the conduct of civil society. Public theology in the twenty-first century will need to address these fundamental changes and realignments taking place in the political process, and work to articulate a rejuvenated theological discourse capable of addressing the complexities and divisions of contemporary society.

Voter Apathy

Two key sources may serve as initial indicators of what really happened in the British General Election: MORI's survey of a sample of the electorate

386

during and after election 2001,[6] and a qualitative study of Basildon in Essex, carried out between 1992 and 1997.[7] A third source, analysis of comparative electorates in the West, also helps to put British evidence in context.[8]

MORI's research was carried out on a sample of 18,000 people in two phases, covering a period early in the election campaign, 9–15 May (Phase 1), and one immediately after the election itself, 9–18 June (Phase 2). The questions covered public attitudes towards voting, the campaign itself and the electoral process in general. The survey found marked variation in reported voter participation, especially by age, the lowest rates being amongst the younger age groups. Thirty-nine per cent of 18–24-year-olds interviewed had voted, rising to 59 per cent (the national average for the electorate as a whole) amongst 35–44-year-olds, to levels of 65 per cent amongst 45–54-year-olds, and 69 per cent and 70 per cent respectively for 55–64 and 65+.

Participation also varied across socio-economic groups, ranging between 68 per cent amongst professionals, to 53 per cent amongst unskilled workers. The differentials are similar depending on type of housing tenure: those who own their house outright were recorded at 68 per cent, mortgage homeowners at 59 per cent (again, the UK average) to council tenants and private tenants at 52 per cent and 46 per cent respectively.

Given Labour's lead in the opinion polls throughout the campaign, and the size of the Commons majority it was defending, it was perhaps unsurprising that many people decided that there was little at stake in the campaign. Certainly, only 36 per cent agreed with the proposition that 'voting would make a difference'.[9] However, the survey finds little evidence of this being a symptom of endemic cynicism with democracy, and concludes that the campaign itself was the cause of most lack of interest. In Phase 1, for example, 65 per cent of respondents reported being actively interested in politics; but, by Phase 2, even 61 per cent of that sample admitted they had not found the election campaign interesting.

MORI's research was sponsored by the Electoral Commission, who made much in its commentary of the fact that two-thirds of the electorate still believed that voting makes a difference, even if they were sceptical about Campaign 2001 itself. Its report concluded: 'civic duty and habit are key motivations to voting; … people have positive attitudes towards voting.… Interest in politics has remained very stable over the past three decades.'[10] Turnout could easily be improved, it went on, by the introduction of new methods of voting, for example by mobile phone or over the internet: 'Voter engagement is an issue, rather than apathy … declining turnout is not a function of declining interest in politics or elections but rather a failure of the campaign to connect with the electorate.'[11]

These conclusions may allay many of the worst fears about 'voter apathy'. Yet given that the voter attitudes survey did not delve more deeply into evidence of wider political activity beyond the ballot box, it is difficult to speculate much further on the significance of this evidence. There is, however, a hint of a mismatch between the importance people attach in principle to the entitlement to vote and the sentiment that the electoral system exercises very little effective accountability over the government of the day. The size of Labour's lead notwithstanding, this report offers small glimpses of a deeper dislocation in the political process: 32 per cent of the sample stated that 'none of the parties stood for policies I would like to see', and 38 per cent that there was 'little difference between ... the main parties'. Predictably, perhaps, those who did not vote were inclined to be more negative about the value of voting, the policies of the main parties and the quality of the campaign. And, arguably, the most serious dimension of voter apathy extends beyond mere boredom or frustration with election coverage to manifest itself as abstention from the democratic process itself. Amongst the non-voters of the MORI sample, 15 per cent did not do so because they had never registered, a figure that stood at 27 per cent of black non-voters sampled, and 29 per cent of 18–24-year-olds.

Attitudes, and a sense of popular investment in the political process, are thus a crucial factor in influencing behaviour, something the Commission itself concedes. New practical measures may prompt a few more to cast their vote, but 'equally important are ... the perceptions people have of the political process in the long term'.[12] Other surveys of voter attitudes represent a more complex, and less reassuring, picture, however, and serve to substantiate rumours of gradual disengagement from public institutions and democratic processes.

Basildon, a new town in Essex, has been called 'a barometer for the mood of the nation'.[13] That may be too expansive a claim, although Basildon's electoral history throughout the 1980s and early 1990s casts it as a model example of the fortunes of post-war social democracy, especially the ability of Thatcherism to steal working-class votes from Labour and to remodel the aspirations of many of the electorate away from 'tax and spend' economics and state intervention towards the ideals, if not the realities, of home owner-ship, lower taxes and private enterprise. In their surveys of Basildon between 1992 and 1997, however, Hayes and Hudson chart the gradual disaffec-tion with the Conservatives and with it a decisive disengagement from the political process itself. The overriding feature of Basildon's political culture was, they concluded, 'a profound detachment from all forms of collective political process or social agency'.[14] However peculiar to its local context – a migrant town, predominantly skilled working-class, created within the very dispensation that brought the Welfare State into being after 1945 – it suggests that the patterns of 2001 may have significant, and inauspicious, antecedents.

For example, Hayes and Hudson produce evidence to suggest that voter disengagement is part of a wider pattern of withdrawal from public association altogether. Those interviewed in Basildon identified themselves overwhelmingly as working class, yet eschew affiliations to trade unions or other labour organizations. This is reflected in national trends: between 1955 and 1995, membership of trade unions in Britain fell by 30 per cent.[15] In other words, the cultural and social context – through which political engagement, public debate, community organization and neighbourhood activism have traditionally been expressed – has atrophied: 'All the evidence of our survey suggests a disengagement from the political sphere and perhaps more importantly from all the intermediary and mediating institutions through which public discussions about priorities used to be conducted.'[16]

When questioning people about habits outside the workplace, a similar pattern emerges. 'Family' is the overwhelmingly most popular focus of allegiance; an obvious choice, perhaps, but standing in contrast to the paucity of alternative foci of association. Basildonians are not disposed to join voluntary associations, clubs or political movements. Leisure preferences outside the family tended to be a session at the gym or the shopping mall; although to share social space with others in these pursuits is more 'an accident of timing'[17] than a conscious search for collective assembly. 'The quality of public life is not sustained merely by resource provision but through participation and active adherence to a public agenda. In Basildon this seems to be largely absent.'[18]

Even allowing for Basildon's special features, Hayes and Hudson's anatomy of the town provides evidence of a far more radical level of disaffiliation from a range of collective organizations than simply boredom with one unspectacular campaign. The people of Basildon do not hold out much hope for government, indeed anybody outside themselves, for delivering long-term improvement to their lot. There is little confidence in any external agency or institution: only education, as a means of self-improvement, is the preferred vehicle of personal aspiration. In short, 'these voters have very little faith in anything other than themselves'.[19]

A comparative perspective on voter attitudes, from a series of surveys of the so-called 'trilateral democracies', provides a further context. For a start, it serves as a reminder that concern for the erosion of public trust in democratic organizations is not new.[20] But it also allows us to extrapolate further from 'voter apathy' towards broader questions of confidence in parliamentary processes, the quality of civil society and so on. Norris and Newton's evidence suggests that disillusion with government is more acute than other measures of investment in public institutions, such as trust of fellow citizens, involvement in voluntary and community organizations or faith in private companies. This has similarities to the mood evoked by Hayes and Hudson, in that Norris and Newton argue that the key to strong democratic institutions is the abundance of 'social capital', especially that represented by civil society.[21] Voluntary and community bodies perform a vital function in linking individuals and communities to local and national decision-making processes, which in turn fosters confidence in government performance and credibility.[22]

After Politics?

What emerges from these studies? Whilst voters' basic motivation does seem harder to stimulate, this may be due to the more fluid nature of political commitment, or the phenomenon of 'social dealignment'[23] amongst electorates throughout the West. Voters are more likely to make decisions on a specific and conditional basis, which may in some circumstances suggest a more critical and discerning electorate. Yet the danger is that it may signal a more fragmented political process, as people cast aside group loyalties (such as social class) in favour of more short-term or sectional interests.

Two issues really stand out, however. Firstly, the greatest drift away from political engagement – in terms of participation in parliamentary elections – is occurring amongst younger people, poorer socio-economic groups and ethnic minorities. This is consistent with research suggesting that 'social exclusion' encompasses a network of economic, cultural and political factors, such that 'deprivation results in a constraint on citizenship'.[24] However, the rhetoric of 'joined-up government' as redressing the multiple and connected indices of disadvantage is seldom matched by the reality of measures to combat social exclusion which have tended to focus on the job market at the expense of other strategies.[25] Whether non-participation in elections is regarded as self-imposed exclusion, or part of a more general syndrome of alienation, therefore, a commitment to social inclusion requires attention to the dynamics of political participation and civic involvement – necessitating a thick notion of *active citizenship*.

Secondly, even though respondents to the various qualitative surveys reviewed above seem to retain a principled belief in the right to vote, there seems to be growing scepticism that it will actually make any difference. This may reflect a lack of faith not so much in democracy per se but in the processes of governance themselves; a loss of confidence in the ability of the state to deliver better welfare provision and economic growth through fiscal management and wealth distribution, and an unravelling of the post-war social democratic manifesto – responsible for the conception of Basildon itself – in which rational centralized government planning was regarded as the means to build a better society. In this respect, the *Observer* newspaper's judgement immediately after the UK General Election on low voter turnout corresponds quite closely with Hayes and Hudson's analysis of Basildon: 'People don't turn out to vote, not because they already know who will win, but because they don't believe that politicians will deliver.'[26]

Some of this is reflected in the uncertainty amongst politicians themselves at the ability of national governments to control their economies given the power of transnational corporations and the fluidity of labour, capital and production in a global economy.[27] There are also the large-scale, long-term problems such as climate change and technological innovation, which far exceed the fiscal or political powers of national governments.

The legacy of neo-liberal economic and social politics during the 1980s and 1990s may also have contributed. Whilst it would be facile to assume a golden age of mass participation, evidence suggests a gradual 'privatization' triggered by an unravelling of the infrastructure of collective association during the 1980s and 1990s. The elevation of the market and dismantling of many intermediate organizations, such as local government and trade unions, privatization and the effects of neo-liberal individualism have worn away the warp and weft of civil society:

> Thatcherism has left no legacy in the shape of prominent individuals or new instit-utions that could carry forward its key tenets. But one achievement did endure: it dealt a death-blow to important forms of collectivism in society … What has emerged in the late 1990s is a landscape in which individuals stand out in isolated relief, without much reference to each other and with only minimal relationships to other institutions and organizations.[28]

For some, however, this is not a short-term aberration that can be redressed by a change of government, because such attenuation of the public domain is an inevitable result of the economic logic inherent in global capitalism.[29] Modernity's emphasis on personal responsibility founded on self-authenticating powers of inherent reason – once a powerful counter to the heteronomy of tradition and deference – weakens the bonds of social solidarity based on common interest. The 'discontinuous, fragmentary, episodic, consequences-avoiding life'[30] is ultimately incompatible with communities built on long-term planning, security and continuity.

At the heart of this, is a kind of social atomism – Basildon's loss of faith in anything beyond themselves – which 'has eroded our capacity to think in terms of common interests and fates, contributing to the decay of an active culture of political argument and action'.[31] Nor do attempts by local policy-makers to connect with the electorate seem significantly to have animated local politics in places like Basildon. Their solutions seem to be about more efficient delivery of 'politics as usual' rather than any means of rebuilding the formal and informal community links – the 'social capital' of local democracy – through which the democratic process has traditionally been mediated: tenants' associations, local ward parties, voluntary organizations (including the churches), which carried authority by virtue of belief in their ability to represent the local community. 'We are left with characteristically top-down policy-making, devoid of any sense of community involvement or social partnership.'[32]

Anyone exercised by the future of democracy – at least in its parliamentary manifestations – is therefore presented with a 'puzzle over how to recreate and renew the civil and political institutions that are the backbone of a thousand towns like Basildon'.[33] Enabling people to vote by mobile phone, as the Electoral Commission recommends, will not address the introversion infecting the political process. Governments cannot simply rely on greater sophistication of technocratic measures without also engendering more robust forms of self-government and consent. Attention to the theory and practice of citizenship, of what Tom Bentley calls not joined-up but 'grown-up' government,[34] will necessitate a root-and-branch reconstruction of the very fundamentals of the body politic. Any constitutional reform aimed at restoring trust in the processes and legitimacy of governance 'must be created with the active participation of the people. It must empower people and give them a sense of belonging. It must protect difference and diversity. It must allow us to claim our rights and protect us from arbitrary authority. It must be based on equality.'[35]

The 'end of politics' may be not so much about its demise, therefore, as an opportunity to rethink the fundamental objectives, or ends, that constitute the public domain.

Public Theology and the Renewal of Civil Society

By establishing a link between a vigorous culture of involvement in local associations which generate 'social capital' and public trust in institutions such as Parliament, the civil service and the legal system, commentators such as Hayes and Hudson, and Newton and Norris, invoke the contemporary debate about 'civil society'. Some of this is close to the 'Third Way' politics which attempts to find an alternative to state socialism or neo-liberal market economics. It seeks to reconfigure the relationship between individuals, communities and the state by emphasizing the importance of strong intermediary organizations – and, in particular, the voluntary sector – for fostering citizenship and directing delivery of welfare services.

It is intriguing to see how religious groups have found themselves centre stage in this new dispensation, both in the UK and the USA.[36] It is clear, however, that a very wide spectrum of opinions and political philosophies is at work here. To involve faith-communities in public life may mean the scaling-down of public expenditure and the promotion of faith-based welfare schemes in its place, as in the right-wing thinking of Marvin Olasky, an adviser to George W. Bush. More towards the centre ground, though, are a number of commentators and politicians who would regard faith-communities as ideal examples of civil society working in partnership with local and national government. Speaking at a rally organized by the Christian Socialist Movement in Westminster in March 2001, Tony Blair expounded a very typical version of this view:

> Community action has always been a central mission of the churches and other faith groups. Looking outwards to the needs of others, beyond your own immediate members, is perhaps the prime expression of how you express your own faith and values. And in carrying out this mission you've developed some of the most effective voluntary community organizations in the country. In many cases you meet urgent social needs directly. In others you work in partnership with central and local government to give a special character to the delivery of public services, which state funds would otherwise have to provide directly.[37]

Note how this touches on the distinctive qualities of faith-communities' contribution: how it emphasizes the fostering of a volunteer ethic; how it touches on the significance of local knowledge and provision; how it synthesizes values with practical service delivery. In this, Blair captures perfectly the hopes of those who see the various components of civil society as capable

393

of complementing state provision but also promoting social cohesion, trust, civic duty and responsible citizenship.

All well and good, but perhaps the spectre of the more right-wing version serves as a reminder that we are looking for a model of civil society which fosters an emergent new form of political establishment that is locally based and values-driven, and not something that allows further unravelling of the links between communities and the state. At one level, the encouragement given by the Blair administration is a genuine acknowledgement of the difference made by religion to public life, and the need to find 'stakeholders' whose activities and organizations can help rejuvenate political participation. In other ways, however, it does little to address the two crucial factors mentioned earlier: a more structural understanding of what makes society tick, and how to meet the growing challenge of social exclusion, especially if civil society only embraces the interests of those sufficiently motivated to participate in the first place. A public theology that tries to be genuinely comprehensive and inclusive, therefore, will need to move beyond an equation of civil society with service delivery on the cheap. Clearly, voluntary action has a complementary role to state provision: but the problem with the churches and civil society is precisely that it precludes public theology from engaging with the values and structures of the state and the market. Civil society must promote the local economy, sustainable regeneration and employment and not be limited to voluntary action alone.[38]

Public Theology

> But is it possible any longer for *religious* images to be reborn, for a religious account of hope to become once more influential? Can the Christian faith any longer sustain a living and relevant hope in cold times?[39]

So is there a task for public theology in an age of 'voter apathy'? The climate of public opinion towards the democratic process suggests that people's faith in politics is increasingly conditional upon government being perceived as responsive and effective; and yet, at the same time, the dynamics of globalization make the task of governmental management more complex. Renewal of trust in the democratic process must also encompass a robust theory of justice, empowerment and inclusion if it is not to fail those on the margins.

These questions go to the heart of public theology. Contemporary writers in the discipline have addressed themselves to a number of related

394

issues: the terms on which shared moral discourse might be conducted in the context of 'the conspicuous absence of unifying narratives that generate moral consensus ... and the consequent difficulty of generating shared values or common assumptions about the nature of "reality"',[40] and whether narratives of faith can effectively contribute to moral and political debate into the twenty-first century. There has also been attention to the ways in which theological insights might contribute to the constitution of public policy such as equality,[41] criminal justice[42] and economics;[43] or how church-sponsored social action and local partnerships might constitute a form of 'practical divinity' (John Atherton, *Public Theology for Changing Times* (2000), p. 3), a kind of performative public theology that clearly owes much to liberationist traditions of *orthopraxis*. Clearly, all these strands of public theology and social responsibility implicitly concern themselves with questions of social justice, and represent a heterogenous set of traditions in public theology concerning the nature of theological interventions in the public forum.[44] The key question is whether public life that is increasingly secular and pluralist is able any longer to connect with the historic insights of Christianity, and whether by clinging to the 'fragments' of that tradition the latter can make a meaningful contribution.[45]

As far as the future of participation, empowerment and the nature of governance is concerned, these debates certainly interrogate the terms on which the various interest groups in an increasingly plural society are prepared to enter and invest in the institutions and procedures on which civil society is deemed to rest – principles of justice, the rule of law, equality, distribution and growth, and so on. Much of this literature assumes implicitly, I think, that 'the public realm' is axiomatic, and that questions of operation, participation and governance are secondary to the primary task of finding a sufficiently 'thick' discourse of moral reasoning by which common consent may be reached. Yet this fails precisely to consider practical and strategic measures for the renewal of social capital.

Universal or Preferential?

A further fault-line within contemporary public theology is also worth introducing into our discussion because it relates directly to the objectives of a renewal of the public realm, and the values informing commitments to social inclusion. On the one hand, we are presented with the challenge of the fragility of the public realm. This invites a reconstruction of the very idea of a common polity, to notions of the common good – the very values seemingly at risk in many of the attitudes expressed above. Yet I would also contend that public theology is faced with the challenge of helping to articulate accounts of polity which are capable of enhancing the 'social capital' of community cohesion, and especially mindful of those at risk from exclusion from the democratic process itself.

In the context of an exploration of inequality and social ethics, Douglas Hicks considers how public theology consistently encounters just such a tension. He illustrates this through the notion of 'social solidarity'. For Hicks, God's actions as creator and redeemer – forming all people in God's image and adopting the human condition in the person of Jesus – guarantee human self-apprehension as uniquely loved; but this also underwrites a fundamental commitment to human equality. This is reminiscent of the work of Gutiérrez, who maintains that the primary task of liberation theology is to proclaim the essential and irreducible *humanity* of all people in the face of dehumanizing structures of poverty and oppression.[46] However, extremes of inequality or exclusion represent a threat to the fundamental concept of human unity under God by virtue of their deleterious effect on community cohesion, or social solidarity.

Hicks thus identifies two important emphases within the notion of solidarity which ostensibly appear paradoxical. An emphasis on the *universality* of human organizations reflects a concern for the common good of all, regardless of status; but a *preferential* attention to the needs of those at risk from exclusion, and a commitment to take their side, is an essential benchmark for the quality of that very community.[47]

These ideas are relevant to a consideration of the nature of public faith in collective organizations and institutions of civil society, the state and politics. On the one hand, 'solidarity' as an achievable objective of faith-based involvement in the political process might be said to relate to a sociological tradition dating back to Auguste Comte, whereby religion is held to articulate the shared moral values that underwrite social cohesion. The role of religion is here to provide the opportunities for individuals to express symbolic obligation to the shared moral order, thereby sealing the bonds of the collective once more. As critics of this kind of functionalist social theory have observed, however, such an equation of the social order with a common moral universe emphasizes the virtues of consensus and hierarchy and obscures the extent to which appeals to 'national unity' or 'traditional values' are often expressions of sectional self-interest masquerading as universal welfare.[48]

Public theology has in the past had many champions who have valued the importance of certain forms of ecclesial dispensation being 'representative' of

the nation.[49] The danger is that in an age of endangered democratic institutions such an arrangement is attenuated into a thin form of civil religion,
colluding in anachronistic notions of Church and state that only serve to
perpetuate public alienation from national symbols. A theologically derived
faith in symbols of transcendence as invoking a reality larger than individual
or sectional self-interest is powerful, but not if it serves to sanctify nostalgic
imaginings of community that do not adequately reflect the complexities and
exclusions of the contemporary polity.

Yet alongside the established traditions of Christian churches in these
islands, there is a parallel dissenting strand as well.[50] This alternative dimension of solidarity articulates a more partisan tradition of social theology 'from
below', in which the faithful are called to identify with God's purposes in
history as representing what the meeting of the Conference of Latin American
Bishops at Medellin in 1968 termed 'the preferential option for the poor'.
This public theology, and the acts of advocacy and solidarity that embody
it, eschews any call that the Church remains neutral or disengaged from the
political fray.

This tension, between the *universal* and *preferential* dimensions of
public theology, needs to be taken into consideration when we consider
the role of Christian social thought and practice in the renewal of civil
society and political culture. For example, there is still a legitimate issue
as to whether religious narratives, symbols and values might be capable of
furnishing concepts of common sociality that genuinely animate people's
understanding of a civil order to which they can claim allegiance. How
might common institutions be embodied and represented in the public
imagination? How would national events be marked in a post-Christian,
post-secular age?[51]

On the other hand, Western theology is still learning of the implicit
biases it has imported into its own canons that have served to silence the
voices of the excluded and the powerless.[52] A 'preferential' public theology
places itself in an explicitly partisan role, as advocate, whose objective in
seeking solidarity is not to silence the voices of dissent but to hear the cry of
the poor. Public theology in liberationist mode is necessary also in order to
introduce structural analysis – something Christians find difficult – and to
think beyond individual voter or consumer behaviour as personal 'choice'
but as embedded in a web of privatization, poverty and alienation that are
systemic and purposeful. 'Perhaps the theologian's task here is not so much
to take part in elegant academic games … as to articulate the cry of the
oppressed, and speak for the dumb.'[53]

These are important when we think about implications for renewal of the 'public' sphere: where is public theology located and embodied? Who are its agents, where are its resources, its convictions, actually located? By what criteria are the effectiveness and legitimacy of public institutions to be judged?

Reconstructing Citizenship

> There is no going back to the old institutions. But it is equally artificial to suppose that they can be invented or declared from above ... Such priorities cannot be established without a shared framework for public decision making, in which the performance of public services is contextualised ... Without finding new ways to engage the latent social and public concerns of these people, better, more efficient delivery of public services is unlikely to make much different [*sic*] to the quality of their lives.[54]

A difficult tension maybe, but perhaps public theology in theory and practice needs to embrace the paradox of these two forms of social solidarity as the twin poles on which debate about a just society might be conducted. This will involve grass-roots partnerships in urban regeneration, working for capacity-building in communities impoverished – in multiple senses – by generations of unemployment and dispossession. Yet it also encompasses the more traditional functions of public theology, one that enshrines the theological values at the heart of government. However, it is important to remember that such participation cannot ignore the fact that in many cases the very institutions of the state, local democracy and civil society through which churches have learned to participate are the very mechanisms that are diminished and faltering. As Hayes and Hudson's research demonstrates, therefore, the very nature of governance and participation will change because the context is changing. Perhaps the most useful lessons might come from consultations between faith-communities and the state which have given consideration to the nature of constitutional reform and national identity. One obvious recent example is the role of the Scottish churches in debates about constitutional reform, national identity and devolution.[55]

Rethinking the nature of citizenship is no longer simply a national dilemma, however. Any renewal of democratic forms needs to acknowledge the global nature of commercial, fiscal, ecological and technological decision-making. It will also need to be flexible and adaptive, ready to engage comprehensively and effectively with the complexities of twenty-first century society. The political process must be capable of addressing such complexities. The acceleration of digital and biotechnological innovation, and their effects on our economic, medical, environmental – even existential[56] – reality will only continue. This will require extra- or supranational agencies and may need transnational legal bodies, as the current debate about human cloning indicates. So public theology will need to be comprehensive, capable of embracing and addressing the complexities of globalization. '[T]he inexorable movement towards a global economy and its interaction with a series of dominating global challenges requires the development of a Christian faith sufficiently *capacious* to engage its nature and extent.'[57]

With the practical agencies, however, must go an adequate theological method capable of discerning the signs of the times and articulating these in terms accessible to ecclesial and secular audiences. Public theology should consider expanding its concerns, in order to engage not only with political and constitutional matters, but the influence of popular culture as well. The power of rapidly proliferating and ubiquitous media will assume an even higher profile and exert an ever greater power over public opinion and popular aspirations – including attitudes to social trust, political processes and global issues.

Conclusion

Measures of ordinary people's engagement with the democratic process call everyone to account because they test the adequacy of our core values and institutions. Whilst surveys of attitudes amongst electorates in the UK and internationally do not fully endorse charges of 'voter apathy', there is evidence to suggest that the processes of participatory democracy require more than passive consent, and that the legitimacy of the 'public' domain is itself an iterative phenomenon. The reconstruction of political will requires a dynamic infrastructure of active citizenship.

In responding to future debates about the nature of participation and democracy, public theology's objective must be to speak about God-in-the-world, *to* the world. So long as public theology prizes the health of public institutions, its contribution will need to adopt a functional *and* sacramental role. That is to say, it will assume material expression in the form of involvement in community, strategies of solidarity and local partnership.[58] Yet, on the other hand, such activity also points beyond itself, as a sign of divine redemption in the midst of human culture. That is nowhere more plain than in the creative interplay between two dimensions of public 'solidarity', the universalist and preferential: whilst affirming the integrity of human energies,

399

there is also a drive towards their transformation. And so public theology into the twenty-first century will embrace both the vision of a cohesive shared polity in which all participants are treated with equal regard, as well as the conviction that the very legitimacy of such governance rests on the authenticity of their claims to equity, inclusion and justice.

Notes

1 A landslide is a majority of one hundred seats or more, and although thirteen out of twenty-six of twentieth-century results qualified as such, not even Mrs Thatcher at her peak could deliver successive parliamentary victories of the magnitude of 1997 and 2001. In terms of net gains and losses, there was relatively little change in the overall standing of the parties between 1997 and 2001. See Pippa Norris, 'Apathetic landslide: the 2001 British General Election' (online), available at http://ksghome.harvard.edu/~.pnorris.shorenstein.ksg/acrobat/BritVote2001%20Norris.pdf (2001), 30 pp, accessed 10 August 2001.

2 Some of the mismatch between the size of the majority and the low turnout is due to the peculiarities of the (Westminster) system of first-past-the-post election. In terms of net gains and losses, there was relatively little change in the overall standing of the parties between 1997 and 2001. Labour lost six seats overall, the Conservatives increased by one, the SNP lost one seat and the Liberal Democrats gained six. See Pippa Norris, 'Apathetic landslide', p. 17, Table 3.

3 Noreena Hertz, 'Why we stayed away', the *Observer* (10 June 2001), p. 15.

4 Glasgow Shettleston constituency had a turnout of 38.8 per cent of the electorate; Liverpool Riverside, 33.8 per cent .

5 Duncan B. Forrester, *Christian Justice and Public Policy* (Cambridge: Cambridge University Press, 1997), p. 198.

6 MORI, 'How Britain voted in 2001' (online), http://www.mori.com/polls/2001/election.shtml (2001), accessed 31 July 2001.

7 Dennis Hayes and Alan Hudson, *Basildon: The Mood of the Nation* (London: Demos, 2001).

8 Pippa Norris, 'Apathetic landslide: the 2001 British General Election' (online), available at http://ksghome.harvard.edu/~.pnorris.shorenstein.ksg/acrobat/BritVote2001%20Norris.pdf (2001), 30 pp, accessed 10 August 2001; Kenneth Newton and Pippa Norris, 'Confidence in public institutions: faith, culture or performance?' (online), available at http://kshome.harvard.edu/.pnorris.shorenstein.ksg/articles.htm (1999), 22 pp, accessed 10 August 2001.

9 MORI, 'How Britain voted in 2001', p. 1.

10 *Ibid.*, p. 5.

11 *Ibid.*, p. 1.

12 *Ibid.*, p. 5.

13 Hayes and Hudson, *Basildon*, p. 3.

14 *Ibid.*, p. 11.

15 Although a key factor in this would also have been the decline in the manufacturing sector over the same period.

16 Hayes and Hudson, *Basildon*, p. 67.

17 *Ibid.*, p. 29.

18 *Ibid.*, p. 37.

19 *Ibid.*, p. 59.

20 Michel Crozier, Samuel P. Huntington and Joji Watanuki, *The Crisis of Democracy* (New York: New York University Press, 1975), quoted in Newton and Norris, 'Confidence in public institutions?', p. 2.

21 Civil society is that part of the public domain independent of the market or the state. For ideas about 'social capital', see Robert Putnam, *Bowling Alone: The Collapse and Revival of American Community* (New York: Simon & Schuster, 2000).

22 Newton and Norris, 'Confidence in public institutions?', pp. 10–12.

23 Norris, 'Apathetic landslide?', p. 11.

24 M. Barnes, A. Knops, J. Newman and H. Sullivan, 'Participation and exclusion: problems of theory and method', Economic and Social Research Council, Democracy and Participation Programme (online), http://www.shef.ac.uk/~pol/Projects/proj1wp1.htm (2001), 19 pp, accessed 31 July 2001.

25 Elaine Graham, 'Good news for the socially excluded? Political theology and the politics of New Labour', *Political Theology*, 2 (2000): 77–100.

26 N. Hertz, 'Why we stayed away', the *Observer* (2001), p. 15.

27 Raymond Plant, 'Crosland, equality and New Labour', in Dick Leonard (ed.), *Crosland and New Labour* (Basingstoke: Macmillan, 1999), pp. 19–34, esp. p. 32.

28 Hayes and Hudson, *Basildon*, p. 42.

29 Zygmunt Bauman, *Alone Again: Ethics after Certainty* (London: Demos, 1994).

30 *Ibid.*, p. xx.

31 Geoff Mulgan, quoted in Bauman, *Alone Again*, p. i.

32 Hayes and Hudson, *Basildon*, p. 12.

33 *Ibid.*

34 Tom Bentley, *It's Democracy, Stupid: An Agenda for Self-government* (London: Demos, 2000).

35 Charter 88, *Unlocking Democracy* (London: Charter 88, 2000), p. 7.

36 Elena Curti, 'God and government', *The Tablet* (1 July 2001), p. 10; Margaret Harris, 'Civil society and the role of UK churches: an exploration' (Birmingham: University of Aston Business School, unpublished paper, 2001).

37 Tony Blair, quoted in David Haslam and Graham Dale (eds), *Faith in Politics* (London: Christian Socialist Movement, 2001), p. 12.

38 Stephen Lowe, 'Should empowerment be important to the urban church?' (Diocese of Manchester, unpublished paper, 2000), 13 pp.

39 Forrester, *Christian Justice and Public Policy*, pp. 256–7.

40 Malcolm Brown, 'Plurality and globalization: the challenge of economics to social theology', *Political Theology*, 4: 102–16, esp. p. 103. See also Jeffrey Stout, *Ethics after Babel: The Language of Morals and their Discontents* (Boston, MA: Beacon Press, 1988); Ian Markham, *Plurality and Christian Ethics* (Cambridge: Cambridge University Press, 1994).

41 Douglas A. Hicks, *Inequality and Christian Ethics* (Cambridge: Cambridge University Press, 2000); Duncan B. Forrester, *On Human Worth* (London: SCM Press, 2001).

42 Forrester, *Christian Justice and Public Policy*.

43 D. Stephen Long, *Divine Economy: Theology and the Market* (London: Routledge, 2000).

44 See Peter Sedgwick, 'Theology and society', in D. F. Ford (ed.), *The Modern Theologians* (Oxford: Basil Blackwell, 2nd edn, 1997), pp. 286–305, for an overview of different theological traditions within twentieth-century social ethics.

45 Duncan Forrester's contention that public theology can only contribute 'fragments' of the tradition to public discourse (Forrester, *Christian Justice and Public Policy*, p. 3) vividly evokes the loss of Christianity as pre-eminent narrative of Western civilization, and warns the theologian against commenting on public debates 'as if their linkage with Christian beliefs will be self evident' (John R. Atherton, *Public Theology for Changing Times* (London: SPCK, 2000), p. 13). However, it also conjures up an image of the theologian as 'scavenger', picking over the detritus of a post-Christian culture, unable to salvage more than a few bits and pieces. Forrester is not saying that the Christian tradition itself is now composed of nothing but fragments, but merely that its correspondence with an increasingly secular culture will be fragmentary and partial. The danger is, however, that the correlation is between the fragments of the (religious) past and the perspectives of the (secular) present. The reality is, though, that theology is more than a recycling of the fragments of the past. It is reshaped in interaction with its changing context. Public theology understood as 'dialogical' does not claim superiority rooted in integrity and coherence unbroken by the fractures of postmodernity, but nor does it abandon the disciplines and continuities of faithful practice. It is better rendered as faithful *praxis* evolving in response to the imperatives of present and future.

46 Gustavo Gutiérrez, *The Power of the Poor in History* (London: SCM Press, 1983), p. 58.

47 Hicks, *Inequality and Christian Ethics*, pp. 168–76.

48 Bauman, *Alone Again*, p. 30.

49 John Habgood, *Church and Nation in a Secular Age* (London: Darton, Longman & Todd, 1983).

50 Forrester, *On Human Worth*.

51 It is possible that the United Kingdom now inhabits a post-Christian, and post-secular age: that the pre-eminence of the Christian West is over and the

mainstream churches in Britain struggle to maintain members, viable ministerial deployment and institutional structures. Yet the signs also are that religion and spirituality endure, albeit in heterodox forms. See Martyn Percy, *Salt of the Earth* (Sheffield: Sheffield Academic Press, 2001).

52 Marcella Althaus-Reid, 'Review of C. Rowland, ed., *Cambridge Companion to Liberation Theology* (1999)', *Political Theology*, 4 (2001): 119–21.

53 Forrester, *Christian Justice and Public Policy*, p. 226.

54 Hayes and Hudson, *Basildon*, p. 67.

55 Church Of Scotland, Church and Nation Committee (online), available at http://www.churchofscotland.org.uk/boards/churchnation/churchnation.htm (2001), accessed 31 July 2001.

56 See E. L. Graham, *Representations of the Post/Human: Monsters, Aliens and Others in Popular Culture* (Manchester: Manchester University Press, 2001).

57 Atherton, *Public Theology for Changing Times*, p. 2.

58 Atherton, *Public Theology for Changing Times*; M. Chester, M. Farrands, D. Finneron and E. Venning (eds), *Flourishing Communities: Engaging Church Communities with Government in New Deal for Communities* (London: Church Urban Fund, 1999).

Chapter 24

Where the Local and the Global Meet: Duncan Forrester's *Glocal* Public Theology and Scottish Political Context

WILLIAM F. STORRAR

The Scottish poet Hugh MacDiarmid once wrote that he always wanted to be where extremes meet. It may also be the place where public theology should be in the twenty-first century. In the history of theology in the twentieth century, one of its distinguishing features was the rise of contextual theologies of identity and political theologies of liberation among the poor and oppressed in the non-Western world, and the growth of emancipatory theologies of gender, race, class or locality all around the world. These emerging theologies tended to include a fundamental criticism of the dominant Western theological tradition, with its theoretical claim to timeless truth and universal significance frequently being unmasked by such critics to reveal the predominantly white, male faces of Western academics and Church leaders, betraying their own local perspective and ideological bias. This tension between the particular context and the universal claim of Christian faith and practice has been a creative one over the last several decades. It has helped to give theological and political voice to the poor and powerless as, in Gustavo Gutiérrez's telling phrase, they irrupted into world history for the first time. And it made some at least in the churches and academies of the rich and powerful West more reflexive and self-critical about the social location of their theology. However, this *particular–universal* tension has also been in danger of stretching public theology to the two extremes of incommensurable local theologies and imperialist grand theological narratives. Is there any possibility of the local and global in Christian theology meeting in some new and fruitful interchange in the public theology of the twenty-first century?

This leads on to the question of how public theology itself should respond to the new world of 'globalization' that also emerged in the later twentieth century, fast on the heels of these contextual theological developments and debates. Globalization has its own apparent extremes of an all-conquering 'McWorld' in conflict with local resistance from those who live in 'Jihad World', as one commentator has described it, all the more poignantly so after the terrible events of 11 September 2001 in New York.[1] Is this the only way in which globalization can be understood? Or can local cultures and global systems also meet in some new and different configuration of globalization?

As one of the editors of this volume in honour of Duncan Forrester, I wish to reflect in this closing essay on the book's overall theme – the twentieth-century legacy and twenty-first-century agenda for public theology. I shall do so in the light of such questions about the interaction between the local and global in theology and in globalization. In order to explore this theme in an appropriately concrete and contextual way, and to conclude this Festschrift, I shall consider two such places where the local and the global meet: Duncan Forrester's work as a public theologian and his own Scottish political context. These two locations are sites where I believe that we can discern what the sociologist Roland Robertson has termed the 'glocal' at work. By 'glocal', Robertson means exactly this interactive local–global dynamic at the core of globalization.[2] Instead of seeing globalization as the conflict or polarization between the extremes of homogenizing global economic, cultural and informational systems and the anti-globalizing resistance of heterogeneous local cultures, traditions and identities, Robertson has argued for another conceptual approach: one that recognizes their meeting and melding in 'glocal' form around the world:

> the debate about global homogenization versus heterogenization should be transcended. It is not a question of *either* homogenization or heterogenization, but rather of the way in which both of these tendencies have become features of life across much of the late-twentieth century world. In this perspective the problem becomes that of spelling out the ways in which homogenizing and heterogenizing tendencies are mutually implicative ... In various areas of contemporary life ... there are ongoing, calculated attempts to combine homogeneity with heterogeneity and universalism with particularism.[3]

In Robertson's account, the term 'glocal' was formed linguistically by the blending of the local and the global, and modelled on the Japanese notion of *dochakuka*, conveying the idea of adapting to local conditions; originally used with reference to farming techniques but later, in business, to the strategy of 'global localization', tailoring global products to local markets.[4] As a student of globalization, Robertson has opted to describe this process of combining the local and the global, which he believes to be empirically observable in the contemporary world, as one of 'glocalization':

> Thus the notion of glocalization actually conveys much of what I have previously written about globalization. From my own analytic and interpretative standpoint the concept of globalization has involved the simultaneity and the interpenetration of what are called the local and the global, or – in more abstract vein – the universal and the particular.[5]

Recognizing the *glocal* character of globalization has profound implications for rethinking the relationship between theology and public issues in the twenty-first century. As the American Catholic theologian and missiologist Robert Schreiter has argued (drawing on Robertson's analysis), cutting-edge work in public theology must now be done in the meeting place 'between the local and the global':

> the important moment for cultural (and theological) production becomes the line of encounter between the global and the local, where the two come up against each other. Roland Robertson describes this encounter as 'glocalization' ... some of the most salient features in religion and theology today can best be described from the vantage point of the glocal. Neither the global homogenizing forces nor the local forms of accommodation and resistance can themselves provide an adequate explanation of these phenomena. It is precisely in their interaction that one comes to understand what is happening.[6]

Studying Forrester's public theology and his Scottish political context as sites of glocalization, places where the local and the global meet in interpenetrative and interactive simultaneity, may help us to understand something of what the kind of *glocal* public theology called for by Schreiter might look like in the twenty-first century. We turn first to Forrester's own theological work, and the way in which its characteristic concerns have been picked up in this volume, to see something of this 'line of encounter between the local and the global' running through them all, before concluding with a case study of his local political context in Scotland. This will be presented as another site of glocal encounter for public theological production but one which suggests a different method of theological engagement with public issues in a *glocal* era than that preferred by Forrester.

407

WILLIAM F. STORRAR

Locating the Glocal in Forrester's Public Theology

Duncan Forrester has been an articulate and passionate advocate of public theology from four distinct but complementary and overlapping perspectives and sets of concerns. As befits a practical theologian, these can only be understood in the context of his own life experience and reflective practice in Church, academy and society. First, he is rooted in his own local Scottish Reformed tradition and political context. For Forrester that Reformed tradition is one that seeks to hold together, in the one Lordship of Christ, the evangelical and trinitarian faith and worship of the Church with radical political commitment to the cause of justice and the poor in an unequal society, both anticipating God's coming rule over all things. He has described this Scottish tradition as one of 'Reformed Radical Orthodoxy', and made the case for its critical retrieval and contemporary relevance in his recent book on the nature of practical theology, *Truthful Action*.[7] His engagement with his own local Scottish political context from this Reformed perspective was expressed in the 1980s and 1990s in the work of the Centre for Theology and Public Issues, which he founded and directed at the University of Edinburgh.[8] Several of the Centre's conferences and publications tackled questions of Scottish identity and constitutional change amid the devolution debates of those decades, and from the wider perspectives of an ecumenical social vision.[9] This was a period when the Centre, under Forrester's leadership and inspiration, was a creative and influential catalyst for doing local theology in the midst of two decades of political turbulence in Scotland, as the campaign for democratic renewal and social justice through a restored Scottish Parliament gained momentum and came to final success. Not least, his work has been a challenge to his own Scottish Reformed tradition to recognize its radical roots and contemporary relevance in the Scottish political context. As he put it himself in 2000, at the outset of the twenty-first century, while his own Church of Scotland seemed to be in decline and to have lost its theological nerve in the late twentieth century, there were grounds for Christian hope in the new Scottish political context:

> In Scotland today a radical impulse and a sense of community which have clear roots in the Scottish Reformation continue to flourish and be influential in politics. This was evident at the opening of the Scottish Parliament in July 1999. The proceedings were markedly informal and started with a wonderful rendering by Sheena Wellington of Burns' great song, 'A man's a man for a' that', a strongly egalitarian poem which pokes fun at a hierarchical ordering of society and appears to be a secular expression of Calvinist egalitarianism. This

408

was followed by the singing of the hundredth psalm to the Calvinist Genevan 'plain tune', which had its origins in the Calvinist insistence that the people should play an active part in the music of worship as in the life of civil society. Could this ecclesiastical and theological crisis and the turning point represented by the establishment of the Scottish Parliament be the moment of opportunity for retrieving and repossessing the Scottish tradition of radical orthodoxy? I think and hope that this may be the case. *And if this time of crisis in Scotland is a moment of opportunity for retrieval, so now, as in the past, stimuli and resources from outside have their role to play. Liberation theology has clear affinities with the radical tradition we are discussing.*[10] (my italics)

This last comment by Forrester is critical for our understanding of his work as an example of glocal theological production. He sees his own local Scottish Reformed tradition as interacting with the external influence and internal resonance of Latin American liberation theology. Robert Schreiter has described several 'global theological flows' that have circulated around the world, and interacted with a variety of local contexts and theologies to produce this glocal public theological outcome. Liberation theology has been one of these major global flows in recent decades, along with feminist theologies, and theologies of the environment and of human rights.[11] For Schreiter, these are the new forms of 'universal theology', but not in the Enlightenment sense. Rather, while each is rooted in its own context, 'They are universal in their ubiquity and in their addressing of universal, systemic problems affecting nearly everyone in the world.'[12] In Forrester's openness to the interaction of his local theological tradition with the global flow of liberation theology, we have an example of exactly the kind of glocal theological production that Schreiter has in mind in his analysis of 'theology between the local and the global'.

Second, as this glocal understanding of his own local Reformed tradition reminds us, Duncan Forrester has been profoundly influenced by his global experience and personally open to a diverse range of 'outside stimuli and resources', challenging his Scottish horizons and self-understanding. As a young educational missionary teaching politics in a college in India with a Scottish Presbyterian foundation, he gazed deep into the human face of local people trapped in extreme poverty, particularly a beggar called Munuswamy whom he encountered daily on his way to work. This led him to wrestle throughout his life and work with the Christian meaning and practice of equality in a shockingly unequal world. That formative primal encounter with the poor in India, in the person of Munuswamy, and the lifetime of theological and practical reflection which followed, bore fruit in his recently

409

published Christian case for a distributive version of egalitarianism, *On Human Worth*.[13] There he recognized the changing global context for problems of inequality that was redrawing the boundaries and character of social exclusion for the world's poor. In an interdependent global economy, local individuals are directly impacted by business and trade decisions taken on the other side of the world but often excluded from consideration when such decisions are taken. And so Forrester comments:

> An argument runs that the old forms of social exclusion which were described and dealt with in terms of poverty, deprivation, welfare and redistribution have been replaced with new radical forms of exclusion which are in many ways the direct consequences of recent fundamental social and economic changes, particularly globalization ... It is now, it appears, easier than ever before to exclude Munuswamy and his interests from our discussion! The new globalized situation may require not only a new language but new forms of treatment and new policies.[14]

The *glocal* line of local–global encounter runs, therefore, right through the middle of both Forrester's contextual Scottish commitment to Reformed Radical Orthodoxy, with its plea for openness to global theological influences like liberation theology, and his evangelical and egalitarian commitment to India's local poor, fated to be forgotten as neighbours by those making the economic decisions that affect them, on the other side of the world.

Third, Duncan Forrester is a profoundly ecumenical and cross-contextual Christian theologian, always trying to relate the riches of the universal Christian faith to the unique insights of particular theologians, traditions, churches and contexts. In his writings, he has drawn diachronically on the history of Christian thought across the centuries, and synchronically on the theological resources of the world Church across the continents, in order to develop his ecumenical understanding of theology, politics and social ethics. Again, such matters are inseparable for Forrester from questions of Church unity and common worship, where particular practices in word and sacrament bear witness to the overcoming of the bitter divisions of the universal Church and its failed witness to that unity-in-diversity held out in Christ. He sees an unbreakable bond between faithful Christian worship in the one Church and the integrity of Christian practice in the one world. As he put it in his short study for the World Council of Churches, *The True Church and Morality*: 'In authentic worship believers are nourished to seek God's reign and God's righteousness, and learn to discern the Lord's presence in the hungry, thirsty, naked, sick and imprisoned neighbour.'[15] Significantly, for our purposes,

410

he draws on particular local church experiences, whether in the struggle of the Confessing Church in Nazi Germany or the disputed position of Dalit Christians in the Indian Church, to explore the meaning of these universal Christian themes. Earlier writings, like his lucid guide to *Theology and Politics*, reflect his serious engagement with the range of Christian thought over two thousand years, from Augustine and Calvin to Dietrich Bonhoeffer, Karl Barth, Gustavo Gutiérrez and Alasdair MacIntyre.[16] Such writings also show his openness to the cross-denominational and contextual breadth of Christian praxis around the world: not least in his early welcome and use of the insights of Latin American liberation theology and constant drawing on the distinctive twentieth-century Indian Christian experience of being a prophetic minority that addressed wider public issues. As one who always seeks the creative inter-penetration of the particular and the universal in his thinking on issues of Christian belief and practice in Church and society, we may properly describe him as a *glocal* Christian theologian and public intellectual.

And, fourthly, as Andrew Morton has reminded us in his opening chapter in this volume, Forrester has been committed to relating theology to public issues and public policy in a critical and public dialogue with other disciplines and other voices, in public forums and not behind the closed door of the academic seminar room. He has had a particular concern for developing appropriate methods for doing public and political theology after Christendom, in a pluralist local and global context.[17] Forrester's published Hensley Henson Lectures, *Beliefs, Values and Policies*, his subsequent major study on *Christian Justice and Public Policy* and the many publications of his Centre for Theology and Public Issues (CTPI) are all examples of his way of engaging in that interdisciplinary and public dialogue.[18] They all pulsate with his characteristic stress on the importance of sustaining a prophetic vision and an eschatological hope in politics, with the power to lift the terms and horizon of public debate and secular social theories to their proper ends. Forrester has also welcomed in CTPI conferences the contribution and, where possible, the direct participation of all those involved in public policy issues and decisions: from policy-makers and social scientists to poor and marginalized people themselves, with their own expertise to give and cries of pain and anger to be heeded. But this kind of interdisciplinary, dialogical and visionary approach in CTPI has always been focused on practical outcomes, whether in the reform of the penal system or the ending of Third World debt, for example. Robert Schreiter, reflecting on the future of liberation theology in a global era, has made a case for exactly this kind of interdisciplinary way of relating theology to local and global public issues, in situations where Christians have the opportunity to help develop concrete proposals for the reconstruction of their society, as in post-apartheid South Africa:

> liberation theologies must be ready to become interdisciplinary, especially in situations of reconstruction. While it may be protested that it is not theology's task to provide concrete proposals for the reconstruction of society, a theology truly arising from and grounded in praxis cannot avoid this kind of concreteness. There is a difference, it seems to me, between getting identified with a single proposal (something that theology should probably not do), and foregoing the hard work of sorting through the vexing issues that make up reality. There is a place in liberation theology for prophetic denunciation. There is also a place for engaged, interdisciplinary work in matters of reconstruction.[19]

When one considers the range of concrete issues that have been addressed by Forrester's Centre for Theology and Public Issues at Edinburgh since 1984, through just such an interdisciplinary approach and with a focus on concrete proposals for the reconstruction of society, then it is evident how much he has pioneered the way of working that Schreiter commends for a glocal era.

Responding to Forrester's Concerns

It is fitting that these four perspectives and sets of concerns have been taken up in the range of essays in this volume, each showing its own kind of critical engagement with Forrester's characteristic approach as a public theologian: his Reformed and ecumenical perspective, interdisciplinary and dialogical method and local–global interaction. Two contributors and Edinburgh colleagues of Forrester engage explicitly with theological and public issues arising from his own Scottish context and Reformed tradition. David Fergusson's study of a theology of tolerance highlights the problematic nature of Reformed theological sources for such a key project for contemporary public theology in a pluralist society, although sharing Forrester's concern to carry out a discerning retrieval of relevant elements in Reformation thought that have the potential to fill the vacuum in modern notions such as tolerance. Drawing on the very different Radical Reformation Anabaptist theology of John Howard Yoder, Michael Northcott's essay on environmental politics and the new Scottish Parliament offers a critique of the kind of Reformed view of Church and state that Forrester's own Church of Scotland has held historically and which it marshalled in support of the establishment of such a parliament in the closing decades of the twentieth century. However,

Northcott's marrying of Eucharist and environmental ethics is very much in harmony with Forrester's recurring Reformed conviction of the inseparable bond between public worship and public witness. And Northcott's relating of local Scottish political developments to global environmental and economic issues challenges public theology done in Forrester's Reformed tradition to respond to the new local–global dynamic of politics in more self-critical, accountable and innovative ways (exactly the qualities needed if Alasdair MacIntyre's notion of a living tradition is to apply to Forrester's own retrieval of a 'Scottish Radical Reformed Orthodoxy').[20]

Christopher Kurien's analysis, as an Indian economist, of the impact of globalization on the world's poor, and the Gorringe and Rowland essays on the relationship between equality and biblical exegesis, radical Christian social experiment or ideology and material culture, all take up themes that Forrester addresses in his own work.[21] They all do so with a similar righteous anger, cool analysis and eloquent articulation of alternative strategies when faced with inequality on a global scale. Max Stackhouse offers a more sympathetic yet equally rigorous study of public theology's constructive engagement with the political economy of the global era that indicates the healthy debate and reasoned argument over differences of approach among public theologians to be found and welcomed in these pages, not least by Duncan Forrester himself. Mary Grey's plea for a global spirituality inspired by Gandhi to fill the moral void of global capitalism reminds us of how important the non-violent spiritual heritage of India has been to Forrester and his thinking on global issues and their resolution.

Forrester's concern to think about public issues through a critical retrieval of the full range of Christian and modern thought, in ways that integrate local and particular insights with global and universal visions, is taken up in several of the earlier essays in this volume which explore some of modernity's most contested ideas about human flourishing. For example, in Richard Bauckham's consideration of the problematic nature of notions of freedom in modernity, Ann Loades's Kantian reflections on the end of history and the possibility of graced action in the face of horror or Raymond Plant's argument for the universal goods which are the precondition of action in a liberal society we see how important modernity's intellectual legacy is for public theology, even in the postmodern times of the twenty-first century. Kees Klop's argument for a pneumatology of environmental stewardship and George Newlands's case for a generous Christology of human rights both show the continuing power of doctrine to shape Christian thinking on these key public issues of our time: an approach which Forrester would warm to as a Reformed theologian who takes Christian doctrine seriously in his own work on public issues.

The authoritative studies by three leading public theologians of our time – Jürgen Moltmann, John de Gruchy and José Míguez-Bonino – of the development of political theology in Germany, South Africa and Argentina – three seminal locations in the unfolding recent history of public theology – highlight the importance of particular local contextual theologies in influencing the emergence of a global discussion on theology and public issues in the second half of the twentieth century. In his teaching and postgraduate supervision, as well as his research and writing, Duncan Forrester has always been alert to these local sources and responsive to their global contribution to public theology and contextual testimony to the worldwide Church.[22]

Finally, we can hear in the range of public issues to be found in the final section of this volume not only a remarkable resonance with Forrester's major public policy concerns as a Christian ethicist and practical theologian, but also the thinking of kindred spirits who are taking up his challenge to find new approaches to relating theology to public life in a changing cultural, economic and political context. Some, like Forrester's distinguished former Edinburgh colleagues, Alastair Campbell and Robin Gill, are addressing mainstream medical and ethical issues in ways that demonstrate the creative methodological diversity by which theology may make a distinctive contribution to public thinking and practice on health matters. But just as Campbell's empirical research, with Teresa Swift, takes seriously the expert voice and values of the virtuous patient in medical ethics and practice, so Forrester's other Edinburgh colleagues contributing to this section, Alistair Kee and Marcella Althaus-Reid, raise the discordant voices and experiences of the excluded that must constitute the core of any authentic political theology of ideological deconstruction and material transformation: exactly the plea that Forrester has made and the practice he has sought to follow in running the Centre for Theology and Public Issues at Edinburgh University.[23] Another development must be noted here. Marcella Althaus-Reid offers a searching feminist and Latin American critique of Forrester's preferred approach of offering theological fragments into the British political arena; and Elaine Graham takes seriously the crisis of apathy for contemporary British politics and the need to hold together universal and particular commitments in doing public theology. Althaus-Reid and Graham both demonstrate that, while Forrester's challenge and example are clearly not going unheeded, the deconstructive critiques and different hermeneutical concerns of women public theologians are questioning the

414

male gendered assumptions of even the best of pioneering British political theology, including Forrester's own work.

Contributors such as Stanley Hauerwas and Alan Torrance show the fruitful possibilities of Forrester's preferred approach of developing theological fragments for the public arena, like Christian notions of punishment or forgiveness.[24] It can be seen from these essays that such fragments may fall uncomfortably into the policy debates of modern liberal democracies. Yet again, they may fulfil Forrester's hopes for them as the prophetic grit in giving purchase to protest movements or as the practical irritant to spin the pearl of fresh policy initiatives, whether in reforming the penal system of the United States or in extending the reach of reconciliation in the Balkans or Middle East.

From the above survey of contributions to a public theology for the twenty-first century, in dialogue with Forrester and the themes that have concerned him as a public theologian over fifty years, since he first studied politics and theology in the 1950s, we can see that the new dynamic at work in this period is the 'glocal' one of local–global interaction at both the public and the theological levels. What makes Forrester's work so significant for the twenty-first century is that he has always sought to relate his own local Reformed theological tradition to wider ecumenical horizons and Christian landscapes, and his own engagement with local public issues to their wider global context. The mutual permeation and interaction of the local and the global in his work on theology and public issues, a process named in a jarring but descriptive way as 'glocalization', makes Duncan Forrester an exemplary public theologian to honour at the outset of a century which is daily manifesting both the predatory features and the emancipatory possibilities of such a glocal era.

Clearly, and very impressively, his work is a place where the local and the global meet. As I noted, in referring to the Hauerwas and Torrance essays in this volume, Forrester has increasingly argued that what public theology must offer the participants in public debate and dialogue in a pluralist and postmodern world are fragments of Christian theological understanding and insight, rather than grand theological systems or mediating ethical middle axioms.[25] But should public theology restrict itself to a diet of theological fragments in the new glocal world of the twenty-first century? I doubt it. By considering our other exemplary location where the local and the global meet and mix, Forrester's own Scottish political context, I shall attempt to show why an earlier ecumenical method in social ethics, the middle axiom approach which Forrester himself criticizes and rejects,

415

should be reconsidered in a revised form as a more appropriate method for doing public theology in a global era – precisely because of its potential to meet the need for concrete responses to public problems in the glocal domain.

Scottish Constitutional Politics: Another Glocal Site for Public Theology

Scotland in the later twentieth century was a place where extremes met. It experienced both the rise of a nationalist movement for political change and the impact of globalization on its social, economic and cultural life. It both gained an autonomous Scottish Parliament, set within the wider political frameworks of the UK and European Union, and lost its old heavy industrial manufacturing economy regulated by the nation state, to be replaced by the weightless economy of electronics, information technology and service industries that operates within global communication networks and market systems.[26]

A modern movement for Scottish self-government within the framework of the United Kingdom, its empire and Commonwealth, existed from the later nineteenth century, along with the stronger Home Rule and nationalist movements in Ireland. After the brief resurgence of a cross-party national campaign for Scottish home rule within the UK in the late 1940s and early 1950s, Scottish nationalism as a political movement had little electoral success until the later 1960s and 1970s. The national Church of Scotland, however, sustained its post-war support for the devolution of power, despite the vicissitudes of party politics. Under pressure from the eleven Scottish National Party Members of Parliament elected in 1974 to campaign for outright Scottish independence from the UK, the then Labour government held a referendum in 1979, on proposals for a limited measure of Scottish self-government. While a bare majority voted for an elected Scottish Assembly, it was judged an insufficient level of electoral support to realize this constitutional change. The very possibility was swept away by the election of a new Conservative government under Margaret Thatcher later in that same year. The continuing electoral support for Scottish self-government after 1979 was resolutely discounted by successive UK governments while the anti-devolution Tories remained in power. As a result, the intransigent Thatcher and Major governments faced the united opposition of a growing cross-party and civic movement, including the churches, campaigning for a consensus scheme to set up a Scottish

Parliament. With the election of a pro-devolution Labour government under Tony Blair in 1997, constitutional change for Scotland was once again a possibility in British politics.

Increased electoral support for devolution since 1979 was confirmed in a further constitutional referendum on 11 September 1997. There were large majorities in support of stronger devolution proposals to set up a Scottish Parliament with both extensive legislative and limited fiscal powers, and democratic responsibility for Scottish affairs, within the wider United Kingdom and European Union. The new Parliament was elected in May 1999, and was officially opened on 1 July.[27] When the new Members of the Scottish Parliament met for the first time after their election, to be sworn in as elected representatives, the oldest MSP, Dr Winifred Ewing, presided. She declared that the ancient Scottish Parliament, which had been officially adjourned rather than abolished in 1707, at the parliamentary union with England, was hereby reconvened. This notion of adjournment, a neat piece of Scottish metaphysical face-saving in 1707, implied that the old Scottish Parliament had not disappeared at the start of the modern era in the early eighteenth century, but had rather gone into a kind of constitutional limbo, awaiting resurrection in more auspicious postmodern times, on the eve of the twenty-first century. This brief history does raise the intriguing question of why a Scottish Parliament did reappear as a democratic legislature with a strong ethos of civic participation in 1999, after almost three centuries of Scottish political acquiescence and patriotic embrace of the unitary British state. How are we to interpret these developments sociologically, and what was the local Scottish Christian theological response to them? To find answers to these questions, within the terms of our local–global theme, we turn to an authoritative external examiner of the Scottish scene.

Scottish Nationalism as a form of Glocalization

The Canadian Catholic theologian and ecumenist Gregory Baum has had a special interest in the relationship between theology and public issues in his work. He has also given particular attention to issues of national identity and nationalism, arising from his own context in Canada and French-speaking Quebec. As someone of German and Jewish origin, he is acutely aware of the ambiguous and often xenophobic and regressive nature of nationalism and religious nationalism in the twentieth century. But, for Baum, that is not the whole story. While he notes the lack of attention given to questions of nationalism in twentieth-century Christian theology and ethics, including

417

the social teaching of his own Catholic Church, he does consider the more nuanced theological and ethical appreciation of national identity by churches and theologians in three later twentieth-century contexts: Quebec, East Germany and Scotland.[28] In Quebec and Scotland, at least, he identifies historical moments, *kairos* moments, from the 1960s to the 1990s, when an affirmation of national identity could be compatible with fresh opportunities to pursue Christian ethical criteria about social justice, the welfare of minorities and strengthened international relations, while always refusing to give an ultimate loyalty to the nation.[29]

Baum sees Scotland as a significant site of two related developments of the later twentieth century: the rise of emancipatory theologies in the context of the rise of both nationalism and globalization. As editor of a collection of essays on *The Twentieth Century: A Theological Overview*, Baum notes that this wide-ranging volume does not mention topics of personal interest to him, including the present Scottish political and theological context:

> the more recent theological reflections on Scotland's self-identity and national aspirations. From the 1960s on, we observe the multiplication of politically responsible theologies that envision the reform or reconstruction of particular societies, exposed to the globalization of the economy and the consumer-orientated monoculture that goes with it. These contextual theologies tend to be progressive, that is, they support social justice, unlike the German Christians under Hitler or the apartheid theology of the Afrikaner church. Through an altogether unique historical development beginning in the 1960s, the emancipatory dimension of divine redemption has assumed, for the first time, a central construction in Christian theology.[30]

And in his recent study of nationalism, *Nationalism, Religion and Ethics*, Baum has noted the way in which this emancipatory theological interpretation of local Scottish identity by Scottish Christians and churches was matched by their acceptance of a sociological interpretation of Scottish nationalism as a postmodern phenomenon inseparable from the interaction of the local and the global:

> Scottish nationalism stresses community against global individualism, social democracy against the dominant neo-conservatism, and self-determination against the central power of the Westminster government. To overcome poverty and unemployment the Scots must rely on their own inventiveness. The Christian literature that looks favourably on Scottish nationalism interprets it as a postmodern phenomenon. In modern times, it is being argued, the small nation of Scotland was firmly embedded in a unitary state; it was overlooked by social

scientists and political observers, and it was reluctant to celebrate its own history and emphasize its own culture. Yet at this postmodern moment, nationalists in Scotland affirm its identity as a nation, demand some form of self-government, look for a closer relationship of Scotland and the European Union, and show greater concern for poverty in the third world. *This appears postmodern because it combines the local and the global in a new dynamic.*[31] (my italics)

For Baum, if this Scottish theological and sociological interpretation of recent Scottish politics is correct, it raises a further question about the need for new categories of thought and analysis that address what Roland Robertson calls glocalization, the dynamic interaction of the local and the global, with the utmost seriousness:

> This takes us to the question of whether the economic, social and political conditions of the present are initiating a new period in human history that can no longer be interpreted with the help of concepts useful for the understanding of the previous period, the age of modernity. *If contemporary nationalism is a phenomenon related to globalization, it would have to be interpreted in categories that relate the local and the global in a new way.*[32] (my italics)

Baum identifies three ways in which the local Christian literature interprets Scottish nationalism in such new glocal categories.[33] First, the affirmation of a local Scottish identity is seen as a way of affirming a cultural heritage and set of shared values against 'the utilitarianism spread by the global monoculture', that, 'creates an emptiness and spiritual homelessness among many people'. Second, Scottish nationalism is seen as a movement for local political autonomy within a larger, interdependent world. As Baum put it, 'the new movements of identity politics do not intend to create sovereign states as independent entities but rather envisage new institutional arrangements for regulating power in the interaction between nations and the global community.'[34] And, third, this literature argues that the national Church of Scotland, in such a changing local and global context, should abandon its modern claim to represent the nation and, instead, act ecumenically and in solidarity with other marginalized minorities, 'in support of social justice and pluralism'.[35]

But Baum is left with other, more fundamental questions about this sympathetic Scottish Christian reading of nationalism and globalization. Perhaps it represents a fatal misreading of the local and global context:

> Are these church people spelling out an impossible dream for the Scottish nation and the Scottish church? Is globalization an earth-shaking event that will provoke the reorganization of society in new patterns of local–global relations? Or should

we follow a pessimistic interpretation of present-day globalization and lament the destruction of human communities and the exclusion of peoples through the spread of the self-regulating market system and the unrestrained power of international capital?[36]

As the essays on globalization in this volume tend to argue, the latter interpretation is the dominant one in contemporary public theology, on strong evidentiary and ethical grounds. But, as this Scottish case study suggests, the pessimists do not give us the whole picture. We need a more discerning account of the complexities and ambiguities of globalization as both a predatory and emancipatory phenomenon.[37] In closing, I wish to revisit the more optimistic Scottish Christian interpretation of nationalism as a potentially emancipatory site of glocalization, as characterized by Gregory Baum above, and ask what lies at the heart of it in terms of its method as a public theology.

Support for Scottish Self-government: A Revised Middle Axiom for Glocal Times

During the Second World War, the Church of Scotland conducted a remarkable collaborative venture in public theology: a 'Commission for the Interpretation of God's Will in the Present Crisis'.[38] It was chaired by a theologian, Professor John Baillie of New College, Edinburgh University, and its wide-ranging work bears the mark of his brilliant mind and involvement in the inter-war ecumenical movement. This Commission on post-war reconstruction adopted the middle axiom method in Christian social ethics first advocated by J. H. Oldham at the Oxford 'Life and Work' Conference held in 1937.[39] Between the general ethical principles derived from the Gospel and specific policy commitments and decisions, the Church needed to develop and advocate middle axioms. These were seen as contingent mediating directives that sought to relate these principles to an informed reading of particular political contexts at a particular time, in ways that would guide the Church and its members, without prescribing detailed action. In Oldham's own words, middle axioms are, 'attempts to define the direction in which, in a particular state of society, Christian faith must express itself'.[40] Such middle axioms should be seen as provisional and context specific, 'for a given period in given circumstances'. The Baillie Commission understood middle axioms to be:

'secondary and more specialised principles which exhibit the relevance of the ruling principles to the particular field of action in which guidance is needed.' These 'are not such as to be appropriate in every time and place and situation, but they are offered as legitimate and necessary applications of the Christian rule of faith and life to the special circumstances in which we now stand.'[41]

For the Baillie Commission, one such relevant but provisional and contextual middle axiom for post-war Britain, with its memories of massive unemployment in the inter-war years, was support for 'a far greater measure of public control of capital resources and means of production', in the common interest.[42] I wish to argue that, in the late 1980s and 1990s, the Church of Scotland returned to this middle axiom approach as it developed a theological argument and contribution to the constitutional debate then being conducted. Given Gregory Baum's reading of that Scottish Christian contribution and political context as examples of glocalization, then the adoption of a middle axiom approach to addressing such local–global political issues is of special relevance. What was its contribution and how does it bear on questions of method for public theology in the twenty-first century? Is this a part of public theology's twentieth century legacy that we should carry over into the global era?

As noted above, after 1945 the national Church of Scotland advocated the devolution of parliamentary decision-making over Scottish affairs to Scotland itself, within the framework of the United Kingdom. It based its support on a claim to represent the higher interests of the Scottish people and a growing consensus of Scottish opinion. This claim proved a house built on sand in 1979, in the months leading up to the first referendum on setting up a devolved Scottish Assembly. The growing unpopularity of the governing party sponsoring devolution led to ebbing support for its constitutional proposals. In these circumstances, anti-devolution voices in the Kirk silenced the General Assembly's 'Church and Nation Committee' from reminding worshippers through a pulpit letter of its long-standing support for devolution, on the grounds that this was presuming to tell church members how to vote. Without the rock of theological conviction to resist these pressures, the Kirk did indeed fall silent in the referendum campaign.[43] After 1979, a younger generation of secular and Christian Scots learned from this experience of collapsing support for devolution in Church and nation. In the 1980s and 1990s, a broad, cross-party and civic movement for constitutional change, including the churches, ensured the resounding success of the Yes campaign for a Scottish Parliament in the 1997 referendum.[44] And in that same period, the 1989 Church of Scotland General Assembly adopted a report on the government of Scotland that analysed the British constitutional situation in terms of a Reformed understanding of power and limited and popular sovereignty under God, drawing on medieval Catholic and post-Reformation Presbyterian theological and political arguments.[45]

The 1989 Church and Nation Report drew a careful distinction between the political ethical principle of limited sovereignty and the various constitutional policy options that were compatible with that principle, which it left open to personal judgement and preference in an election or referendum vote: recognizing the legitimacy of a vote for a devolved assembly, a federal settlement or outright independence. Between these two levels of a theologically grounded political principle and the personal judgement of electoral preference, the report supported what was in fact, if not in name, a middle axiom: it called for democratic control of Scottish affairs through self-government. The exact form of that self-government was to be decided in a national referendum on the range of constitutional options. This is a middle axiom because it clearly stands as a provisional directive stance, mediating between a Reformed understanding of Christian faith, with its derived political principle of limited sovereignty, and particular electoral decisions about the shape and form of constitutional change. The fact that this middle axiom was linked to theology and political ethical principle is recognized by secular and academic commentators.

Lindsay Paterson is one of the leading analysts of contemporary Scottish politics. In surveying the communitarian values and practices in Scottish society that undergirded support for a Scottish Parliament in the closing decades of the twentieth century, against the neo-liberal individualism espoused by Margaret Thatcher, Paterson notes the theological contribution to Scottish communitarian political thought:

> The same kinds of communitarian principles were generalised in the debates on the constitutional question from 1988 onwards. One of the striking features of these discussions, compared with the 1970s, was the interest in sovereignty and the emerging conclusion that Scottish ideas about legitimate government rested on the principle of popular sovereignty. Again the religious origins are unmistakable, and indeed Church of Scotland theologians in particular were eloquent in their contribution to the debate, modernising the Knoxian idea that the people have the right to overthrow unjust rulers. Sovereignty, they argued, is intrinsically limited. Federalism is not just a way of organising a constitution, but a principle based on human fallibility. Because we have a duty to respect our fellow human beings, governments should seek to share power, not to monopolise it. Once again, similar conclusions were reached by Catholic thinkers, drawing also on the European tradition of subsidiarity, which entered Scottish debates through discussions about the character of the European Union.[46]

422

The dynamic behind Scottish constitutional politics in this period was the particular interaction of local, theologically informed communitarian values and institutional practices with globalizing movements in support of participatory democracy, accountability and solidarity, against the dominant counter-force of global market systems and consumer values. At what Gregory Baum has called a *kairos* moment of historic opportunity, when social justice and democratic renewal are real possibilities for a nation, Scotland became a political site of glocalization, where the local and the global interacted, and created a new democratic political institution and process.[47] By adopting a middle axiom approach, the Church of Scotland was able to respond effectively to this Scottish experience of nationalism as glocalization.

As the Scottish sociologist of nationalism, David McCrone, has expressed it, addressing the postmodern Scottish political situation: 'State-based societies become heavily porous. Globalisation carries with it an implication for locality; the global and the local become part of the same dialectic. We enter a world not of standardisation and homogenisation, but of difference and unpredictability ... a global-local nexus emerges, a process of relocalisation.'[48] The middle axiom of support for the democratic control of Scottish affairs through political autonomy in an increasingly interdependent world allowed the Church of Scotland to be heard and heeded in that local–global nexus of Scottish constitutional politics. But note the way in which this middle axiom was developed. It was not done deductively, as a critic like Forrester would think of middle axioms.[49] It was the experience of failed support for devolution in the 1979 referendum that prompted some Scottish Christians to revisit the basis of the Church of Scotland's support for Scottish self-government. This reflection led them to see the urgent need for the critical retrieval of their own Reformed tradition of theological reflection on power, and its relevance to their particular constitutional dilemmas. What emerged in that Scottish political context was a *revised* middle axiom that was interactive rather than simply deductive in its operation: with the concrete experience of constitutional politics leading to the retrieved ethical principle and theological tradition of limited sovereignty, which together acted as the catalytic elements in re-creating the middle axiom of support for a greater democratic control of Scottish affairs in an explicitly local–global context. Given that this was a middle axiom that was also fiercely debated and finally endorsed in the Church of Scotland's 1989 General Assembly, after careful consideration in the collaborative processes of policy deliberation and formation in the Assembly's Church and Nation Committee, and public scrutiny in the media, it can hardly be accused of the deductive and elitist faults that Forrester finds with this method in ecumenical social ethics.[50]

This Scottish case study of a revised, interactive middle axiom approach, which proved fruitful in a period of national reconstruction in the context of globalization, does not stand alone in the late twentieth-century political world. When Charles Villa-Vicencio considered appropriate methods for developing a theology of reconstruction in post-apartheid South Africa, linking this activity of local nation-building with the relevance of global human rights, he turned his attention to the potential of middle axioms.[51] He offers a nuanced case for their contemporary relevance to a country like South Africa that is worth quoting at some length:

> The immediate task of an ethic of reconstruction involves placing certain values and structures in position to *begin* the process of social renewal. A neglected ethical device designed to serve this need emerged from the work of J. H. Oldham in 1937, as he faced the social crisis that ultimately engulfed the world in war. Speaking at the Oxford Conference on Life and Work, he referred to the urgent need for the creation of 'middle axioms' to facilitate social construction. He saw these axioms as 'not binding for all time', but rather as 'provisional definitions' of the kind of society required to meet the challenges of the time. John Bennett suggested that they constitute 'the next steps that our own generation must take' ... It is at the same time always important to locate the 'middle axioms' of society under the renewing power of the gospel which demands more than a society can deliver at a particular time. To fail to do so could result in a form of civil religion which is sometimes used merely to legitimate the existing social order. Concerned to emphasise the tentative and changing nature of 'middle axioms' Oldham saw them to be less rigid than fixed laws or moral codes. They were for him *evolving principles.* Constantly being reshaped by the eschatological vision of the gospel, middle axioms function as a lure, drawing society beyond values to which it holds at any particular time of its history, while specifically addressing the challenges of the time. As such they constituted a theological incentive to a society in perpetual growth, while seeking to provide specific content for a specific context.[52]

Villa-Vicencio recognizes the force of Forrester's criticisms of middle axioms, including the difficulty today of establishing the consensus in Church and society that they require to be effective, and the weakness of abstract principles compared with the power of the Christian narrative to offer a compelling theological and ethical account of life.[53] But for Villa-Vicencio, while recognizing that 'Story, tradition and biblical teaching are important', they are not sufficient for a theology of reconstruction in a South African context: 'Ultimately ... if the Church is to share creatively in the reconstruction process it is obliged to translate this heritage into concrete proposals.'[54] For Villa-Vicencio, this means developing middle axioms that are not seen as abstract, deductive principles but as a conceptual and contextual device 'that integrates the contextual and transcendental demands of the gospel'.[55] I agree with his argument at this crucial point: offering theological fragments from the Christian narrative, as advocated by Forrester, is a necessary but not a sufficient step in developing a public theology which can help generate concrete proposals for social reconstruction. The story must be translated into such concrete proposals, with all the risk and guarding of the Christian narrative's integrity against ideological co-option that this requires. In my view, the Scottish case study of constitutional politics adds weight to this South African analysis in support of an interactive middle axiom approach as one effective way to realize public theology's constructive contribution to public life in a pluralist society.

In closing, I return to Robert Schreiter's reflections about the nature of 'theology between the global and the local', in his seminal book for understanding public theology's twentieth-century legacy and twenty-first-century agenda, *The New Catholicity*. That new catholicity for Schreiter will be found in the glocal interaction of global theological flows like twentieth-century liberation theology with the new local political contexts that Christians and others find themselves inhabiting in the twenty-first century. In these new political localities of a global era, such as Scotland or South Africa, Schreiter argues that emancipatory public theologies like liberation theology must embrace a repertoire of approaches to public engagement, from their founding stances of *resistance*, *denunciation* and *critique* to more recent challenges to embrace *advocacy* and *reconstruction*. And, Schreiter concludes, if a theology of reconstruction is the appropriate response in a local context, then two theological tasks become paramount – the development of appropriate middle axioms and the adoption of an interdisciplinary way of working. Schreiter defines such middle axioms as 'provisional definitions of the human and of a just society to which the message of the Gospel can contribute'. And he envisages such middle axioms being found 'in the values of community and solidarity present in civil society'.[56] The Scottish political case study outlined above, in which the Church of Scotland contributed its theologically grounded communitarian political principles and middle axiom of support for democratic renewal through a Scottish Parliament, to a wider movement in Scottish civil society for constitutional change, is a late twentieth-century example of the middle axiom approach which Robert Schreiter is commending for public theology in the twenty-first century. But middle axioms for a glocal era can only offer provisional definitions of the human and of the just society, as he reminds us.

The Scottish Christians who advocated such a middle axiom of support for constitutional change in Scotland knew this very well, as they set it within the dual horizons of an emerging local–global world and the coming of God's reign over all things:

> We do not identify any 'programme' with the coming of God's kingdom, and recognise the provisional nature of all attempts to speak and act for good in human society. Yet in [these constitutional proposals] we see a concern for what will bring Scotland peace in the fuller biblical sense of justice and right relationships; and we recognise a timely opportunity to work out proposals which will allow the people and not any one party to decide Scotland's future. Subject to the claim of Christ over all life, we welcome this claim of right for Scotland, with its positive implications for our partnership with other nations in Britain and Europe.[57]

It is this meeting of the provisional and the possible that makes public theology between the local and the global in the twenty-first century an exercise in humility and an unfinished task of love. The authors of this volume dedicate it to a public theologian who offers not only theological fragments but a glocal feast to sustain and inspire us all in that common endeavour.

Notes

1 B. R. Barber, 'Jihad vs. McWorld', *The Atlantic*, 269(3) (1992), cited in R. Robertson, below.

2 R. Robertson, 'Glocalization: time-space and homogeneity-heterogeneity', in M. Featherstone, S. Lash and R. Robertson (eds), *Global Modernities* (London: Sage, 1995), pp. 25–44.

3 *Ibid.*, p. 27.

4 *Ibid.*, p. 28.

5 *Ibid.*, p. 30.

6 R. Schreiter, *The New Catholicity: Theology between the Local and the Global* (Maryknoll, NY: Orbis, 1997), p. 12

7 D. B. Forrester, *Truthful Action: Explorations in Practical Theology* (Edinburgh: T&T Clark, 2000).

8 See D. B. Forrester, 'The political service of theology in Scotland', in W. Storrar and P. Donald (eds), *God in Society: Doing Social Theology in Scotland Today* (Edinburgh: Saint Andrew Press, 2003), pp. 83–121, for his own understanding of the relationship between the Scottish Reformed tradition and the work of the Centre.

9 See, for example, the following Occasional Papers published by the Centre for Theology and Public Issues, Edinburgh, in this period: *Christianity and Social Vision: Looking to the Future of Scotland*, No. 20 (1990); G. Hand (ed.), *Seeing Scotland, Seeing Christ*, No. 28 (1993); and G. Hand and A. Morton (eds), *Catholicism and the Future of Scotland*, No. 39 (1997). See also D. Forrester, 'Theology and constitution: some reflections', in J. Stein (ed.), *Scottish Self-Government: Some Christian Viewpoints* (Edinburgh: Handsel Press, 1989), pp. 32–3, for his own understanding of Scottish constitutional matters from a Reformed perspective.

10 Forrester, *Truthful Action*, p. 183.

11 Schreiter, *The New Catholicity*, pp. 15–21.

12 *Ibid.*, p. 20.

13 D. B. Forrester, *On Human Worth: A Christian Vindication of Equality* (London: SCM Press, 2001). On Munuswamy's lasting impression on Forrester and his theology, see pp. 2–7 and *passim*.

14 *Ibid.*, pp. 217–18.

15 D. B. Forrester, *The True Church and Morality: Reflections on Ecclesiology and Ethics* (Geneva: WCC Publications, 1997), p. 60.

16 D. B. Forrester, *Theology and Politics* (Oxford: Basil Blackwell, 1988).

17 *Ibid.*, p. 55: 'there remains an urgent need for a post-Christendom political theology ... not wistful but forward-looking and missionary.'

18 D. B. Forrester, *Beliefs, Values and Policies* (Oxford: Clarendon Press, 1989); *Christian Justice and Public Policy* (Cambridge: Cambridge University Press, 1997). For the range of CTPI publications, see the Centre's website: www.div.ed. ac.uk/research.

19 Schreiter, *The New Catholicity*, p. 114.

20 See Alasdair MacIntyre, *After Virtue: A Study in Moral Theory* (London: Duckworth, 2nd edn, 1985), Ch. 15.

21 See Forrester, *On Human Worth*.

22 Forrester's classroom and home, with his wife Margaret, a pioneering and gifted minister, have always been crossroads of the world for ideas, hospitality and visiting colleagues, like Moltmann, de Gruchy and Bonino; as those of us who have been privileged to be his students know to our lasting benefit and gratitude.

23 See Forrester's essay in Storrar and Donald, *God in Society*, pp. 101–7, for his reflections on a public theology that puts the voices, experience and expertise of the excluded, marginalized and powerless at the centre of its work, as exemplified in several CTPI projects.

24 For Forrester's own exposition of this approach, see *Christian Justice and Public Policy*, Part IV: 'Theological fragments'; his essay in Storrar and Donald, *God in Society*, pp. 116–20; and his *Afterword* to this volume.

25 For Forrester's critique of the middle axiom approach, see his *Beliefs, Values and Policies*, Ch. 2.

427

26 For an overview of these changes in Scottish politics and society, see D. McCrone, *Understanding Scotland: The Sociology of a Nation* (London: Routledge, 2001, 2nd edn); and G. Hassan and C. Warhurst (eds), *Tomorrow's Scotland* (London: Lawrence & Wishart, 2002), and *Anatomy of the New Scotland: Power, Influence, Change* (Edinburgh: Mainstream, 2002). For a longer historical perspective on these changes, see C. Harvie, *Scotland: A Short History* (Oxford: Oxford University Press, 2002), Chs. 5, 6.

27 For an account of these political developments, see A. Marr, *The Battle for Scotland* (London: Penguin Books, 1992); and C. Harvie and P. Jones, *The Road to Home Rule* (Edinburgh: Polygon, 2000).

28 Gregory Baum, *Nationalism, Religion and Ethics* (Montreal: McGill-Queens University Press, 2001), Ch. 1, pp. 5–13.

29 *Ibid.*, pp. 9–10, 103–4.

30 Gregory Baum (ed.), *The Twentieth Century: A Theological Overview* (Maryknoll, NY: Orbis, 1999), pp. 247–8.

31 Baum, *Nationalism, Religion and Ethics*, pp. 133–4.

32 *Ibid.*, p. 134.

33 *Ibid.*, pp. 134–5. The Scottish Christian literature that he cites includes two Occasional Papers from the Centre for Theology and Public Issues, University of Edinburgh: *Christianity and Social Vision*, No. 20 (1990); and *Seeing Scotland, Seeing Christ*, No. 28 (1993). In particular, Baum notes the postmodern sociological analysis of the nature of Scottish nationalism, and its relationship to globalization, by D. McCrone, 'Understanding Scotland: a sociological perspective', in *Seeing Scotland, Seeing Christ*, pp. 3–13, 5. See also D. McCrone's *Understanding Scotland: The Sociology of a Nation*, for a fuller analysis.

34 Baum, *Nationalism, Religion and Ethics*, pp. 134–5.

35 *Ibid.*, p. 135.

36 *Ibid.*, pp. 135–6.

37 For different interpretations of globalization, see R. Robertson, *Globalization: Social Theory and Global Culture* (London: Sage, 1992); R. Falk, *Predatory Globalization: A Critique* (Cambridge: Polity Press, 1999); J. H. Mittelman, *The Globalization Syndrome: Transformation and Resistance* (Princeton, NJ: Princeton University Press, 2000). For a theological interpretation, see the three-volume series edited by Max Stackhouse *et al.*, *God and Globalization: Theological Ethics and the Spheres of Life* (Harrisburg, PA: Trinity International Press, 2000–2002).

38 For an edited version of its wartime reports, see *God's Will for Church and Nation* (London: SCM Press, 1946). For commentary on the work of the Baillie Commission, see Andrew Morton (ed.), *God's Will in a Time of Crisis* (Centre for Theology and Public Issues Occasional Paper No. 31, Edinburgh, 1994); D. Fergusson (ed.), *Christ, Church and Society: Essays on John Baillie and Donald Baillie* (Edinburgh: T&T Clark, 1993); and G. Newlands, *John and Donald Baillie: Transatlantic Theology* (Oxford: Peter Lang, 2002).

39 For an account of the Commission's use of middle axioms, see Forrester, 'God's will in a time of crisis: John Baillie as a social theologian', in D. Fergusson (ed.), *Christ, Church and Society*, pp. 221–33.

40 For Oldham's account of middle axioms, see W. A. Visser't Hooft and J. H. Oldham, *The Church and its Function in Society* (Chicago, IL: Willet, Clarke & Co., 1937), pp. 209ff. For a sympathetic account of Oldham's middle axiom approach, see R. H. Preston, *Church and Society in the Late Twentieth Century: The Economic and Political Task* (London: SCM Press, 1983), pp. 141–56.

41 *God's Will for Church and Nation*, p. 156.

42 *Ibid.*, p. 157.

43 For this history of the Church of Scotland's post-war support for devolution up to 1979, see H. Sefton, 'The Church of Scotland and Scottish nationhood', in S. Mews, *Religion and National Identity* (Oxford: Basil Blackwell, 1982), pp. 549–55; for an informed theological critique of the Church of Scotland's approach to devolution up to the 1979 referendum, see W. B. Johnston, 'Church and state in Scotland today', in A. Elliot and D. B. Forrester, *The Scottish Churches and the Political Process Today* (Centre for Theology and Public Issues and Unit for the Study of Government in Scotland, University of Edinburgh, Edinburgh, 1986), pp. 4–10.

44 For an account of the churches' role in this broad civic constitutional movement, see N. Shanks, 'Constitutions, conventions and values: the Scottish churches and the constitutional debate', *Scottish Affairs*, 16 (Summer 1996): 18–35. For a perceptive analysis of the broader civic movement for self-government, see Jonathan Hearn, *National Identity and Liberal Culture* (Edinburgh: Polygon, 2000), Chs 1–4.

45 See 'Church and Nation Report', in *Reports to the General Assembly* (Church of Scotland, Edinburgh, 1989); reproduced in J. Stein (ed.), *Scottish Self-Government* (Edinburgh: Handsel Press, 1989), pp. 14–24.

46 Lindsay Paterson, 'Scottish social democracy and Blairism: difference, diversity and community', in Hassan and Warhurst, *Tomorrow's Scotland*, p. 119.

47 Baum, *Nationalism, Religion and Ethics*, pp. 103–4.

48 D. McCrone, 'Understanding Scotland: a sociological perspective', pp. 5–6.

49 See Forrester, *Beliefs, Values and Policies*, Ch. 2, for this charge that the middle axiom approach moves deductively in one direction from general Christian belief and ethical principle to specific decisions, via such intermediate directives; and R. H. Preston, *Church and Society in the Late Twentieth Century*, Appendix Two, and *Explorations in Theology 9* (London: SCM Press, 1981), Ch. 3, for a reply that denies the deductive nature of middle axioms. I write below of revised middle axioms, to stress their interactive rather than deductive nature and operation: i.e., they are formed out of the two-way and mutually influential catalytic interaction of theological belief and ethical principle with concrete political experience and decisions.

50 Forrester, *Beliefs, Values and Policies*, p. 20.

51 Charles Villa-Vicencio, *A Theology of Reconstruction: Nation-building and Human Rights* (Cambridge: Cambridge University Press, 1992).
52 *Ibid.*, pp. 9–10.
53 *Ibid.*, pp. 280–3.
54 *Ibid.*, p. 283.
55 *Ibid.*, p. 281.
56 Schreiter, *The New Catholicity*, pp. 108–15.
57 From, 'The claim of right and the claim of Christ: a statement in support of the Scottish Constitutional Convention', in J. Stein (ed.), *Scottish Self-Government*, p. ii.

Working in the Quarry:
A Response to the Colloquium

DUNCAN B. FORRESTER

What an energizing intellectual feast we had at the Carberry Colloquium in the late summer of 2001! I have been thrilled by the splendidly contextualized and grounded papers that have been presented, by the real honesty and penetration in discussion and critique, by the capacity of this company of friends, colleagues and collaborators to challenge and encourage one another in the common endeavour of developing public theology that is rigorous and constructive, theology that makes a difference. I have learned so much both from the papers and from our discussions that I am in debt to everyone who took part, and especially to those who organized this notable occasion and edited the volume. The papers were too rich and varied for me to give a considered and adequate response to each. Instead I intend to make some comments on the colloquium as a whole, and perhaps suggest some ways forward.

Sailing between Scylla and Charybdis

Public theology needs, I think, to steer a course between Scylla and Charybdis. On Scylla, we learn, there dwelt a fearful monster, that barked like a dog, with twelve legs and six long necks and heads, full of fearsome teeth. Who are the theological equivalents of Scylla? Rather naughtily, might I suggest that the many-headed Scylla represents those who denounce modernity and all its works and insights, proclaiming that social theory in particular and modern thought in general are heretical. We must not look there, suggests Scylla, for help or illumination. Rather, we must go back, to the Bible, they say, or to Aquinas or Augustine, sources unsullied by the acids of modernity.

Scylla stands for a theology so distinctive, so orthodox (to use that tricky term rather loosely), so unrelated to today's world as to be effectively irrelevant to the actual dilemmas facing people day by day, and almost unintelligible to those who are outside a charmed circle.

But Scylla is a monster that nonetheless reminds us of the necessity of quarrying into the tradition, to explore and understand the past, to dig deep and value what is found there. Yet to be shipwrecked or to make landfall on Scylla is to be condemned to irrelevance and an inability to communicate to contemporary people. For the possibility that God is speaking to us today in and through the secular world and its problems is dismissed out of hand.

On the other rock dwells Charybdis, who thrice every day swallows down the waters of the sea, and thrice throws them up again. Charybdis represents the extreme liberal, with a banner proclaiming godless morality, and a wonderful ability to communicate acceptably to secular men and women. I say acceptably, because the question is how much the message is simply the surrounding sea that has been swallowed now regurgitated. The standing question is how much there is in the message which is challengingly relevant, how far it is rooted in the household of faith, how far it communicates the Gospel. But at least Charybdis endeavours to address today's world and today's issues, to challenge and to call to action.

In between these two tempting and dangerous rocks there is open, if straitened and stormy, sea. As the barque called 'Public Theology' steers its way ahead and avoids both shipwreck and enticement from port or starboard, it may make a modest but truthful, constructive and challenging contribution to public debate, and beyond that, one hopes, to human flourishing in community. Public theology seeks to be a theology that makes a difference, a theology which engages with the real issues of today and tomorrow, that focuses on the places where people are hurting, where there is conflict, where there are seeds of vision and of hope. As it navigates between Scylla and Charybdis it uses the tradition as chart and compass, but the voyage is often into uncharted waters where the dangers and opportunities cannot be anticipated in advance, but must be responded to as they arise.

Church and God's Reign

If you wish, like me, to affirm that public theology is necessarily *ecclesial* theology, we have a problem of identifying the form or forms of Church that are appropriate today, eschewing the powerful temptations of the ghetto or sectarianism on the one hand, and easy identification of the Church with the nation, or indeed with humanity as a whole, on the other. The ghetto is the way of withdrawal from the public square. The traditional establishment engages in a thoroughly archaic way with public life, but its assumptions about the Church are quite out of touch with the realities of today's world. We can no longer regard, with Richard Hooker, being English and being a member of the Church of England as effectively the same thing. And the statement in the Articles Declaratory of the Church of Scotland of 1926 that the Church is 'representative of the Christian Faith of the Scottish people' rings hollow today. But there are surely some affirmations that we can and should make about public theology as ecclesial theology.

In the first place, the Church is called to manifest the Gospel it proclaims. It never does this completely or adequately, but in bits and pieces, in fits and starts. Manifesting the Gospel also means prefiguring God's Reign, manifesting a little bit of God's future. So the Church becomes an appetizer for God's Reign – or at least this is what the Church is called to be and to do.

Public theology is not a free-floating wisdom (or rather, foolishness!) in the public sphere. Nor is it simply the ideology of the empirical community called 'Church'; it is caught in the constant tension between the Church and God's Reign. The Church, meaning at this point primarily the congregation, is called to be a kind of Utopian community, nurturing hope and giving shape to expectation, providing a working model of reconciliation, and transforming anger and despair. The Church, meaning now both the congregation and the *oikumene*, is also a community of moral discourse, honest, hard-hitting and attentive.

We *ought* to be able to speak of the Church as a place of truth, perhaps as *the* place of truth, a community whose lifestyle and actions at least make people ask questions and become open to new possibilities. That is its calling; but the empirical reality is often very different. Similarly, it is fashionable to speak of the Church of the poor, or the Church as a community of the excluded. Alistair Kee reminds us of the need to examine why mainstream society excludes, and how often the Church actually colludes in exclusion. It is not easy in the West in talking of the Church as a community of the excluded to get beyond the rhetoric to some reality.

Whose Agenda?

Public theology is for the most part located in the university as well as in the Church. The academy sets standards and expects each discipline to give a public account of itself. Some of the issues here can be explored in relation to economics and biblical studies. These are particularly clear instances of tensions which are widespread in the academy. Is economics a science which is, or ought to be, detached and value free? Or is the economist called, in the distinguished Indian economist Christopher Kurien's words, to discern the visible fist behind the invisible hand?

For me it was particularly encouraging to find professional exegetes of distinction who took part in the colloquium taking people's readings of Scripture with real seriousness. There was mention of Rembrandt's great painting of the nativity in which the Virgin Mary is holding the Christ child in one arm, but reading a book, which on closer inspection has no writing. The child is the incarnation of the Word. But the page in the book is today no longer blank, but covered with much writing, which may in fact direct us to Christ, or tempt us to collude in the process so vividly depicted by Edwin Muir in a poem on Scotland: 'the Word made flesh is here made word again.' Some academic study of the Bible lends itself to Kierkegaard's rather naughty critique:

> Suppose that in the New Testament it were written, for example (a thing that we can at least suppose), that every man should have $100,000 ... do you believe that then there would be any question of a commentary? – or not rather that every one would say: That is easy enough to understand, there is absolutely no need of a commentary, for God's sake, let us be delivered from any commentary ...
>
> But what actually is written in the New Testament (about the narrow way, about dying to the world) is not a bit more difficult to understand than that about the $100,000. The difficulty lies elsewhere, in the fact that it is not to our liking – and therefore, therefore we must have commentaries and professors and commentaries.
>
> It is to get rid of doing God's will that we have invented learning ... we shield ourselves by hiding behind tomes.[1]

Many of us have had experiences when a people's reading has gone right to the heart of the meaning of a passage of the Bible. And often enough this was a meaning which was hidden from the wise and learned, scholarship veiling rather than revealing the meaning of the text. And reading and rereading the Bible in contexts of crisis and difficulty can have dramatic consequences. I think, for instance, of the dramatic reaction when two prominent white South African Dutch theologians – B. B. Keet and Beyers Naudé declared that the reading of Scripture to support apartheid was not tenable.

The slogan of the 1960s, 'The world sets the agenda', is, and always has been, inadequate. This is because the world's priorities are often radically skewed, and in any case, the world has a multitude of conflicting agendas. The agenda is given where people suffer and call out for help, where people want to be useful and often do not know how, where people need encouragement, grace and forgiveness, where great injustices and fears are to be found. In my *On Human Worth* I try to show how much of my theological agenda has been set by my encounters with the leper who begged on the railway bridge outside the college in which I taught as a missionary in India, and by my continuing difficulty in knowing what to do. If we are honest, our agendas in public theology are often, quite properly, set in this sort of way.

Rekindling Utopian Energies

Mary Grey speaks very movingly of the loss of the power of dreaming. 1989 has left a deep suspicion of Utopias. And the Culture of Contentment reminds us that the comfortable no longer wish to dream dreams. Fukuyama's *End of History* suggests that there are no realistic hopes left. And when Lesslie Newbigin returned to Britain after many years in India he declared that the most obvious difference between India and Britain was that, even in the worst slums in Chennai, people still hoped for a better future, while in Britain there had been an evacuation of hope.

Is there perhaps a special responsibility laid on public theology today to dream, and to keep dreams alive, especially as we know that so many millions of our fellows, our brothers and sisters, live in a real-life nightmare? And have we not also to challenge the selfish and escapist pipe dreams that sustain so many? Do we need today to reassert faith as hope, a faith which disturbs the slumbers of comfortable people like most of us?

But how do we do it?

Theology in Public Debate

A number of chapters raise questions about how theology can or should take part in public debate in modern secular societies, which are no longer deferential to religious views and impatient with biblical or theological language. Does public theology have to adopt a different language and style of argument if it is to be heard in the public forum? Can Christian insights any longer be commended in Christian language? And if we have to translate out of Christian language, are we in danger of losing our Christian distinctiveness and simply jumping on the bandwagon of secular liberal discourse?

435

Translation can be a salutory exercise, demanding clarification of meaning and precision in expression. I remember vividly years ago when I chaired for the Church of Scotland a working party on the distribution of wealth, income and benefits, I was asked along with a bright young German theologian to prepare the key theological paper on justice, community and sharing. We worked hard, and were fairly satisifed with the result. We were rather abashed when a distinguished senior social scientist spoke up for the rest of the group, and told us that they did not really understand what we were getting at. Could we translate it into 'ordinary language' that they could cope with? Our hours spent wrestling with how to communicate what we had to say in more direct and accessible language, shorn of technical theological jargon, and without any Greek, Hebrew or Latin words or citations, was a very important intellectual – and I think, also spiritual – discipline for me and my German colleague. What we stripped off was mainly pretentious ornament to what we had to say, which in fact obscured the message rather than illuminating it. In a way this was for me what R. H. Tawney would call an 'intellectual conversion' to a new understanding of public theology.

What we need is a theology which makes a difference, a theology that heals, reconciles, helps, challenges. Perhaps we need more theologians who are angry, and determined to make a difference when they read statements like C. T. Kurien's: 'Towards the end of the decade (and century) 20 per cent of global population living in the highest income countries had 86 per cent of world GDP while the bottom fifth had just 1 per cent.'

Theological Fragments

I have written a good deal recently about what I call 'theological fragments', and I am indebted to several papers and passages in the discussion at our colloquium which challenged or clarified the idea of theological fragments.

I agree emphatically with Marcella Althaus-Reid that the most important, challenging and constructive theological fragments often come from the 'underside of history', and that they can be, and often are, subversive. Theological fragments can be missiles landing unexpectedly in the theologians' playground, as it were. I also agree that we need to look with suspicion at the quarry face from which the fragments come, for this can often be not 'revelation', or 'the Gospel', but what Tim Gorringe calls a 'hegemonic matrix'.

But with all necessary caveats, I still think that the idea of theological fragments is useful both in challenging an oppressive and oversystematic understanding of theology, and also developing theology's contribution to public debate. Theological fragments can play many roles in public theology – as irritants, as illumination, as road metal, as lenses and, ultimately, perhaps, as building blocks once again.

I want to suggest that serious theological work is rather like working in a quarry, and quite specifically the kind of quarry which we find in India, where men and women, and often young children, in the heat of the day hack away at the rock face with simple implements, exposing themselves to danger, and committing to the task all their reserves of energy, intelligence, determination and strength.

I am not thinking of the modern fully mechanized quarry, where everything is done at a safe distance, at the flick of a switch, or the pressing of a button, where danger and sweat are minimized, and people do not themselves engage directly with the rock face. That might be an image of the modern academic assumption that we are most likely to encounter truth in detachment, that objectivity is all, that commitment is a distraction, or leads to distortion of the truth.

No, I am thinking of the kind of quarry that we find in India and elsewhere, where:

- The work is hard, demanding, exhausting.
- The work does not bring high status or tangible rewards, indeed the very opposite. You work because of an inner compulsion or constraint.
- Most of the work is invisible, rarely noticed or applauded. People in their cars pass by the quarry with hardly a glance as they go about their business.
- The work is sometimes dangerous, full of unexpected hazards.
- Co-operation is essential. No one can work the quarry alone; one must work as a team with others.
- The quarriers seldom see the end product. The stones they quarry are normally used and fashioned far away.

The cliff face in our theological quarry is the Bible and the rich resources and insights into truth which are to be found in the Christian tradition, and the other world faiths and ideologies that have interacted with the Christian tradition.

If we are faithful in our quarry work in the heat and sweat of the day, we produce:

- Rough blocks of stone, which others may fashion and shape and use for building strong and lasting edifices – homes, and hospitals, schools and churches, places of welcome and of service, places of stability, constancy and love, built of living stones.

- And from our quarry we also produce the small rubble stones called *road metal*, used for making firm, straight paths on which God's people may move forward.

- Occasionally we find a gemstone in our quarry, which delights by its beauty, sparkling in the sun.

- Sometimes we come across a crystal, acting like a lens, helping us to see more clearly into the depths of things, to glimpse another world, to find a vision that others may share.

- And then, as in every quarry, there is loads of grit and dust, apparently useless, untidy, pervasive, irritating the eyes and coating the nose and throat. But if perchance a piece of that grit might ultimately find its way into an oyster, it gathers around the irritant layer upon layer until the grit becomes the nucleus of a pearl. The grit stands for the awkward, probing, irritating questions that a lively theology should address to Church, society and culture.

So, after our colloquium, back to the quarry, to obtain the fragments that serve as road metal, the living stones that make our homes and churches, the grit that provokes the oyster to produce pearls, the crystals that concentrate light into visions, the fragments that generate Utopias, that build up jigsaws of meaning and that nourish the activity of truthfulness, love and justice which is the practice of God's Reign.

Note

1 S. Kierkegaard, *Efterladte Papirer*, Vol. II, p. 389, cited in W. Lowrie, *Kierkegaard* (New York: Princeton University Press, 1962), p. 539.

Duncan B. Forrester:
Selected Bibliography

1963

Chapters on Martin Luther, John Calvin and Richard Hooker in Leo Strauss and Joseph Cropsey (eds), *History of Political Philosophy* (Chicago, IL: Rand McNally, 1963), pp. 277–323; 2nd edn (1973), pp. 293–339.

1964

'Some thoughts on religionless Christianity', *Indian Journal of Theology*, 22(1) (Jan–March 1964): 11–19.

1965

'Parliamentary privilege – an Indian crisis', *Parliamentary Affairs*, 18 (1965): 196–200.

1966

'Changing patterns of political leadership in India', *The Review of Politics*, 19(3) (1966): 308–18.

1969

'Approaches to the study of Indian politics', *Political Studies*, 16 (1969): 277–84.

1970

'Towards a theology of protest', *Indian Journal of Theology*, 19(1) (1970): 30–6.

1972

'The attack on Christendom in Marx and Kirkegaard', *Scottish Journal of Theology*, 25 (1972): 181–96.

1973

'The development game', *Frontier*, 16(2) (Summer 1973): 105–9.

1974

'Western academic sophistry and the Third World', *Economic and Political Weekly*, 9(40) (1974): 1695–799.

1975

'Indian Christians' attitudes to caste in the nineteenth century', *Indian Church History Review*, 8(2) (1975): 131–47.

'Indian Christians' attitudes to caste in the twentieth century', *Indian Church History Review*, 8(1) (1975): 3–22.

1976

'Professor Hick and the Universe of Faiths', *Scottish Journal of Theology*, 29 (1976): 65–72.

1977

'The depressed classes and conversion', in Geoffrey Oddie (ed.), *Religion in South Asia: Religious Conversion and Revival Movements in Mediaeval and Modern Times* (London: Curzon, 1977).

1979

'The ecumenical renovation of the Gospel', *Christian Faith and Political Hopes* (London: Epworth, 1979), pp. 34–46.

1980

Caste and Christianity (London: Curzon, 1980).

1982

'What is distinctive in social theology?', in M. H. Taylor (ed.), *Christians and the Future of Social Democracy* (Ormskirk and Northridge: Hesketh, 1982), pp. 33–45.

1983

Studies in the History of Worship in Scotland, ed. with D. M. Murray (Edinburgh: T&T Clark, 1983).

Encounter with God, with J. I. H. McDonald and G. Tellini (Edinburgh: T&T Clark, 1983).

'Worship since 1929', in D. B. Forrester and D. M. Murray (eds), *Studies in the History of Worship in Scotland*, Ch. 11 (Edinburgh: T&T Clark, 1983).

1985

Christianity and the Future of Welfare (London: Epworth, 1985).

1986

The Scottish Churches and the Political Process Today, ed. with A. Elliot, (Edinburgh: CTPI, 1986).

1988

Theology and Politics (Oxford: Basil Blackwell, 1988).

Just Sharing: A Christian Approach to the Distribution of Wealth, Income and Benefits, ed. and co-author (London: Epworth, 1988).

'Lazarus wasn't the problem', broadcast response to Mrs Thatcher's 'Sermon on the Mound', *Movement* (Autumn, 1988), pp. 15–16.

1989

Worship Now Book 2, joint edn (Edinburgh: Saint Andrew Press, 1989).

Beliefs, Values and Policies: Conviction Politics in a Secular Age (Oxford: Clarendon Press, 1989)

1990

Theology and Practice, ed. (London: Epworth, 1990).

'Divinity in use and practice', in D. B. Forrester (ed.), *Theology and Practice* (London: Epworth, 1990).

'Lex orandi lex credendi', in D. B. Forrester (ed.), *Theology and Practice* (London: Epworth, 1990).

441

1991

'Theological and philosophical accounts of justice', *Studies in Christian Ethics*, 6(2) (1991): 15–30.

1993

'The place of the Church in the New Europe', Ch. 4 in Jurgen Wiersma, (ed.), *Discernment and Commitment* (Kampen: Kok Pharos Publishing House, 1993), pp. 67–98.

'God's will in a time of crisis: John Baillie as a social theologian', Ch. 10 in David Fergusson (ed.), *Christ, Church and Society: Essays on John Baillie and Donald Baillie* (Edinburgh: T&T Clark, 1993), pp. 221–34.

1994

'Can Liberation Theology survive 1989?', *Scottish Journal of Theology*, 47(2): 245–54.

1995

'Ecclesiology and ethics: a reformed view', *The Ecumenical Review*, 47(2) (1995), pp. 217–24; reprinted in Thomas Best and Martin Robra (eds), *Costly Commitment* (Geneva: WCC, 1995), pp. 21–7.

1996

Co–editor with Douglas Murray, and author of one chapter in *Studies in the History of Worship in Scotland*, 2nd edn (Edinburgh: T&T Clark, 1996).

Joint author with J. I. H. McDonald and Gian Tellini of *Encounter with God: An Introduction to Christian Worship and Practice* (2nd edn), radically revised and expanded (Edinburgh: T&T Clark, 1996).

1997

The True Church and Morality: Reflections on Ecclesiology and Ethics (Geneva: WCC, 1997).

Christian Justice and Public Policy (Cambridge: Cambridge University Press, 1997).

1998

'Practice and passion in theology', *Studia Theologica Islandica*, 12 (1998): 41–50.

'A free society today?', in Marjorie Reeves (ed.), *Christian Thought and Social Order* (London: Cassell, 1998), pp. 210–20.

1999

'Ecclesia Scoticana: established, free or national?', *Theology*, 102 (800) (March/April 1999): 80–9.

'Theology in fragments: practical theology and the challenge of post-modernity', in Paul Ballard and Pam Couture (eds), *Globalisation and Difference: Practical Theology in a World Context* (Cardiff: Cardiff Academic Press, 1999).

2000

'Social welfare and human nature: public theology in welfare policy debates', *Studies in Christian Ethics* 13(2) (2000): 1–14. Reprinted in Paul Ballard and Pamela Couture (eds), *Creativity, Imagination and Criticism: The Expressive Dimension in Practical Theology* (Cardiff: Cardiff Academic Press, 2001), pp. 285–97.

Truthful Action: Explorations in Practical Theology (Edinburgh: T&T Clark, 2000).

2001

On Human Worth: A Christian Vindication of Equality (London: SCM Press, 2001).

2002

'Lesslie Newbigin as public theologian', in Thomas F. Foust *et al.* (eds), *A Scandalous Prophet: The Way of Mission after Lesslie Newbigin* (Grand Rapids, MI: Eerdmans, 2002), pp. 3–12.

The End of Equality? A Strange Silence in Public Debate. The John Baillie Memorial Lecture 2001 (Edinburgh: Centre for Theology and Public Issues, 2002).

2003

'Ecclesiology and ethics', in *Dictionary of the Ecumenical Movement*, 2nd edn (Geneva: WCC, 2003).

'Citizens of Heaven', in Rebecca Dudley and Linda Jones (eds), *Turn the Tables: Reflections on Faith and Trade* (London: CAFOD, 2003), pp. 39–47.

Duncan Forrester

Index of Subjects

Individuals named in this index were active before 1850;
individuals active after 1850 may be found in the names index.

Index of Names

The names index refers to those people who were active after 1850; other names will be found in the subjects index.